STANDARD
LOAN

UNLESS RECALLED BY ANOTHER READER
THIS ITEM MAY BE BORROWED FOR
FOUR WEEKS

To renew, telephone:
01243 816089 (Bishop Otter)
01243 816099 (Bognor Regis)

Education Policy Perspectives

General Editor: **Professor Ivor Goodson,** Faculty of Education,
University of Western Ontario, London,
Canada N6G 1G7

This series aims to fill the academic gap between the study of education and
the formulation of education policy, to reflect the politicalization of
education, and to provide practitioners with the analysis for informed
implementation of policies that they need. It will offer studies in broad
areas: a General Section which will seek to provide exemplary policy
studies and will shop-window a range of methodologies and modalities
employed in education policy analysis (Professor Ivor Goodson, *University
of Western Ontario, Canada*) School organization and improvement (David
Reynolds, *University College, Cardiff, UK*); Social analysis (Professor Philip
Wexler, *University of Rochester, USA*); and Policy studies and evaluation
(Professor Ernest House, *University of Colorado-Boulder, USA*).

Education Policy Perspectives

Private Schools and Public Policy: International Perspectives

William Lowe Boyd
and
James G. Cibulka

 The Falmer Press

(A member of the Taylor & Francis Group)
London ● New York ● Philadelphia

UK   The Falmer Press, Falmer House, Barcombe, Lewes,
            East Sussex. BN8 5DL

USA   The Falmer Press, Taylor & Francis Inc., 242 Cherry Street,
            Philadelphia, PA 19106 –1906

© Selection and editorial material copyright W. L. Boyd and J. G. Cibulka 1989

First published 1989

Library of Congress Cataloging-in-Publication Data

Private schools and public policy : international perspectives /
   [edited by] William Lowe Boyd and James G. Cibulka.
      p. cm. — (Education policy perspectives)
   Based on two symposia held during the 1986 annual meeting of the
American Education Research Association at San Francisco, Calif.
   Includes index.
      ISBN 1-85000-446-3. — ISBN 1-85000-447-1 (pbk.)
      1. Private schools—Congresses.   2. Education and state—
Congresses.   3. Federal aid to private schools—Congresses.
4. Comparative education—Congresses.   I. Boyd, William L.
II. Cibulka, James G.   III. American Educational Research
Association. Meeting. (1986 : San Francisco, Calif.   IV. Series.
LC47.P72   1989
379.3—dc20   89-32018
                                                            CIP

British Library Cataloguing in Publication Data

Private schools and public
   policy: international perspectives.—
(Education policy perspectives)
   1. Developed Countries. Independent schools.
Policies of government.
   I. Boyd, William Lowe.   II. Cibulka, James G.
III. Series.
379.3

   ISBN 1-85000-446-3
   ISBN 1-85000-447-1 Pbk

Jacket design by Caroline Archer

Typeset in Bembo by
Mathematical Composition Setters, Salisbury,
Wiltshire, UK
Printed in Great Britain by Taylor & Francis (Printers) Ltd,
Basingstoke

Contents

Contents

Introduction: Private Schools and Public Policy

James G. Cibulka and William Lowe Boyd

One of the major purposes of political institutions, apart from protecting a nation's security and preserving domestic order, is to determine how a society's other institutions (family, schools, churches, and so on) will be preserved and protected. Political theorists and political activists have long debated what the proper role of government is in relation to these institutions. Marxist, liberal, and conservative theorists differ dramatically in the purposes which they attribute to government and its legitimate scope. Liberal theory, for example, maintains an important distinction between the public and private realms, on the premise that in this private realm outside governmental reach individuals best pursue their self-interests and satisfactions. At the same time, governmental authority, in the liberal view, should be extended to cover any situation in which individual or social harm results. Thus, in the case of education, the creation of state-supported 'public' schools could be justified.

This liberal ambivalence toward governmental power, then, sanctioned the coexistence of public and private institutions in many societies. In the United States, for example, where the liberal political tradition has reigned supreme, the expansion of public schools was justified as an expression of individual fulfillment and as an antidote to social harms such as ignorance and poverty. Yet private schools have been permitted to exist on the theory that individuals cannot be coerced to accept the state's orthodoxy in matters so closely related to the well-being and happiness of their children and family. Moreover, as a practical matter, political conservatives also support private schools, on various grounds of quality, economy, and maintenance of privilege.

How to draw the invisible line between public and private, then, or whether to honor it at all, is a matter of ideology and the social interests behind these ideologies, a theme we shall expand on below. Even apart from ideologies, however, national traditions have led to quite different organizational arrangements. Further, these arrangements are not fixed over time, but have evolved to accommodate changing national and international circumstances.

During the current period the merits of the private sector have enjoyed renewed recognition and support. Many have come to see private institutions such as private schools as a legitimate provider of social requirements that are, they argue, 'public' in purpose. Even in socialist systems such as the Soviet Union, *perestroika* has led to experimentation with market-oriented activity in spheres heretofore monopolized by state bureaucracies. However, this development has not led as yet to restructuring of the state educational system, merely to calls for its decentralization.

Insofar as educational institutions in much of the world are concerned, their history in the last century has been one of expansion, however gradual and intermittent, of state purposes. Of course, elementary and secondary schools were not always a dominantly state-provided function, and in some nations this still is true. Indeed, through most of history, education was provided informally and privately by guilds, tutors, charities, religious organizations, and the like. But as education has been formalized into schools and expanded to cover an ever more inclusive proportion of the population (by age, geography, social class, etc.), governmental apparatuses have been an indispensable tool for rationalizing the educational enterprise. Moreover, the creation of state-supported schools has been a means of expanding the power and legitimacy of the state itself both in Western and other nations.

Despite this large historical trend toward creation of universal public education, many factors have prevented the historical process from unfolding completely in all settings. Consequently, it is quite common in many countries for some mix of public and private schools to coexist, with or without state support or regulation.

As we point out below, and as many authors in this book argue explicitly or implicitly, there are no easy answers as to how public or private in its purpose and organization the educational enterprise should be. Nevertheless, changing ideological preferences, often driven by changing national and international circumstances, have rekindled this debate in recent years.

Aims of the Book

The idea for this book emerged as the result of two symposia held during the 1986 annual meeting of the American Educational Research Association at San Francisco, California. A majority of the authors represented here presented papers there and have since revised the papers for publication here. Other authors were invited to contribute chapters which addressed the major topics of the book.

This volume has two interrelated aims. First, it introduces the reader to recent public policy developments in various Western countries affecting private schools and their relation to government schools. The reader may be struck, as we were, by the diversity of national (and even regional) traditions within which this issue arises. Some countries have a long history of government aid to certain private schools, others practically none. Such diversity alerts us to the importance of understanding each national context before attempting generalizations which reach across the driving events in each nation.

At the same time, our aim here is to do more than describe recent policy developments. Our second objective in this book is to provide a basis for interpreting the analyses presented in this book, some of which are case studies, while others are comparative in focus. For this purpose, later in this chapter we introduce an analytical framework for discussing the role of private schools in a society, particularly their relationship to the size and well-being of a nation's public sector schools. (For reasons of space, our focus in this book is primarily on elementary and secondary schools, despite the fact that the reader will find references to higher education in some of the chapters.)

Taken together, we believe the issues raised in the chapters can be organized around the following questions:

1. What values and standards are used in democratic societies to evaluate the appropriate role for private schools and how should public policy shape that role?

2. What trends in various countries (social, cultural, economic, political) have triggered the many recent proposals to alter the existing political balance between public and private schools? (Increased support for private schools can come in any of several ways — through direct financial support or favorable tax policies to private schools, through monetary transfers to patrons, either directly or through state tax policies, and through favorable judicial rulings and regulatory policies.)

3. What issues emerge concerning private schools, what configurations of social and political power shape the issues, and what policy settlements have resulted? In other words, whose interests have prevailed in the various countries as policy changes have been proposed, and what do these outcomes suggest about the future expansion of government support for private schools?

The above three questions, in turn, offer the foundation upon which we will build the analytical framework to which we have alluded.

Overview of the Book

Before taking up these questions, readers need an overview of the organization and content of the book. Part I is a normative discussion of rationales which underpin arguments for *the existence of* private schools. It concerns the principal arguments which supporters of private schools advance. We believe this is an important starting point for the book, since it raises the issue of what role private schools should play in a democratic society. As will be evident, even advocates of private schools disagree. Four particular perspectives are examined.

In chapter 1 Donald Erickson (University of California, Los Angeles) offers a libertarian defense of private schools. He examines the limitations of arguments frequently advanced to justify public policy favoring government schools rather than private schools. His analysis reflects the libertarian concern for dangers to individual liberty. posed by government power.

In chapter 2 Denis Doyle (The Hudson Institute) offers a religious defense of private schools by examining family choice arrangements in Denmark, Holland, and Australia. He shows how religious values are integral to the educational process and how the organization of schooling should reflect the contest among values which democratic societies honor.

In chapter 3 Jacob Michaelsen (University of California, Santa Cruz) builds a rationale for private schools around the conceptions of efficiency and quality, drawing on public choice theory to demonstrate how the competitive process in private schools promotes entrepreneurship, which in turn favors such important goals as character development.

Finally, in chapter 4 Barbara Schneider (National Opinion Research Center) offers an egalitarian defense of private schools. Drawing on the American context, she asserts that government-operated schools often are inegalitarian, while many private schools offer socially equalizing opportunities for youth.

In chapter 5, the conclusion of this section of the book, James Cibulka (University of Wisconsin-Milwaukee) offers a comparative analysis of these four defenses of private schools. He addresses whether they really are alternative explanations, showing points where they overlap or conflict, and how they might be integrated by appealing to the communitarian values associated with private schools.

Part II of the book, covering chapters 6–17, contains empirical analyses of policy developments in various nations. Chapter 6, written by Tony Edwards (University of Newcastle upon Tyne), and John Fitz and Geoff Whitty (Bristol Polytechnic) examine the Assisted Places Scheme introduced by Great Britain's Conservative government in 1980. The Scheme is a scholarship ladder designed to permit 'bright children from less affluent homes' to attend independent (non-government) schools. Edwards and his colleagues analyze the claims of supporters and detractors of this policy in light of their own empirical evidence. They ask, for example, whom the program has benefited and what new opportunities, if any, have resulted.

In chapter 7 Don Smart (Murdoch University) examines public-private school policies in Australia between 1983 and 1986, under the

Socialist Hawke government. Smart explains Hawke's surprisingly limited steps during this period to phase out federal aid to wealthy private schools.

Chapter 8, written by William Lowe Boyd (Pennsylvania State University) addresses the policy problems faced in trying to achieve a fair balance between public and private schools, drawing on the implications of the Australian experience for the United States. He questions the view that Australia is a successful model for the United States, of how public dollars could be distributed beneficially to private schools without harming the public schools, pointing to problems and successes in the Australian experience.

Stephen Lawton (Ontario Institute for Studies in Education) in chapter 9 examines public policy toward public, private, and separate schools in the Canadian province of Ontario, particularly a new policy of extending government funding of former Roman Catholic separate schools from grade 10 to grades 11 through 13. This policy reopened old conflicts which had been resolved when Ontario entered the Confederation in 1867.

Chapter 10, written by Manfred Weiss (German Institute for International Educational Research), reviews and interprets the growth of pupil enrolments at private schools in West Germany since the mid-1970s, as well as legal regulations affecting private schools. Weiss evaluates probable policy consequences flowing from greater public financing of private schools.

In chapter 11 Estelle James (State University of New York, Stony Brook) uses an economic analysis to explain why different industrialized and developing countries choose widely varying systems for providing education. She analyzes the difference made by public versus private management of schools in such matters as segregation, elitism, and educational quality.

Chapter 12 is a commentary provided by Berry Durston, past Executive Director of the National Council of Independent Schools in Canberra, Australia, and now with the Curtin University of Technology. Durston examines the themes raised in chapters 6–11. He compares developments in the various countries on such matters as the scope of the private sector, the thrust for privatization, the nature of public funding for private schools, the implications for public schools of providing public funding for private schools, and related public policy concerns.

In chapter 13 Bruce Cooper (Fordham University) discusses what he terms the politics of privatization in the USA and Great Britain. He defines privatization and the various public policy options falling between the extremes of total state control over education and total private control, and then analyzes policies in both countries designed to foster privatization.

Dan Inbar (Hebrew University of Jerusalem) explains in chapter 14 that privatization is occurring even in Israel, a country with a strong egalitarianism and a centralized school system. He interprets the major forces driving this thrust and turns to an examination of the basic options available to Israeli society in addressing public expectations for privatization.

Drawing on the American context, Patricia Bauch (Catholic University of America) in chapter 15 addresses a critical issue in the American debate over public policy toward private schools. That issue is whether poor parents can make wise educational choices. Based on her in-depth studies of inner-city Catholic high schools, Bauch argues that there is strong evidence to answer this question affirmatively.

Chapter 16, written by Peter Mason (Independent Schools Information Service, England) discusses the factors which determine the degree of elitism in independent schools, with examples drawn from trends in West Germany, Denmark, the Netherlands, and other countries.

In the final chapter (17), Irene Fox (Polytechnic of Central London) investigates the role which Britain's famed 'public' schools play in reproduction of the nation's social classes. The various kinds of private schools given the label 'public' are reviewed. The author offers empirical evidence on the recruitment base and class orientation of those attending high status boys' 'public' schools, including the reasons parents select these schools.

A Conceptual Approach to Policy Developments Affecting Private Schooling

Standards for Evaluating Private Schools

We believe it is useful to use a 'competing values' model for understanding how private schools are judged and treated by government policy. This competing values model has been applied to educational policy generally by Guthrie, Garms, and Pierce (1988), who highlight three different values which influence policy makers — equality, efficiency, and liberty.

For instance, policy makers can emphasize the right of individuals and groups in the society to freedom of choice or *liberty*. This value emphasizes the voluntary activity of individuals and their freedom from external restraint, whether by governments or private action. As we pointed out earlier, the tradition of liberal individualism makes sharp distinctions between the autonomous sphere of voluntary action and the legitimate sphere of state intervention. The right to autonomous pursuit of privately held values is assumed sacrosanct unless a compelling state interest can be shown, such as protection from the intrusion on some individuals' rights by other individuals. Although the value of liberty or choice gives rise to a variety of claims, it tends to limit the role of state action to the protection of individual rights. In the case of private schools, this value provides their *raison d'etre* alongside a state-organized and supported system of education.

Choice may even require a public policy which actively protects the right to choose private schools through financial support for the schools or their patrons. At the other extreme, the tenor of the liberty argument may be anti-statist, striving to minimize the intrusive state regulation of private schools. Suspicion of state intrusion is so strong in some cases that any form of state support is rejected.

When the value of *equality* is the starting point for constructing social and political theory, an entirely different set of assumptions follows. While equality is an ambiguous concept, frequently it is operationalized to mean equal access to social and political resources, fair treatment according to procedural due process and, in the extreme, equal outcomes for individuals.

When equality is the primary value anchoring discussions of private schools, two alternative policy issues tend to be raised. First, the question arises as to whether all children are treated equitably by the state system of education and, if not, how greater access to private schools would improve the equitable distribution of educational benefits in a society.

Second, the elitism of private schools is questioned, by virtue of their social class makeup, superior resources (in some instances), and frequent access to privileged occupational and social adult roles. Several chapters in this book (those by Fox, Mason, and Schneider) make this question their major focus, while a number of others (for example, James) offer interesting relevant evidence. Because the authors focus on different contexts and issues, and perhaps because of different personal beliefs and values, they do not all come to similar conclusions.

The value of *efficiency* focuses as a point of departure primarily on the relationship between the costs and the outcomes of schooling, particularly on how to improve outcomes at a given expenditure level or, alternatively, how to achieve the greatest gains per unit of increased costs. At its simplest, the value of efficiency is operationalized by taxpayer watchdog groups to mean economy: cut costs even if it requires cutting services 'to the bone'. In the hands of more sophisticated persons, the tools of cost-benefit analysis are used to calibrate dollar investments to the best possible benefits.

Because efficiency is partly concerned with outcomes, it overlaps with the outcome approach to defining equality. Unlike equality, however, efficiency raises nothing explicitly about the distribution of educational outcomes. Whether to focus educational expenditures at the margin on the most academically able, the average pupil, the underachiever, or all three is determined, within the framework of efficiency considerations, largely by which approach maximizes benefits in relation to input costs.

Consequently, the goal of efficiency provides little guidance outside the logic of cost-benefit ratios concerning many important decisions facing educators and society. Is the most efficient system one that helps each child to reach his or her highest potential, using some acceptable definition and measure of individual ability? Is the standard some level of mastery of content, and how is that level determined? Alternatively, is efficiency to be understood through a *comparative* standard of reference? If so, what constitute fair comparisons among nations, states, districts, schools, and pupils? These dilemmas prove no less vexing than problems of defining and measuring equality, as evidenced by the many debates about educational testing and the growing accountability movement in the United States focusing on comparisons among schools and school districts.

When the efficiency of private schools is debated in relation to public schools, similar problems of measurement and interpretation arise. Are private schools more efficient because they may spend less per pupil than comparable public schools? Is the fact that they may spend less with more favorable outcomes the critical fact? Critics of such comparisons charge that private schools have many hidden input costs and that their student bodies are less difficult to educate than those in public schools.

Advocates for private schools make their claims both on grounds of technical and allocative efficiency. Private schools demonstrate technical efficiency when they can demonstrate better cost/benefit ratios than the public schools. To the extent that a different mix of public and private schools would reduce total societal costs for elementary and secondary education, changing the financing and governance arrangements would prove allocatively efficient for the nation as a whole.

These competing values emerge throughout the chapters which follow. For example, in part I of the volume the four different normative defenses of private schools use one or more of the values as a starting point. Erickson's libertarian defense of private schools is, of course, an argument built on considerations of choice. Doyle's argument for the religious foundations of schooling is essentially a more specific argument for the value of choice as well. Since religious values are assumed to be at the heart of the educational process, and since these religious values are diverse, the argument runs that a nation's educational governance and financing system should protect, indeed encourage, religious choices.

Schneider finds inequality in the present state-run educational system, from which she infers that efforts to broaden access to private schools for the poor would be a more equitable societal policy.

Michaelsen's public choice argument draws heavily on technical efficiency arguments. Although choice is important to the public choice perspective, it is defended less as a political right than as an economic tool. Choice creates competition, thereby creating organizational incentives for improved performance and cost-management.

As Cibulka points out in his commentary on these four chapters, the different rationales are to some degree in tension. Consider the possibility that a social policy which offers unlimited access to private schools might lead to reduced equality for the children who might be left behind in qualitatively poor public schools deprived of middle-class patrons. This is a fear which Weiss raises in considering the possible consequences attending further expansion of private schooling in West Germany. Similarly,

Edwards, Fitz, and Whitty describe this as one of the criticisms directed at the Assisted Places Scheme by those in Great Britain who fear the possible enlargement of that policy to a voucher system. Cooper describes the attack on City Technology Colleges in Great Britain in similar fashion; these new magnet secondary schools are a cross between independent and government schools designed to train academically able students in math, science, and technology. Boyd's analysis of Australian developments raises the same concern that systems which maximize choice do so at some cost to equality. Pushing from the other side, Schneider points to inequities in the American system which afford differential access to high quality public schools to those who can afford to locate in residential locations with such superior schools.

In some respects, to be sure, these alternative values are mutually reinforcing. Advocates of greater choice, such as the former United States Secretary of Education, William Bennett, assert that higher standards for everyone assure equality of intellectual opportunity for the poor as well (Bennett, 1988).

By this logic, educational excellence achieved in the pursuit of efficiency should contribute to greater educational equality. Some evidence supports this assertion. Dropout rates from American public schools have not increased since the first wave of reforms in 1983, and have actually decreased slightly. Transcript studies do indicate a modest increase in the percentage of American youth who take the 'new basics' coursework (four years of English, three years each of mathematics, science, and social studies, one-half year of computer science and, for students planning to attend college, two years of a foreign language). While racial differences persist among students taking the 'new basics' curriculum, they have narrowed since 1982 (Bennett, 1988, pp. 14–17).

Although much more needs to be known about the impact of the American educational reform movement on underachievers and minorities, the above data do suggest that caution should be exercised before predicting with certainty that values such as efficiency and equality must operate in tension.

Such caution also is appropriate when discussing what policy consequences flow from expansion of the value of liberty or choice, through public support for private schools. At the level of values, choice and equality appear to work somewhat at cross purposes. One of the benefits of this volume is the actual empirical evidence it brings to bear on that issue; the problem is addressed in many of the chapters, which span various national contexts. The reader may draw his or her own conclusions about what these data 'prove'. We will not attempt to air or resolve in this chapter all of the points made by the authors on that issue. However, it is important to note that the authors offer conflicting evidence, and many of them, because of incomplete information, are forced to speculate. Such speculation is apt to be tainted by the ideological preferences which any of us brings to public policy and research problems. Indeed, it would be naive to assume that additional factual evidence alone, devoid of ideology, will answer definitively whether further government support for private schools will increase educational and social inequality. Yet further research, which is desperately needed, will push the debate beyond speculation and clarify the issues. If public policy is to be improved, it needs to be informed by this evidence. What is offered in this volume, while rich in cross-cultural detail, is merely a beginning point for such understanding.

Recent Trends Favoring Expansion of Private Schools

From the chapters in this book one can identify three intersecting factors fostering value shifts which have heightened public policy attention to private schools in many countries. We refer to them as intersecting because while each factor has separate origins, the three do reinforce one another. However, not all three have been operative in each country, nor have they been of equal significance.

First, in many countries the equality and efficiency of the public education system has become an issue because of growing concern over national economic well-being. The emergence of a global economy, as well as the existence of trade imbalances in some nations, have caused policy makers to refocus their attention on education as an instrument of national economic policy. Related to this concern about economic competitiveness was the effect of inflation and recessions in some countries during the late 1970s and early 1980s.

The best example of this may well be the United States, which is faced with the prospect of no longer being the dominant economic power among its allies, due to a constellation of complex causes both within the country (for example, low capital investment in some economic sectors, monetary, taxing and spending policies) as well as external causes (the emergence of the Pacific basin economies in international markets, the instability of the international banking and monetary system, etc.). In a country without any tradition of (or inclination for) national economic planning, educational reform has been appealing across the American political spectrum.

This inclination to see education in economic terms has strengthened the hand of reformers who measure educational performance in terms of outcomes such as achievement test scores. In this regard, Coleman, Kilgore, and Hoffer (1982) triggered a national debate with their findings that private schools enjoy an achievement advantage over comparable public schools.

One rationale for private schools, according to Durston, is that they provide a benchmark against which public schools can be compared. Indeed, many economists see competition between the sectors as contributing to efficiency in both sectors. (See, for example, Michaelsen, in this volume.)

In some other countries, concern about national economic productivity also played as an element rekindling interest in private schools. According to Edwards, Whitty, and Fitz in this volume, such concerns among others led to the passage of the Assisted Places Scheme for England and Wales. In his review of English developments, Cooper portrays the controversial City Technology Colleges plan as embracing the same logic. Similarly, Smart's chapter interprets the moderation of the Hawke labor government in Australia as due in part to national concerns about the need for a closer fit between the education system and labor market needs, leading to the emergence of the controversial Quality of Education Review Committee.

A second factor contributing to further interest in private schools, related to the above, has been an increasingly demanding population of educational consumers in many countries. The specific impetus for this heightened scrutiny varies from country to country. As Durston points out, undoubtedly contributing to this trend has been the demographic decline in school populations in many countries, now reversed in some nations, still continuing in others. This decline led to concern about the costs of education in relation to quality received, particularly in countries with national economic downturns.

Feeding into this concern over efficiency has been a growing citizen interest in a broader array of educational choices from which to select, rather than relying on the judgments of professional educators. This is an element to be found in West Germany, according to Weiss, and Inbar describes its impact on the traditionally centralized Israeli educational system. Judging by public opinion polls in the United States, the concept of choice has wide appeal, although aid to private schools remains controversial. What may be at work here is a confluence of growing disenchantment with bureaucratic authority, increasing levels of education among consumers, and growing parental recognition about the critical role education plays in their children's life chances. (Wirt and Harmon, 1986). In any event, parents want a greater role in selecting their children's school, and greater influence on other matters in state education systems. In countries where the boundaries between public and private schools are not as sharply drawn as in Israel, the United States, and West Germany (among others), this interest in exercising choice has made it legitimate to talk about the value of educational markets and state aid for private schools or their patrons.

Finally, a third factor has been the election of politically conservative national governments in some countries, which had the effect of making these frequently inchoate public expectations more organized and transforming them to particular policy proposals which themselves embraced the specific agenda of conservatives now in office. The 1980s has been a period of national political conservatism in many countries, among them England, the United States, and West Germany, triggered by a backlash in social values and concern about economic stringency. As we discuss below, these policy proposals have had different degrees of success, but this aside there can be no doubt that the emergence of conservative governments contributed to whatever success proponents of 'privatization' have had.

James' chapter is a reminder that the expansion of private schools in some countries has not been so much a response to 'differentiated demand', (what we have referred to as greater public interest in choice) as a problem of excess demand. Excess demand continues to exist in some countries without a fully developed public system, such that some patrons must be accommodated in private schools. By and large, however, the factors which we have discussed above contributing to growing legitimacy for private schools have occurred in countries with government systems which already offer close to universal coverage.

Power Configurations Shaping the Issues

We argued at the outset that conflicting values drive the growing public policy interest in private schools. In advancing this position, it seems important to distinguish this argument from a simple functionalist perspective. If the latter were our frame of reference, the argument might run something like this: Among the conflicting values of liberty, equality, and efficiency, changing socioeconomic needs in many countries have raised efficiency or productivity to a new level of importance, replacing earlier national concerns about equitable distribution of government expenditures.

At the heart of a functional perspective is the idea that social structure reflects social needs. Within functional theory, the driving force of social action is not ideas and values, but rather objective social requirements. By contrast, in introducing the concept of competing values, we employ an explicitly *political* model. The particular values which are called upon to justify public policy are quite flexible, depending on national tradition, institutional specifics, and the role-interests of the protagonists (their social class, race, age, gender, etc.). Consequently, given this potential for variation, to understand how proposals for altering the balance between public and private schools have fared in each country, we must carefully study the politics of each national situation as well as changing socioeconomic 'needs'. The issues have been articulated in different ways and the coalitions for and against policy change are not always identical, not only among nations, but in the same country over time.

Cutting through this diversity, though, is the salient fact that proposed policies to aid private schools or to give individuals a wider choice of schools typically trigger *redistributive* rather than *distributive* politics (Lowi, 1964). By this we mean politics which mobilize a wide spectrum of constituencies who cast their claims in emotional, symbolic terms said to benefit or harm whole groups of persons and, indeed, society itself. Coalitions congeal along ideological lines, however unlikely their other common interests or values may be. Redistributive politics are conflictual, characterized by considerable public posturing and appeals for support through the media. By contrast, the classic case of distributive politics is narrowly construed benefits whose conferral on some group is viewed as of little consequence to other affected parties, permitting compromise, fluid coalitions, and covert bargaining over shared goals.

As Mason, Durston, James, Cooper and others in this volume point out, the degree to which private schools are regulated by the state varies considerably among countries. Under Lowi's classification of political processes, such regulatory matters generate still a third kind of politics, which typically mobilizes very narrow interests. In this context, however, such regulatory questions are not easily separable from the broader public policy question of the state's support for private schools. Undoubtedly, examples could be found where state regulation of private schools generates a narrow, non-conflictual politics of primary interest only to the immediately affected parties. More often, however, such regulatory matters are interpreted as symbolic of wider public policy considerations, thus generating redistributive issues.

Aid to private schools is redistributive because it raises conflicts over fundamental values, (for example, liberty, equality, or efficiency), affecting social classes (for example, rich v. poor, middle-class v. rich) or affecting social status groups. For instance, as regards social class, some argue that aid to private schools benefits the rich, while others see it as an avenue to improve the social mobility of the poor.

The principal status categories arising here tend to fall into two groups. First, religious, ethnic and racial groups are affected. Thus, some argue for aid to private schools in order to help a particular religious minority felt to be discriminated against, while others oppose such aid because it could legitimate further racial segregation.

A second status group distinction arising in such disputes often occurs between those attending private schools and those in government schools. Indeed, the status distinction frequently extends to their respective supporters, also. In many national contexts, greater prestige is attached to attending a private school, because of the academic and/or social advantages such enrollment may confer. Accordingly, the public policy debate on private schools becomes a platform upon which broader ideologies concerning social privilege and social redistribution are argued. Whether public or private schools are labeled egalitarian or elitist depends on the country, as James' and Mason's chapters point out, but support for one is often seen as occurring at the expense of the other institution, requiring that one resort to a broadly-conceived social and political ideology to defend one's position on the private school issue.

With these conceptual categories in mind, several concrete examples can be examined. Let us take the status-group category of religion first, contrasting Canada with the United States. In both cases the religious issue has engendered rancorous redistributive politics when aid to private schools has been discussed, but with different policy outcomes. As Mason notes, the national constitutional provisions in both countries are silent on parent choice and the rights of private schools. Lawton's chapter on Ontario, Canada illustrates how one province has made religious accommodations in the funding of education. Since this decision has been decentralized to the regional level, a majority of the provinces has chosen not to provide such aid. Lawton describes, among other developments, the politics surrounding extension of public support to Catholic separate (secondary) schools.

Although controversial, the idea that aid to religious schools might be held constitutional would have far less political support in the United States, where the federal constitution speaks clearly on the separation of church and state. Indeed, the church-state issue has been the Achilles heel facing supporters of aid to private schools in the United States. It has even siphoned off some potential political support from religious schools themselves, as they have feared government entanglement in their religious missions. At the heart of such religious debates in the United States is the question of how to protect religious liberty: Does it require extending the same access to religious schools as is available to those desiring a secular state-sponsored education, or is religious liberty protected only by strict avoidance of state entanglement? Because such questions are so value-laden and raise conflicts between liberty and equality, among other values, they tend to find their way from legislatures to courts for some resolution which may prove durable for a time. Of course, the religious issue does not arise as such in every country, depending on the degree of religious pluralism to be found and whether there is a tradition separating church and state. Mason and Doyle's discussions of the Netherlands show how peaceful accommodations among religious groups have occurred in that country.

Another set of political arguments, also redistributive, is focused around the social consequences of aiding poor or wealthy private schools. Here the underlying issue, of course, is equality, which raises the politics of class as contrasted with status group cleavages which emerge when religion is the focus. Sometimes, however, class and status group issues become intertwined. For example, Smart discusses the intent of the Hawke government in Australia during 1983 to reduce aid increases to the wealthiest private schools. The government met not only with their opposition but also that of less affluent Catholic schools, who had been receiving aid since 1973 and were reluctant to endorse the government's proposed new community standard for distributing funds, since they feared the policy would inevitably affect some additional schools. The issue played itself out as a classic redistributive game — public, confrontational, with extensive media coverage, and predictable ideological cleavages.

When the government's policy has been to give aid to needy individuals, who in turn may attend private schools, the redistributive social class issues have become blurred, but only in some cases. England's *Assisted* Assisted Places Scheme was passed without extraordinary rancor, even if *places* many on the political left saw it as a wedge in the door for greater state aid to private schools. Similarly, the Hawke government in Australia was able to establish a policy designed to improve high school retention rates, the Participation and Equity Program (PEP), justifying aid both to private and government schools on the grounds that the nation needed to confront its youth unemployment problem. The lack of controversy may have been due to the fact that the policy was advanced by a Labor government, rather than a conservative one, and because the PEP program did not aid private schools primarily but rather government schools.

By contrast, the reaction in the United States to Reagan administration proposals for vouchers, including the 'voucherization' of chapter 1, the nation's major compensatory education program, was most acrimonious, as Cooper's discussion reveals. The proposals created such unlikely allies as school boards, teacher unions, and consumer groups, thereby transcending political party boundaries. Indeed, many in Mr. Reagan's Republican party did not support the proposals, feeling opposition from all sides, including some on the political right. Opponents successfully redefined a social class issue (aid to poor children and their families) with largely distributive implications (benefits to a particular group) into a status-group issue with strongly redistributive overtones (favoring elite private institutions to the detriment of egalitarian public ones).

Thus far, proponents of family choice arrangements in the United States have been unable to make any headway by proposing to target aid on worthy individuals rather than schools. On the other hand, choice arrangements *within* the public school sector, either among school systems or within them, have gained growing political support, as Cooper points out. School officials readily adopted magnet and specialty schools. They have been opposed to cross-district open enrollment plans, but without consumer groups to support them, have not always prevailed. (In Minnesota such an open enrollment plan passed the state legislature in 1988, and plans were under serious consideration in other states). In other words, when family choice arrangements confine themselves to reform within the public schools, it is more difficult for the public school establishment (unions, school boards, administrative associations, and others) to frame the status group issue in ways which disguise their own self-interest in preserving the status quo.

It is hard to predict how public interest in greater choice of schools will affect the public-private school balance. In some countries like Israel, the United States, and West Germany, public demands for greater choice have been accommodated primarily in the public school sector rather than by expansion of the relatively small private school sectors in these countries. If public schools are unable to retool themselves to meet growing consumer and business expectations for greater efficiency (excellence and productivity), tax support for private schools or their patrons may gain political support and become a serious redistributive issue.

This political debate undoubtedly would be rekindled if politically conservative national regimes return to or remain in power in the 1990s in these various countries. But we think it unlikely that a political regime analysis will adequately explain future policy developments. Public interest in liberty and its handmaiden, choice, is unlikely to subside and can be expected to grow. Traditional deference to professional judgment is breaking down throughout the world as more consumers are themselves better educated and better informed by electronic media. Further, both the new and old middle classes recognize that education is critical to their children's life chances in the newly emerging, unpredictable economies of the post–industrial period. From a producer point of view, pressures to view the educational system as a form of national economic investment will increase as the world economy (ownership, investment, consumption, etc.) becomes more interdependent and comes to penetrate national boundaries and traditional notions of national hegemony. This increasing internationalization, if it is not cut short by global war or the unexpected emergence of a political superpower which dominates by force, is likely to maintain educational policy as one of the highest domestic policy concerns and to continue causing it to be viewed as an indirect tool to achieve foreign policy. Under such competitive circumstances in an economically tumultuous world, educational institutional arrangements which show the most promise to advance a nation's interest will enjoy great advantage. Old ideologies about public and private, about elitism and social redistribution will scarcely disappear, of course. Yet the age of uncertainty only now unfolding will force older ideologies to adapt to new challenges no less dramatic than those which reshaped educational systems in the new industrial period and in the post–World War II world. The balance between public and private schools in the new post–national era before us promises to be caught up in the redistributive politics of national economic productivity. Those politics cannot be charted with any more precision than we can predict the far-reaching, frequently startling changes reshaping our world economic system itself.

References

BENNETT, W. B. (1988) *American Education: Making It Work* Washington, DC, United States Department of Education.

COLEMAN, J. S., KILGORE, S. and HOFFER, T. (1982) *High School Achievement: Public, Catholic, and Private Schools Compared* New York, Basic Books.

GUTHRIE, J. W., GARMS, W. I. and PIERCE, L. C. (1988) *School Finance and Education Policy: Enhancing Educational Efficiency, Equality, and Choice* Englewood Cliffs, NJ, Prentice-Hall.

LOWI, T. W. (1964) 'American Business, Public Policy, Case Studies, and Political Theory' *World Politics*, 16, 4, pp. 677–715.

WIRT, F. and HARMON, G. (1986) *Education, Recession, and the World Village* Lewes, Falmer Press.

Part I
Philosophical Foundations of Public Policy Towards Private Schools

Chapter 1
A Libertarian Perspective on Schooling

Donald A. Erickson

I begin with the following libertarian assumptions: government has a dramatic tendency to limit liberty, a fundamental condition of human happiness. Government generally lacks the limiting discipline of the marketplace and the softening compassion of primary human relationships. Especially in matters of the family, when the most precious values are at stake, government intervention should be permitted only if demonstrably essential to the common weal. Both as private individuals and as government agents, humans are fallible, but errors and unwillingness to take advice are particularly destructive when embedded in far-reaching bureaucratic structures and backed by state power.

Even when government intervention is needed, the response should be limited, strictly commensurate with the need. Government intervenes selectively, for example, when certain children are seriously neglected or abused by their parents or guardians. It does not respond by taking custody of all children. In matters of child nutrition, we assume that most parents by far will treat their children reasonably well, with more compassion and concern than a government agency could exhibit. Government provides welfare money when parents cannot afford food. It does not establish tax-supported public kitchens where all children may eat free. It does not require all children to patronize those kitchens unless obtaining food from government-recognized private cafes. It does not require all cafes to offer a long list of required dishes, to hire only state-certified cooks, and to use the same recipes. It does not harass and occasionally shoot parents who prefer to provide their children with home nutrition.[1]

In the matter of shelter from the elements, similarly, we assume that the vast majority of parents will do reasonably well. Government provides financial assistance when parents cannot afford a roof over their children's heads. With the exception, to some extent, of Indian reservations where most citizens cannot see what is happening, government does not set up tax-supported public dormitories where all children may slumber free. It does not require all children to spend a certain number of hours in those dormitories unless bedded down in private government-recognized 'equivalent sleeping space'. It does not require all private hotels to conform to the standards of public dormitories, hiring only state-certified maids. It does not harass and occasionally shoot parents who insist upon sleeping their children at home.

The state intervenes selectively in other areas, but universally in education. Most parents may be trusted to see that their children are nourished and sheltered from the elements, but cannot be trusted, our legal framework says, to see that their children are educated. Children who do not spend the required learning hours in the state's own instructional service stations (commonly known as public schools) are often permitted (depending on the state) to spend the same amount of time learning *only in private instructional service stations* (commonly known as private schools) *which the state approves*. In some states all children must do their required learning under teachers whom government certifies. Though forbidden to specify what people will learn through the mass media, the state lays out a lengthy list of things that all children, the most impressionable humans of all, must learn through schooling. When parents who feed, clothe, and shelter their children at home dare to educate them at home as well, state officials become particularly upset, and harassment and prosecution often follow.[2]

This disproportionate distrust puzzles me. Perhaps it serves professional educators well to depict themselves, in league with the state, as the only trustworthy custodians of essential learning for the bulk of the nation's youth. Perhaps our current policy framework for schooling is less a matter of logic and demonstrated need and more a reflection of the fact that educational policies are influenced by a far more powerful lobby of public bureaucrats than are policies on nutrition and shelter.

I cannot analyze that possibility within the confines of the present chapter, nor many other possible reasons why this nation, while fundamentally libertarian in other areas of child-rearing, permits such extensive state influence in education. Neither can I discuss at any length the many possible alternatives to our current framework of public intervention in matters of schooling.

If sufficient space were available, I could easily demonstrate, I believe, that US courts have been discouragingly insensitive to these issues, though the nation's highest court has on occasion, *in dicta*, enunciated principles which I wish the judiciary as a whole would keep in mind. 'The child', the US Supreme Court once said, 'is not the mere creature of the state. Those who nurture him and direct his destiny have the right, coupled with high duty, to recognize they prepare him for additional obligations'.[3] The state, according to the Court, may demand 'that certain subjects *plainly essential* to good citizenship be taught, and that nothing be taught that is *manifestly inimical* to the general welfare'[4] [my italics].

It may be useful to observe at the outset that government intervention into schooling assumes several configurations. One form, not considered in this chapter, is exhibited when the state takes custody of children who *demonstrably and seriously* have been neglected or abused by their parents or guardians. I think that tactic is clearly justified, though subject, of course, to abuse.

A much more pervasive mode of state intervention into the upbringing of the young is found in the public school, for here the state itself assumes extensive child-rearing functions. The state sculpts the minds of its future citizens during a period of approximately 15,000 hours. After that — after individuals have undergone the most enduring aspects of personality development, and are equipped with prejudices that will influence them for the rest of their lives — we suddenly become interested in protecting them from what government might teach them through the mass media.

A third form of state intervention consists of measures that limit the liberty of families to opt out of the state's child-rearing efforts. Such intrusions take the form of financial frameworks that penalize alternatives to public education, and of regulatory frameworks that discourage or outlaw various approaches to private schooling and home instruction for compulsory attendance purposes. Limitations of time and space prevent proper analysis here of the nature, extent, and consequences of the above-mentioned state influences. I will assume for present purposes that most readers are reasonably well aware of them, though perhaps not fully cognizant of the lamentable impact that dissenters often suffer.[5]

The bulk of this chapter analyzes the logic of state interventions into the child-rearing process by examining four major rationales that may be advanced to justify the intervention. The rationales are not mutually exclusive, but often complement and reinforce each other.

Rationale 1: Encouraging Individual Autonomy

State involvement in the upbringing of children is often defended on the grounds of the child's right to choose freely from among available ideologies, vocations. and life styles. This freedom cannot be a reality unless individuals develop the understandings and skills that make choice more than a fiction. If the state must limit the freedom of parents, educators, and even, in the short run, of children themselves, the intervention may be defended in terms of this rationale.

The ideal of using educational institutions to help produce autonomous human beings lies at the heart of the concept of a liberal (or 'liberating') education. Booth speaks, for instance, of 'the knowledge or capacity or power of how to act freely as a man.'[6] Redfield defines education as most fundamentally a quest for autonomy, the 'necessary condition of happiness.'[7]

According to this liberal definition, educational institutions should promote the rationality of their students, offering forums in which a wide range of options may be examined freely. This approach is at odds with the state's attempts to mold children to some selected vision of the good life. It also conflicts with parental efforts to curtail their children's freedom to strike out in directions which the parents may not approve.

From the standpoint of a 'liberal education', the state has no business complaining if, after examining the options freely, the youngster rejects mainstream culture and decides to live as an Amishman, hippy, or radical intellectual. Neither does the parent have a right to complain if the youngster departs from the family's religion, ideology, or life style. The purpose of the liberal education was to make self-determination possible, not to exalt one alternative over another. Choice means little, after all, if it is limited to those options which state or parent select in advance.

Justice Douglas expressed this point of view in his dissent in the famous 'Amish school case' of 1972. If given only the primitive education the Amish approve, Justice Douglas argued, Amish children might lose the right to choose vocations:

> While the parents, absent dissent, normally speak for the entire family, the education of the child is a matter on which the child will often have decided views. He may want to be a pianist or an astronaut or an ocean geographer. To do so he will have to break from the Amish tradition... If a parent keeps his child out of school beyond the grade school, then the child will be forever barred entry into the new and amazing world of diversity that we have today.[8]

The individual autonomy rationale has two big problems, unfortunately. One problem concerns the impossibility of determining objectively the prerequisites of individual autonomy. The second problem is the fact that *all* schools are biased in some way against the exercise of autonomy. These two problems will now be discussed in sequence.

Problem 1: Who Can Be Trusted to Specify the Understanding and Skills that Make Humans Autonomous?

One major limitation of the 'individual autonomy' rationale inheres in the difficulty of achieving consensus on the understandings and skills that are truly essential to autonomy. If we cannot reach consensus on this issue, we must either let people follow their differing preferences or let government make the relevant decisions arbitrarily. I believe there is ample evidence, in the recent history of state legislation, regulation, and litigation concerning private schools and home instruction, to suggest that the state simply cannot be trusted to make reasonable decisions in an area so plagued by powerful prejudices and lobbies.

The educational profession has come up with virtually interminable grocery lists of what all children should learn, but nothing that identifies the truly essential prerequisites of autonomy. The National Education Association's famous 'Cardinal Principles', for example, whose title suggests a focus on the *cardinal*, or primary, or essential, relate instead to well-nigh everything, providing almost every educational specialist with a claim to employment.

Perhaps the claim to employment was a primary consideration in the identification of 'cardinal' principles. The process was perhaps like one often used in universities, where efforts to identify the courses all students logically must take to complete a particular program often turn out, after high-sounding discussions, to include the favorite course of each professor on the committee. In the light of the self-serving impulses of human beings, one should not expect a list of the essential competencies of individual autonomy — or the essentials of anything else, for that matter — to emerge from the unavoidably political efforts of the people who stand to benefit directly from the contents of such a list.

Nevertheless, certain elementary understandings and skills are probably essential to responsible, autonomous adulthood, at least for the majority of people. Though questions may be raised about the cruciality twenty years hence of the three Rs (for most communicating and calculating may soon be done electronically), it seems unjust to burden a child with the risks inherent in the lack of these capabilities, especially since the lack will hamper forms of learning that the individual may elect in the future. It seems tenuous to assert, similarly, that there is no need to familiarize all youngsters with the fundamental workings of our political, legal, and economic structures, so long as the familiarization involves no imposition of particular world views. Without such understandings and skills, most individuals will probably fall far short of the decision-making capacities they would otherwise develop, and will probably find many options beyond their reach.

These arguments seem enough to warrant the demand that every child be given at least the above-discussed core elements of an elementary education. There is evidence to suggest that these simple elements make available a surprising range of options, especially for people whose cultures equip them with habits of versatility and responsibility. In a brief study in Kansas, I discovered that children who grew up in the old order Amish fold experienced remarkable success later on, despite Justice Douglas' predictions to the contrary, when they defected and prepared themselves for college through correspondence courses or independent study.[9] There is evidence from history to suggest, along this line, that success in school instruction is less a cause of upward mobility than a consequence, at least for some once-oppressed minorities.[10] Even if we agree, however, that it is essential to give all youngsters the above-mentioned core elements of schooling, that agreement does not necessarily justify the degree of state intervention common today, as expressed through compulsory school attendance laws and related regulations. We could give parents and children complete freedom to decide how the specified competencies would be developed, so long as each child demonstrated periodically — by jaunting off to the nearest testing station, perhaps — that at least normal progress was being made. It is surely not more difficult to determine whether a child can read than it is to determine whether the child has been given the right combination of physical nutrients. One may hand a child a book of appropriate difficulty and say, 'Please read this page out loud'. One may then ask questions to determine whether the child understood the passage. When attorneys for the State of Maine argued recently that a process of this kind would be incredibly difficult and expensive, the judge observed that the state had no great problem setting up a mechanism to determine whether people could drive automobiles.[11]

Should anything *beyond* the above-discussed essentials of autonomy be required? A further prerequisite of adult autonomy, perhaps, is an introduction during adolescence and early adulthood to options that are too complex for adequate consideration in the pre-adolescent years. The freedom to choose means little if the individual is unaware of alternatives — unacquainted with ideologies, life styles, and vocations not characteristic of the immediate community. Decision-making skills may need more honing than occurs in the elementary grades if one is to make rational choices in the complex modern world. A familiarity with the modes of inquiry of several disciples might help. More problems should be manageable, more occupations accessible, and more leisure activities available after an intensive study of mathematics, belles-lettres, and rhetoric. An involvement in group discussion of historical and contemporary issues seems advisable. Exposure to various sports, fine arts, practical arts, and crafts is a good way to open up vocational and avocational worlds. Great ideas from religion, philosophy, and jurisprudence help illuminate the fundamental dilemmas that humans often must confront choosing. Well planned studies of ethnic and religious groups, of various parts of the globe, and of alternative approaches to ethical issues can be argued for quite cogently.

But educational desiderata of this type can be listed almost indefinitely, far beyond the bounds of student time in the high school and even the undergraduate college. We are forced, then, to confront questions pondered for generations by proponents of liberal education: What knowledge is of *most* worth? What knowledge is *utterly* essential? At this point, we encounter many enigmas. To master any area of human endeavor to the extent some scholars think essential, we must neglect areas that other scholars think essential. Available, potentially vital knowledge has become an infinite ocean. If thinkers in the tradition of Herbert Spencer had their way, all students capable of benefitting therefrom would be given exten sive tutelage in science.[12] But if overdone, this approach might produce a good many technically competent barbarians, insensitive to beauty and morality. Many Bernsteins, Hemingways, and Calders might never uncover and develop their talents. Similarly, if we grant all children sufficient training in music, art, crafts, creative writing, and various sports to ensure that potential virtuosi in those areas will be discovered, we may end up with many people essentially naive in several other crucial sectors of knowledge and skill. As a further complication, we must remember that if schools and colleges monopolize too much time, many individuals may be robbed of the capabilities they should develop outside classroom walls. And to add to these conundrums, in planning today's education we must cope with the demands of tomorrow's unknown world in an era of precipitous change.

State officials who act as if they know what areas of knowledge are essential for everyone must possess insights as yet undiscovered by leading scholars, must be unaware of their own ignorance, or must be guilty of colossal pretension, for there is little agreement or certitude among thinkers who have pondered these dilemmas most deeply. As Booth observes:

> Whether from the baffling confusion reigning in higher education today we can extract forms of learning demonstrably more worthy of pursuit than others is not a settled question...[13]

> When C. P. Snow and F. R. Leavis exchanged blows on whether knowledge of Shakespeare is more important than knowledge of the second law of thermodynamics, they were both, it seemed to me, much too ready to assume as indispensable what a great many wise and good men have quite obviously got along without.[14]

But if we cannot identify what everyone must master, by what warrant do we specify what everyone must undergo? It is understandable that the late Robert Hutchins, a leading proponent of liberal education, found the logic behind conventional school programs 'incomprehensible'.[15] Incomprehensible, perhaps, but compelled by force of law.

Special attention should perhaps be given to a kind of learning given systematic analysis only in relatively recent years — the kind that occurs as a consequence of the 'hidden', 'covert', 'unstudied', or 'tacit' curriculum. One argument often advanced in this connection asserts that some essential skills for future citizens must not be permitted to pursue all their studies independently, at home. The argument, if pursued to its logical conclusion, would let the state take custody of all children who live in remote, isolated areas. Dreeben suggests, for instance, that customary forms of schooling may be an essential mechanism for developing the 'sentiments and capacities' that are imperative for all people who wish 'to participate as adults in an industrial nation whose dominant political and economic institutions have not experienced *fundamental* structural change over the past century'. [16] In schools, according to this view, children learn, not so much from their studies as from the patterns of behavior that organizational structure generates, to relate to others in ways basically different from those learned earlier in the family. In the family, there is a tendency to treat everyone as a unique human being. In the bureaucratic spheres that pervade the larger society, the individual must be capable of working with universalistic norms (which treat all people in a given category the same, disregarding differences among them); of interacting with other people in a segmented, specific way (as, for example, when a surgeon deals with the person merely as a patient of a particular type); of differentiating the attributes of an organizational position from the characteristics of the individual occupying the position (as when a worker calmly obeys a foreman he dislikes); and of forming and tolerating the transient, shallow social relationships that are so common in organizational life. Dreeben thinks 'formal schooling ... may provide psychological capacities that individuals "require" in their daily activities as the clients (customers, patients, renters, litigants, depositors, passengers) of others in *their* occupational pursuits'. [17] While agreeing with Dreeben in many respects, Gintis emphasizes the other side of the coin, viewing patterns of daily life in schools as designed primarily to make people effective *producers* (not consumers or clients) in a bureaucratic society. [18] For instance, Gintis thinks people learn in schools to tolerate long periods of boredom, to master tasks that have no meaning to them, to follow schedules dependably, to compete, to subordinate current interests for the sake of future pay-offs, etc., because these are the behavior patterns valued by most employers.

But is Dreeben on target when he suggests that people who have not benefitted from the unstudied curriculum of conventional schools will have great difficulty functioning in a bureaucracy-dominated world? In this connection, again, the example of the old order Amish people is illuminating, for though the simple elementary schools they usually attend exhibit few of the norms of which Dreeben speaks, and though the Plain People almost never attend high schools, they seem typically viewed by employers as superb producers and by bankers and other business men as superb clients. [19] There are still many examples, furthermore, of non-Amish individuals who, despite extremely limited formal schooling, achieve extraordinary success in our bureaucratic world. It seems obvious, then, that some people can acquire the competencies of which Dreeben and Gintis write without being conditioned for many years by the hidden curriculum of the conventional school. For all we know, most people can. Even without examining the desirability or essentiality of preparing children to be good cogs in organizational machinery, then, it seems that the clear, agreed-upon essentials of individual autonomy are very limited, in this respect as well as those discussed earlier.

Problem 2: Can Anyone Create a Neutral Child-Rearing Forum?

Liberalism's logic argues that children must be given a neutral forum in order to be given the power to choose from among competing ideologies, values, and life styles. If humans are pushed or coerced in one direction or another, by their families, their communities, their ethnic groups, or some government agency, choice becomes apparent rather than real in varying degrees.

Many writers on liberal education are sensitive, in this regard, to the bias of 'parochial' groups, but seem surprisingly oblivious to bias in the institutions designed to 'rescue' students from parochialism.

To quote Leonard Fein, 'liberal intellectuals have cast their lot ... against tradition, ritual, and community... The traditional liberal perspective maintains its utopian commitment to a world ... in which the private community would be obsolete'.[20] The liberal traditions school, ostensibly free from parochialism, is a school maintained by the public at large. In the view of most American courts, as well, the liberating, neutral forum for the young is the public school, once all religious trappings have been removed. The public school is a cafeteria of sorts, in which the young confront a wide range of options and presumably have opportunity to develop the capacity to make informed, independent decisions. But is the forum liberating? Is the cafeteria neutral?

The question of whether the state can (and will) guarantee school neutrality is both crucial to the analysis and generally neglected. If the state cannot or will not ensure that an educational forum is unbiased, it obviously cannot invoke the ideal of individual autonomy as a justification for coercing most children into that forum. It may be forced, as the most logical approach to neutrality, to encourage a diversity of educational approaches, none of them neutral, but all tending to balance each other off in the national dialog. Let us consider, then, the factors involved in making a school neutral.

Official school observances seem at first glance to be the easiest segment of school activity to neutralize. There is nothing subtle or hidden about them. But evidence on the ineffectiveness of legal directives in education is sufficient to give anyone serious pause. Whatever one may think of Supreme Court rulings on prayer and Bible reading in public schools, the record is clear: the rulings were widely flouted for years, and apparently no one could do much about the flouting. In the words of one study,

> ...there is no necessary and direct relationship between a Supreme Court decision (or, perhaps, other national enactments as well) and actual local practice. The tangible consequences of national efforts at change, we have seen, are the product of an extended process involving many forces and people. The process only starts with

enunciation of a new national policy; groups, corporations, individuals, and public officials then interact as their priorities and power permit, shaping the eventual outcome as nearly as possible to their preferred image.[21]

Many scholars insist that it is unrealistic to expect any society's schools to maintain an unbiased stance. Such neutrality can hardly be achieved unless school officials disregard demands for privileged treatment from the same social order that granted them their power. After examining several societies, especially our own, the late sociologist-anthropologist Jules Henry asked, half-despairingly, 'Is education possible?'[22] He concluded that education (which he defined in the autonomy-promoting sense under consideration here) was *not* possible in schools maintained by any society or cultural group. The logic of his analysis is straightfoward: No social system can be expected to take deliberate self-destructive steps. Since every social system Henry had examined or read about, including our own, seemed based partly upon obviously illogical assumptions, every one of these social systems depended for its survival upon the inculcation of 'socially necessary ignorance.' Most citizens, he stated, must believe that their form of political economy is the best, or the system will not work. In societies like ours, officially sponsored schools must not counteract compulsive spending — by encouraging such groups as the Amish, for example. Nothing of consequence must be done to interfere with the readiness of citizens to march off and kill on command. Henry listed numerous other components of the stupidity that 'pays off in the social and political areas over the short run.'[23]

There is room to suggest that some of Henry's charges are extreme. For instance, what the leaders of a society think essential to its survival often turns out to be dispensible. So far as I can determine, however, no respected body of opinion in the social sciences regards the schools of any society as neutral with respect to the ideologies and life styles they present for the consideration of the young. At least one major historical treatise has as its central theme the remarkable correspondence of schools with the social orders that sponsor them.[24]

One widely discussed theme in this regard concerns the role of schools in perpetuating privilege and disadvantage. Some writers accuse the public schools of deliberate failure in the education of disadvantaged minorities.[25] Others, seeing formal education as much less efficacious than most people assume, declare that its main function is not to promote social mobility, which it allegedly cannot do, but to maintain the *fiction* that it promotes social mobility.[26] Another body of literature asserts that the bulk of American schools, dedicated to the 'melting pot philosophy', have attempted for many years to destroy ethnic diversity, with the effect, not of creating a new way of life, but of promoting Wasp culture at the expense of other heritages brought to these shores by immigrants.[27]

Part of the explanation for biased schools is the myopia that comes naturally with socialization to any life view. When people in a given locality find a school congenial, they tend to assume that others find it congenial as well, and thus consider complaints about discrimination to be unreasonable. For example, few mainstream Americans around Amish communities seem to display much understanding of why the Amish think public high schools are hostile.[28] (The high schools do not appear hostile to Methodists, Catholics, and agnostics.) Among numerous striking examples that he cites along this line from the Jewish standpoint, Himmelfarb cites the following:

> The society many liberal Christians have seen as secular, either gladly or sadly, is less secular and more Christian from a Jewish perspective. Even those who call themselves secularist rather than Christian tend to have different standards from Jews for judging a culture's secularism and religious neutrality. Two tests of this proposition are the place of Christmas in American life and the question of religious influences in the public schools. For a Jew, no matter how secular, Christmas must be more problematic than it is for a Christian (or ex-Christian) of equal secularity. Despite all the efforts, frequently by Jews, to show that Christmas is no longer Christian (or never was), even Jews removed from Jewish tradition find themselves obliged to engage in casuistries: a tree in the parlor but no wreath on the door or windows, 'Seasons' Greetings' rather than 'Merry Christmas' — the list is long and wryly comical.[29]

It is ridiculous to proclaim educational neutrality when a child from a pacifist minority attends a public school in wartime, when Jehovah's Witness children are required to rub shoulders with peers who consider 'Russellite' doctrines inane, when Navaho children, reared to practice mutual assistance, are placed in a school where most students compete ruthlessly, and in a hundred other settings where merciless social sanctions are exercised against children who behave in accordance with minority ideologies, values, and life styles. It is a travesty to view these situations as liberating, conducive to individual autonomy.

Whether capitulating to these pressures or not, the individual may acquire permanent scars. When Rosenberg compared Catholics, Protestants, and Jews who had been reared in communities where their religious group was dominant with those reared in communities where they were in the minority, he discovered a uniform tendency for the minority-reared to exhibit more anxiety, as reflected in psychosomatic symptoms, many years later in adulthood.[30] On the basis of hundreds of relevant studies, Bloom concludes:

> Where the home and the school are mutually reinforcing environments, the child's educational and social development are likely to

take place at higher and higher levels. Where the home and the school are contradictory environments, it is likely (though our evidence is not very systematic on this point) that the child's development will be slower, more erratic, and, perhaps, with a good deal of emotional disturbance for the child.[31]

The school curriculum may be particularly difficult to neutralize. Every few years, educators are alerted to curriculum bias that escaped earlier scrutiny. They have returned to the drawing boards at different times to obliterate a distorted view of political life, and of ethnic minorities, and of women. They have been urged, on the one hand, to rid science classes of all discussions of creationism, and condemned for doing so on the other hand. Much religious material has been omitted, to the joy of some people and the anger of many others. Some authors now accuse public schools of a pervasive secular humanism.[32] Others complain most of ideological blandness, a lack of emphasis on values, a plague of directionless inconsistency.[33] The library books that some constituencies love, others burn. Whose view of neutrality and fairness will prevail, and when it does, will it not simply be exposed, a few years later, as another dreadful prejudice?

As another complication, children are profoundly influenced by the relatively few adults with whom they identify strongly. The Supreme Court worries about this tendency, but only when it occurs in church-related schools.[34] How can anyone prevent teachers and administrators, who inevitably are committed, knowingly or unknowingly, to one ideology or another, one set of values or another, one life style or another, from influencing children in directions that these children might not choose in a truly neutral forum? As one approach, we could forbid discussion of all value-related topics, since few individuals seem capable of presenting positions with which they disagree as cogently as they present positions with which they agree. But since virtually every aspect of life is fundamentally significant to someone, this policy would place a taboo on almost everything, and make the widely documented boredom of the classroom more deadly than ever. And even if we could prevent teachers from presenting unbalanced discussions of value-related topics, we would have to reckon with such non-verbal influences as an attractive or repugnant personality. When admiring and beginning to identify with a teacher, a youngster is likely to acquire some of the teachers' tacitly exhibited attitudes and values. We could forbid all teachers to reveal their positions concerning issues on which minorities differ fundamentally from the local majority. Then what if the teacher's position becomes known to students, in spite of efforts to conceal it? Should the teacher be required to resign, or failing that, to desist at once from impressing students favorably, lest they begin to identify with him or her and in the process to view his or her position in an increasingly positive light? We could try not to hire any charismatic teachers, since they all have attitudes they may transmit powerfully to the young. At the same time, we should screen out all cantankerous instructors, lest students develop antipathy towards the positions these teachers embody. We could require a variety of ideologies and cultures to be represented proportionately among the attractive and repellent members of a faculty, so as to cancel each other out. Each child could be instructed, during a given school year, by at least half a dozen charismatic teachers, each representing a different position, to avoid unidirectional influences.

But all of these approaches are ridiculous! There apparently is no feasible way of neutralizing the tendency of teachers to influence children one way or another on important questions. Furthermore, we cannot expect teachers even to *attempt* to hide those biases of which they are totally unaware. (One need not study much anthropology to discover that every culture is shot through with unexamined assumptions that members of other cultures find totally unacceptable and repugnant.)

Another aspect of the school that is potent, yet difficult to neutralize, is the student subculture, particularly during the pre-adolescent and adolescent years. Educators as yet know little about it, to say nothing of learning how to control it. As James Coleman's study suggests, conformity to the norms of student peer groups is apparently induced by the 'rating and dating system', which mercilessly dispenses popularity, respect, acceptance into the crowd, praise, awe, support, aid, isolation, ridicule, exclusion, disdain, discouragement, and disrespect.[35] The system's blunt estimation of the student's worth has a profound effect.

As if these impediments to school neutrality and individual autonomy were not enough to cause despair, I must add the contention considered earlier — that the organizational structure of a school, in its formal and informal aspects, far from being a mere container into which ideas of many sorts can be poured, is itself a potent instrument (a 'hidden curriculum') for socializing children to a particular life style. In this light, since it seems difficult to conceive of continuing, purposive social activity bereft of structure, the notion of an unbiased education seems equally difficult to conceive. Some life style must be maintained in any school, but every life style is odious and threatening from some cultural and ideological standpoint.

On the basis of the foregoing analysis, I am forced to conclude that the ideal of the neutral educational forum, being unattainable by any means now discernible, can hardly be used to justify state intervention in the child-rearing process. There is no neutral school. If it could be demonstrated that some schools, even if not neutral, were much more conducive than other schools to the development of individual autonomy, one might be able to construct a somewhat plausible case for channelling children into the former schools rather than latter, but I can discern no reliable criteria for making such distinctions among schools. What many people consider a close approach to neutrality may turn out, on closer analysis, to close off important options, and what many people consider unusually confining approaches to education may have a surprisingly liberating effect. Pertinent here is the previously discussed fact that graduates of Amish schools seem to move readily into mainstream society when they decide to do so, whereas the public high school appears to create a trained incapacity to live as an old order Amishman. The Black Muslim schools, which send some state legislators into tirades, teach that white people are devils, but apparently have the effect, when combined with other aspects of the Black Muslim social system, of imbuing children with a very traditional middle-class Protestant ethic.[36]

There are other severe limits, generally unrecognized, on the liberal dream. Most members of our society, it appears, are not liberated but mutilated when torn loose from their backgrounds.[37] Most individuals adapt best, it appears, when carried along in the stream of their adapting groups. Ironically, then, the most liberating educational settings may often be parochial-looking settings! The possibility deserves more attention than it gets.

Rationale 2: National Unity and Other Demands of 'Good Citizenship'

As every textbook on school law makes clear, US courts generally justify state intervention into the child-rearing process by asserting that the welfare of the state (not the child) is in question. The individual autonomy rationale, considered earlier, emphasizes the learning that will maximize informed choice. The welfare-of-the-state rationale, on the contrary, may often lead to suppression of inquiry and choice. A preoccupation with national unity will cast jaundiced eyes on dissent. Fear of ideologies that seem to threaten the state may lead, as in the McCarthy era, to extreme steps designed to keep the national mind-set 'pure'. If I may revert to the comment of Jules Henry, no known culture can exist without important elements of culturally essential ignorance.

The 'national unity' or 'good citizenship' rationale has three major problems. First of all, definitions of the nature of the sought-for national unity and good citizenship vary widely, depending on whose view of the good life is involved. Secondly, much concern for national unity may be anachronistic in light of the powerful homogenizing influence of the mass media. Thirdly, in attempting to promote the general weal by molding the values of its future citizens, government may be violating the most basic tenets of democracy.

Problem 1: Who Can Be Trusted to Identify the Essential Attitudes and Skills?

As has been suggested, the learnings that are essential to the blooming of individual autonomy will be somewhat different from those that promote the welfare of the state. There is apparently no more agreement, however, concerning the latter than concerning the former, so many problems discussed earlier are equally applicable to the rationale that the state must intervene to ensure an adequate preparation of 'good citizenship'. Even from the standpoint of the welfare-of-the-state rationale, there is justification, then, only for intervention focused upon the relatively limited, widely agreed-upon essentials. In this regard, too, the most defensible mode of intervention seems to be one that focuses upon a demonstration, through simple testing, that the relevant understandings and skills have been acquired, rather than on the context in which, or the methods by which, these competencies must be acquired. It seems sensible to assess culinary wizardry by sampling the pudding, not the recipe.

In the face of all the disagreement, to permit the state to specify long lists of requirements is, in effect, to give the state the arbitrary power to mold its future citizens in terms of some selected vision of the good life. State officials are probably the last group we should trust to decide how much commonality, and of what type, is essential to the general weal. It is in the interest of these officials to discourage the dissension and diversity that may jeopardize their positions, subject them to challenge, and make public institutions more difficult to govern.

If the state requires schools to promote commonality of viewpoint and experience, some programs must be mandated in schools and some must be outlawed. Otherwise, since the ocean of available materials and styles of learning is so vast, there may be little commonality among the offerings of different schools. Who then should be trusted to decide what all educational programs must hold in common? Whose version of national unity should be enforced upon everyone?

A device frequently used to obliterate this issue is the fiction that the common schools simply emphasize what 'all groups have in common'. Even a cursory look at educational history reveals, however, that the unity the public (and often many private) schools promote is neither limited in compass nor composed exclusively of what 'all groups have in common'.

Reactions to the tide of immigration which hit American shores in the late 1800s and early 1900s made this state of affairs particularly clear. 'Let us now be reminded', Calvin Stowe declared, 'that unless we educate our immigrants, they will be our ruin... It is altogether essential to our national strength and peace, if not even to our national existence, that the foreigners who settle on our soil should cease to be Europeans and become Americans'.[38] The word 'Americanization' was soon incorporated into the lexicons of educators and politicians. But for such influential educators as

Ellwood Cubberley, to Americanize meant 'to assimilate and amalgamate these people ... and to implant in their children, so far as can be done, ... the *Anglo-Saxon* conception of righteousness, law and order, and popular government'.[39] The intent of Americanization was clear, at least in the minds of many influentials: the dominance of Anglo-Saxon culture. Diversity, ethnic and religious, was characterized as a 'problem' that needed to be obliterated. Historians began to praise the American frontier as the 'crucible' and the common school as the 'melting pot' of 'spiritual transformation.'[40]

So pervasive is the domain of common experiences and understandings promoted through state intervention that some scholars think government has adopted an official 'civil religion' and designated the public school as an established church.[41] That religion, such scholars assert, is comprised of the values, beliefs, myths, loyalties, ceremonies, etc., generally subsumed under the rubric, 'The American Way of Life'. The nation's civil religion is reflected in the rhetoric and visual symbols of many public ceremonies (for example, Presidential inaugurations, celebrations on Memorial Day and July 4). Civil religion is not a substitute for, or rival of, Protestantism, Catholicism, Judaism, or any other instrument of personal piety, but rather a somewhat parallel device that performs vital civil functions.

Government, while purporting to accentuate the values all groups hold in common, intervenes to promote a distinctly biased version of national unity. It is difficult to see how anything else *could* occur.

Problem 2: A Preoccupation with National Unity May be Anachronistic in an Era of Powerful, Ubiquitous Electronic Media

The argument may be raised that this nation now suffers far less from any lack of common ideas and values than from a diminishing opportunity for alternatives. The masses of Americans may have an unprecedented background of common knowledge and experience, and it may be derived far more from television and cinema than from the schools. To become more aware of the homogenizing influence of the mass media, one need only visit Canada, a country possessed of a long-standing, intense, and perhaps intensifying concern with the difficulty — some think, the impossibility — of maintaining national distinctiveness when no one can shield Canadians from the electronic bombardment across the southern border. If we were properly aware of the impact of the media, we might be well advised to view schools as one of the few remaining institutions for preserving a modicum of diversity. This is another issue demanding more discussion than it gets.

Problem 3: In Attempting to Protect the General Weal by Molding Values, Government May be Violating the Most Basic Democratic Tenets

There is something basically contradictory about a nation which, while ostensibly dedicated to the free expression of ideas and an uninhibited examination of alternatives, allows government to determine how the minds of its young will be molded. In Meiklejohn's view, it is precisely this effort by the state to tailor the thought of its citizens that the First Amendment was written to forbid. Followed to its ultimate conclusion, the First Amendment would demand, not so much the often-discussed separation of church and state, but, far more important, separation of school and state — or, more broadly, the removal of government from all major devices for forming human minds, including the press, other mass media, religion, and educational institutions. These ideas, fortunately, are discussed at length by Arons.[42]

Rationale 3: Education as an Expert Function

One often hears in American courts the argument that the state must intervene in schooling because education is essentially a scientific enterprise, requiring the well developed competencies of professionals. Private schools may be permitted, and sometimes home instruction, but only when the state ensures, by mandating certain 'minimum requirements', such as teacher certification, that the needed competencies will be applied to the education of children.

This rationale often falls on sympathetic ears. The belief seems widespread that, since no one may practice as an attorney without gaining admission to the bar, and no one may practice as a physician unless being licensed, the public thus gains substantial protection against incompetence. The notion of protecting against educational incompetence by specifying who may function as a teacher seems a logical extension of the strategy of protection through licensing arrangements. Little attention is given to the possibility that licensing provides more protection to the members of a profession than to the general public; so while prices may rise, the quality of service may not, or may even decline.[43] Even less attention is given to the fact that teaching is at best a 'truncated profession', lacking the powerful training mechanisms and procedures of peer evaluation of the established professions, and particularly lacking the benefits of a firm knowledge base.[44]

It is unfortunate when reputable scholars write as though the recent meager findings on teacher behaviors associated, generally modestly, with superior student learning, now constitute a scientific basis for teaching.[45]

The research on teaching, though voluminous, does not reveal many consistent attributes of good instruction. Some prominent scholars still argue, in fact, that the search for consistent attributes is misguided, since different subjects and different levels of cognitive functioning may necessarily demand different teaching approaches.[46]

The attributes of good teaching that do seem reasonably consistent in the research apply mostly to basic, well structured academic subjects and the lower levels of cognition.[47] It is important to note, moreover, that the attributes seem largely a matter of common sense, rather than of esoteric training.

My UCEA colleague, Madeline Hunter, who has advocated the pertinent teaching techniques for many years, informs me that she has been able to turn intelligent lay persons into good, and sometimes excellent, teachers rather quickly by instructing them rather briefly. Her successful experiences in this area have led her to publish a book, in collaboration with Sally Breit, on *Aideing in Education* , a book designed to tell lay people how to follow certain simple practices of good teaching.[48]

As followers of research on teaching well know, the initial prevailing approach of that research, much like the early research on leadership, was to attempt to find the secrets of good teaching (like the secrets of leadership) in the personal *attributes* or traits of teachers. Were good teachers more verbal or less verbal, more outgoing or less outgoing, more nurturant or less nurturant, younger or older, child-centered or subject-centered, experienced or inexperienced, trained in major universities or in institutions devoted exclusively to teacher training, certified or uncertified? That body of research, most scholars concluded, was essentially a waste of time. Good teachers and bad teachers often had the *same* personal attributes. What differentiated them was not what they *were*, but how they performed in the classroom.[49]

State regulators seem not to have learned that lesson. In the face of the vast preponderance of evidence on good teaching, they still seek to guarantee good teaching to every child by demanding a teacher attribute that has no demonstrated relationship to teaching quality — namely, teacher certification.

One reason why I tend to be slightly cynical on this issue is found in an inconsistency often manifested in US courtrooms. I have often heard the state's expert witnesses argue that the state cannot rely on testing as a way of ensuring that students have learned what the state is entitled to demand, for tests often have only limited validity. A far better way, these witnesses insist, is to demand, through certification requirements, that all teachers be trained in the competencies associated with student achievement in recent research. But this research is just as invalid as the achievement tests on which it is based. The state's 'hired guns' cannot logically have it both ways. They cannot reject achievement tests as invalid and then demand regulations based upon findings from the same achievement tests.

Rationale 4: Beyond the Clear Essentials, Education Needs State Encouragement

One may argue that it is not enough for the state to demand that every child be provided with the understandings and skills essential to individual autonomy and good citizenship. Though there may be extensive disagreement about the further knowledge that is of most worth, there is widespread agreement concerning the advantages of further knowledge. But education is complex and expensive. Without state encouragement, education often simply does not occur, as this argument goes, and many of the young will spend their time, instead, in wasteful and sometimes destructive activities. The nation may suffer from a shortage of scientists and engineers.

This argument would be rejected out of hand by many conservative economists, since they contend that, in the long haul at least, especially when government intervention does not distort the interaction of supply and demand, the market's 'hidden hand' elicits all the goods and services that a society needs, and does so more effectively than the state could possibly do. The argument is repugnant to libertarians as well, who see government action as inevitably destructive, especially in the long run, of liberty and human happiness. The argument could be assessed more logically if we had better evidence on the extent of the need for state encouragement. Some scholars insist, for example, that in both England and the United States there was much greater educational opportunity *before* the modern era of state intervention than is generally recognized.[50]

Whatever the merits of the argument, political realities probably guarantee that considerable government involvement in education will continue to occur. Realistically, it may be important to discover ways in which that involvement may be channeled so as to minimize its negative impact.

Conclusion

None of the four rationales for state intervention into child-rearing and schooling is without significant problems. Two particular difficulties beset the individual autonomy rationale — the impossibility of objective definition and the inevitable cultural biases embedded in schooling. The 'national unity' and 'good citizenship' rationale has similar definitional problems, in addition to being anachronistic and undemocratic. The rationale that state intervention is needed because education is an expert function is no more sound than the preceding rationales; expertise about the best methods of teaching and learning is limited. Finally, the premise that education needs state encouragement is grounded in no clear or consistent conception of national purpose. Virtually any argument can be made about the need for

Donald A. Erickson

state investment in education to justify a policymaker's goals. Because this
rationale is subject to much potential abuse as it pertains to regulation both
of public and private schools, a libertarian perspective requires skeptical
vigilance.

A libertarian argument does not require that no state intervention into
child-rearing and schooling will occur. Justifiable basis may exist, but it
is the task of others, not libertarians, to make that case. The distinctive
libertarian contribution is to challenge existing rationales and the abuse that
too frequently attends these unchallenged assumptions that state intervention is beneficial.

Acknowledgment

I gratefully acknowledge the reactions of James Cibulka to an earlier draft.
This paper was prepared in some haste, in response to an invitation to
explore the educational implications of libertarianism. The ideas are
preliminary and tentative, requiring much further thought. They appear
here to stimulate discussion.

Notes

1 The 'shooting' reference is to John Singer, who was killed in a confrontation with
Sheriff's deputies over his insistence upon educating his children at home. For a
brief account of this episode, see: MOORE, R. and MOORE, D. (1982). *Home-Spun
Schools: Teaching Children at Home — What Parents Are Doing and How They Are Doing
It*, Waco, TX, Word Books, pp. 129–132.
2 See numerous instances of state harassment of home-schoolers, *ibid.*; Arons,
examining other episodes, asks why it is that 'millions of children who are
pushouts or dropouts amount to business as usual in the public schools, while one
family educating a child at home becomes a major threat to universal public
education and the survival of democracy'. ARONS, S. (1983) *Compelling Belief: The
Culture of American Schooling* New York, McGraw-Hill Book Company, p. 88.
3 *Pierce v. Society of Sisters* , 268 US 510, 45 S Ct. 571 (1925), at 573.
4 *Ibid.*
5 See instances discussed in Moore and Moore, *Homespun Schools*; Arons, *Compelling
Belief* ; ERICKSON, D. A. (1968) 'The "Plain People" and American Democracy',
Commentary 45, January, pp. 36–44; ERICKSON, D. A. (1969) 'The Persecution of
LeRoy Garber', *School Review* 78, November, pp. 81–90.
6 BOOTH, W. C. (1967) 'Is There Any Knowledge That a Man Must Have?' in
BOOTH, W. C. (ed.), *The Knowledge Most Worth Having* Chicago, University of
Chicago Press, p. 21.
7 REDFIELD, J. M. (1967) 'Platonic Education', in Booth, W. C. *op. cit.* pp. 158–59.
8 *Wisconsin v. Yoder*, 406 US 205 (1971), at 244–45.
9 Erickson, (1969) *op. cit.*.

10 JENCKS, C. *et al.*, (1972) *Inequality* New York, Basic Books; BERG, I. (1970) *Education and Jobs: The Great Training Robbery* New York, Praeger Publishing Company.

11 The comment appears in the court record, though not in the decision itself, in *Bangor Baptist Church v. Maine*, 576 F. Supp. 1299 (D.Me. 1983).

12 SPENCER, H. (1911) *Essays on Education, Etc.* London, J. M. Dent & Sons, Ltd., p. 42.

13 BOOTH, W. C. 'Preface', in Booth, W. C. (1967) *op. cit.*, p. xi.

14 BOOTH, W. C. 'Is There Any Knowledge That a Man Must Have', in Booth, W. C. (1967) *op. cit.*, p. 4.

15 HUTCHINS, R. M. (1971) 'Toward a Learning Society: The Institutional Illusion', *National Elementary Principal* 51, October, p. 39.

16 DREEBEN, R. (1971) 'American Schooling: Patterns and Processes of Stability and Change', in BARBER, B. and INKELES, A. (eds), *Stability and Social Change* Boston, Little, Brown and Co., p. 101.

17 *Ibid.*

18 GINTIS, H. (1972) 'Towards a Political Economy of Education: A Radical Critique of Ivan Illich's "Deschooling Society",' *Harvard Educational Review* 42 February, pp. 87–88.

19 ERICKSON, D. (1969) *op. cit.*

20 FEIN, L. (1970) 'The Limits of Universalism', in LEVIN, H. J. (ed.), *Community Control of Schools* Washington, DC, The Brookings Institution, pp. 89–90.

21 DOLBEARE, K. M. and HAMMOND, P. E. (1973) *The School Prayer Decisions: From Court Policy to Local Practice* Chicago, University of Chicago Press, p. 33. Also see: MUIR, W. K. (1967) *Prayer in the Public Schools: Law and Attitude Change* Chicago, University of Chicago Press.

22 HENRY, J. (1969) 'Is Education Possible?' in ERICKSON, D. A. (ed.), *Public Controls for Nonpublic Schools* Chicago, University of Chicago Press, pp. 83–102.

23 *Ibid.*, p. 87.

24 EDWARDS, N. and RICHEY, H G (1963) *The School in the American Social Order* 2nd ed.,; Boston, Houghton Mifflin.

25 STEIN, A. (1971) 'Strategies for Failure', *Harvard Educational Review* 41, May, pp. 158–204.

26 GINTIS, H. (1972) *op. cit* ; KATZ, M. B. (1972) *Class, Bureaucracy and Schools* New York, Praeger; GREER, C. (1972) *The Great School Legend* New York, Basic Books.

27 SHRAG, P. (1982) *The Decline of the Wasp* New York, Simon and Schuster; NOVAK, M. (1972) *The Rise of the Unmeltable Ethnics* New York, Macmillan.

28 ERICKSON, D. A. (1968) 'The "Plain People" and American Democracy', *Commentary* 45, January, pp. 36–44.

29 HIMMELFARB, M. (1967) 'Secular Society? A Jewish Perspective', *Daedalus* 96, Winter, p. 223.

30 ROSENBERG, M. (1964) 'The Dissonant Religious Context and Emotional Disturbance', in SCHNEIDER, L. (ed.), *Religion, Culture, and Society: A Reader in the Sociology of Religion* New York, John Wiley & Sons, pp. 549–559.

31 BLOOM, B. S. (1966) 'Stability and Change in Human Characteristics: Implications for School Reorganization', *Educational Administration Quarterly* 2, Winter, p. 46.

32 McCARTHY, R., OPPEWAL, D., PETERSON, W. and SPYKMAN, G. (1981) *State, Society, and Schools* Grand Rapids, MI, William E. Eerdmans Publishing Company.

33 ARONS, S. (1983) *Compelling Belief.*

34 *Aquilar v. Felton*, 105 S. CT. 3232 (1985).

35 COLEMAN, J. S. (1961) *The Adolescent Society* Glencoe, IL, The Free Press of Glencoe.

36 VONTRESS, C. E. 'The Black Muslim Schools', *Phi Delta Kappan* 47, October, pp. 86–90; PARENTI, M. (1964) 'The Black Muslims: From Revolution to Institution', *Social Research* 31, Summer, pp. 180–83.

37 FEIN, L. (1970) 'The Limits of Universalism'.

38 Quoted in CREMIN, L. A. (1961) *The Transformation of the School* New York, Vintage Books, p. 68.

39 MARDEN C. F. and MEYER, G. (1962) *Minorities in American Society* 2nd ed., New York, American Book Company, p. 30.

40 TURNER, F. J. (1920) *The Frontier in American History* New York, Henry Holt & Company, pp. 22–23.

41 BELLAH, R. N. (1967) 'Civil Religion in America', *Daedalus* 96 Winter, pp. 1–21; HERBERG, W. (1960) *Protestant, Catholic, Jew* rev. ed., Garden City, NY, Anchor Books; MICHAELSON, R. (1970) *Piety in the Public School* New York, Macmillan Company.

42 ARONS, S. (1983) *Compelling Belief. op. cit.*

43 FRIEDMAN, M. (1963) *Capitalism and Freedom* Phoenix ed., Chicago, Univerity of Chicago Press, pp. 137–160.

44 LORTIE, D. C. (1975) *Schoolteacher: A Sociological Study* Chicago, University of Chicago Press.

45 GAGE, N. L. (1977) *The Scientific Basis of the Art of Teaching* New York, Teachers College Press.

46 STODOLSKY, S. S. 'Teacher Evaluation: The Limits of Looking', *Educational Researcher* 13, November, pp. 11–18; PETERSON, P. E. (1979) 'Direct Instruction Reconsidered', in PETERSON, P. E. and WALBERG, H. J. (eds.), *Research on Teaching: Concepts, Findings, and Implications* Berkeley, CA, McCutchan Publishing Corp., pp. 57–69.

47 BROPHY, J. and GOOD, T. L. (1986) 'Teacher Behavior and Student Achievement', in WITTROCK, M. L. (ed.), *Handbook of Research on Teaching* 3rd ed.; New York, Macmillan Publishing Company, pp. 328–375.

48 HUNTER, M. and BREIT, S. (1976) *Aide-ing in Education* El Segundo, CA, TIP Publications.

49 This emerged as a major theme, discussed in several chapters, in GAGE, N. L. (ed.), (1963), *Handbook of Research on Teaching* Chicago, Rand McNally.

50 See, for example. WEST, E. G. (1965) *Education and the State* London, Institute of Economic Affairs.

Chapter 2
Family Choice in Education: The Case of Denmark, Holland, and Australia*

Denis P. Doyle

The essence of education is that it is religious. Pray, what is religious education? A religious education is an education which inculcates duty and reverence. Duty arises from our potential control over the course of events. Where attainable knowledge could have changed the issue, ignorance has the guilt of vice. And the foundation of reverence is this perception, that the present holds within itself the complete sum of existence, backwards and forwards, that whole amplitude of time, which is eternity.

Alfred North Whitehead
The Aims of Education

Introduction

This essay offers a preliminary examination of family choice in elementary and secondary education in three foreign countries — Holland, Denmark, and Australia. Its purpose is to stimulate American thinking about family choice systems and what approaches might be appropriate in an American setting.[1]

Choice, in an American context, is typically exercised between the public and private sectors, in large part because in the public sector schools are more alike than different. (That we have more than 15,000 'independent' school districts has no observable effect on school differences. The American public school is the product of a shared culture of schooling which overwhelms almost all differences.)

There are, to be sure, differences among American schools that people do choose, but these differences fall across a 'quality' gradient. Thus, a newcomer to the Washington DC metropolitan area who has children and

* Commission by the National Institute of Education Contract # EPA 30032

is in a position to select a neighborhood in which to live, does so with the 'quality' of the schools very much in mind. But in the case of public school 'quality', the differences are almost entirely attributable to the social class of the school, its staff, and students. Thus, a school in the depressed inner city is structurally the same as the school in the affluent suburbs: children are grouped by age, in classrooms, before a teacher who lectures and uses publicly-approved textbooks.

The quality differentials the education consumer finds in this example are not a matter of education policy but an accident of housing patterns and social class. In only a few communities in the United States are quality differences a matter of explicit education policy. Thus, in New York City, Boston, Philadelphia, and San Francisco, there are a limited number of 'fast track' public schools designed to serve the needs of a limited population of academically ambitious and talented youngsters. Bronx Science and Peter Stuyvesant in New York, Boston Latin, Lowell in San Francisco, and Central in Philadelphia are public schools which have been established to provide real choice for a select few. That they work is beyond dispute. The principal of Bronx Science, for example, proudly reports that forty per cent of his incoming class is drawn from private schools.

These schools are designed on European models that to this day are widely followed in all the developed countries — the grammar school in the UK and Commonwealth countries, the gymnasium in Germany, and the lycée (with the Baccalaureate examination and degree) in France and the former French colonies. But even these schools are structurally similar to their less prestigious counterparts. The only choice models of consequence are those that permit children (or their families) to choose among schools with different value systems. And these schools in most countries are described as 'private' schools. But are they private as we would use that term?

Private Meets Public

To the American researcher or policy analyst beginning to examine school practices in other countries, the difficulty occasioned by developing a working definition of the term 'private school' is surprising. It is surprising because the American experience has conditioned us to assume that a straightforward definition exists and is widely used and widely understood. Thus, in America a private school is a school which is privately owned and operated, sets its own standards, and is subject to only marginal state control. (Most observers also assume that private schools are part of the so-called third, or independent, sector; while most private schools are organised as not-for-profit organizations, not all are, and there is no *a priori* reason that most must be organized that way.)

Similarly, in America a public school is one which is owned and operated by the government, regardless of who it serves and how its expenditure levels are determined. Thus, a wealthy suburban enclave, which serves only upper-middle class white students is considered public if the residents in that area tax themselves to support the school their children attend. (Taxes that may be deducted from the federal income tax, it must be added, are a do-it-yourself tuition tax credit for the well-to-do.) A struggling Roman Catholic parish school, with a high proportion of poor and minority students, which has an open-enrollment policy, is regarded by most Americans as a 'private' school.

The issue is not rhetorical — there are today dozens of inner-city 'private' schools that serve the poor and racial minorities.[2] Similarly, there are thousands of 'public' enclaves, deliberately created to provide amenities, financed out of public revenues, that are as exclusive as the most exclusive 'private' club. To most middle-class families with children of school age, the most important 'amenity' is the local school. Real estate agents in most communities are self-styled 'experts' on the quality of local schools, and few prospective home buyers fail to make judgments about the quality of the local public school; it is one of the central reasons for purchasing a house at all.

Ironically, in other areas of national life — clubs, hotels, restaurants, airlines, buses, trains, taxis — we employ a different and more useful definition of the term 'public'. It is based not on who owns and operates the institution that provides the service, but who is served. A hotel organized to serve the public is a public accommodation. So too is a restaurant, train, drugstore, gas station, bus, or an airplane. There, public character derives not from ownership but patronage; or, in the case of civil rights questions, who would like to be a patron. Indeed, this definition lies at the heart of the interstate commerce clause; it permits the federal government to protect the rights of minorities.

There is, then, a long tradition of law and custom which leads us to define as public certain institutions which serve the public but which themselves are not publicly owned. Indeed, in many areas of national life we deliberately use private instrumentalities to achieve public policy objectives.[3] Of equal interest in this connection is the way in which American society deals with collateral human capital issues of which education is only the most prominent part. (Human capital is the acquired set of skills, knowledge, traits, and attitudes possessed by an individual. In addition to formal and informal education, human capital includes health and welfare.)[4]

Thus, public sector health care programs have shifted away from reliance on publicly owned and operated hospitals, to financial aid programs for individuals to purchase privately offered health care in the market. Similarly, food stamps are used to improve the diet of poor Americans, rather than publicly owned and operated soup kitchens or food distribution centers. In the same vein, a shift away from public housing is occurring, replaced by housing vouchers, rent supplements and other programs. The reasons for these shifts in policy are not administrative expedience or cost savings (though those frequently occur as a consequence); rather, they reflect a belief that the dignity and self-respect of the recipient are enhanced by such program design.

The Sacramento, California, County Welfare Department made national headlines precisely for this reason. A 'conservative' welfare administrator decided that public aid could be more efficiently dispensed by providing a county facility in which food, housing, and bathroom facilities would be made available at no cost to the indigent. For his pains, the county administrator was sued because of the allegation that changing from a cash grant for the indigent to the provision of service and goods by the government stripped the recipient of his dignity. Indeed, in a flight of hyperbole rarely seen even in the legal profession, counsel for plaintiff asserted that Sacramento County was re-establishing the 'poor house' of the nineteenth century. (It is an interesting commentary on the nature of the times that in this and similar cases it is often difficult to determine the philosophical or political predilections of the various actors without a scorecard.)

Indeed, expanding the review of the world of social services beyond those mentioned above reveals a set of programs that rely very heavily on the private sector as well. Working parents may claim daycare tax credits for children 14 and under in private (or public) fee-charging daycare centers (including private kindergarten, suggesting that the IRS knows more about the educational content of kindergarten than educators do). Grants and loans for higher education have been in place at the federal level for a number of years, and have a long history in many states.

Education and Values

The reason for this disquisition is to make a simple point: in America, in almost all walks of life, the line between the public and private sectors is beginning to blur.[5] But there is a special reason, unique to this country, that Americans have tried to maintain a line between public and private schools. Most American private schools are religiously affiliated, but so too are most non-government schools in developed democracies. It explains much about American practice and much about the experience of other countries. America is alone among the developed democracies in not providing aid to private schools. This is perfectly natural to many Americans, but it obscures an important point.

Not aiding private schools is a part of a more important public policy: not providing aid to religious schools. Because the overlap between the two categories is so great, the two types of schools are often thought to be one and the same. They are not. Even the most ardent supporter of a narrow construction of the First Amendment must admit that this is no constitutional barrier to the provision of public funds for non-denominational private schools. The constitutional barrier that was once thought to exist was limited to religiously affiliated schools (That barrier may have crumbled under the terms of *Mueller* v. *Allen*, the recent Supreme Court case in which Minnesota's system of tax deductions for school expenses, public and private, secular and religious, was upheld.[6])

Because American public schools were so overtly and openly Protestant, Catholics thought it only fair that they have their own school system, as indeed they did in many parts of the country until the late 1840s. The most famous was the Lowell Plan, which euphemistically described Catholic schools (in the public sector) as 'Irish schools'. The process of disestablishing these schools and denying them public funds was not the work of the court. Rather, it was the work of legislatures.

So self-obvious was this that enthusiastic opponents of aid to Catholic schools such as Speaker of the House, James G. Blaine and President Ulysses S. Grant never thought to raise constitutional arguments against it. It simply never occurred to anyone of the time that aid to religious schools might be unconstitutional. The way to stop it was to outlaw it, plain and simple. This they did with such effect that Catholics could only secure a Catholic education in private Catholic schools, and so the nation's private Catholic schools appeared. Protestants had the luxury of a Protestant education at public expense.

As an historical note, it is important to remember that for many years in the United States, public schools were Protestant institutions in which Protestant prayer was conducted daily and the Protestant Bible was used.[7] The importance of this should become apparent in the discussion and analysis of other countries' systems of support for education choice.[8]

Before discussing the choice systems in Denmark, Holland, and Australia — independent systems which receive government funds — we should look briefly at choice exclusively within the government sector. Does it exist, and if so, what does it look like? It does exist in almost all developed democracies *and* totalitarian systems. But to most Americans it is a 'choice' system as surprising as a system of 'public' education which is not owned and operated by the government. It is, in a word, a part of the 'elite' education system characteristic of almost all other developed and undeveloped countries, free and totalitarian.

In these systems, choice is secured by passage of an examination at successive educational levels. Each higher level is progressively more difficult than the preceding lower level, and the number of seats in each higher level is strictly rationed. It is a true status pyramid, in which the band of students served is narrowed at each upward step. The reasons for this are twofold: in most countries there is explicit recognition of real intellectual and academic differences among students. No one in France or Germany would seriously propose that all children can be educated to the same level. At the same time, the other nations of the world have not been so fortunate, in economic terms, as the United States. Limiting the number of seats in education institutions was encouraged for budgetary as well as pedagogical reasons. Together, budget constraints and 'assumptions' about student ability have led to an education system characterized by a degree of hierarchy which does not exist in this country, even in the post-secondary realm.

There is, then, a well developed system of elite public schools in all the developed countries, which provide for some real measure of academic choice in the government sector for those students who can pass the examinations (or who are effective influence peddlers).[9]

To understand these developments more fully, and to see if they might have some relevance to the American experience, let us turn to Denmark, a country renowned for toleration and civility.

Denmark

In the early years of the nineteenth century, Danish interest in free public education for young children began to build, as it did in most of the enlightened and more developed nations of the day. And in 1814, seven years of compulsory education was introduced. The notion of 'compulsory education' had a special meaning in Denmark:

> It should, however, be noted that compulsory education did not mean compulsory schooling. It meant that people were free to educate their children in whatever way they saw fit as long as the children received instruction in the principal school subjects and that this instruction was of a standard comparable to that given in municipal schools.

> This freedom of choice of education has always been a leading principle of Danish education and is particularly stressed in the 'free school movement'. This movement resulted from the ideas of N. F. S. Grundtvig, a famous Danish poet, clergyman and philosopher who, during the 1830s, was a strong critic of the contemporary practice especially in grammar schools, which he found too scholastic.[10]

(Free public high schools were a much later development in all countries.)

The importance of free public education was self-obvious to most reformers interested in education. The burden of establishing and maintaining schools exceeded the capacity and willingness of the private sector. Indeed, in a moral sense (if not an economic one) those children most in need of a decent education were precisely those least likely to receive one if it were left to the vagaries of the private sector; i.e., a system restricted to fee-charging schools worked a hardship on the poor. Church schools had long been organized, but their principal mission was to teach enough reading to permit parishioners to understand the Bible. The greater knowledge necessary to work and succeed in a mercantile society called for more thorough and complete schooling, precisely the kind made available to the more well-to-do in the private sector.

The Danes, then, created a national system of public elementary schools designed to serve all young children in the nation. (Interestingly, the Danes still do not start compulsory education until age 7, a practice with roots deep in the nineteenth century.) At the time they started the public school there was a national church, as there is today. Danish Evangelical Lutheranism found its way into the Danish public school and its curriculum as naturally as did the study of Danish. And it was not rote devotional activity, but serious business.

Ever concerned about the rights of minorities, however, the Danes developed a system to preserve the religious freedom of non-Lutherans — Jews, Catholics, and free thinkers. They were given the right to start their own schools at public expense. Any group of parents — to this day — who among them have twenty-eight children, is permitted to claim government funding for their own 'private school'. The term is set in quotation marks for a reason. Although the Danish *Freischolen*. represent about thirteen per cent of the elementary and secondary schools in Denmark, they enroll only about six per cent of the population. Their enrollment has hovered at about five per cent for many years, a commentary on the vitality and strength of the government-run sector. Indeed, the Danish government regards the private schools as only natural, because not all parents have the same taste in education.

The government is quite explicit about its reasons for providing the opportunity to parents to start their own schools:

> Today, various kinds of 'free' or independent schools exist, all of them subsidized by up to 85 per cent of their operational expenditures. Subject to certain conditions, loans on favourable terms can be obtained for the establishment of new schools.

> The principle behind these large subsidies is that, although Denmark has an efficient education system providing educational opportunities for all, it should be possible for people to choose an alternative kind of education for their children should they wish, whether their reasons for this be ideological, political, educational or religious.[11]

They do escape the necessity of offering Danish Evangelical Lutheranism as both a course of study and as a devotional activity. This is no small thing, because there are large areas of the curriculum which are heavily freighted with religious values — sex education is only the most obvious example. Literature as an expression of deeply held religious values may more subtly embody religious precept, but it is every bit as imbued with religious value. Courses in comparative religion or the Bible as literature (the American public school stratagem to get the Bible back into the school) deliberately and self-consciously avoid this point. [12]

To most American observers it is a fine bit of irony that the Danes assert that the way to preserve religious freedom is to provide public funds for religious (and non-religious) schools. At the same time, and with the same enthusiasm, many Americans argue that religious freedom is best preserved by not providing public aid to students who attend religious schools. [13]

Australia

The antipodes offer a most interesting and striking comparison to the United States. [14] A continental democracy, inheritors of English common law and language, Australia is in many important respects more like America than any other country on earth. Indeed, the similarities are so strong and so striking the observer must remind himself that differences exist as well. The principal difference is population. With a land mass approaching that of the contiguous forty-eight states, Australia's total population is about fifteen million — approximately seven per cent of the population of the US. But Australia's relatively small population is among the most urbanized on earth, with the vast majority of Australians living in and around eight cities — Darwin, Brisbane, Sydney, Melbourne, Canberra, Adelaide, Tasmania-Hobart, and Perth — all but Canberra located coastally. (Canberra, the capital, established in 1908, was deliberately sited inland, out of the range of the longest naval guns of the day.) And until only recently, the Australian population was much more homogeneous than that of the US (in the past two decades, Australian immigration has drawn heavily on non-British stock, principally central and southern Europeans. The native aboriginal population is very small.)

One of the most striking aspects of Australian intellectual and political life is the set of close ties between our two countries.

Most Australian academics and senior civil servants have traveled extensively in the US and many have also studied here. They read American journals and magazines, and are extremely well informed about American practice and history. Indeed, there is a long history of Australia–US information exchange, exemplified by Australian adoption as a part of their constitution important parts of the US constitution.

Although the Australians have a Westminster form of government — a parliament, in which ministers are drawn from the lower house of the legislature — there is a division of power, with a strong judiciary. And to ensure the rights of all Australians, the first amendment to the US constitution was adopted virtually word-for-word when the Australian colonies formed the Federation in 1901. Article 116 of the Australian constitution reads: 'The Commonwealth shall not make any law for establishing religion, or for imposing any religious observance, or for prohibiting the free exercise of any religion.' By way of contrast, the First Amendment to the US Constitution reads: 'Congress shall make no law respecting an establishment of religion, or prohibiting the free exercise thereof.' So similar is the wording between the two, that upon challenge before the Australian High Court, American precedent and the terms of the constitutional debate were discussed to illuminate the eventual interpretation. (It should be noted that the Australian decision was based on organic Australian law and did not employ American precedent or interpretation as a basis for the High Court's finding.) In the instant case, the Australian High Court upheld the government program of aid to religious schools so long as the Australian government was scrupulously neutral and treated all religions (including non-religion) equally, and did not prefer one to another. [15] Australian interest in private education was not abstract. As it happens, a sizeable portion of the Australian population is Catholic; in fact, in most of Australia's six states a third of the population is Catholic. The pressure, then, for Catholic education has been very intense. [16]

The argument about the appropriateness of including Catholic schools as part of a system of public funding for education began to unfold in a most interesting way, however. Because of limited financial resources (the 'free' labor of religious orders notwithstanding), Catholic schools had overcrowded physical plants, unfavorable student–faculty ratios, poorly trained teachers (in at least some areas), and limited curricular offerings.

The effect of all this was to create a popular belief that Catholic education was 'inferior' to public education. [17] Whether or not it was inferior in any measurable sense is probably beyond resolution, except to note the common sense views that lower student–teacher ratios are usually to be preferred to higher ones, just as better physical plants and more textbooks are generally to be preferred to run-down buildings or out-of-date books. There is a curious footnote to this. Australians have never shared American reticence about comparing school outcomes; i.e., school-by-school test scores, and the Australian Council for Education Research (ACER) reported in 1976 that Catholic schools had higher test scores than government schools. Nevertheless, the view persisted that Catholic schools were less well-off than public schools; in terms of financial resources this was most certainly true.

The power of this public sentiment was important in one special dimension. The Australian Catholic Church was determined to maintain its schools if at all possible, and to this end it launched an all out campaign to do so. Whether Catholic school academic quality was good, bad or indifferent, the bishops and Catholic parishioners would continue to support Catholic schools. They would go the extra mile, but it was clear that public funding for Catholic schools could make a crucial difference. (At the same time in the US the Catholic bishops had reached the diametrically opposite decision — they would not build new Catholic schools in the suburbs, which was precisely where the American Catholic population was moving. These decisions were not centrally orchestrated by Rome; each was arrived at independently in terms of the conditions extant in each country. Thus, Catholic education in America became progressively weaker as its enrollment began to plummet. The attachment of American Catholics to their schools had begun to diminish, and the base of political support began to erode.)

The bishops' decision in Australia was to try to strengthen Catholic education precisely because it was 'weak': that is, the network of 'inadequate' Catholic schools would not be diminished in number, even if their quality was second-rate. Thus arose a most interesting political argument about public support for private schools. Because Catholic schooling was inevitable, and because it was inevitably 'weak' so long as its primary source of funds was the Church, the only way to bring it up to acceptable levels was to provide public funds. The architect of this unusual approach was James Carroll, co-adjutor archbishop of Sydney, a 'people's padre' of enormous sophistication and ability. A major figure in Australia, many of his 'parishioners' were members of the Labor Party. (Although the first major Australian aid scheme was enacted under a liberal rather than a labor government, labor acquiescence was important — both to secure original enactment and to assure support during periods of labor ascendancy. Like the Democratic Party in the US Australia's Labor Party is ambivalent about aid to Catholic schools, but on the whole is more favorably than unfavorably disposed to support it.) Carroll was an indefatigable campaigner for aid to private schools. The result of his work, and the work of colleagues and supporters, was the enactment of one of the most comprehensive systems of aid to non-public schools in the world. Today all of Australia's private schools receive some form of government support, but the poorest receive the most. Indeed, it is a commentary on the political coalition marshalled to gain enactment of public aid that the largest share of the aid goes to the poorest schools. To use the terminology of the American school finance community, private school aid in Australia is 'power equalized.'[18]

The argument is especially interesting when juxtaposed to the argument about aid to private schools that was unfolding in America. Although the dates do not fit precisely, the issues do. The most lively and persuasive article on the subject was written by a United States Senator. In 1978 Daniel Patrick Moynihan wrote an article for *Harper's* magazine entitled 'Government and the Ruin of Private Education'.[19] His thesis was simple

— private schools, particularly religious schools, most particularly Catholic schools — were in immediate danger of collapse and disappearance because there was no public money to support them. Their numbers were fewer because they were penniless and their quality was not sufficient to hold their traditional clientele. Not surprisingly, the weaker American parochial education became, the weaker became its claim on the public purse. In short, while nothing succeeds like success, nothing fails like failure. Australian Catholic schools, by refusing to contract, had created a political coalition leading to public support. And find it they did.

It is not surprising that one of the terms of public aid is public standards; the private schools are held to the same standards as the public. But in Australia this has a special meaning. Private schools are not 'regulated'; they are not held to a narrow and prescriptive set of rules. Rather, private school graduates must take 'leaving' exams to get a diploma, and they must take 'entry' exams to secure a place at college or university. The standard to which the Australian private school is held, then, is one of performance. In almost all respects, then, they are 'public' schools even if they serve a special 'sub-set' of the public. By any measure, they are more public than American suburban schools.

What impact has public funding of private schools had in Australia? About this matter there is general agreement, among both supporters and opponents of aid to private schools. First, there is general agreement that the quality of the Australian Catholic school has improved. It is at least as good as the public schools and frequently better. Indeed, the major sign of private school vitality is private school growth. As political determination led to funding in the first instance, funding has improved the quality of the private school, further strengthening its position. Indeed, the head of the Australian Schools Commission, Peter Tannock, under both Prime Ministers Fraser and Hawke, believes that generous funding for private schools will lead to their continued growth in the foreseeable future.[20]

Second, the emergence of the private school as an institution of similar or even better quality has 'stimulated' some public schools. In South Australia in particular, the public schools feel pressured and have taken vigorous measures to strengthen their own position. Most significantly, they have initiated a comprehensive, state-wide, open–enrollment policy designed to create in the public sector some of the diversity and choice that exists in the private sector.[21]

Having said all this, what does the nomenclature 'Catholic school' or 'private school' mean in an Australian context? To Australians it means a good deal. They believe that they have a vigorous private school network which happens to receive generous public support. They do not think that by accepting public funds they have compromised their integrity, nor do they think that they are in danger of being compromised. They most definitely do not think that their 'private' schools are public schools.

Holland

To the American visitor, imbued with the notion that the natural order of things is a small, vigorous private school system together with a large public school system, the Dutch system is remarkable.[22] In the context of one of the world's most orderly and bourgeois societies, the Dutch system of public support for education is startling. A century ago one-third of Dutch children attended private schools, two-thirds attended public schools. Today those numbers are reversed. Indeed, so extensive is the Dutch network of private schools that it is hard to believe that they are fully funded by the Dutch government, and they are required to meet Dutch academic standards.

Teachers in both the public and private schools must meet the same licensing requirements, the core curriculum is the same, and students are held to the same academic measures, as tested by national examinations. (Indeed, although standards are high, large numbers of Dutch students meet them. The result is that there are more qualified students than places in graduate and professional schools. How then are Dutch pre-med students selected? By lot.) Government and private schools, then, not only look very much alike in Holland, their outcomes are very much alike.

What distinguishes Dutch private from Dutch public schools? The major difference is the value system around which the school is organized. And because most value systems are derived from the great religious traditions, it is no surprise that most private schools in Holland are religiously affiliated. (There are secular schools, but they are the exception.)

The history of Dutch support of private schooling is perfectly rational. A country characterized by deep religious divisions, but also characterized by deep and lasting traditions of religious toleration, Holland was convinced that education and religion were inextricably bound together. (The American Puritans, it should be remembered, went first to Holland, then to America.) As education could not be separated from a confessional tradition, so too it could not be artificially joined *across* confessional traditions. As Muslims and Christians can talk to one another but do not share devotional practices, so their views about education diverge. The example is not a theoretical one in Holland. Muslims from the Dutch colonies are an important part of Dutch society today. Where do they go to school? Some attend Muslim schools, but a large number attend Christian schools because the academic standards are high. But the preference for academic excellence over religious purity is no less a value decision.

Equally, then, it is no surprise that the major difference between Dutch schools is curricular, because even the most humble subject contains within itself (or can be made to reveal) normative significance. Thus, literature, art, poetry, philosophy, and music are deeply imbued with religious significance and meaning. Although the natural sciences have less overt religious content — as recent debates in this country about so-called 'creation science' reveal — even biology and botany can be taught within a religious context. And while it is difficult to imagine how mathematics might be offered within the context of different religious traditions, perhaps Unitarians or Trinitarians, given the chance, might develop their own 'new math'.

Other Countries

The examples developed so far in this essay could be expanded upon almost indefinitely. In Belgium, Canada, France, Japan, Ireland, and Spain, to name only a few, public support for private education is well developed, at least at the level of elementary and secondary education. Indeed, in most of these countries, as well as in a number of developing countries, the distinction between public and private education does not have the meaning that it does in America. It does not have that meaning because of the American passion for distinguishing between religious and non-religious education, not public and private. Indeed, the public-private distinction is a stalking horse; the real issue in America is whether or not religious education should receive public assistance.

That is as the issue should be. Not because we should be forced to deal with religious issues, but because we should be forced to deal with educational issues. The real question raised by choice systems has to do with the ultimate purpose of education. Why do we educate children at all? The answer is deceptively simple — it is to transmit values, to maintain a living culture. In a vast continental democracy there are competing values, particularly in a pluralistic and heterogeneous society. But there are also non-competing values — openness, toleration, acceptance of differences, and democratic decision-making. And these lay the foundation for our economic and political life.

They are the foundation for our national community. But they do not lay the foundation for the more intimate communities which form the ties that bind. Those communities are of many kinds, but principal among them are religious communities. They are the fount of values, they are the essence of the normative life. Without them, education is an empty exercise. Education is nothing if not value-laden; to think otherwise is an exercise in futility. It is this simple truth that lies at the heart of 'choice' systems in other countries. They are not attempting to provide alternatives for the sake of alternatives, but because they mean something. If there is to be a choice system in America, it must exist because it is worth doing.

Choice within or among wholly secular educational offerings is to be preferred to no choice at all, but only barely, because choice that matters is concerned with the underlying values a school embodies. The private sector is home to a wealth of different schools — Quaker day and boarding schools, military academies, fast-track Jesuit high schools, Hebrew day schools, old order Amish schools, Hutterite grade schools, Mennonite grade schools (where 'Luther German' is taught); the list is virtually endless, because the range of value systems is so broad.

A shift to a choice system which recognized the importance of religious values would represent a fundamental change in the way American education has been organized and operated in the twentieth century. It would not be a change that should be entered into lightly or easily. To the contrary, it should be entered into carefully and cautiously, the product of reasoned thought and mature deliberation. But it is a policy debate we should join.

For many years choice in American education was the exclusive province of the select few. The well-to-do could always choose a private alternative, frequently an expensive and exclusive one. Failing the private alternative they could choose a suburban, 'public' alternative; the less well-to-do but ambitious could choose heavily subsidized religious schools; and in some unusual communities, like New York, the ambitious student who did well on standardized tests could enroll in highly selective public schools like Brooklyn Tech, Peter Stuyvesant, or Bronx Science. But the rest, the vast majority, were simply out of luck. Indeed, elementary and secondary education turned into a sort of social IQ test — where you ended up indicated what and how much you knew about the world.

Conclusion

What, then, are the lessons of choice systems in other parts of the world? They are several. First, they provide alternatives for families with different interests and values, pedagogical as well as spiritual. And in all but totalitarian countries the state is not hostile to religious values in education. (There are very good reasons for the state to refrain from supporting or endorsing one set of religious values as against another, but no persuasive reason for the state to adopt policies that are hostile to the religious experience.)

Second, they are perfectly practical from an administrative standpoint; that is, they are easy to make work. Because choice systems explicitly recognize differences in values, curricular, pedagogical and philosophical differences are not only tolerated, they are expected. At the same time, because public funds are involved, some measure of public accountability is also involved. In other countries the need to have an accountable choice system is resolved by an approach not widely used in America. Students are expected to pass examinations that reveal how much they know about different subjects — an elegant idea, but one that is unnecessary if all schools are the same, as they are supposed to be in the US. But today this is no more than a deeply held myth.

Third, the most important thing Americans can learn from choice systems is that they are not code for racism or religious exclusivity. To the contrary, they can be systems designed to increase personal freedom and autonomy by reinforcing the empowering communities that protect people from the state.

Fourth, religion and choice can not be separated, for their separation creates a distinction so artificial that the meaning of choice systems is lost. To be sure, it is possible to imagine schools for existentialists, atheists, or agnostics; one can even imagine schools in which 'secular humanism' is the dominant philosophy. But such schools are few among many, they are not the rule in a diverse society. The rule would be schools in which the dominant values flow from the great religious traditions. In the West, for many years that meant the Judeo-Christian tradition; and even if its dominance is no longer so certain or complete, it is still the dominant tradition.

It is possible to design choice systems on an exclusively pedagogical foundation, but that is not the pattern revealed by foreign example. The lesson offered by our friends and allies is that choice is important precisely because values are important to education, and some sympathetic set of shared values will not suffice. The answer is revealed in the way in which we respond to apparently shared values. We all believe in the sanctity of human life — or do we? What of just and unjust wars, capital punishment, Baby Doe, abortion, the right of a woman to control her own body? These are binary questions. There are no agnostic answers; temporizing will not do. The answers are yes or no. Two thousand years ago such questions were answered by Caesar as he dispensed life or death in the *circus maximus* . Today as then 'maybe' will not do. Relativism can not respond to absolutes — except in one important respect. In light of conflicting values, societies have broad ordering principles available to themselves. By far the oldest and most effective is the totalitarian model, modern Russia or Iran, in which all wisdom and all legitimacy originate in all-powerful rulers. Driven by ideology or religion, or both, there are two sides to every question — the right side and the wrong side. Woe to the individual who selects the wrong side.

The more fragile system is constitutional democracy, in which the state *qua* state deliberately suspends judgment. The continuing political process pits idea against idea; and as a corollary, it permits communities of shared values to form, coalesce, and reform. In the modern state they have many names: neighborhoods, fraternal organizations, churches, political parties. Why they should not include schools is a curiosity.

How, then, is the democratic tradition of toleration of competing ideas reconciled to the notion that about some matters agnosticism is not to be expected? Both the philosophical and instrumental purpose of toleration is the recognition that one person's compelling belief is not the same as another's. The purpose of toleration is not to force belief to some lowest common denominator, but precisely to give full sway to diversity of belief.

And the reason that we would institutionalise diversity of belief is because we have no absolute guarantee that one set of beliefs is superior to another.

John Stuart Mill in 1859, in his celebrated essay *On Liberty*, supported voucher systems in education because he was convinced that government-owned and -operated schools would become devices for the state to advance the prevailing orthodoxy.[23] Today, the nation's severest critics of education share that view. Neo-Marxist interpretations, like those of Bowles and Gintis, left-wing Libertarian analysis like Arons', *laissez-faire* market criticisms like that of E. G. West, practitioner reaction like that of Nathan, and centrist liberals like Coons and Sugarman are agreed that a system of government-owned and -operated schools leads inevitably to attempts to standardize children in terms of the prevailing value structure of the larger society.[24]

To have meaning then, choice systems, supported by the government, must be systems that recognize that value systems are at the heart of the education process. In the political arena — at least in democratic states — we treat as a virtue the fact that we have no final political answers. We have institutionalized a process in which a succession of provisional answers is identified, adopted, and eventually replaced with a new set of provisional answers as it becomes clear that the first set is no longer appropriate. So it might be with education. There could, for example, be the educational equivalent of constitutional federalism, in which the rules, procedures and processes — including a balance of powers — could be established within which the educational process would unfold. To do so would require a definition of public education new to America, but well developed abroad. Public education is the education of the public at institutions that serve the public. The old definition, that public schools are only those schools owned and operated by the government, is today an anachronism.

Acknowledgments

I owe a special debt of gratitude to Peter Karmel, Vice-Chancellor of the Australian National University, for his careful reading and critique of the Australian section. His comments have permitted me to revise and strengthen that section, sparing me embarrassment and providing greater accuracy of fact and interpretation. Any errors that remain are solely my responsibility.

Author's note

The opinions expressed herein are those of the author and do not necessarily reflect the views of the scholars, trustees, or staff of the Hudson Institute or NIE.

Notes

1   It builds on an entry prepared for the *International Encyclopedia of Education* (co-authored with Bruce Cooper of Fordham University) which dealt with private schools around the world. The research for that work began with a comprehensive questionnaire, submitted to the education attaché of each country with an embassy in the United States. The four-page questionnaire was sent to 120 countries, and fifty-seven completed questionnaires were returned. In addition, this work is based on extensive site visits in the UK, Holland, and Australia, as well as extensive interviews with senior government and private sector officials in those countries. As well, secondary sources, principally government publications, have been used as appropriate.

2   For a more complete treatment of this subject BLUM, V. (1981) *The Inner City School*, Milwaukee, Wisc, Catholic League for Religious and Civil Rights.

3   For an elegant and powerful exposition of this theme, see SCHULTZ, C. L. (1977) *The Public Use of Private Interest* , Washington, DC, The Brookings Institution.

4   For the definitive discussion of this theme see SCHULTZ, T. (1981) *Investing in People*, Berkeley, CA, University of California Press.

5   For a more complete description of this phenomenon, see LEVINE, M. and DOYLE, D. P. (1982) 'Private Meets Public', in *Meeting Human Needs*, Washington, DC, The American Enterprise Institute for Public Policy Research, June.

6   A large number of state constitutions are more restrictive than the US. Constitution. In the last quarter of the nineteenth century, a number of states adopted so-called Blaine Amendments, named after the enthusiastic anti-Catholic Speaker of the House James G. Blaine, who had been an ardent supporter of President U.S. Grant. (Grant returned the favor — he was an ardent supporter of Blaine, and shared his anti-Catholic proclivities.) Although Blaine and President Grant were unsuccessful in getting a federal Blaine Amendment adopted, a number of states were so moved. The language of the California Constitution is typical: 'No public money shall ever be appropriated for the support of any sectarian or denominational school, or any school not under the exclusive control of the officers of the public schools, nor shall any sectarian or denominational doctrine be taught, or instruction thereon be permitted, directly or indirectly, in any of the common schools of this state.' (Article IX, Section 8, Constitution of California.) The situation reached a fever pitch in Oregon in the 1920s when the state legislature, in a fit of nativist enthusiasm, outlawed attendance at any school except public school. It was a fine bit of Catholic baiting, and the act was declared unconstitutional in a landmark US Supreme Court case, *Pierce* v. *Society of Sisters*, 1927.

7   See MOYNIHAN, D. P. (1978) 'Government and the Ruin of Private Education', *Harper's*, April, pp. 28–38.

8   For a complete discussion of this see REICHLEY, J. *Church and State in Modern American Democracy*, The Brookings Institution, forthcoming. Reichley carefully documents the long and tangled history of the 'disestablishment' of Catholic schools, and their transition from public institutions for Catholics to private Catholic schools.

9   For a more complete description, see DOYLE, D. P. and LEVINE, M. *Magnet Schools*, National Science Foundation, September. A conceptual and theoretical framework, with great explanatory power, has been developed by Estelle James, Professor of Economics, SUNY Stony Brook. On the basis of extensive fieldwork, she advances the idea that the private sector — in education and other fields — is well developed if

consumer demand is not satisfied in the public sector. This is particularly the case in countries with dispersed, heterogeneous populations. Thus, in Scandinavia, with highly homogeneous populations and shared value systems, the private sector is very weakly developed. In Sweden, for example, the private sector is almost non-existent (even the church is part of the public sector).

In contrast, Holland has a culturally and religiously diverse population that is geographically dispersed: there are here pockets of Calvinists, there groups of Catholics, here a few Muslims, there some Jews. The effect is schools built around communities of interest to which various members 'commute' from their geographic communities.

In the middle lies a country like Belgium — culturally heterogeneous, but where large population groups (with similar cultural beliefs) live together. In that setting, there are 'neighborhood' denominational public schools. The pattern is the same in Canada. For a more complete description, see JAMES, E. *International Comparative Studies*, PONPO WP No. 28, and PONPO WP No. 30 Program on Non-Profit Organization, Institute for Social and Policy Studies, Yale University, New Haven, Connecticut.

10   See *Danish Education*, The Danish Ministry of Education, Copenhagen Denmark 1980.

11   *Ibid*. For a more detailed description, see FUCHS, E. (1979) 'The Danish Freischolen', *The Saturday Review*, August.

12   Anyone who thinks this is a small matter would do well to remember the apocryphal colloquy attributed to the eminent nineteenth century Catholic cleric Cardinal Newman and a Protestant devine full of ecumenical good will. The Protestant devine is reported to have said, 'After all, we do worship the same God.' To which Newman is reported to have responded, 'Yes, you in your way, I in His.'

13   This issue has begun to attract the attention of a number of revisionist legal historians many of whom are convinced that the recent history of Supreme Court interpretation of church-state relations, particularly as it relates to aid to religious schools, is seriously flawed; in fact, many are convinced that it is flatly in error, and that all that remains is for a 'new' court to deliver itself of a new opinion, in just the way the Warren court reversed 'separate but equal.' For two exemplary treatments of this, see MOYNIHAN, D. P. (1979) 'What Do You Do When the Supreme Court is Wrong? *The Public Interest*, Volume 57, Fall, pp. 3–22; and John Baker, Roscoe Pound Memorial Lecture, the Roscoe Pound Trial Lawyers Association, Washington, DC, June 1981.

14   Much of the material in this section was gathered in in-depth interviews conducted in Canberra, Sydney, Melbourne, Adelaide, and Perth, Australia, during two lengthy visits in 1977 and 1979. Interviews were conducted with the heads (in succession) of the Australian Schools Commission, the Tertiary Education Commission, officials of the Ministry of Education, the Minister of Education in the government of Malcolm Fraser, senior faculty of the Australian National University, the heads and senior staff of the state education agencies of New South Wales, the Australian Capital Territory, South Australian and Western Australia, and a host of other individuals and institutions too numerous to name. Support for this work was generously provided by the Ford Foundation, the sponsor of the US–Australia Policy Project.

15   The case in question was infelicitiously known as the DOGS suit (Defenders of Government Schools). Brought by citizens opposed to public aid to children in

religious schools, the decision was handed by the Australian high court on February 10, 1981. In a six to one decision, the Court ruled in favor of Australia's practice of aid to non-government schools. See, High Court of Australia, Her Majesty's Attorney General for the State of Victoria (at the Relation of Black and Others) and Others, (Appellant) and Commonwealth of Australia and Others (Respondents), February 10, 1981.

Interestingly, the Australian system had evolved from an earlier arrangement in which tax deductions had been permitted for education expenses (in either public or private schools). The deduction was so small it was thought to have little effect, and the Australians decided to develop a system of direct government transfer payments to schools based on the number of children enrolled; it is analogous to American systems of state support to schools on the basis of ADA (Average Daily Attendance) or ADM (Average Daily Membership), which, over the past fifty years have come to replace state 'foundation' programs which provided funds on the basis of teacher or classroom units. The existing Australian system is likely to stay in place so long as the Labor Party remains in power. But if the Liberal Party (read 'conservative' in an American context) is returned, serious proposals to transit into a full-fledged voucher system will be debated. (Interview with former Prime Minister Malcolm Fraser, Vail, Colorado, AEI World Forum, August 26, 1983.)

16 Denominational education in the United Kingdom has been the norm throughout British history and was in no way limited by constitution or statute. It is the norm in Great Britain as it is in the Commonwealth countries — most of which did not separate themselves from the mother country by violent revolution as we did. Australian debate about the appropriateness of Catholic schools was very much like the same debate in America.

Unlike Great Britain, however, where there has been a long tradition of state support of non-public education, the Australians had a more limited tradition. Financial exigencies and the pressure of the frontier had led to a pattern of public schools as the responsibility of government, with private schools the responsibility of the private sector. But one major similarity between Australia and the US appeared — the Australian Labor Party — the analogue of the American Democratic party — was the overwhelming party of choice of Australian Catholics, yet it was the party most against state aid. The more liberal political party, then, became the focus of political pressure to deal Catholic schools into a system of public support. (The issue of non-Catholic private schools was virtually moot; they play so small a role that whatever happened to Catholic schools was decisive.)

17 It is of interest to note that a similar view obtained in America; that is, that Catholic schools were inferior to public schools. Poorly trained nuns, overcrowded classes and buildings, out-of-date physical plants, and poor textbooks were all cited as reasons for American public school superiority, and at the same time (the late forties and fifties) American Catholic schools reached their historic high point in terms of enrollment. It may be that there is an inverse relationship between enrollment and quality. In this context it is interesting to note the findings of James Coleman, *et al.*, about the high quality of some American Catholic schools today. See COLEMAN, J., KILGORE, S. and HOFFER, T. (1981) *High School Achievement: Public, Catholic and Private Schools Compared*, New York, Basic Books.

18 The source for this material is interviews conducted by the author with Archbishop Carroll in Washington, DC, in 1980, and interviews with members of the Australian

Schools Commission, Peter Tannock (now head of the Schools Commission) and Gregory Hancock (now Superintendent of School in the Australian Capital Territory) in Sydney, Australia, in 1977, and in Canberra, in 1979.)

19 See MOYNIHAN, D. P. (1978) *op. cit.*
20 Speech delivered by Peter Tannock on the occasion of the 1983 School Finance Conference held at the Spring Hill Conference Center, Wayzata, Minnesota, September 1983.
21 Most of the foregoing is based on lengthy interviews with the Head of the South Australia Schools John Steinle, and his senior staff, meetings in Adelaide. Australia, in 1979. Steinle's office also designed the Choice and Diversity Project, an examination of 'choice models in public education' funded by the Australian Schools Commission.
22 The material for this section is based on Dutch publications and site visits and interviews in The Hague in 1980 with public and private school officials, officials of the Dutch Ministry of Education and the Dutch Inspector General.
23 The full quote, cited in ARONS, S. (1983) *Compelling Belief: The Culture of American Schooling*, New York, McGraw-Hill, p. 195, is

> (state education) ... is a mere contrivance for molding people to be exactly like one another: and as the mold in which it casts them is that which pleases the predominant power in the government, whether this be a monarch, a priesthood, and aristocracy, or the majority of the existing generation, in proportion as it is efficient and successful, it establishes a despotism over the mind...

24 See BOWLES, S. and GINTIS, H. (1976) *Schooling in Capitalist America*, New York, Basic Books; ARONS, S. (1983) *Compelling Belief: The Culture of American Schooling*, New York, McGraw-Hill; WEST, E. G. (1965) *Education and the State*, London, Institute of Economic Affairs; NATHAN, J. (1983) *Free To Teach*, New York, Pilgrim Press; and COONS, J. and SUGARMAN, S. (1982) *Family Choice in Education*, Berkeley, University of California Press.

Chapter 3
A Public Choice Perspective on Private Schooling

Jacob B. Michaelsen

Introduction

Perhaps the chief contribution of public choice economists to the debate on the organization of schooling has been the systematic application of the notion of utility maximization to individual conduct in governmental settings. This characterization of individual conduct has made it possible to bring a wide range of standard economic ideas to bear, first on the analysis of governmental organization, and later on the organization of schooling. To illustrate, let us consider the implications of the circumstance that most public school systems are monopolies. In standard economic analysis, competitive markets constrain self-aggrandizing conduct. Thus, when the airline industry, which had effectively been a cartel under the Civil Aeronautics Board, became competitive under deregulation, both airline costs and fares fell dramatically. Public choice theorists have argued that the combination of monopoly power and self-interested individual conduct will lead to significant inefficiency in the productive activity of public bureaux. The evidence from studies of resource allocation in a wide range of public bureaux supports this view (Borcherding, 1977). This argument has been extended to show that large, public school systems with diverse constituencies are likely to be both wasteful of resources and unresponsive to the divergent needs of their clienteles (Michaelsen, 1981). If we accept these results, decentralized, private schooling becomes a standard against which the public schools may be judged. It is but a short step to justify policy proposals like vouchers and tax credits as means to undercut the monopoly position of the public schools and thereby increase their effectiveness and responsiveness.

While the idea of an educational marketplace has gained a respectable, if modest, following, it has also elicited strong opposition. It is tempting to respond to this opposition by elaborating the public choice approach to demonstrate once again its pertinence to the policy debate. However, many who remain unconvinced about the efficacy of market arrangements in schooling question the standard economic ideas more than they do this particular application of them. I wish here to examine these more fundamental objections and show that a more sophisticated understanding of the opportunities competitive markets afford can meet these objections while, at the same time, reinforcing the more narrow policy implications for efficiency of the public choice approach.

Some opponents of educational markets believe privatization would undercut the role the schools play in the political socialization of the young. For them inefficiency is not the central issue. They see the public schools as sustaining, in a fundamental way, the core values citizens must share in a democracy if it is to survive and prosper. Private schools in the United States have not appeared to threaten these core values largely because they have been a small, privately funded segment of schooling here. Proposals that could enhance and enlarge private schooling at public expense could dramatically alter the relative size of the two sectors and have consequently been regarded with suspicion. Others, associations of teachers and administrators for example, oppose the marketplace, not only because they may believe it undercuts democratic values, but chiefly because they believe it threatens the settled positions they have in public education as it is presently organized.

It is an open question whether the significant growth of alternatives to the public schools would undermine core democratic values. But there are reasons to believe that a state school monopoly is not essential to the functioning of a pluralistic democracy. There are, after all, agencies other than the schools that socialize the young. More importantly, private school authorities have every reason to support pluralism and democracy since these schools exemplify the values of pluralist democracy and are protected by them. The question deserves careful consideration: it should not be ignored. The opposition of those with vested interest at stake poses a practical, rather than an intellectual, challenge. I will touch on it below.

There is another critique of the educational marketplace that goes more directly to the heart of the economic argument on which public choice analysis is based. Critical theorists such as Jurgen Habermas take issue with certain general features of neo-classical economic analysis. They are especially concerned with what they perceive as the tendency of markets to suppress the discussion of important questions that can only be resolved by open and free public debate. Public choice economics, being solidly grounded in the neo-classical tradition, thus is subject to this critique. Applied to schooling, the critique asserts that educational markets would stifle the discussion necessary for the sound formulation of educational policy. This concern for keeping schools in the political arena to insure the possibility of 'communicative action' about educational policy is quite compatible with the concern for the role the public schools should have in political socialization of the young but it goes beyond it. The claim that intelligent public policy toward schooling is not possible without public organization of the schools is a strong one which public choice theorists must address.

Critical theorists go far beyond calling for keeping schools public monopolies. They find democratic governments dominated by the interests of the powerful whom they serve. In their vision of an ideal democracy, such domination could not arise. In this ideal democracy, the standards for the formulation of public policy — that it rest on publicly acknowledged principles and be acceptable to all — virtually require the elimination of private power. Such standards are certainly not met in the United States, nor anywhere else for that matter.

Public choice economists also claim to have identified systemic flaws in the political process. They find the origin of these flaws, not in the existence of dominant classes, but in the susceptibility of democratic politics to the influence of organized interest groups. Thus, groups of teachers and administrators, who could hardly be regarded as members of a power elite, have organized to benefit from the centralization of public schools into larger and larger systems. Were we to meet the objections of critical theorists to educational markets, we would still be left with the opposition of those groups where interests would be adversely affected by a radical decentralization of the schools. Perhaps we can, like critical theorists, make arguments for a more equitable distribution of power, if not its elimination, while deferring to another time the question of how to achieve it.

A Critical View of Market Decentralization

A central feature of the standard, neo-classical economics that opponents of educational markets find particularly troublesome is its treatment of wants. The wants served by markets are taken as given, fundamentally private matters largely outside the scope of governmental concern. As a consequence, proposals for an educational market seem to make the education of the young simply a matter of private, unregulated taste. Since our future as a democratic republic depends to a considerable extent on how our children are educated, relying on an educational market appears to rule out the possibility of taking responsibility for this future. Whatever their present condition, the public schools are seen by many to offer the opportunity to act on behalf of this future. For them, to exchange the public system for an educational marketplace is to trade something for nothing.

In an insightful paper, Sheffrin (1978) has provided an interesting point of departure from which to examine the consequences of the standard treatment of wants in consumer theory for thinking about how schooling can best be organized. Sheffrin (1978) begins with the concern of Habermas and other critical theorists that organized markets can 'suppress or interfere with the expressions of wants and needs of individuals' (p. 785). He then attempts to reconcile this concern with traditional consumer theory in which markets serve as a paradigm for the efficient satisfaction of wants. This reconciliation results in a practical critique of the standard assumptions about consumer tastes and preferences. Sheffrin identifies two kinds of consumer wants: discrete and conceptual. A discrete want is a simple, primitive relationship between a person and an object 'that is irreducible, finite and not subject to any rational scrutiny' (p. 786). An example of such 'mere' taste is a preference for chocolate ice cream. For such objects there is little, if any, serious public discussion of what ought to be preferred.

This stark characterization of preferences, with its implied simplification of how preferences are formed, is sufficiently common in the economic literature, in the textbooks and in the press to raise grave doubts about the efficacy of an educational marketplace. It must be noted that Sheffrin's treatment, which closely follows that of the critical theorists, is focused on a particular theoretical version of consumer behavior in markets. In many ways this view is a straw man. Modern mainstream economics, not to mention the views of the Austrian economists that I will consider below, is much more sophisticated than this. Nevertheless, because of its wide currency, it must be taken seriously.

Matters are not so simple for conceptual wants and the objects to which they refer. The example here is art. For art there are 'public or cultural canons of knowledge or behavior' (*ibid.*, p. 787). And there is a strong hierarchy of tastes as well. Finally, and what is very important for our consideration of education, 'since conceptual tastes depend on publicly established standards of criticism, group interaction is essential, indeed, mandatory'; that is, we cannot know what we want except through actively encountering the views of others about the substantive matters involved. Sheffrin argues, and rightly so, that for a wide range of important instances, including education, the received theory of consumer choice omits essential features of the world we wish to understand.

Sheffrin's notions of discrete and conceptual tastes and goods parallel quite closely the key ideas of work and communicative action in critical theory. To work is to achieve given, discrete goals with given means. This is the kind of instrumentally rational activity that is the subject of standard economic analysis. In common usage work includes a much broader spectrum of activities in which instrumental rationality is only a component. For the moment it will be convenient to work with this simplifying distinction, considering later the implications of the circumstance that work is seldom merely instrumental. In contrast, communicative action is a venture in substantive rationality. Here ends are not given but must be discovered and rediscovered by the community through a process of mutual encounter and accommodation. If all wants were reduced to 'mere' discrete tastes in actual markets, the development of important conceptual tastes would indeed be suppressed in the practical world. Communicative action would be rendered very difficult and this would certainly be true of the social interaction required for establishing norms for education.

If markets seem to rule out communicative action, one way to facilitate it is to move the good in question to the political arena. Sheffrin takes it for granted that because education requires communicative action, educational policy should be determined largely, if not entirely, through governmental processes. In this he follows the critical theorists. However, actual markets do not have all the suppressive power that Sheffrin and the critical theorists attribute to them. 'Publicly established standards' need not derive their authority from acts of government. To use his own example, we do not look to government for authoritative canons of art. Conceptual goods form a very substantial part of what interests us as consumers. Our tastes for these goods are formed in a wide range of social contexts which, for the most part, involve government only tangentially. In my view, education falls in this large class of conceptual goods. Nevertheless, a case for more than tangential government involvement in setting standards for it can be made. Well educated persons benefit the community as well as themselves and their families. Poorly educated persons may harm themselves as well as the community. Concern for these benefits and costs falls properly within governmental purview. But the case for governmental regulation of these externalities should be undertaken with great care because the current, extensive role of government in education can easily lead us to take the case for governmental monopoly for granted.

The Challenge

Critical theory poses the challenge to go beyond the strictly instrumental considerations of efficiency to find a moral basis for the reliance on the marketplace in schooling. In a paper on the influences of market institutions on the development of wants and personality, McPherson (1983) makes a strong case against the pervasive assumption in standard economic theory of the 'givenness' of wants . He identifies the 'neo-Austrian' approach as one rich and complex enough to offer a defense of the market on moral as well as instrumental grounds. A brief review of McPherson's critique of the standard approach will set the stage for a closer examination of the Austrian case for the market and for reliance on the marketplace in schooling.

Once we agree that wants are not simply given but derive in important ways from the political economy in which we live, we are driven to ask whether we ought to prefer wants different from those we now have. If we find that we do, and those seeking to change the way schooling is organized often wish to improve the opportunities for enhanced personal development of the young, we need to discover the changes in the political economy required to encourage the kind of personal development that would support these more desirable wants. Rather than asserting a set of such wants, McPherson proposes to guarantee 'a desirable social background for preference development'. This desirable background is one in which autonomous persons, capable of knowing their own interests and how to pursue them, exercise substantial control over their own development. The autonomous person thus has, in addition to the consumer sovereignty of standard theory, 'protection from constricted or distorting environments for developing wants' (*ibid.*, p. 116).' McPherson believes that the cognitive conditions necessary for autonomy, 'like awareness of alternatives, scope for reflection, {and} opportunities for free discussion and questioning' (p. 115) could provide criteria on which people with differing views about particular ends could agree.

He acknowledges that 'market economies do have important features which protect certain aspects of personal autonomy' such as extensive opportunity for experiment and an absence of overt social control. He also recognizes that, while persons in market economies have an imperfect grasp of the available information and a limited capacity to process it, they have access to a vastly richer store of information than those in non-market economies. Offsetting these features are the implicit coercion of, for example, advertising and the more standard market failures like pollution and combinations in restraint of trade. He believes it important 'in advancing alternative conceptions of political economy' that the features which protect personal autonomy be preserved.

In the Austrian analysis, the complexity of the human economy in which individual initiative and creativity are driving forces, places major obstacles before any system of organization that requires extensive centralization of detailed technical knowledge. These obstacles to centralized decision-making give market institutions a decided edge over alternative political economies in facilitating autonomy. Moreover, the systemic defects of government under democratic pluralism limit the range of alternative ways personal autonomy may be advanced. Bluntly put, improving market institutions and limiting the field of governmental activity may be the best way to protect and enhance the development of the autonomous person.

Competition as a Discovery Process

In his essay 'Competition as a Discovery Process,' Hayek (1978) commented that economists have long discussed competition on assumptions that, 'if they were true of the real world, would make it wholly uninteresting and useless' (p. 179). One of these assumptions, that the data about wants and about the means of satisfying them are fully known, was only partially challenged by critical theorists. Like many economists, critical theorists have taken technical knowledge about means for granted. For them, it is knowledge about wants, not work, that is problematic. Hayek argues that we can never fully know in advance all the facts necessary to achieve given ends. Indeed, because of the continuing incomplete and imperfect state of our knowledge of both of means and ends, a clear distinction between instrumental and substantive rationality is often hard to make in practice. Recognizing the problematic character of all knowledge, Hayek proposes 'to consider competition as a procedure for the discovery of such facts as, without resort to it, would not be known to anyone, or at least would not be utilized' (*ibid.*, p. 179).

In the 1930s Lange and others argued that central planning could achieve an allocation of resources identical to that by competitive markets. In the *Road to Serfdom*, Hayek (1944) showed that these results depended on the same implausible assumptions that economists had long been making in their analyses of market economies. It may seem surprising that so many of the economists who have acknowledged the soundness of Hayek's case against central planning have often proceeded as if he had not made it. Central to Hayek's case is the proposition that competition is a procedure for the discovery of 'particular facts' relevant to achieving practical aims. In this its procedures parallel those of scientific inquiry which produce knowledge of 'general facts' about the more permanent patterns of things which the scientist aims to understand. Thus, the needs of the entrepreneur and the scientist to discover are the same, only the character of their goals, one practical and the other theoretical, differ. The parallel extends further: competition among scientists is a necessary and central feature of scientific procedure. In this sense, competition can be considered an essential element in all discovery.

What does all this have to do with schooling? Large, centralized public school districts are very much like centrally planned economies. The opportunities for an entrepreneur to discover and exploit new ways of doing things is drastically limited in these large systems. In the Austrian tradition entrepreneurship is not limited to the classical owner/entrepreneur. Everyone is a potential entrepreneur, especially with regard to his or her own talents, capacities and opportunities. In the schools this means, not only administrators and teachers, but students and their families are critical actors. For effective and responsive education all the actors need the knowledge of the particular facts necessary to exploit the opportunities potentially available in their situations. Large, centrally controlled systems afford very little incentive for the discovery of this knowledge. Indeed, in such systems, discovery is systemically inhibited. As a consequence, the system must run without the knowledge of important 'particular facts' and will, therefore, run badly.

Educational research is a well-established field. Perhaps this branch of the knowledge industry, which is run on competitive principles, could provide the knowledge that educational markets would generate. It is notorious that the findings of educational researchers have seldom had much impact on educational practice. Such findings, to be sure, shed little light on the particular facts necessary for the actors in the schools to pursue their goals effectively. Of equal importance is the lack of incentive for these actors to mine this vast stock of findings. Competition in schooling would, as in other areas, give scope to the entrepreneurial talents of all concerned, providing the opportunity and incentive for them to find out how best to achieve their goals. Such an environment would provide an incentive to mine the output of the educational research industry as well, thus affording the opportunity to discover what is truly valuable in that vast effort to understand mostly large monopoly public school systems.

We live in a pluralistic society. Much of the knowledge necessary for effective education is of the transient, particular facts specific to the persons and families who would join together around a school as its staff and clientele. Indeed, many of the particular facts will be about the character, needs and habits of the individual students enrolled in the school. If the entrepreneurial spirit of all those who join together is supported by a radical decentralization of control, this knowledge is likely to be discovered and effectively utilized. Moreover, those who join together around a school are likely to share important values which they wish to transmit to their young. In such a school the distinction between knowledge about means and knowledge about ends cannot be sharp. The actors' values will influence the means they use and these means will affect how their values are realized in practice. Learning by doing will lead to the discovery of knowledge of both means and ends. Under such circumstances, learners may well leave the distinction between work and communicative action to disinterested observers.

Personal autonomy can be best achieved in a school setting in which meaningful parental involvement can easily be achieved. Such involvement has been exceedingly difficult to achieve in large and diverse public school districts. Inexpensive access to private schools for children who would otherwise be placed in schools in such districts would greatly facilitate the kind of parental involvement that fosters the growth of personal autonomy. In such school settings of choice, conflict about fundamental values is likely to be minimal. I have argued (Michaelsen, 1981) that in such large and diverse districts, the consensus and community that arise when shared values inform the conduct of students, parents and staff in schools of choice, are greatly impeded. Bureaucratic interests inimical to personal autonomy can more easily flourish when conflict about goals creates serious confusion about the directions educational policy should take. Without shared goals informing daily life and educational practice, other goals which serve the narrower interests of school administrators and teachers displace what ought to be a coherent force guiding the conduct of families, students and staff. Where there is effective community and shared values, students will have unambiguous examples of adults taking responsibility for their education in ways consistent with values they have learned at home. The strength that coherent practice provides to the young greatly abets the development of personal autonomy. This is why I believe private schooling should play a central educational role in a pluralistic democracy.

As an epigraph to his discussion of education in *The Constitution of Liberty*, Hayek (1960, p. 376) quotes J. S. Mill in part as follows: 'A general state education is a mere contrivance for moulding people to be exactly like one another.' In keeping with his idea of the role of competition in the discovery of knowledge, Hayek believes that many, if not most, of the problems in education are questions of value that arise within the state monopoly. He concludes that 'the very possibility that, with a system of government education, all elementary education may come to be dominated by theories of a particular group who genuinely believe that they have scientific answers to those problems ... should be sufficient to warn us of the risks involved in subjecting the whole educational system to central direction' (*ibid.*, p. 380).

If competition among schools will lead to the knowledge necessary for effective and responsive schools and stand in the way of 'moulding people to be exactly like one another', it will lead to the development of personal autonomy. It seems clear that the large public schools systems in which a large fraction of the young are educated in the United States do not support the development of autonomy particularly well. Under a radical decentralization of the schools, the people who value personal autonomy in a political democracy can undertake to build schools that do this. In the process of such an effort they may learn more precisely what autonomy and democracy mean as well as how schools can support these values. If the values of autonomy and democracy are important to Americans, giving power to the people through radical decentralization of the schools will assist greatly in their realization. If we do not try, we will never know whether it can be done because large, government school systems are not engines of discovery.

Concluding Remarks

I have not developed here a detailed analysis of the more narrow implications of the public choice approach for the ways in which we can expect large and diverse public school districts to display the systemic effects of self-interested action within the political arenas of the district and the state legislature. Such analyses of efficiency losses are available elsewhere as I indicated earlier. Instead of focusing on questions of instrumental rationality, I have concentrated on the contributions market arrangements can make to substantive rationality in the education of those who will become citizens of a pluralistic democracy. I have argued that the freedom to choose will lead to the consensus and community needed to

Jacob B. Michaelsen

give proper scope to the entrepreneurial capacities of the young, and of the adults who serve as role models in such communities, to develop both the personal autonomy and the intellectual and practical capacities requisite for a productive life and responsible citizenship. This line of argument is, of course, not new. Unfortunately, the widespread and shallow depiction of the market as a rather simplistic mechanism in the service of instrumental rationality tends to mask the more subtle, richer and deeper perception of the market as an engine of discovery, not only of means, but of ends as well. The richness and depths of writers like Hayek, and the Austrians more generally, is well known in the economics profession. That it is so often submerged in mainstream economic argument goes a long way toward explaining why it is so little understood by even the educated public.

References

BORCHERDING, T. E., (ed.) (1977) *Budgets and Bureaucrats: The Sources of Government Growth*, Durham, Duke University Press.
HAYEK, F. A. (1944) *The Road to Serfdom* Chicago, University of Chicago Press.
HAYEK, F. A. (1960) *The Constitution of Liberty* Chicago, University of Chicago Press.
HAYEK, F A (1978) *New Studies in Philosophy, Politics, Economics and the History of Ideas* Chicago, University of Chicago Press.
McPHERSON, M. (1983) 'Want Formation, Morality, and Some "Interpretive" aspects of Economics Inquiry', in HAAN, N., BELLAH, R., RABINOW, P. and SULLIVAN, W. (eds), *Social Science as Moral Inquiry* New York, Columbia University Press.
MICHAELSEN, J. B. (1981) 'A Theory of Decision-Making in the Public Schools: A Public Choice Approach,' in BACHARACH, S. B. (ed.) *Organizational Behavior in Schools and School Districts*, New York, Praeger.
SHEFFRIN, S. (1978) 'Habermas, Depoliticization, and Consumer Theory,' *Journal of Economics Issues*, 12, December, pp. 785–97.

Chapter 4
Schooling for Poor and Minority Children: An Equity Perspective

Barbara L. Schneider

One of the principles of American public education is that schools exist to teach children specific academic and socialization skills necessary for attaining productive adult roles in a democratic society. What makes this assumption problematic from an equity perspective is that some schools help children learn more than other schools regardless of the children's family backgrounds, ability, and motivation. Research indicates that children are more likely to achieve scholastically in schools that establish high academic standards, enforce disciplinary policies, and involve parents in school decision-making. Unfortunately, schools that exhibit these characteristics are not the ones that typically serve poor and minority children.

Children who are at risk of failing academically should be placed in schools that minimize the negative impacts that poverty, family disorganization, and cultural differences can have on their academic performance. Unfortunately, the majority of poor and minority children often find themselves in schools that compound rather than alleviate their educational problems. Disadvantaged students are more likely than other students to attend schools where academic performance receives limited emphasis, where violence on school grounds is commonplace, and where nearly a third of the student body are chronically absent and score well below grade level on national reading and mathematics tests. The American public education system is inequitable because it tends to confine poor and minority students in schooling environments where the staff, facilities, curricular materials, and instructional practices are inferior to those found in many suburban and advantaged urban schools.

Few families, rich or poor, would choose to send their children to poor quality schools. Most public school districts have policies that make it nearly impossible for families to send their children to schools outside designated attendance areas regardless of the reputed quality of the school inside the district. Poor and minority families are usually thwarted in their attempts to alter the quality of the schools within their districts as they often lack the power or resources necessary to achieve reform. Unable to change the system, these families are dually trapped, since they do not have sufficient resources to move out of their school districts or access private schools.

The educational problems of disadvantaged students have attracted the attention of educators and government officials, but it appears that recent federal and state policies may be misdirected. One must question whether today's educational reform movement, with its emphasis on changing academic standards and course requirements, will ultimately provide students at risk of academic failure with greater opportunities for social mobility. Requiring a competency exam for graduation from high school can do little to improve the reading performance of an adolescent who has only basic or rudimentary literacy skills. Raising course requirements for high school graduation is unlikely to help retain a teenager planning to drop out of school.

Instead, if we are to improve educational opportunities for poor and minority children, we will need to examine more closely those schooling environments that mitigate the negative impact that poverty and family disorganization can have on academic achievement. This chapter reviews the evidence on the problems in public inner city schools, and contrasts this information with the accumulating research on the positive impact private schools are having on disadvantaged students. Several explanations are presented as to why private schools are successful. The chapter concludes by recommending ways in which public education could become more equitable for poor and minority children.

Differences Between Public and Private Schools: A New Look at the Evidence

Concern over the effectiveness of America's public education system has generated volumes of data on student academic performance. Subject to interpretation, these data present an uneven picture of academic success, particularly for poor and minority students. Scholars optimistic in their views cite rising achievement scores (in some grade levels and in some subject areas), increasing high school completion rates, and college entrance statistics among certain minority groups as substantive proof that the gap in academic performance between minorities and other students is narrowing. Others take a more pessimistic perspective, arguing that changes in academic achievement have been minimal and that the nation's disadvantaged students are in danger of academic failure and likely to become even more so in the future.

A crucial element in the debate over the effectiveness of public education is the position taken by some educators and policymakers that private schools produce better academic results for disadvantaged students then public schools (Coleman, Hoffer and Kilgore, 1982; Coleman and Hoffer, 1987; Greeley, 1982). From a review of some of the national data on private and public school student test scores, dropout rates and college matriculation figures, it appears that private schools are particularly effective in providing poor and minority students with knowledge and skills that can increase their opportunities for social mobility.

The National Assessment of Educational Progress (NAEP), considered to be the most representative and complete measure of student academic performance, reports that from 1971 to 1984 there has been an improvement in the average reading performance of Blacks and Hispanics (US Center for Education Statistics, *Condition of Education*, 1987). However, upon closer inspection the situation remains very problematic. For example, while there has been some improvement in Black and Hispanic reading scores, the absolute numbers of those minority students with limited reading skills at various ages measured by NAEP remain considerable. The average reading proficiency of Black and Hispanic 17-year-olds is similar to that of White 13-year-olds (Applebee, Langer and Mullis, 1987). Furthermore. in 1983–84, only 16 per cent of Black 17-year-olds demonstrated 'adept' reading skills, compared to 45 per cent of White students at this age. Results for mathematics are also disheartening. Blacks and Hispanics tend to score on the average at least 10–18 per cent lower than Whites (US Center for Education Statistics, *Digest of Education Statistics*, 1987). In fact, Black and Hispanic scores are consistently lower than Whites for all age cohorts (that is 9, 13, and 17 year olds) on 'subject' achievement tests measured by NAEP (*ibid.*, pp. 87–93).

Poor and minority students in private schools do not appear to fall as far behind as students in public ones. Using data from the US Center for Education Statistics national longitudinal study, 'High School and Beyond', Coleman, Hoffer, and Kilgore (1982) found that poor and minority children attending Catholic schools outperform poor and minority students in public schools. It is not surprising that these findings, which questioned the efficacy of public education, were met with a rash of criticism and debate (see *Harvard Educational Review*, 1981 and *Sociology of Education*, 1982, 1983, and 1985). However, subsequent reanalyses of the 'High School and Beyond' data failed to produce results that could conclusively refute the academic effects of the Catholic schools as reported by Coleman, Hoffer, and Kilgore (1982). Moreover, further analysis of the first follow-up survey of 'High School and Beyond' confirmed Coleman *et al.*'s earlier findings (Coleman and Hoffer, 1987).

The controversy over Coleman *et al.*'s initial (1982) findings centered primarily on issues pertaining to 'magnitude': that is, how much better were the test scores for private school students, and how much did private schools reduce the inequities between advantaged and disadvantaged students, at least with respect to their achievement test scores (Haertel,

1984). This focus on issues of 'statistical magnitude' distracted public attention from other findings by Coleman *et al*. that clearly pointed to the ability of private schools to produce a more equitable schooling environment for poor and minority children. For example, Coleman found that Catholic schools seem to be more effective in maximizing the social opportunities of poor and minority students by helping them 'stay in school.'

'High School and Beyond' data also reveal that graduates of private high schools are more likely to enroll in post-secondary institutions (Coleman and Hoffer, 1987). The ability of private schools to send their students to post-secondary institutions highlights another important equity consideration. National figures indicate that Blacks and Hispanics are more likely than Whites not to go to college (US Center for Education Statistics, *Condition of Education*, 1987). Yet, in private schools, Black, Hispanic, and White students are not only more likely to go on to college but are also more likely to matriculate to four-year institutions.

Several factors contribute to the low college matriculation rates of Black and Hispanic students in public schools. Data from 'High School and Beyond' reveal that Blacks and Hispanics are less likely to take as many academic units in high school as White students (US Center for Education Statistics, *Digest of Education Statistics*, 1987). High school course selections in public school are determined in large part by school type and 'track' to which the student is assigned.

Furthermore, recent changes in the organizational structure of many large urban public schools are having calamitous effects on the education of poor and minority students. Many large urban public school systems have begun establishing special schools for the scientifically or artistically talented youngster. While seemingly replicating the private school admission selection concept, in reality 'choice' as it exists in many public schools further stratifies the schools by removing the most gifted students from neighborhood public schools. Whether by family choice or public school selection criteria, poor and minority students in many of these special schools are underrepresented in proportion to the total school population (Raywid, 1985). The consequence of this is that many urban educational districts have a two tier system — one layer of desegregated advantaged urban schools for academically gifted and talented students, and another layer of segregated schools that serve poor and minority students and a large number of students with academic problems. Thus this two tier system is at odds with the American rhetoric of equal opportunity associated with public schools.

In addition to being underrepresented in special academic high schools, poor and minority students are more likely to be assigned to vocational or non-college bound programs. Placement of students into various programs has been shown to be related to ability, race, and socioeconomic status (Goodlad, 1984; Oakes, 1985; Rosenbaum, 1976;

Sebring, 1987). Poor and minority students often find themselves in classes where their teachers expect less, are presented with curricular materials below grade level, and are more likely to interact with students who have feelings of low self-esteem and control over their lives (Rowan and Miracle, 1983; Hotchkiss, 1984; Kerckhoff, 1986). Given the type of high school and program many poor and minority students are assigned, it is not surprising that their college entrance tests are so low. In Chicago, for example, half of the city's public high schools rank in the bottom one per cent of schools in the United States based on results of student American College Test scores.

The public schools that serve America's disadvantaged students are in crisis conditions. Evidence on student academic performance in private schools in many ways has highlighted the plight of public education by offering a sharp point of comparison. Private schools are reducing the educational inequities among racial and economic groups by improving student academic performance and providing disadvantaged families with a viable schooling alternative.

Within the past decade, a significant change occurred in the conduct of private school studies. During the sixties and seventies, researchers interested in school organizations tended to study the nature of administrative relationships among teachers, students, and parents; the social and ideological forces that shape curricular content; and ways to improve student productivity and school efficiency (Bidwell, 1965; Erickson, 1979; Boyan, 1982). Such research generally focussed on public schools. Even though scholars recognized administrative and organizational distinctions between public and private schools, few of them comprehensively examined differences between the two sectors. Study of private schooling was perceived as out of the mainstream of educational research, and openly regarded as politically divisive to public education (Erickson, 1986). Notable exceptions to this trend were Kraushaar's (1972) detailed historical overview of private schools in America, and Erickson's (1978, and Erickson and Nault, 1980) insightful work on family school choice and private school enrollments.

Spurred in part by Coleman, Hoffer, and Kilgore's study (1982), scholars proceeded to take a close look at variations between the two sectors (James and Levin, 1988). Several important findings have emerged from these 'new' studies of private schools. Many commonly held assumptions about the differences between the two sectors, particularly with respect to certain student background characteristics, are not supported. For example, one frequent explanation for the success of private schools has been that the majority of students who attend private schools come from economically advantaged families. New evidence suggests that differences in student background characteristics between the two sectors may be considerably less than previously assumed (Williams, 1986).

Scholars studying the organization of schools outside the United

States have focussed on examining historical social class distinctions between public and private schools (Boyd, 1984, 1986; James, 1984, 1986). Private schools in some countries were established to educate the children of the wealthy, elite ruling class, whereas in other nations private schools have been created for individuals not accepted into the competitive high quality public schools (James, 1984). It appears that social class differences between private and public schools in at least some foreign countries mirror the social class stratification system within those societies. In the United States, social class distinctions between public and private schools do not seem to be nearly as rigid or as apparent as in other countries.

In the US, it is often concluded that private schools enroll more students from higher income families than public schools (Kraushaar, 1972). Recent enrollment data seem to dispel this notion (US Center for Education Statistics, *Condition of Education*, 1986, pp. 191–5). Doyle (1981), in examining data from California, found that there was an underrepresentation of the very poor and an underrepresentation of the very wealthy in private schools in this state. The trend Doyle reports for California, seems to be prevalent throughout the country. US Census data for 1980 reveal that both public and private school systems enroll students from all income levels (US Center for Education Statistics, *Condition of Education*, 1986, p. 191). Contrary to commonly held assumptions, Williams (1986), citing 1980 Census data, reports that the majority of private school students are from low and middle income families. Fifty-six per cent of all public students come from families reporting incomes from $15,000 to $49,999, whereas sixty-three per cent of all families in private schools report family incomes in this same bracket (Williams, 1986).

The homogeneity of the student population in many public and private schools appears not to be the result of restricted admission policies, but the consequence of the geographical location of the school (Schneider and Slaughter, 1984). Although private schools are racially and economically stratified to a certain degree, this stratification process is neither as dramatic or rigid as the one in public schools. Private schools do not consign children to schools based on their residential locations. In the private sector, families have the opportunity to exercise self-determination with respect to their child's education. The public educational system permits this type of self-determination only to middle and high income families and those with gifted children. Middle and high income families have greater opportunities for school choice because they can select the public school community in which they want to live and they have the resources and information to access other types of schools if they desire (Vitullo-Martin, 1982). Low income and minority families have limited choices over their residential locations. In spite of continuing anti-discrimination legislation, Blacks living in many urban areas remain isolated and highly segregated (Massey and Denton, 1987).

Despite their poverty status, a number of poor and minority families are choosing to send their children to private schools. In absolute numbers, most poor children are White. However, Blacks and Hispanics are more likely to live in poverty. US Census data reveals that one out of every six Whites live at poverty level, whereas two out of every five Hispanics and one out of every two Blacks live at poverty level (US Center for Education Statistics, *Condition of Education*, 1986). As more Blacks and Hispanics enroll in private schools they are likely to increase the concentration of students at poverty level in private schools.

These poor families are making considerable financial sacrifices to send their children to private schools (Bauch, 1985; Cibulka, O'Brien, and Zewe, 1982; US Center for Education Statistics, *Condition of Education*; Slaughter and Schneider, 1986). Poor families pay a greater proportion of their family income than do middle income families for private school tuition (US Center for Education Statistics, *Condition of Education*, 1986). Moreover, families of Black students are more likely to pay higher tuition and fees than families of White and Hispanic students (*ibid*). For these families, the financial hardships of selecting private schools are confounded by the fact that tuition and fees in private schools have risen more sharply than the cost of living since 1979 (*ibid*). The only financial assistance poor and minority families are likely to receive is in the form of scholarships and fellowship programs.

Why Private Schools Are Successful

Perhaps the most compelling reason why private schools provide such a successful learning environment for disadvantaged students can be traced to their organizational structure. Because they do not encounter the myriad of bureaucratic problems that beset public schools, private schools can accomplish their goals with minimum interference and resource misuse (Schneider, 1986, Chubb and Moe 1985).

Increasingly, life in public schools is being influenced by changes and controls in the external environment. Critical decisions in public schools are often made by political interest groups or individuals who have only a marginal interest in the educational system. For example, state legislators are more likely to respond to the pressures of various interest groups who demand that more of the curriculum be devoted to 'arts education' than to the educational needs of students at risk, whose families are perceived as having little political clout. Contract negotiators, hired to represent administrators, parents, and teachers, end up specifying what teachers can do in their classrooms. And finally, in many school districts, decisions on whether to increase the school tax rate are being determined by voters on fixed incomes with no children in their homes.

Autonomy and Accountability

Public education is increasingly finding itself in an environment where there is no filter or protective seal to insulate the system so that it can establish and accomplish its goals. Meyer and Rowan (1983) maintain that the impact of these external forces on the 'work' of the schools is continuously increasing in scope and intensity. The result of this is that the public school system, unsheltered from these external forces, has had to adapt its own internal mechanisms to meet outside imposed changes. Often times these externally imposed changes can interfere with the school and deflect it from its mission. Moreover, as changes are externally derived rather than internally determined, resistance increases and goals are less likely to be achieved.

Private schools are protected from some of these external forces that impact on a public school. Because private schools do not have to be responsive to the fragmented external environment of the public school, they can look inwardly when establishing goals. This inward focus encourages greater goal clarity and consensus. In comparison to public school goals, which are often variegated and contested, private school goals are more likely to be shared and integrated into the work activities of the school.

Another major organizational difference between private and public schools is their hierarchical structure. Most urban pubic school systems have numerous administrative layers. In these large superstructures, the principal is frequently perceived as a middle manager having little impact on major school policy decisions. The principal in many private schools is more likely to act as an instructional leader and decision-maker. The private school community expects the principal to exercise leadership over the instructional program and be accountable for the consequences of those decisions. Because private schools tend to have fewer students and be more streamlined administratively than public schools, how and what the principal does is open to the purview of the entire school community. This level of accountability raises the expectation and likelihood among the school community that goals will be accomplished.

It would, however, be incorrect to assume that all private schools have similar types of goals and similar success in reaching them. Diversity in educational program, disciplinary style, and cooperation with parents varies from one private school to another (Slaughter and Schneider, 1986). However, diversity among private schools' goals also creates opportunities for the schools to be more responsive to their clients. Parents selecting private schools have potentially more choices, and when exercising their choice option are more likely to select schools that more closely match their expectations. It is this matching phenomenon that helps private schools establish a clear set of goals formulated by and shared among the school community (Cibulka, 1987).

Expectations and Communications Policies

Another major organization issue that seems to distinguish the two sectors is that in private schools, norms for parent and student behavior are more likely to be clearly articulated both explicitly and implicitly. Students know what is expected of them, as do parents. Open-houses and other teacher contacts with parents are designed to communicate to parents what the school expects the home to assume responsibility for in the students education. This socialization activity helps the parents formulate reasonable expectations for their child's academic performance. As Bloom (1981) and others have found, clearly articulated parent educational aspirations are directly linked to student academic achievement.

In politically fragmented public schools, norms are seldom articulated, much less shared. However, the very existence of private schools is directly tied to a shared ideology among teachers, parents, and students. A private school would be unable to remain operational if its constituency did not support its mission. Thus, there are economic as well as intrinsic values for private schools to build and reinforce consensual goals among staff, parents, and students.

One study that details the relationship between parent and school goals and expectations was conducted by Slaughter and Schneider (1986), *Newcomers: Blacks in Private Schools*. In examining four private elementary schools, Slaughter and Schneider found that Black middle and low income families selected private schools because they perceived that the high educational aspirations they had for their children were more likely to be realized in private school environments. Frequently commenting that the quality of public education in their neighborhoods and communities was inferior to the quality of the education their children were receiving, these parents thought the private schools their children were attending had a stronger emphasis on reading, writing, and mathematical concepts and skills than did the public schools.

Concerning issues of social equity, several of the Black parents in the Slaughter and Schneider study expected the school to provide experiences that would positively influence the social development of their children. Some of these parents stated during intensive interviews that they or their extended families and communities could not provide these socialization experiences. These parents were confident that the schools would provide their children with knowledge and skills that would allow them to access high-quality post-secondary schools and eventual occupational and social success. Their expectations were grounded in a reality of academic equity, as administrators and teachers treated Black and Non-Black students with the same performance standards and provided them with similar opportunities to fulfill these academic expectations.

Findings of Slaughter and Schneider (1986) are also reported by Cibulka *et al.* (1982) and Erickson and Nault (1980). In examining private

Catholic schools, Cibulka *et al.* (1982) found that low-income parents were choosing private schools because they perceived that the schools were committed and upheld certain standards that they believed important to their views of education. Erickson and Nault (1980), in their initial study of British Columbia Catholic schools, also found that the parents perceived the schools as committed to their ideas of the purpose of schooling and how that should be accomplished.

School policies, rules, and procedures are particularly useful for understanding how goals are fulfilled. The link between school policies and academic achievement has been clearly documented. Schools that have high attendance rates produce higher levels of academic performance (Coleman, Hoffer and Kilgore, 1982). Private schools, partially because of their unified goal structure and small organizational size, are more able than public schools to establish, monitor, and uphold school policies.

The school policies examined in the Slaughter and Schneider (1986) study included disciplinary rules, suspension procedures, administrator and teacher hiring and retention policies, teacher and student evaluation policies, admission policies, and curriculum policies. While all of these rules, procedures, and policies were present in each of the private schools, they were established under different conditions and upheld differently. Moreover, the way they were upheld was consistent with the school's culture. At the Catholic school, children who missed homework assignments had to pay a penance (usually a penny to the school fund); whereas students at the independent school who missed homework assignments received a detention, their names were posted on the school bulletin board, and they were expected to come to school early for a certain number of times, depending on the severity of the problem (Schneider, 1986).

Although the schools in the Slaughter and Schneider study differed in the ways they carried out school policies, they shared several important properties. Administrators and teachers held high academic standards for all students and assumed major responsibility for ensuring that students met these expectations. Children had homework assignments that were graded and monitored, the emphasis being on the acquisition of skills and the development of critical thinking ability. There were few discipline problems, and time in the classroom was devoted to teaching the subject matter. Full, descriptive accounts of the child's academic progress were routinely reported to each family. Special classes and one-to-one tutoring sessions were available to children who needed additional academic help. And finally, each school gave explicit attention to parent involvement in school life.

Similar private school qualities were also found in Bauch's (1987) study of five secondary high schools, which surveyed 1070 parents. The schools were selected from 106 schools serving low income communities and were viewed by teachers as 'particularly effective'. Parents reported being satisfied with these schools because the teachers frequently communicated with them over issues of student progress. The parents also indicated that the teachers carefully monitored their child's homework. Parents felt encouraged to attend school meetings and communicate with teachers and administrators over school policy matters.

Parent involvement in school activities is widely considered to be an important factor in a child's success in school. Researchers have maintained that parent involvement in school activities is critical for low income and minority families because they are likely to feel excluded from school life (Connell, Ashenden, Kessler and Dowsett, 1982; Comer, 1980; Lightfoot, 1978). Private schools appear to offer families greater opportunities for participation (Coleman and Hoffer, 1987; Schneider and Slaughter, forthcoming).

Schneider and Slaughter (forthcoming) examined parent participation in the context of a school's culture, and found that each school has its own norms and rituals for parent participation. In some private schools, parents are expected to participate actively on school policy boards and committees, whereas at another school this type of activity was not encouraged by the school or desired by most parents. However, each school had specific types of activities that involved parents in school life. Providing opportunities for parent involvement helps schools form strong ties with their constituents and reinforce academic and social goals. Low income and minority families who feel excluded from the public school system and who may feel excluded and discriminated against generally are made to feel part of the private school's community, because the school explicitly encourages their participation.

There are several organizational reasons that help to explain why private schools are able to encourage open parent-teacher communication and involvement. First, private school teachers are accessible: they can and will contact parents about their child's academic performance. In public schools, union contracts often have stipulations that limit the amount of time teachers can spend on out-of-school evaluations (Cresswell and Murphy, 1980). Although there is nothing to prohibit a public school teacher from contacting a parent, and many do, the normative social structure as well as the explicit policy standards set by contracts or administrative policy discourage such action. It is important to point out that one reason unions have stipulated time allocations is so that schools will not take advantage and abuse teachers' time without adequately compensating them for their efforts.

The state of public school teaching is problematic. Teaching has consistently been viewed as an occupation with high attrition rates and low professional status (Lortie, 1975; Heyns, 1972). Teacher morale in public schools is particularly low among teachers in secondary schools, among young teachers and men, and in large urban high schools. Morale is not the only concern, as the number of malpractice lawsuits against teachers has increased (Leary, 1981). These conditions certainly discourage teachers from communicating frequently with parents. While there are certainly other factors that discourage public school teachers from being as accessible to parents as private school teachers, the bottom line is that in a private school the teacher still is more likely to be viewed by parents as approachable, knowledgeable, and interested in their children's education.

Thus, even though public and private schools share fairly basic structural characteristics, such as a designated chief school administrator, instructional and support staff, and some form of grade-level distinctions, the processes by which educational goals are articulated and fulfilled are quite different (Bauch, 1987; Peshkin, 1986; Slaughter and Schneider, 1986). Because of their emphasis on learning, perceptions of student abilities, and opportunities for parent involvement, private schools seem to create educational environments that are especially conducive for raising the academic performance of poor and minority students (Bauch, 1987; Cibulka, O'Brien and Zewe, 1982; Coleman and Hoffer, 1987; Greeley, 1982; Slaughter and Schneider, 1986).

Directions for Public Policy

Various studies have implied that poor and minority families are liable to lack information that would make them sophisticated or careful shoppers of private schools if they had the resources to make those choices. However, Slaughter and Schneider (1986) found that most families in their sample — regardless of socioeconomic level or minority status — made private school choices based not on programs or teaching styles, but rather on their beliefs about the type of schooling environment that best suited their own educational philosophies and the needs of their children. Poor and minority families, like other families in the study, espoused distinguishable values about what constitutes quality education, and these beliefs helped to guide their selections of specific private schools. The process by which disadvantaged families selected a private school reflected their personal educational ideologies. Although middle and higher income families had the financial resources to consider more private school options, their ultimate decisions were philosophically based as well. Thus there were few differences in the school selection process, employed by disadvantaged, middle or high income families.

School choice for the families in the Slaughter and Schneider (1986) study was in large part an issue of selecting a school that enhanced their child's academic and social development. Clearly, many of America's poor and minority students attend large urban public schools that impede rather then enhance learning and social development, as evidenced by low test scores, high dropout rates and low college matriculation figures. Disadvantaged families do not send their children to inferior public schools by choice, but rather as the result of an archaically organized educational system that reflects racially segregated residential housing patterns.

Increasingly, poor and minority families are becoming more aware and articulate about the obvious long term results of the inequitable public education their children are receiving (Schneider and Slaughter, 1988). Some families have chosen private education as a means to alleviate the educational plight of their children. Unfortunately, the number of private schools that poor and minority students can choose to enroll in is declining. While urban school-age populations have become primarily minority, it now appears that the number of private schools in inner-city areas is decreasing, while the number of private schools in suburban and non-metropolitan areas is increasing slightly (Williams, 1986). This change has come about in part because the number of Catholic children in many urban areas has declined. These population declines have not been offset by the considerable number of low income and minority students attending Catholic high schools (National Catholic Education Association, 1986). This demographic trend has resulted in the closing of a number of inner-city Catholic schools.

Hence, while the number of minority and poor families is increasing, the number of private schools they can access is decreasing. Poor families, even those willing to make extreme sacrifices to send their children to private schools, may be increasingly unable to do so in the future. Thus, even if there were a government program to provide assistance to private schools, there are currently not enough private schools in urban areas to accommodate the needs of the population.

What then can be done to make educational opportunities for poor and minority students more equitable? Various policy initiatives have been suggested to increase the opportunities for high, middle, and low income families to access private educational alternatives. Recent legislative proposals are unlike other prior public aid programs for private schools in three major respects. First, new proposals target state and federal appropriations for various types of private schools; in the past such aid was directed primarily to religious schools (Carper and Hunt, 1984). Second, the amount of aid being proposed for private elementary and secondary schools is substantially more than in previous assistance programs (Erickson, 1983). And finally, the aid would be given *directly to the parents* who choose private education for their children, rather than to the private schools. The two family choice initiatives currently being debated at state and federal levels are tuition tax credits and educational vouchers. Under the tuition tax credit system, a family's federal or state income tax liability would be reduced equal to a specified portion of the cost of a child's tuition at a private school. Under the voucher system, parents would receive tuition certificates that would be redeemable at either public or private schools.

Neither vouchers nor tuition tax credit systems have received wide-spread political support. The likelihood of either type of initiative being passed in the Congress at this time is virtually nil. The number of public school employees who potentially stand to lose their hold on their captive clientele will prevent such action. Moreover, the amount of federal money needed to mount either initiative is considerable and unlikely to be allocated in the current political environment, where Gramm–Rudman solutions are passed to balance the budget. No matter how convincingly either side tries to make the case that such benefits will assist in the education of poor children or will make little difference to them, the issues will ultimately be resolved through interest group politics in an economically constrained environment.

An equitable schooling experience for poor and minority children cannot be sustained under the current educational system. Disadvantaged families should have the opportunity to access quality schools, be they public or private ones. School choice should not be the consequence of race, ethnic background, or economic resources, particularly in a country that prides itself on providing a free public education to all students. Because of their organizational structure, many private schools are offering positive educational environments for low income and minority families and could be used as models for reform. If we are serious about providing high quality education we need to look more closely at how private schools are able to accomplish these objectives for all students.

Acknowledgments

I gratefully appreciate the time and helpful comments my colleagues Dr James Cibulka and Dr Elizabeth Sulzby made on the content of this chapter.

References

APPLEBEE, A, LANGER, J. and MULLIS, I. (1987) *Learning to Be Literate in America* Princeton, New Jersey, Educational Testing Service.

BAUCH, P. (1985) Five Low Income Schools: A Sketch, in BENSON, P. (ed.) *A National Portrait of Catholic Schools* Washington, DC, National Catholic Educational Association.

BAUCH, P. (ed.) (1987) 'Family Choice and Parent Involvement in Inner-City Catholic High Schools: An Exploration of Parent Psycho-Social and School Organizational Factors', Paper presented at annual meeting of the American Educational Research Association, Washington, DC.

BIDWELL, C. (1965) 'The School as a Formal Organization', in MARCH, J. G. (ed.) *Handbook of Organizations* Chicago, Rand McNally.

BLOOM, B. (1981) *All Our Children Learning* New York, McGraw-Hill Book Company.
BOYAN, N. (1982) 'Administration of Educational Institutions' in MITZEL, H. E. (ed.) *Encyclopedia of Educational Research* New York, The Free Press.
BOYD, W. (1984) 'Competing Values in Educational Policy and Governance: Australian and American Developments, *Educational Administrative Review*, 2, pp. 4–24.
BOYD, W. (1986) 'Educational Choice and the Dilemmas of Elitism: The Australian Experience and American Implications'. Paper presented at the annual meeting of the American Educational Research Association, San Francisco, California.
CARPER, J. and HUNT, T. (1984) *Religious Schooling in America* Alabama, Religious Education Press.
CIBULKA, J. (1987) 'Responsiveness to Community Needs Among Catholic Secondary Schools: The Role of Markets, Politics, and Organizational Structure'. Paper presented at the annual meeting of the American Educational Research Association, Washington, DC.
CIBULKA, J., O'BRIEN, T. and ZEWE, D. (1982) *Inner-City Private Elementary Schools: A Study* Milwaukee, Marquette University Press.
CHUBB, E. and MOE, T. (1985) 'Politics, Markets, and the Organization of Schools'. Project No. 85-A15 to the National Institute of Education, Grant No. NIE-G-83-0003.
COLEMAN, J. S., HOFFER, T. and KILGORE, S. (1982) *High School Achievement* New York, Basic Books.
COLEMAN, J. S. and HOFFER, T. (1987) *Public and Private High Schools: The Impact of Communities* New York, Basic Books.
COMER, J. (1980) *School Power: Implications Of An Intervention Project* New York, The Free Press.
CONNELL, R., ASHENDEN, S., KESSLER, S. and DOWSETT, G (1982) *Making the Difference: Schools, Families and Social Division* Sydney, George Allen and Unwin.
COOPER, B. (1983) 'The Latest Word on Private School Growth' *Teachers College Record*, 85, pp. 88–98.
CRESWELL, A. and MURPHY, M. (1980) *Teachers, Unions and Collective Bargaining in Education* Berkeley, Ca, McCutchan.
DOYLE, D. (1981) 'A Din of Inequity: Private Schools Reconsidered' *Teachers College Record*, 82, pp. 66–673.
ERICKSON, D. (1978) 'Recent Enrollment Trends in U.S. Nonpublic Schools', in ABRAMOWITZ, S. and ROSENFELD, S. *Declining Enrollments: The Challenge of the Coming Decade* Washington, DC, National Institute of Education.
ERICKSON, D. (1979) 'Research on Educational Administration: The State-Of-The-Art', *Educational Researcher*, 8, pp. 9–14.
ERICKSON, D. (1983) 'Private Schools in Contemporary Perspective', Institute for Research on Educational Finance and Governance, Stanford University.
ERICKSON, D. (1986) 'Research on Private Schools: The State of the Art', Paper presented at the conference on Research on Private Education: Private Schools and Public Concerns What We Know and What We Need to Know, Catholic University of America, Washington, DC.
ERICKSON, D. and NAULT, R. (1980) *Effects of Public Money on Catholic Schools in Western Canada* San Francisco, CA, Center for Research on Private Education.
GOODLAD, J. (1984) *A Place Called School* New York, McGraw-Hill.
GREELEY, A. (1982) *Catholic High Schools and Minority Students* New Brunswick, NJ, Transaction Books.

HAERTEL, E. (1984) 'The Question of School Outcomes: A Synthesis of Competing Arguments.' Paper presented at the conference on Comparing Public and Private Schools, Institute for Research on Educational Finance and Governance, Stanford University, Stanford, California.

Harvard Educational Review (1981) 'Report Analysis: Public and Private Schools.' 51, pp. 481–545.

HEYNS, B. (1972) 'Down the Up Staircase: Sex Roles Professionalization, and the Status of Teachers', in ANDERSON, S. (ed.) *Sex Differences and Discrimination in Education* New York, Charles Jones.

HOTCHKISS, L. (1984) *Effects of Schooling On Cognitive, Attiudinal, and Behavioral Outcomes* Columbus, Ohio, The National Center for Research in Vocational Education.

JAMES, E. (1984) 'The Public/Private Division of Responsibility for Education: An International Comparison'. Paper presented at the conference Comparing Public and Private Schools, Institute for Research on Educational Finance and Governance, Stanford University, Stanford, California.

JAMES, E. (1986) 'Comment on Public-Private School Research and Policy.' Paper presented at the conference, Research on Private Education: Private Schools and Public Concerns, What We Know and What We Need to Know, Catholic University of America, Washington, DC.

JAMES, T. and LEVIN, H. (eds) (1988) *Comparing Public and Private Schools: Institutions and Organizations Volume I.* Lewes, Falmer Press.

KAUFMAN, P. (1986) 'Trends in Elementary and Secondary Public School Enrollments', in *Condition of Education 1986* Washington, DC, US Center for Education Statistics, pp. 140–157.

KERCKHOFF, A. (1986) 'Effect of Ability Grouping in British Secondary Schools', *American Sociological Review*, 51, pp. 842–858.

KRAUSHAAR, O. (1972) *American Nonpublic Schools: Patterns of Diversity* Baltimore, Maryland, John Hopkins University Press.

LEARY, J. (1981) *Educators on Trial* Michigan, Action Inservice Inc., Publisher.

LIGHTFOOT, S. (1978) *Worlds Apart: Relationships between Families and Schools* New York, Basic Books.

LORTIE, D. (1975) *Schoolteacher: A Sociological Study* Chicago, The University of Chicago Press.

MASSEY, D. and DENTON, N. (1987) 'Trends in the Residential Segregation of Blacks, Hispanics, and Asians: 1970–1980', *American Sociological Review* 52, pp. 802–825.

MEYER, J. and ROWAN, B. (1983) 'The Structure of Educational Organizations', in MEYER, J. and SCOTT, W. (eds) *Organizational Environments* Beverly Hills, CA, Sage.

National Catholic Education Association (1985) *The Catholic High School: A National Portrait* Washington, DC, National Catholic Education Association.

OAKES, J (1985) *Keeping Track. How Schools Structure Inequality* New Haven, Yale University Press.

PALLAS, A. (1986) 'School Dropouts in the United States', in *Condition of Education, 1986* Washington, DC, US Center for Education Statistics, pp. 158–170.

PESHKIN, A. (1986) *God's Choice* Chicago, University of Chicago Press.

RAYWID, M. (1985) 'Family Choice Arrangements in Public Schools', *Review of Education Research*, 55, pp. 435–467.

ROSENBAUM, J. (1976) *Making Inequality: The Hidden Curriculum of High School Tracking* New York, Wiley.

ROWAN, B. and MIRACLE, A. (1983) 'Systems of Ability Grouping and the Stratification of Achievement in Elementary Schools', *Sociology of Education*, 56, pp. 133–144.

SCHNEIDER, B. (1986) 'Studying Social Relationships in School', Unpublished manuscript.

SCHNEIDER, B. and SLAUGHTER, D. (1984) 'Accessing Educational Choices: Blacks in Private Urban Elementary Schools'. Paper presented at the conference on Comparing Public and Private Schools, Institute for Research on Educational Finance and Governance, Stanford University.

SCHNEIDER, B. and SLAUGHTER, D. (1988) 'Educational Choice for Blacks in Urban Elementary Schools', in JAMES, T. and LEVIN, H. (eds) *Comparing Public and Private Schools: Institutions and Organizations Vol. I.* Lewes, Falmer Press.

SCHNEIDER, B. and SLAUGHTER, D. (forthcoming) 'Parents and School Life: Varieties of Parent Participation', in BAUCH, P. (ed.) *Private Schools and the Public Interest: Research Issues and Policy* Conn., Greenwood Press.

SEBRING, P. (1987) 'Consequences of Differential Amounts of High School Coursework: Will the New Graduation Requirements Help?' *Educational Evaluation and Policy Analysis*, 9, pp. 258 –273.

SLAUGHTER, D. and SCHNEIDER, B. (1986) *Newcomers: Blacks in Private Schools. Final Report to the National Institute of Education. Volumes I and II.* (Contract No. NIE-G-82-0040). Northwestern University, ERIC Document ED 274 768 and ED 274 769.

Sociology of Education (1982) 55 (April/July). Special two volume Series on the debate surrounding Public and Private Schools (1981).

Sociology of Education (1983) 56 (October). Series of papers on the Public and Private School Debate. See pp. 170–234.

Sociology of Education (1985) 58 (April). Third special issue devoted to Public and Private School debate.

UNITED STATES CENTER FOR EDUCATION STATISTICS (1986) *Condition of Education*, Washington, DC, US Center for Education Statistics.

UNITED STATES CENTER FOR EDUCATION STATISTICS (1987) *Condition of Education*, Washington, DC, US Center for Education Statistics.

UNITED STATES CENTER FOR EDUCATION STATISTICS (1987) *Digest of Education Statistics*, Washington, DC, US Center for Education Statistics.

VITULLO-MARTIN, T. (1982) 'The Impact of Taxation Policy on Public and Private Schools', in EVERHART, R. E. (ed.) *The Public School Monopoly* Cambridge, MA, Ballinger Publishing Company.

WILLIAMS, M. (1986) Private School Enrollment and Tuition Trends', in *Condition of Education* Washington, DC, US Center for Education Statistics.

Chapter 5
Rationales for Private Schools:
A Commentary

James G. Cibulka

The first thing that may be said about the four preceding chapters is that because all are written by Americans, they reflect a concern which is peculiar to the United States and perhaps a few other countries. In many nations, it would not be necessary to fashion a philosophical defense of private schooling because the distinction between public and private is not so sharply drawn. As Doyle observes in his chapter, elsewhere people are not accustomed to think of the government-run schools as public and all others as private. (And in Great Britain public schools are, in fact, privately-owned.) Private schools, depending on their patronage, are assumed to serve a public purpose and frequently are eligible for government aid.

The greater acceptance of private schools in most countries other than the United States has made it less compelling that they defend their purposes. Quite the opposite in the United States, where private schools are not regarded as part of the public culture, but rather carry the connotation of embodying narrow, sectarian, or exclusive values. Among the social democracies of the West, the United States, owing to its liberal Lockian tradition of individualism and limited government, has the least developed social welfare state. Yet Americans have supported a strong system of universal public education, in order to pursue their enlightenment faith in individual fulfillment as well as to unify a diverse nation.

Thus, the four chapters upon which this commentary is based and the discussion which follows speak to some degree to an American interest and need. At the same time, the issues raised here about the purposes of schooling and how to organize that enterprise are so fundamental as to be universal. Each philosophical perspective will carry somewhat different relevance as it is applied to various national circumstances. At the end I will return to this point.

For reasons of exposition, the chapters will be discussed in slightly different order from their appearance in the book. After analyzing Donald

Erickson's libertarian argument, I turn directly to Jacob Michaelsen's public choice rationale, then to Denis Doyle's discussion of religious values and finally, Barbara Schneider's egalitarian approach. In entertaining the libertarian, public choice, religious values, and equity arguments in turn, I will focus on two considerations. In what ways are these positions compatible and in what respects do they operate in tension? Also, how can each rationale contribute to an overarching, comprehensive philosophical position on the need for private schools in a democratic society? An underlying premise I bring is that no one position, as presently formulated, adequately states the case for private schools. Accordingly, I examine how these positions might be restated and juxtaposed so as to contribute to a philosophical synthesis. In this effort I intend to examine another rationale which complements and augments the four chapters included here and which contributes toward the broader rationale I believe is needed.

The Libertarian View

The thrust of libertarian thought is largely protectionist and anti-statist. It is protectionist in its concern with preserving the rights of individuals and groups from infringement by hostile social institutions, whether these be the media, law enforcement agencies, schools, or whatever. It is anti-statist in its deep suspicion of government's capacity to address and protect these rights. Donald Erickson's chapter reflects both these pervasive aspects of the dominant libertarian view — the implicit liberal vision of society as a collection of individuals and groups striving to protect their autonomy and the conception of government as having limited inclination and capacity to protect individual rights or cultivate individual happiness.[1]

As they apply to schooling, these libertarian concerns are most likely to be advanced in countries where a strong institution of public schools has emerged and where some individuals and groups in the society feel that their rights are threatened. Both situations exist in the United States. Since nearly nine out of ten American youngsters are educated in public schools, there can be no question of the preeminence and strength of public schools in the United States, despite their political problems in recent years. At the same time, the growth of evangelical schools suggests the depth of feeling held by some segments of the population that their values are not being recognized or 'protected' in the public schools.

The libertarian perspective, like liberalism generally, is a loose collection of views whose proponents bring varying analyses to the common ideological core mentioned above. Some approaches emphasize political liberty to the exclusion of economic liberty, or vice-versa, or both. Those concerned with political liberty stress the potential for abuse of human rights when government has the capacity to compel persons in the name of the majority.

On the economic side, most libertarians see excessive state intervention into the economy through planning or other means as a threat to liberty as well. Hayek (1944) believed that government works less efficiently and ultimately less effectively than market institutions. From this starting premise about market superiority, however, economic libertarians move in many directions. Hayek, for example, supported government regulation of the economy and certain elements of the welfare state. Others such as Friedman (1953) are critical of most forms of government action wherever the market can otherwise operate. This illustrates the point that libertarians are more united in the abstract about the evils they wish to protect against than they are agreed about how such liberty is to be protected through specific institutional arrangements.

Erickson's chapter does not really address solutions, for he does not argue in detailed fashion for one or another institutional approach to parental choice and private school regulation. He thus avoids the ambiguities about remedy which seem endemic to libertarianism. He believes it sufficient to document the propensity for government abuse of individual liberty, and offers a compelling argument that such compulsion cannot be avoided.

Yet even Erickson's diagnosis of the problem, solutions aside, indirectly reveals the limits of libertarian analysis. If formalized schooling inevitably results in indoctrination of youth, as Erickson argues, the problem is not confined to government-sponsored schools, but rather pervades private schools as well. Individual liberty is threatened by formal organizations, paradoxically even at same time these formal organizations protect human liberty in other respects.

As economists recognize, any formal organization represents an alternative to a pure market exchange, and many economists would characterize this hierarchy as a market failure. Yet organizations sometimes can accomplish what simple market exchanges cannot, and hence their attraction. In formal organizations, however, the owners have difficulty maintaining control, managing discretion of their agents, creating proper incentives against shirking and other abuses. It follows that these universal organizational problems presumably are to be found in private schools, as well as in government-sponsored ones.

This being true, as an alternative it is possible to see the libertarian problem as one of learning how to counteract the distortions imposed on human affairs by formal organizations, not merely by government. Indeed, the relatively new field of organizational economics speaks to this problem; it addresses how motivational problems are to be resolved in organizational hierarchies (Barney and Ouchi, 1986; Moe, 1984.) This is a shift of focus away from the traditional libertarian preference for market relationships rather than governmental regulation. Under certain market conditions competition may well improve organizational performance, but organizational economics alerts us to the fact that this is not inevitable.

Unfortunately, a libertarian perspective has yet to provide a theory of organizational performance which links internal organizational attributes (goals, structure, achievement, etc.) to broader economic and political institutional arrangements. It does not concentrate, for example, on a detailed explanation of why private schools can protect individual liberty better than public ones. What it does offer is a defense of individual autonomy as a social goal and a criterion by which governmental performance may be judged. As we shall see in the following section, public choice theory concerns itself principally with the latter problem of government productivity, and thus does begin to address in a partial way the problem of organizational performance and its relationship to existing institutional arrangements, a matter which is left unaddressed by the libertarian paradigm.

Public Choice Theory

'Public choice theory has concentrated on developing a theory of why governments fail. Built from microeconomic assumptions, this theory stresses the insularity of government bureaucracies from public accountability, leading to goal displacement which favors the interests of employees rather than the true owners of the polity, the people themselves.

Implicit in this theory is the ideal of the competitive marketplace, whose discipline introduces a tangible goal (profit-maximizing) to which employees can be held accountable by owners. The argument must be adapted somewhat for schools, the large portion of which, even in the private sector, are non-profit corporations. Accordingly, Michaelsen has argued elsewhere (1981), that the size and heterogeneity of parental tastes in many public school systems makes it impossible to articulate clear goals for employees, thereby rendering it difficult to measure their performance and reward them commensurately. By implication, a market system would better match consumer wants with responsive schools. To the extent that private schools must compete for clients, public choice theory offers an explanation for why they are more likely to perform well than public schools, which are monopolies operating in heterogeneous environments.

Michaelsen has added a novel element to public choice theory in this chapter. First, he has introduced a moral imperative in discussing the superior performance of private schools. As conceived previously by Niskanen, (1975), Orzechowski, 1977, and Michaelsen himself (1981), public choice theory has reflected the American economist's concern for technical efficiency and productivity. Hence, the problem with government, it is said, is that it is less efficient and productive than market forms. In the realm of productivity, Michaelsen now carries the logic a step further. Private schools are able to cultivate better individual autonomy, personal initiative, creativity, and self-fulfillment. These moral virtues presumably must be modeled by the school's faculty. They tend to be in short supply in many American schools, most likely because of the bureaucratic structure within which most teachers are compelled to work and which denies them full status as professionals. Private school teachers, on the other hand, consistently report that their relatively low pay is offset by considerable freedom and a collegial, family-like atmosphere. Therefore, based on what is known about these overall differences between public and private schools, Michaelsen's conjecture seems quite plausible. Although it is known that character development is stressed very heavily in many private schools, available research does not speak clearly to this issue.

Michaelsen's chapter also extends public choice theory by asserting that a market system would (and presumably already does in the private school sector) foster entrepreneurship. He makes the very perceptive point that we need in education an institutional structure which builds incentives for school officials to advance our knowledge base about school effectiveness and which inclines them to be responsive to parental expectations. In point of fact, there is little evidence that rates of innovation are higher in private than public schools (Powell, 1987), but perhaps innovation is not the only or most important measure of entrepreneurial behavior. The latter might as well be defined as the propensity of school officials to anticipate and respond to parental wishes. Whether this responsiveness is due to school officials' perception that parents make a sacrifice deserving their respect, whether it is due to competitive market conditions, or some other combination of reasons is not understood. Yet Michaelsen points us in the right direction.

Indeed, his public choice argument does not depend entirely on demonstrating greater entrepreneurship in private schools. If more market alternatives were created in America, permitting greater family choice options either within public school or among both sectors, the level of experimentation might well rise as a result of increased competition. It is important to note, though, that if demand for school slots exceeded supply, producers would have little incentive to act as entrepreneurs.

Michaelsen's chapter therefore pushes public choice theory beyond being principally a critique of public school bureaucracies. He begins to specify here what conditions are needed for institutional reform to take place.

His analysis has considerable affinity with Erickson's libertarian thesis. Both perspectives offer a rationale for private schools indirectly through their trenchant disaffection from government schools and state regulation. Each is intellectually indebted to the discipline of economics for insights. Both authors are concerned about individual autonomy in modern society, although Michaelsen may have more faith that good private schools can teach this quality. Despite their common philosophical starting point, where these two theorists depart is important. Erickson's libertarian argument reflects a fear of state involvement; he seeks only to create sanctuaries for the individual to pursue happiness beyond the reach of state action. Michaelsen's public choice theory, on the other hand, envisions a broad restructuring of educational governance in line with market principles. Thus, Michaelsen's contribution here moves both beyond libertarian thought and beyond traditional public choice theory. He provides a positive rationale for private schools and the institutional framework which facilitates their effectiveness. The chapter charts a direction rather than defining all the territory, but in so doing makes an important contribution.

Education for Religious Values

Denis Doyle's chapter uses cross-national comparisons to build his argument. A principal aim of education, he says, is inculcation of values, both those national values which are widely shared in a culture (openness, tolerance, etc.) and those which are in competition and embraced by different groups. In this second category Doyle places special weight on religious values advanced by intimate religious communities. At the start he quotes Alfred North Whitehead on the religious essence of education.

Doyle, then, uses 'religious' in two senses in this chapter: as a doctrinal descriptor distinguishing the orthodoxies of various churches and in a more general sense as a moral virtue which transcends allegiance to particular religious institutions. This second use of the word is not described at length, but beyond some general terms such as Whitehead uses (duty and reverence) presumably there would be little consensus on what constitutes morally virtuous behavior. According to Doyle, while we all agree on the sanctity of human life, we demur on more specific questions which involve the taking of human life — war, capital punishment, abortion, and so on.

The typical approach to such contentious matters in American schools, at least recently, has been to maintain neutrality, either by purging them from discussion or by seeking to help students 'clarify' their own values. While Doyle does not openly attack this second approach, he hints at his disdain for approaches which fail to acknowledge that these issues are 'binary' and must be presented as 'yes' or 'no' propositions.

He goes on to offer an argument for these matters being addressed in the context of a religious education. The assumption is that religious groups would be less inclined toward relativism in approaching moral questions.

In point of fact, however, much of religious teaching leaves certain matters to individual conscience, taking us back toward the relativism Doyle seeks to avoid. Indeed, his argument for accommodating religious values in education is pluralist. He likens the problem to the accommodation of dissent in constitutional democracies. Competing ideas are allowed to flourish because there is no guarantee that one or another view is right. Pluralism does not tolerate all views as equally valid. Rather, it sets forth institutional procedures to guarantee their right to be aired.

It is this pluralism which Doyle believes is lacking in the American system of education. After arguing that other countries do not maintain such an anachronistic distinction between public and private, he asserts that the resistance is really to public support for religious education.

The separation of church and state is a thorny political and constitutional issue in the United States. The country often has turned to the judiciary to resolve the issue temporarily until another legal challenge settles the matter again. Doyle avoids a discussion of this legal thicket, but anyone familiar with it knows that the long tradition of separation of church and state in America is not likely to be reversed quickly. For one, many religious groups would not have it so any more than civil libertarians would favor blurring the separation.

Doyle's premise, then, is that religious values are the essence of education and that institutional arrangements should accommodate diverse religious preferences and sponsorship among schools. Doyle illustrates how this has been done in Denmark, Holland, and Australia. For example, in Denmark it is accepted widely that the system should permit dissenting groups of various persuasions the right to form their own school with government support.

Doyle's presentation has much in common with Erickson's libertarian and Michaelsen's public choice arguments. Like Erickson, he finds the prevailing orthodoxy of public schools a threat to diverse preferences. While not critical of public schools, like Michaelsen he finds the governmental structure in the United States a barrier to goal fulfillment. Whereas Michaelsen stresses values such as individual autonomy, personal initiative, and creativity, Doyle stresses religious values. Like Michaelsen, he believes that public schools cannot accommodate diverse preferences by excluding segments of the population. This point of view assumes that it is better for homogeneous groups to compete.

These differences are important to underscore. Doyle's support for religious values is built not from premises about individuals or from an analysis of the dysfunctions besetting public monopolies. Rather the argument is erected around an analysis of the content of the educational process itself as well as a pluralistic conception of the political and social order as a means of protecting our search for the truth underlying these values. If Michaelsen's analysis is 'micro' in its understanding of organizational behavior, Doyle offers a broader reaching 'macro' argument about the proper interplay between education and politics.

Yet in constructing his argument, Doyle has made an assumption that the critical facet of social organization around which to construct such a theory is religion. At the start he takes note of the class inequity in the

American system of education. Yet he does not explore how a family choice system would improve upon this degree of inequality.

This raises the problem of how any analysis of private schools can ignore issues of social class and other status categories besides religion such as race and gender. That consideration points us to the question of how equitably educational resources are distributed among various groups.

It is this concern which animates Schneider's analysis.

An Equity Perspective

Until recently, private school advocates in the United States have treated the equity issue as a matter of taxpayer fairness, not pupil rights. It has been argued that private school patrons are, in effect, taxed twice, once for sending their children to private schools while parents of public school pupils enjoy a reduced tax price for schooling due to the existence of private schools, whose pupils would otherwise be educated at taxpayer expense.

The objections to this conception of equity have been many. Public school education, it is said, is a constitutional right. The right to attend a private school, while constitutionally protected, does not extend to public financing of such schools. Private school patrons must meet their tax obligations for support of public schools, at the same time that tax support for private schools repeatedly has been struck down by the courts. (Minnesota's policy of allowing income tax deductions for public or private school expenditures has, however, been upheld as constitutional.)

Schneider's chapter represents an important reformulation of this traditional equity argument. Given the elitist image of American private schools, frequently they are accused of being anti-democratic. Hence, it is novel for Barbara Schneider to fashion a defense of private schools around the idea of equity. In America equitable treatment for rural children, for poor blacks and Hispanics, or for poor children of whatever background, has been associated with improving their access to higher quality *public* schools. This is, after all, the American ideal of universal public education. The image of private schools as serving a private interest for an exclusive audience — the rich, religious groups, the culturally alienated, or any other group which is partisan — seems at odds with this ideal. Therefore, for many Americans fair treatment for the disenfranchised means equalizing educational opportunity within the existing public school framework. Political liberals, for example, accept the reality that this decentralized public school structure falls far short of affording full equality to all pupils. Indeed, they accept this fact because they concede other competing values of high importance. Paramount among these is local control, which ostensibly favors greater choice for consumers and a more responsive system matching local tastes.

Yet this liberal commitment to incremental progress, one readily embraced by public school educators and their allies, is deeply shaken by the evidence which Schneider reviews; many public schools, particularly those in urban areas, are not successfully educating poor children, particularly minorities. Thoughtful observers of this American tragedy have begun to take note that many Catholic schools educate the urban poor successfully, and at less cost.

This fact has yet to lead to a reevaluation by the political establishment of what equity means. Schneider suggests that it should mean access to high quality education for the poor, wherever that education can be obtained. This same position has been argued more recently by the former United States Secretary of Education, William Bennett, who called for 'equal intellectual opportunity'. Equity, in other words, must entail not merely access to educational resources but evidence that school officials apply those resources effectively to benefit the educational goals and needs of children.

This definition will trouble many liberals, however, who see in Schneider's approach a threat to the democratic ideal. Will it lead to greater racial segregation? Will the public schools become even worse than now if the most articulate and motivated among the poor are given greater freedom to exit public schools through a policy of supporting private schools or their patrons?

These concerns direct our attention to the narrow platform upon which Schneider has constructed her equity defense of private schools. Schneider's approach to equity has limitations if its purpose is to offer a broad defense of private schooling. By concerning herself with the access of the poor to quality education through private schools, this equity rationale is necessarily constructed more narrowly than either the libertarian or public choice rationales. Equitable treatment for disenfranchised students is not the same as arguing that in the aggregate private schools are more equitable in their enrollment and other policies than the public school sector. To be sure, such claims have been made; for example, Coleman, Kilgore, and Hoffer (1982) asserted that the private school sector is no more racially segregated than the public. However, such claims are disputed, and in any case only rest on the limited assertion that private schools are no more inequitable than public counterparts. Schneider's chapter offers a more valid but equally limited point about particular private schools being more equitable than public ones.

To realize Schneider's defense of equity as comparable access to quality education, two things would have to occur in the United States. More poor parents would have to choose private schools, and more private school choice would have to be available. This immediately raises two questions. Do the poor desire private schools and, second, what public policy would guarantee greater choice best?

The answer to the first question is not clear. Some inner-city private schools have closed for lack of enrollment. Yet one would be surprised if this were not the case, since private school attendance requires some additional financial sacrifice for poor families already in dire circumstances. While many minority and poor parents remain committed to public education, they routinely report high levels of dissatisfaction with public school quality in public opinion polls. It can be expected that poor and minority parents, like most parents of any background, will choose higher quality educational alternatives for their children when these become available.

The answer to the question 'what public policy would guarantee choice best?' already has been addressed in broad outline. A public choice perspective supplies the methodology by which the equity implications of Schneider's argument could be more widely available to the poor and minorities. As Michaelsen argues, the conditions found in private school markets are conducive to productive, responsive school policies. Assuming that vouchers or tax credits would not cause private schools to be less productive or responsive than at present (owing to excessive state regulation, loss of 'shared jeopardy' (Erickson, MacDonald, Casimir-Manley and Busk, 1979) or some other factor, then these private school advantages could be more broadly available to the disadvantaged. Even if some public schools remained intact largely as we know them today, they might well be influenced to improve their performance if they were in competition with high quality private schools. As an indication of this likelihood, the present limited market arrangements in the United States have led to increased competition between public magnet schools and private schools, providing incentives for both sectors to improve their responsiveness to consumers. With increased choice and competition, educationally disadvantaged children in both public and private schools could benefit.

A full treatment of the equity argument, then, could be expected to include Schneider's focus on equity for particular pupils, but also must reach beyond that argument to explain what structural conditions will improve equity for the greatest number of children in a nation.

Private Schools As Embodiments of Communities

While each of the above rationales for private schooling has merit, there is another which deserves serious consideration, at least for its applications to the American context. A growing body of evidence suggests why private schools are unusually productive. I shall refer to this property as the 'community ethos' of private schools. It has been characterized as *gemeinschaft* by Erickson *et al.* (1979). Coleman and Hoffer (1986) refer to the social capital available at Catholic high schools. Schneider alludes to the unique communal climate in the schools she studied. Michaelsen emphasizes in the same vein the virtues of small institutions as more capable of fostering a quality of communication and innovation which eludes many public schools. Cibulka (forthcoming) has studied the various ways in which this community 'responsiveness' is operationalized in Catholic high schools, embodying in different ways the school's ownership, its mission, the views of parents and school supporters, and staff, to name only some.

This community ethos has a number of defining elements. First, it involves a reasonably clear statement of school mission and academic goals which flow from that mission. The staff, owners, students, and patrons of the school generally can articulate this mission and these goals. The school, in other words, has a well-defined purpose which establishes boundaries for the participants.

Second, the community ethos we find in private schools is built on voluntary self-affiliation. Parents, students, and staff generally have sought the school out as a special place. The perception of control over entrance and exit opportunities for the participants has important motivational implications. All things equal, people are more willing to invest their energies and talents in such institutions.

Third, these schools must work hard at having all the actors share ownership of the school's mission and goals. People are participating voluntarily, and frequently the students, their parents, and staff are making a personal sacrifice to participate. In all but the wealthiest of these schools, financial well-being and survival cannot be guaranteed, either. In these circumstances, private schools must develop shared commitment and emphasize cooperation. Private schools with social systems which do not develop these attributes are at a disadvantage, and the school may not survive.

Fourth, the relative absence of government regulation of these schools, compared with public ones, frees them to work cooperatively in shaping their mission. While autonomy is not itself the same as community, it is a defining element since autonomy motivates participants to shape their own school's destiny rather than being preoccupied with responding to outside controls. The opportunity for internal self-regulation gives rise to the idea of community as a process in which participants can define their own needs best and resolve their problems themselves.

How does this ideal of community which I have outlined relate to the libertarian, public choice, religious values, and egalitarian perspectives already presented? I believe it augments them and strengthens each. The idea that private schools embody a community of values recasts the libertarian argument from an essentially negative defense of *freedom from* state intervention. Instead, it adds a positive rationale for *freedom to* create a private school community without the necessity for state intervention. Indeed, from a libertarian perspective, state authority and regulation, however well-intentioned, is inherently in conflict with the right of persons to build private school communities. Of course, libertarians may well have other values which they wish to protect from state intervention, such as high learner productivity. Yet the thrust of Erickson's defense of private schools from state regulation is squarely in this area of values. What is needed is a more fully-elaborated libertarian critique of the public school approach to defining community, and a libertarian argument on behalf of private schools' embodiment of community.

The ideal of community is implicit in the public choice argument. Consumers should have choices of entry and exit in an educational marketplace where they can ' group' their preferences efficiently with other like-minded consumers. Indeed, constellations of schools with distinct preferences ('communities') lead to greater accountability and respon-siveness by school officials who supply educational services. Michaelsen's conception of moral autonomy fits well with the community ethos. Moral autonomy is more likely to be learned in a school where the hidden or explicit curriculum emphasizes the interplay of individual responsibility and collective purpose. In general, the community ethos offers an organiza-tional explanation for how people are motivated and held responsible for organizational goals, a central concern of organizational economists. Similarly, Doyle's ideal of religious communities as an organizing framework for schools is a specific example of how the ideal of community can work. While Doyle leaves room for the possibility that other non-religious bases may exist for affiliating around a school, his idea of community is somewhat narrower than the conception of community advanced here.

The egalitarian argument on behalf of private schools also is strength-ened by this notion of community, as Schneider recognizes in her chapter. The community ethos explains how and why low income and minority pupils do unusually well in such schools, particularly Catholic ones. Schools such as the ones Schneider and her colleague Slaughter studied have a community ethos which encourages shared responsibility for these pupils and holds out high expectations for them.

In sum, as a rationale for private schools, a community ethos conception broadens libertarian, public choice, religious values, and egalitarian perspectives.

Conclusion

I have argued here for a broader, more integrative statement of the role of private schools in a democratic society than can be offered by the libertarian, public choice, religious values, or egalitarian perspectives, if each were taken alone. I have tried to demonstrate in what respects each falls short of a comprehensive rationale. At the same time, these four frameworks, brought together by the 'community ethos' rationale I sketched above provide the building blocks for a comprehensive rationale for private schools. The components should include first, an emphasis on the individual's educational needs and rights, operating as freely as possible from unnecessary and possibly pernicious governmental intrusion. A second component would stress the teaching of values, both in the explicit and implicit curriculum of private schools. A third component should allude to the governance and finance structure in private schools, whose features of autonomy and competition encourage responsiveness to patrons' preferences and whose emphasis on community sustains the school. A fourth component of the rationale would stress the availability of private schools as an equitable alternative to public schools for disadvantaged segments of the population who are currently poorly served by the public school system. Finally, a rationale for private schools should include a conception of community which shapes the school's mission and organizational climate.

Private schools operating in other national contexts presumably would find this framework applicable, although emphases and particular arguments may differ. Some democratic societies cherish individualism less than the United States, and might find the libertarian thread less appealing. In some countries, as Doyle points out, the teaching of values is more explicitly accepted in government schools. Therefore, the argument that private schools do a better job teaching values may be less relevant for those contexts. Unlike the United States, disadvantaged groups elsewhere may not see private schools as a sanctuary against unequal treatment in public schools.

Yet the broad issues raised in these chapters will arise in any national context and must be addressed in any philosophical defense of private schools. For example, the argument that private schools enjoy an advantage over public ones in being effective and responsive is likely to have appeal in many national situations. Further, the 'community ethos' advantages of private schools appear to be universal. From these common elements, then, each nation can fashion a rationale for private schools most appropriate to its traditions and values.

Note

1 I do not address here libertarian views from the political left such as those of Arons, (1983). Despite its commonality at certain points with Erickson's and others' libertarian arguments, Arons' views are outside the 'mainstream' of libertarian thought, which is my principal interest in this essay.

References

ARONS, S (1983) *Compelling Belief: The Culture of American Schooling* New York, McGraw-Hill.

James G. Cibulka

BARNEY, J. B. and OUCHI, W. G. (1986) *Organizational Economics* San Francisco, Jossey-Bass.

CIBULKA, J. G. (Forthcoming). 'Environmental Responsiveness Among Catholic Secondary Schools: Toward An Integration of Theoretical Perspectives, in BAUCH, P. (ed.) *Private Schools and the Public Interest: Research and Policy Issues* North Scituate, Mass., Greenwood Press.

COLEMAN, J. S., KILGORE, S. and HOFFER, T. (1982) *High School Achievement: Public, Catholic, and Private Schools Compared* New York, Basic Books.

COLEMAN, J. S. and HOFFER, T. (1986) *Public and Private High Schools: The Impact of Communities* New York, Basic Books.

ERICKSON, D. A., MACDONALD, L., CASIMIR-MANLEY, M. and BUSK, P. L. (1979) *Characteristics and Relationships in Public and Independent Schools* San Francisco, CA, Center for Research on Private Education.

FRIEDMAN, M. (1953) *Essays in Positive Economics* Chicago, University of Chicago Press.

GREELEY, A. M. (1982) *Catholic High Schools and Minority Students* New Brunswick, NJ, Transaction.

HAYEK, F. A. (1944) *The Road to Serfdom* Chicago, University of Chicago Press.

MICHAELSEN, J. B. (1981) 'A Theory of Decision Making in the Public Schools: A Public Choice Approach', in BACHARACH, S. B. (ed.) *Organizational Behavior in Schools and School Districts* New York, Praeger.

MOE, M. (1984) 'The New Economics of Organization', *American Journal of Political Science*, 28, pp. 739–77.

NISKANEN, W. (1975) 'Bureaucrats and Politicians', *Journal of Law and Economics*, 18, pp. 617–43.

ORZECHOWSKI, W. (1977)'Economic Models of Bureaucracy: Survey, Extensions and Evidence', in BORCHERDING, T. E. (ed.) *Budgets and Bureaucrats: The Sources of Economic Growth* Durham, NC, Duke University Press.

POWELL, A. G. (1987) 'Private School Responsibilities: Are They As Important as Private School Rights?' *Private School Monitor: An Occasional Paper*, Washington, DC.

TYACK, D. B. (1974) *The One Best System: A History of American Urban Education* Cambridge, Mass., Harvard University.

Part II
Private Schools and Public Policy Issues

Chapter 6
Private Schools and Public Funds:
A Case Study of an English Initiative

A. Edwards, J. Fitz and G. Whitty

Much of the controversy about state aid to private schools has centred on the acceptability of using government money to help maintain schools or school systems which compete with those provided wholly out of public funds. The legitimacy of direct state-aid to non-government schools has been at the heart of the issue in Australia, while in the USA the illegality of direct aid to most such institutions has focused argument on various forms of indirect support. In its introduction of the Assisted Places Scheme in 1980, the British conservative administration might seem to have side-stepped some of the issues by its claim that it was not aiding the independent schools involved, but rather enabling relatively low income parents to exercise the same right of choice as is available to those from wealthier backgrounds.[1] Each school participating in the scheme signs its own contract with central government to offer a certain number of places each year on which fees are remitted according to a sliding scale of parental income. The school then recovers the residue of the fees from the government. It remains entirely 'independent', its only obligations to the Department of Education and Science being to check the financial eligibility of pupils for assistance (their academic suitability being left to the school except for a requirement to recruit not less than 60 per cent from maintained schools), and to report any proposed increase in fees. This might seem to accord well with monetarist preferences for aiding individuals rather than institutions (Seldon, 1981; Tullock, 1986). We would argue, however, that the device used by the British government to evade issues encountered elsewhere does little to overcome them. A case study of this particular initiative may therefore be more useful than a straightforward contrast between policies being adopted in different countries.

Before proceeding, it is necessary to clarify some aspects of the English situation. First, we use the term 'English' rather than 'British' because of significant differences between the education systems of England (and

Wales), and those of Scotland and Northern Ireland. Secondly, we emphasize that, quite apart from the evident difficulty of distinguishing between the effects of state aid to individuals and to institutions (Edwards, Fitz and Whitty, 1985), there are recognizable ways in which the British government also aids independent schools themselves. For example, it pays the costs of training teachers for the public and private sectors, and it grants 50 per cent relief on rates to the many schools (including all the market leaders) which have the legal status of 'charities'.[2] Thirdly, it is important to note that the Assisted Places Scheme is essentially a 'scholarship' ladder for academically able children; those who saw it as a pilot experiment for a fully-grown voucher system, or who wanted assistance extended to much broader categories of 'need' (for example, the need for boarding education) have so far been disappointed. Fourthly, the question of state aid is not directly linked to controversies about support for sectarian education, as it is in many other countries. Although independent schools are often religious foundations, and may be chosen by parents for that reason, there are large numbers of Anglican and Roman Catholic schools within the state system because of a series of historical compromises between church and state (Cruikshank, 1963). Finally, it should be borne in mind that, largely because of this incorporation of sectarian schools within the state system, less than 7 per cent of secondary-age children are in the private sector and the majority of them are at schools which have traditionally been highly selective both socially and academically (Halsey, Heath and Ridge 1980, 1984; Salter and Tapper, 1985; Walford 1986). Where private schools in other industrial countries are widely defended as expressions of religious, ethnic and cultural diversity, their predominant function in England has been to provide training for high-status occupations within the cultural mainstream (Mason, 1983, 1985; and the chapters by Boyd, James, and others in this volume).

In this English context, it is understandable that the essential defence of the Assisted Places Scheme has been that it makes a real contribution to social mobility by enabling 'bright children from less affluent homes' to attend independent secondary schools 'of proven academic worth' from which they would otherwise have been excluded by their parents' inability to pay.[3] By 1985–6, the fifth year of the scheme's operation, £33.8 million government money was paid to 226 English independent schools to waive or reduce the fees, and to meet some incidental expenses arising from the taking up of places.[4] There were then 21,412 assisted-place holders in English independent schools, about 40 per cent of them having qualified for free places; the average parental contribution for new 1985 entrants was £360, and the average government payment per pupil was £1603.[5] This sponsoring of pupils in independent schools was justified as an extension of parental choice valuable for its own sake; as a restoration of 'real' academic opportunities to many pupils who would not have been fully 'stretched' in schools which had to cope with the full range of ability; and as a protection both for those individuals and for the nation's resources of talent against the levelling-down effects attributed to comprehensive reorganization. Opponents of the scheme saw it as an offensive declaration by the government that the public sector of education was incapable of providing for able children.

Our own initial interest in studying the scheme lay partly in the relationship between claims made by its advocates and critics at the time of its inception, and its actual operation and effects.[6] Some of these predictions were confident, specific, and directly contradictory — for example, that 'able children from our poorest homes will once again have the opportunity of attending academically-excellent schools', or that 'a scheme designed to attract working-class children who would otherwise go to a poor neighbourhood comprehensive may simply attract middle-class children who would otherwise go to a good comprehensive'.[7] Other arguments exchanged during the controversy have reflected irreconcilable differences of principle which are not open to empirical testing, although they certainly shape decisions about what empirical effects are to be studied. For example, 'individualist' advocates of the scheme have often insisted that the only relevant criteria for judging it are the benefits it brings to the assisted-place pupils themselves, while 'collectivist' critics concentrate on its consequences for the image, intakes and morale of maintained schools. To focus entirely on either would be vulnerable to the charge of being a politically-biased restriction of view. Yet while much of the debate expressed predefined positions on (for example) the relative claims of 'individual freedom' or of 'social justice' to inform the ordering of society, no research could adjudicate between their respective merits. What we have done elsewhere is to locate supporting and opposing arguments in the context of these broader philosophical positions, and within the ideological repertoires of the various political parties (Edwards, Fulbrook and Whitty 1984; Edwards, Fitz and Whitty, forthcoming).

Despite such evident limits, some claims made by supporters and critics are susceptible to empirical investigation. The most obvious example is the extent to which the scheme has reached its intended target group. Over time, some of the scheme's effects can also be studied both on the participating schools, and on state primary and secondary schools around them. To what extent, for example, has it enabled the independent schools to recruit still more academically selective intakes? Given that by far the best predictors of school outcomes are the social and cultural characteristics of school intakes, that question has considerable significance for the schools' market appeal as academically-excellent schools (Gray, 1981; Gray, Jesson and Jones 1984). While the private sector needed no rescuing in 1981 from the prospect of unfilled places, there seems to have been a significant decline in the academic quality of intakes to those schools affected after 1976 by the Labour government's phasing out of direct grants and its pressure on local education authorities not to take up places in independent schools. The scheme may therefore have constituted a timely defence of a 'lead' in academic output which is of especial importance to the private sector at a time of intensifying competition for high status employment — the high proportion of its pupils who leave with a clearly-stamped passport to higher education (three 'good grades' at GCE Advanced-level) and to those occupations which recruit graduates. While that sector contains only 7 per cent of pupils aged fourteen, its share of those leaving school with three A-levels is approaching one-third (Halsey *et al.*, 1984). The scheme may well be enhancing this strategic 'success' rate. Certainly its predicted 'creaming effects' on post-sixteen provision in the public sector has been a main source of opposition to it, especially since it has coincided with growing pressure from falling school rolls on the viability of sixth forms, to which it has therefore posed a direct threat to numbers as well as to quality.[8] At the point of entry to secondary schools, we could also enquire whether the revival of a fairly substantial 'scholarship' scheme had brought a return in some primary schools to the kinds of scholarship-coaching previously produced by the competition for entry to grammar schools, and whether parents' interest in the scheme is related to the pattern of state provision and the academic reputation of state schools in their area. Finally, and crucially, we were interested in testing the claim that assisted-place pupils will gain tangible benefits in relation to their peers in the state sector. This is the crucial question, because advocates of the scheme have insisted that it 'complements' that sector by providing academic opportunities difficult to maintain in 'schools catering for the majority', while its critics have argued that it represents an unjustifiable expenditure of public money unless (or until) it can be demonstrated that the pupils receiving assistance needed to move out of the public sector to obtain those opportunities.[9] These were the main considerations shaping our decisions about what evidence to collect.

That evidence was collected at three levels — from national statistics, in selected areas with high concentrations of assisted places, and in individual schools. We therefore tried to focus down on individual pupils and parents affected by the scheme while maintaining in view its broader contexts. At the national level, we analyzed the scheme in relation to previous attempts to link the public and private sectors, and to other aspects of contemporary social policy. We also made a detailed study of how it originated within the private sector, of its subsequent appearance as a Conservative party commitment, and of its unusually rapid formulation as a workable scheme following the Conservative election victory of May 1979. Of particular interest has been the extent to which the scheme can be 'read' as manifesting some of the main themes in the new educational ideology constructed by the Right during the 1970s, especially its emphasis on the incompatibility of equality with equality of opportunity and the reduced opportunities open to able working-class children brought about by the 'destruction' of grammar schools. Given the scheme's attractions as an inexpensive way of displaying simultaneously the new government's commitments to preserving academic standards, extending parental choice, and rewarding the 'deserving', it was tempting to see it in this way. In practice, however, our documentary and other evidence did not reveal a universal enthusiasm for it within the Conservative party, nor any contributions to its formulation from those (in and around the Centre for Policy Studies or the Institute for Economic Affairs) who were actively engaged in reconstructing the party's ideological base. It is more realistically seen as the product of a close alliance between a few enthusiastic politicians and a well-organised pressure group from within the private sector, an alliance which both reflected and reinforced a close articulation between independent schools and a 'grammar school education'.

Nationally, the distribution of places is highly significant in relation to initial claims that priority would be given to inner-city areas without grammar schools and the opportunities so firmly associated with them: that the nature of local provision in the public sector would be carefully considered in determining allocations to avoid duplication or competition, especially with the remaining state grammar schools; and that the scheme's declared objective was to secure 'a network of highly academic schools to which any child regardless of income would be free to apply'.[10] Whatever the intentions of creating a new national scholarship system, however, an equitable distribution of places around the country was impossible without creating new independent schools or enticing far more voluntary-aided grammar schools out of the state sector than actually made that move. Assistance with boarding education was and remains excluded from the scheme's provisions, so that it is hardly surprising that almost 90 per cent of places are in day schools despite the participation of many prestigious 'public' boarding schools. The former direct-grant and other grammar schools which offer most of the places are relatively highly concentrated in and around the cities of London, Bristol, Liverpool, Manchester and Newcastle. As a consequence, 42 per cent of all assisted place pupils in 1985 were in schools in those areas (Fitz, Edwards and Whitty, 1986), which raises obvious questions about the national network.

The take-up of places nationally has risen from 77 per cent in 1981 to 96 per cent in 1986 — figures which indicate that the scheme is pushing hard against Treasury imposed limits on the total number of places available and might also seem to indicate that it should be expanded. However, the overall figure conceals a considerable diversity between over-recruiting and under-recruiting schools. Although there has been some slight redistribution of places in response to demand, major changes would increase the regional disparities already mentioned and so be difficult to justify on the scheme's own terms as a scholarship 'system' based on merit. In addition, over 20 per cent of new sixth-form places remained unfilled even in 1986, while two-thirds of the rest taken were by pupils already in independent schools. An initially lower allocation of places for girls has been made more unequal by lower rates of take-up, the proportion remaining around 42 per cent. These national statistics show a scheme which rapidly attracted a clientele, which is nevertheless very uneven in its operation as a scholarship system based on merit alone, and which has been strongly shaped by the philanthropic activities of individuals and merchant companies long ago who decided where 'their' grammar schools should be founded.

Our local studies have included urban, suburban and semi-rural catchment areas in both the south and north of England. While their choice was shaped by their accessibility to the research team, the most significant factor was obviously the willingness of schools and LEAs to co-operate in research into a scheme which has been defended and attacked with a ferocity apparently out of all proportion to its modest scope. We return to this 'opportunity sampling' later in the chapter. Within each area, we interviewed the heads of independent and state secondary schools, senior staff in independent schools who had particular responsibility for selecting assisted-place pupils and monitoring their progress, and the heads of primary schools some of whom were experiencing pressures to prepare children for the entrance examinations (sometimes despite an explicit local education authority ban on any co-operation with the scheme). In independent schools, we interviewed equal numbers of assisted-place and full fee-paying pupils from the same year groups, using semi-structured interviews which include questions about their home backgrounds, their reasons for coming to the school, their views of the school, their plans for higher education and for employment, and any contacts they continued to have with friends made at primary school. The same interviews were conducted with some of their contemporaries in state schools. Where parents also agreed to be seen, the interviews were much longer; they extended from pre-coded items on their own (and their parents') education and occupations to open-ended questions about their choice of school, their objectives and strategies in making that choice, and their more general views about educational opportunities and the 'openness' of British society. Here, again, we talked with parents (or pairs of parents) of assisted-place holders and full fee-payers in the independent sector, and with parents whose children are in state schools. Altogether, we interviewed 675 pupils, and 319 parents and pairs of parents.

The state schools we studied were among those which had been available to the assisted-place pupils, might have been attended by them if the scheme had not existed, and were attended by former friends from primary school. This component of the research enables us to make detailed comparisons between the characteristics and educational careers of assisted-place holders, full fee payers in the same school, and state secondary pupils from the same local areas. There are clearly insuperable objections to comparing the actual careers of pupils with what they 'might have been' in some other school, and it was disturbing that one national newspaper report of our research included the entirely invented 'finding' that many assisted-place pupils 'would have done better' in their local comprehensive schools (*The Guardian*, 4 September, 1986). Nevertheless, it is possible to make some systemic comparisons of resources, curriculum and subject choice in schools participating in the scheme, and neighbouring schools in the state sector. Indeed, it is difficult to see how such comparisons can be avoided, given those references to rescuing able children from inappropriate or inferior schools which have figured so prominently in the scheme's justification.

In all this data collection, equal attention has been given to boys and girls. That might have been taken for granted had several major studies of social origins and educational destinations in England not focused entirely on boys, and had the prestige and elite-reproduction functions of boys' 'public' schools not dominated debate about the entire independent sector (Halsey *et al.*, 1980; Fox, 1985; Salter and Tapper 1985). At least before the sixth form stage, most schools participating in the scheme are single-sex, and so (within the constraints imposed by schools' willingness or reluctance to take part in the research) we included equal numbers of girls' schools and girl pupils.

Though the data are still being analyzed, hence a necessary reticence about 'findings', a number of issues have emerged or become more sharply defined in the course of the research. Some of these have resulted from provisional empirical conclusions, others from the continuing national debate about the effects of the scheme to which we hope our analysis will contribute. Of particular concern to us at present are the social backgrounds of those participating in the scheme, the extent to which the scheme itself has been instrumental in their taking up places in independent schools, the effects of their doing so on the life chances of other pupils, the institutional effects of the scheme on different types of school, local and regional differences in the take-up of places, and the more general question of how the scheme is changing the systemic relationship between the state and the private sector. We concentrate on some of these issues in the remainder of the chapter.

At the individual level, there have been claims that some pupils are benefiting who could not be held to 'need' assistance in any accepted sense of need. The evidence suggests, however, that only a small minority of parents are able, by clever accountancy, to mislead school bursars much as they mislead their tax inspectors. Others raise questions about the appropriateness of parental income as the criterion of eligibility, when some parents qualify for full assistance even though co-habiting with affluent partners and others would otherwise have received assistance from more wealthy members of the child's extended family (usually grandparents). Far more interesting, in our view, is the social composition of that group which *is* clearly entitled to assistance within the terms of the scheme. The frequency of one-parent families, for example, is apparent in all the national statistics. Less obvious, partly because of the way occupations are categorized in official figures, is the possible under-representation of manual working-class parents. In our view, their participation is vital to any claim made in defence of the scheme at the time of its introduction. If it appears that a high proportion of assisted-place holders come from 'submerged' middle-class backgrounds already well-endowed with cultural capital, then a major justification for withdrawing children from the public sector would be called into question.

This would still be so even if many able children from financially modest backgrounds were taking up places, as national statistics clearly indicate is the case. In 1986, for example, 40 per cent of places were awarded to children from families whose 'relevant income' was less than £6838, and so qualified for full remission of fees; two-thirds were taken by children of parents earning less than the national average wage of £9776. These figures are cited to support the conclusion that the scheme was indeed reaching those for whom it was intended, the 'largest categories of beneficiaries' being again 'the unemployed and one-parent families' (press release, Independent Schools Information Service, 8 December 1986). It is worth looking more closely, however, at the full range of beneficiaries.

Although our own data on the social backgrounds of assisted-place holders have still to be fully analyzed, it is already clear that they will not differ substantially from the findings of Douse (1985), who studied the scheme's operation in different areas from ourselves. On the basis of a questionnaire returned by the heads of ninety-three participating schools containing 42 per cent of all assisted-place holders in England in 1984, he identified the following characteristics in his sample — less than 0.1 per cent were from ethnic minorities; 19 per cent were from homes where the main wage-earner had recently spent a significant time unemployed; 41 per cent were from single-parent families; 32 per cent had at least one parent with graduate or professional qualifications; 20 per cent had a brother or sister attending, or who had attended, an independent school and 9 per cent were the sons or daughters of former independent school pupils. Of the 199 pupils whom Douse interviewed in six of his sample schools, only thirteen described parental occupations which could be reliably classified as skilled, semi-skilled or unskilled manual work while no fewer than 167 cited occupations generally regarded as being 'middle-class'. From both his general and detailed evidence, Douse concludes that relatively few assisted-place holders come from 'unambiguously working-class backgrounds', that many come from single-parent families or from other families where a low income reflects 'unusual' circumstances, and that a large minority are already within what he calls 'the independent school frame of reference'. Our own evidence from a sample of 157 assisted-place pupils in ten schools gives a similar picture:

1   A third come from single parent families, almost all of them headed by women.
2   On the basis of information from the pupils, only about 9 per cent of fathers and about 4 per cent of mothers had occupations which the Oxford Mobility Study classifies as working-class (Halsey, Heath and Ridge, 1980). Initial analysis of the more explicit information provided by parents suggests that even these figures are too high, although one-third of the others are in routine non-manual jobs which some critics of the Oxford classification suggest should be reclassified as being working-class occupations *for women.*
3   About half the fathers, and over 20 per cent of the mothers, were in service class occupations as classified in the Oxford Study, though these proportions were significantly lower than in our comparable samples of pupils paying full fees and of academically able children in state schools.
4   About 7 per cent of the fathers and 30 per cent of the mothers were not in paid employment, although almost none of the mothers were registered as being officially unemployed.
5   Fifty-eight per cent of the mothers has attended academically selective secondary schools themselves, and a further 10 per cent had been to fee-paying schools. The relative figures for fathers were 40 per cent and 10 per cent.
6   Forty-four per cent of our sample qualified for full fee remission, while a further 11 per cent paid less than £100 a year in fees — figures which closely match the government's national statistics.

Our own evidence, and Douse's, provide some of the details needed to support the conclusion which Tapper and Salter (1986) take from published statistics — that the scheme is providing 'real financial assistance to relatively impoverished but educationally aware members of the petite bourgeoisie'. They go on to cite from the minutes of a meeting of independent school headmasters in June 1981 a clear statement that the main purposes of the scheme would be frustrated if too many of its beneficiaries turned out to be 'distressed gentlefolk', and then comment themselves on the lack of answers since to the question of how many would be too many (Tapper and Salter, 1986, p. 325).

Publicly, such evidence is not treated as a problem by government ministers. The relevant legislation merely states that the scheme is intended to help 'pupils who might not otherwise...be able to benefit from education at independent schools', while the high proportion of existing place holders receiving full remission of fees (a rather higher percentage than the government itself originally anticipated) is often used to support the claim that the scheme is proving conspicuously successful in directing aid to those from 'disadvantaged and poor homes' who are being selected on academic merit alone. [11]

In the context of the evidence we have cited, it is clear that the terms 'disadvantaged' and 'poor' are being used here not only in a rather broader way than is usual within educational discourse, but in a way that actually disguises the low proportions of pupils fitting the more usual definition of those categories. Yet Douse (1985, p. 216) claims that his own findings do not 'constitute a criticism of the scheme' because the legislation which created it was never couched explicitly in terms of reaching out to the 'working class'. He suggests that 'aiding bright youngsters from single-parent homes or from ones in which the main wage-earner is unemployed, even if the family might reasonably be characterized as "middle-class", is well within the terms of the scheme as planned and justified'.

In our own research, however, which seeks explicitly to explore the operation of the scheme in terms of the claims made by its advocates and critics, it is certainly pertinent to ask whether funds are being allocated to the groups originally anticipated. To this extent, Douse's defence of the scheme minimizes the significance of a change in the representation of the typical assisted-place pupil within the rhetoric of legitimation employed by ministers since the scheme's initial announcement. While there was certainly little reference to any concept of 'class' in the official justifications for the scheme 1979–81, there can be little doubt that parliamentary references to (for example) 'children from inner urban areas', 'academically-minded children of poor parents' and 'children from deprived backgrounds' conjured up images of working class children for whom opportunities for upward mobility through educational success were being restored. This is particularly clear in a statement by Rhodes Boyson, a junior education minister, at the time when the first assisted-place pupils were entering their independent schools:

> Once again the boy or girl from an inner city area, where the aspirations and achievements of his (*sic*) local comprehensive aren't such that he will be stretched the way he should be, can once again join the ladders of social and economic mobility, and to me that's part of an open society. And I'm astonished anybody opposes it. [12]

Similarly Mark Carlisle, the Secretary of State for Education at the time when the scheme was introduced, emphasized to us that he had promoted it as both a scholarship system and as a 'general widening of choice for parents'

> Particularly in my mind always was that in inner-city areas for the children to be able to benefit from the education that was available at such places as King Edward's (Birmingham), Bradford Grammar School, and Manchester Grammar School (Interview. 16 November, 1982).

There is little evidence in our own sample of assisted-place holders that even those children from single parent families or from families where parents are unemployed come from the kinds of material and cultural backgrounds which are conjured up by these images. Though ministers have always been careful to point out that children from inner-city areas were only one of the disadvantaged groups which the scheme might benefit, it is clear that there is some unease among its promoters about their failure to appear in large numbers among its beneficiaries. This is indicated by the fact that, while the numbers eligible to have all or most of their fees remitted can be cited as vindication of the scheme, the annual publicity exercises mounted by the Independent Schools Information Service and by the DES place particular emphasis on those pupils from manual working class occupations 'mentioned more than once' in the participating schools' annual returns to the ISJC, or on those pupils from evidently disadvantaged circumstances who are sometimes persuaded to pose for the media alongside an appropriate minister. To this extent, the celebration of the unanticipated consequences of the scheme for the submerged middle classes may not be adequate compensation for its failure to reach the core target group as this has been consistently defined by the scheme's leading advocates within the private sector and by their political allies — namely, 'the clever working-class child in a deprived area', denied the chance of a 'real academic education' by the virtual disappearance of academic selection from the state sector.[13]

The claim that the scheme is reaching a group that might otherwise not have received the same standard of education also needs to be subjected to careful scrutiny. Certainly there was little suggestion in public debates about the scheme that one of its purposes was to give assisted places to pupils who would have attended the same schools without them. Yet the Heads who responded to Douse's questionnaire estimated that between 30 per cent and 40 per cent of assisted pupils would have attended their schools anyway, while among the pupils in his smaller sample, 46 per cent believed that they would have attended an independent school of some sort had the scheme not existed. In our own sample, the majority would certainly not have attended their schools without assistance from public funds, and a minority had been led to consider the possibility of private education for the first time. On the other hand, a quarter of the siblings of the sample were or had been in an independent school, indicating families already within the 'independent school frame of reference'. For these pupils, it is difficult to argue that the scheme has significantly widened choice, while the justification for subsidizing the choice they had anyway made is not self-evident in a period of severe restraint on public expenditure. Nevertheless, the official view has been that a widening of choice for at least the majority of assisted-place pupils is to be welcomed as an extension of freedom valuable for its own sake, and because it brings enhanced opportunities for these particular pupils and exerts an additional competitive pressure on state schools to improve their own standards. These are the claims upon which it is most important and most difficult to adjudicate.

Our interviews with parents of assisted place holders certainly indicate that, by and large, they believe that their children are getting a better education than that available to them in the public sector. They feel this as strongly as those parents who pay full fees. State school parents were less likely to hold this view, although some parents of state school pupils, especially in working-class areas, also expressed belief in the superiority of independent schools. Sometimes this was because of the better facilities and teachers attributed to them, but more often it was because of their social selectiveness and the self-confidence which they were believed to instil. The complex relationships between parents' own educational experiences, their ambitions for their children, and the opportunities they perceive as being offered by schools of different kinds are the focus of much of our current analysis of parental interviews, and will provide a useful comparison with the work of Fox (1985) and Johnson (1987) among more 'traditional' clients of the private sector. What is already apparent, however, is the extent to which many parents of assisted-place and full fee-paying pupils in schools which formerly had direct grant status see those schools primarily, even entirely, as grammar schools. It is their academic selectiveness, not their independence or (at least directly) their social exclusiveness, which is highly valued.

We now turn from these parental perceptions to the corresponding assumptions made by the architects and advocates of the Assisted Places Scheme about the opportunities which it would make more widely available. Much of the momentum behind the scheme came from belief in the distinctive academic education offered by good grammar schools, and from equally entrenched doubts about the capacity of some comprehensive schools, or even of any comprehensive school, to extend very able children. Both belief and doubt rest on a presumed association between academically-selective schools and academic achievement which is by no means conclusively demonstrated in the literature (Gray *et al.*, 1984). The assumptions are that high academic standards are only safe in grammar schools, which therefore offer 'poor but able' children opportunities which comprehensive reorganization would deny them. Very able children from any background, but especially those from homes unable to provide much of an educational or cultural 'inheritance', 'will perform more effectively in the special, the hothouse, atmosphere of the high academic school'.[14] Extending access to such schools is therefore seen as making 'a real contribution to social mobility', to that open society to which Rhodes Boyson referred, while also reinforcing the distinctive function of independent schools, which is to 'complement the public sector by offering a quality of provision hardly available within it (Independent Schools Information Service, 1981).

Contrary claims have been alluded to already — notably, that there is no firm evidence that comprehensive schools cannot cater for the full range of ability, but that their chances of doing so are significantly diminished (especially at the sixth-form stage) by the 'pirating of scholastic talent' which the Assisted Places Scheme is said to have encouraged.[15] We can do no more here than indicate some of the evidence which might be relevant to these claims and counter-claims. Nationally, the take-up of assisted places has risen from 77 per cent in the scheme's first year to 92 per cent in 1985. Yet there are individual schools where unfilled places have brought a reduction in their allocations, and areas of the country where the take-up is generally lower than might be expected of such apparent bargains. Nor are these exclusively affluent areas where the 'pool' of financially eligible parents might also be low. One would expect the scheme to have least appeal where state schools are seen to be doing a relatively good job. We are therefore looking with particular interest at those state schools which do seem to be both competent and confident in nurturing the talent of academically able pupils and we are exploring how far they do actually meet the aspirations of those pupils who, in other areas, might be tempted into the private sector. How far such schools have been encouraged to do an even better job by the existence of the scheme itself is doubtful, given the high proportion of assisted-place pupils who would not have considered a state school anyway, and the possibility (to which we have already referred) that the scheme may be increasing the academic selectivity of independent schools, and so enhancing their academic results, beyond what would have been attainable through the operation of 'pure' market forces. This, in turn, could have important long term consequences for the capacity of state schools to compete with them.

It seems then that even a policy of aiding individuals to attend independent schools, rather than giving direct aid to those schools, has the potential to bring about systemic changes in the relationship between state and private education. Indeed, it has been argued that this sponsored withdrawal from state schools for reasons which explicitly identify them as second-best is only part of a planned large-scale intrusion of private provision into the state sector (Pring, 1986). Certainly, some members of the government have urged more radical ventures in extending parental choice. Boyson, for example, has been quoted as saying that — 'If choice is a good thing and variety a good thing, which I obviously believe it is, then it should be open not only to academically able children but to all children'. The logical conclusion of that belief was some form of voucher system which would carry the benefits attributed to the Assisted Places Scheme much further.[16] In such pronouncements, it may be possible to detect the preparation of the ground for a redefinition of the Assisted Places Scheme as the precursor of a radical new policy of privatization rather than as a 'natural' extension of the traditional scholarship ladder. Yet there has remained a degree of diffidence in government circles about such a redefinition — a diffidence which persisted through the 1983 election campaign, has continued ever since, and which greatly disappoints those who are most enthusiastic about enhancing consumer choice and thereby subjecting state schools to the discipline of consumer preference (Seldon, 1986; Barnes, 1986). As though to keep their hopes alive however, voucher experiments, an expansion of the Assisted Places Scheme, and even the return of direct grant schools have all been floated as possibilities from time to time by a government which remains explicitly committed in its social policies to reduce the share of national resources taken by the public sector. Meanwhile, the political climate has certainly become much more favourable to the private education sector during the past few years. This is because independent schools have seemed to be models of good practice by many on the Right; they are seen as upholding traditional standards of behaviour and academic achievement, as being far more accountable to parents and responsive to market forces, and as providing an essential defence against state monopoly of educational provision (Salter and Tapper, 1985; Edwards, Fitz and Whitty, forthcoming). From other political perspectives, there is a fear that encouragement of the private sector, and the presentation of entry to independent schools as a legitimate aspiration for all, could lead to state provision becoming little more than a 'safety-net' of elementary education for those families unable or unwilling to compete in the market (Pring, 1986).

Speculation of this nature can itself have a powerful backwash effect throughout public sector provision and help foster a climate in which a more full-blown attempt at privatization could become a real possibility should the balance of forces within the Conservative party change still further and wider support seem more attainable. Such a development would be likely to have particularly dire consequences for those living in the inner cities. Not only would they be unable to attain access to educational and welfare services beyond a bare minimum provided by the state, they would increasingly become the only groups receiving this form of public provision. While in those circumstances a few children might 'escape' from the inner cities into the middle classes via assisted places and similar 'rescue' operations, they would be relatively few on present evidence. Those remaining would, in turn, lack even present levels of middle class support in their efforts to improve the quality of state provision.

Even though such speculation gains some credence from our observations of the limited effects of Assisted Places Scheme to date, it has to be recognized that the scheme remains the most tangible expression of the present government's policy 'preferences' in education to date, and that 'logical' next steps predicted at its inception have not yet materialized into legislation. [17] The scheme has therefore had only marginal effects so far on the education system as a whole. This illustrates the difficulty of seeking to inform future policy with research of the kind we are undertaking, for as soon as we try to interpret our data for this purpose, we are forced to make informed guesses about the effects of an initiative which has hardly yet taken root. What is apparent to us, however, is that any 'creaming' of the state sector through the operation of the Assisted Places Scheme is less significant than its capacity to reinforce belief in the inability of that sector to match the quality of private provision, or to develop credible alternatives to the type of 'academic' education which that scheme has so powerfully sponsored.

Notes

1 In using the term 'independent' to refer to non-government schools, we realize that critics of such schools usually prefer the labels 'private'. We also recognize that establishing the term 'independent', with all its positive 'connotations' as the normal usage in England has been a considerable public relations victory for the schools themselves.
2 In its statement to the House of Commons Select Committee enquiring into charitable status, the Independent Schools Joint Committee (ISJC) estimated the total value of the benefits of charitable status at 5–10 per cent of schools' fee income. For a discussion of that status and its legal defences, see Salter and Tapper (1985), pp. 71–95.
3 Statement by the Secretary of State, Mark Carlisle, introducing the 1979 Education Bill which included the Assisted Places Scheme.
4 The scheme also extends to Wales, where nine schools had agreed to participate when it began in 1981. A somewhat different scheme operates in Scotland.
5 Summary statistics, Department of Education and Science, 1986.
6 Our research was funded 1982–1986 by the Social Science Research Council/Economic and Social Science Research Council (Award no. C00230036).
7 The first prediction was made by a junior Education minister, Rhodes Boyson, writing in the *Daily Mail* 25 June, 1981; the second was quoted in an editorial in a private sector journal, Conference, February 1982.
8 In recognition of that danger, or at least of widespread demands to curtail it, LEAs were initially given the right to veto the taking up of assisted places at sixteen-plus where the consequent moves from state schools could be shown as damaging to their own post-sixteen provision. Because of what the government described as overuse (and 'prejudiced' use) of this veto, the right was removed in 1983.
9 The first claim is made in *The Case for Collaboration* (ISIS, 1981); a prominent exponent of the counter-argument, from within the private sector, has been Rae (1981, pp. 178–193).
10 Sexton, 1977; as political adviser to successive conservative 'shadow' spokesmen and Secretaries of State for Education, Sexton was the politician most actively and continuously involved in constructing the scheme.
11 Education Act, 1980; statement by Bob Dunn, then the junior minister responsible for the scheme, in the House of Commons 15 May 1984.
12 Interviewed on the London Weekend Television programme *Starting Out*, 11 September 1981.
13 Rescuing such children from the effects of the 'cult of egalitarianism' was one of

the main themes in the successive collections of *Black Papers* published 1969–1977, to which Boyson was a prominent contributor. See also Cox and Marks (Eds), *The Right to Learn*, Centre for Policy Studies, 1981.

14 Stuart Sexton, interviewed by us 2 February, 1984.

15 This comment by Neil Kinnock, then Labour's 'Shadow' minister of education (*Guardian* 29 September 1979) has been a consistent theme in Labour opposition to the scheme. When the party's National Executive wrote to the Heads of participating schools in December 1981 warning them that the next Labour government would abolish the scheme immediately, it referred to them as a 'gang of poachers'.

16 Quoted in T. Albert, 'The cheapest way to help the brightest and best', *Guardian*, 23 November 1982.

17 This was largely true until the 1987 Conservative election victory and the Education Reform Act which followed it. It is possible to see the new funding arrangements for schools, and the encouragement to opt-out of local authority control, as precursors of larger scale privatization.

References

BARNES, J. (1986) 'Political pressure and government inaction', *Journal of Economic Affairs*, 6, pp. 22–23.

COX, C. and MARKS, J. (eds) (1981) *The Right to Learn*, Centre for Policy Studies.

CRUICKSHANK, M. (1963) *Church and State in English Education*, London, Macmillan.

DOUSE, M. (1985) 'The background of assisted places scheme students,'*Educational Studies*, 11, pp. 211–17.

EDWARDS, T., FITZ, J. and WHITTY, G. (1985) 'Private schools and public funding: a comparison of policies and arguments in England and Australia', *Comparative Education* 21, pp. 29–45.

EDWARDS, T. FITZ, J. and WHITTY, G. (1989) *The State and Private Education: An Evaluation of the Assisted Places Scheme*, Lewes, Falmer Press.

EDWARDS, T., FULBROOK, M. and WHITTY, G. (1984) 'The state and the independent sector: policies, ideologies and theories', in BARTON, L. and WALKER, S. (eds) *Social Crisis and Educational Research*, London, Croom Helm.

FITZ, J., EDWARDS, T. and WHITTY, G. (1986) 'Beneficiaries, benefits and costs: an investigation of the Assisted Places Scheme', *Research Papers in Education*, 1, pp. 169–93.

FOX, I. (1984) 'The demand for a public school education: a crisis of confidence in comprehensive education', in WALFORD, G. (ed.) *British Public Schools: Policy and Practice*, Lewes, Falmer Press.

FOX, I. (1985) *Private Schools and Public Issues*, London, Macmillan.

GRAY, J. (1981) 'A competitive edge: examination results and the probable limits of secondary school effectiveness', *Educational Review*, 33, pp. 25–35.

GRAY, J., JESSON, D. and JONES, B. (1984) 'Predicting differences in examination results between LEAs: does school organization matter?' *Oxford Review of Education*, 10, pp. 45–68.

The Guardian (1986) 4 September.

HALSEY, A. H., HEATH, A. and RIDGE, J. (1980) *Origins and Destinations*, Oxford, Clarendon Press.

HALSEY, A. H., HEATH, A. and RIDGE, J. (1984) 'The political arithmetic of public schools', in WALFORD, G. (ed.) *British Public Schools: Policy and Practice*, Lewes, Falmer Press.

INDEPENDENT SCHOOLS INFORMATION SERVICE (1981) *The Case for Collaboration: the Independent Schools and the Maintained System*, London, ISIS.

JOHNSON, D. (1987) *Private Schools and State Schools: Two Systems or One?* Milton Keynes, Open University Press.

MASON, P. (1983) *Private Education in the EEC*, London, ISIS.

MASON, P (1985) *Private Education in the USA and Canada*, London, ISIS.

PRING, R. (1986) 'Privatization of education', in ROGERS, R. (ed.) *Education and Social Class*, Lewes, Falmer Press.

RAE, J. (1981) *The Public School Revolution: Britain's Independent Schools 1964–1979*, London, Faber.

SALTER, B. and TAPPER, T. (1985) *Power and Policy in Education: the Case of Independent Schools*, Lewes, Falmer Press.

SELDON, A. (1981) *With the Welfare State*, London, Institute of Economic Affairs.

SELDON, A. (1986) *The Riddle of the Voucher: an Inquiry into the Obstacles to Introducing Choice and Competition in State Schools*, London, Institute of Economic Affairs.

SEXTON, S. (1977) 'Evolution by choice', in COX, B. and BOYSON, R. (eds) *Black Paper Five*, London, Temple Smith.

TAPPER, T. and SALTER, B. (1986) 'The Assisted Places Scheme: a policy evaluation', *Journal of Education Policy*, 1, pp. 315–30.

TULLOCK, G. (1986) 'No public choice in state education', *Journal of Economic Affairs*, 6, pp. 18–22.

WALFORD, G. (1986) *Life in Public Schools*, London, Methuen.

Chapter 7
The Hawke Labor Government and Public-Private School Funding Policies in Australia, 1983–1986*

Don Smart

Undoubtedly two of the most unexpected education policy shifts attributable to the Hawke Labor government have been its somersaulting to a position of support for Federal aid to the so-called 'wealthy private schools' and its significant downgrading of the role of the Labor-created (and equity-inspired) Commonwealth Schools Commission.[1] How could a socialist Labor government traditionally committed to a redistributionist and reformist platform adopt such policies? This chapter explores the often conservative and pragmatic policies adopted in the schools area by the Hawke government and seeks to explain the economic, social and political factors underlying them.

Introduction: The Political Context of Hawke

Education policy under the Hawke Labor (ALP) government from 1983–1986 has frequently been characterized by paradox and contradiction. The strong reformist commitment to education and equality of opportunity usually associated with Labor governments has been put under severe test by economic and electoral considerations. In the process, ALP platform and principles have, in the view of some within the party, often taken a battering at the hands of pragmatism and pressures for privatization. Characteristically, in the pursuit of a broad-based community consensus settlement on education issues — as with other major issues such as uranium, American nuclear ships and Aboriginal land rights — Hawke has been prepared to confront the ALP caucus and challenge established party

*Reprinted with permission from Boyd, W. L. and Smart, D. (1987) *Educational Policy in Australia and America*, Lewes, Falmer Press, 1987.

policy. In the process, he sometimes seems to be supporting policies more appropriate to his predecessor, Malcolm Fraser, and the conservative Liberal government than to a party supposedly committed to reform. For a fuller account of Hawke education policy including higher education see Smart *et al.*, (1986).

Such contradictions should come as no surprise to students of public policy, for education, like other areas of government policy, is locked in a complex historical web of political, economic and social relationships and understandings. This pre-existing web heavily constrains the degree of freedom which policy-makers have in seeking to reshape the amorphous and slow-moving education enterprise in new directions.

A key constraint on Hawke — as on his conservative counterparts in the UK and US — has been serious concern about the state of the economy and in particular, worry about the massive federal budget deficit (currently estimated at about US $9b). In fact, concern about the twin economic problems of the deficit and historically high youth unemployment have been dominant forces shaping (some would say distorting) the education and other policies of the Hawke government. 'Sound economic management' has been an understandable preoccupation of the Hawke government, particularly given the widespread popular perception of the previous Whitlam government as notoriously spendthrift and economically profligate.

Internalizing the history lesson inherent in the brevity of the radical reformist Whitlam government's occupancy of the Treasury benches, Hawke's approach has been to go cautiously and occupy the middle-ground of Australian politics. Thus Hawke's inclination is generally to eschew traditional left-wing Labor ideology in favour of pragmatism and to show a strong preference for a consensual approach to decision-making. Nowhere has this been more evident than in the sensitive policy areas of funding for 'wealthy' private schools and the proposed reintroduction of tertiary tuition fees. On both these issues, having initially argued for a policy preference consistent with its ideological opposition to social and financial privilege, the government (or in the case of fees, more correctly Hawke, Finance Minister Peter Walsh, and several other powerful Cabinet members) pragmatically sized up the mounting political costs of pursuing such policies and then – at least temporarily — deferred to well-organized vested interests.

This chapter will focus its attention on four key related schools policy developments which have occurred under Hawke: the so-called 'historic schools funding settlement' of 1984, the Participation and Equity Program, the highly political Quality of Education Review Committee Report, and the downgrading of the Schools Commission.

Before examining these four issues, however, let me briefly spell out the major value orientations evident in Hawke's education policy.

Value Orientations Evident in Hawke Education Policy

First, the ALP government has shown itself to be more committed to maintaining a strong federal role in education than its Fraser predecessor.

Second, this commitment is reflected in a willingness, so far, to improve or maintain levels of Federal funding in education and in a centralist approach to coordination and policy-making in relation to that Federal expenditure.

Third, the Hawke government has sought to reverse the swing of the excellence-equity pendulum. In contrast to Fraser, equity issues in education are with some notable exceptions, being given greater attention — though cynics would argue that this has been done more at the level of rhetoric than at the level of practical implementation.

Fourth, the Hawke government has adopted a more economistic view and approach to education than might have been expected. There has been a tendency to stress the vocational/competitive/technological role of education and even, on occasions, to resort to the old Fraser routine of blaming education for youth unemployment. In addition, there has been a growing Federal emphasis on accountability for the educational dollar — not just in financial input terms but a much greater insistence on evidence of educational outcomes in terms of progress and efficiency indicators.

Pressing School Issues Confronting the Hawke Government in 1983

There were two pressing school issues confronting the Hawke government when it came to power in 1983. One was the long-standing and divisive 'state aid' (aid to private schools) problem. This problem had been temporarily submerged since the creation of the generously funded Commonwealth Schools Commission under Whitlam in 1973. However, it had re-emerged during Fraser's conservative government (1975–1983) and the Hawke-led ALP opposition, in its pre-election statements in 1983 had promised to tackle the problem if elected to government. The other problem was the disturbingly low national level of student retention to Year 12 (in 1982, 64 per cent of students were leaving school without completing grade 12). This problem had a special salience for Hawke because of the potential which increasing school retention had for reducing the alarming levels of youth unemployment (25 per cent in the 16–19 age group). On assuming power in 1983, the ALP government tackled both the state aid and the school retention problems.

Don Smart

State Aid

The Whitlam and Fraser Legacy

In 1969, Malcolm Fraser as Federal Minister for Education in the conservative Liberal-Country Party government introduced a novel system of recurrent grants to private schools based on a standard per capita grant. By 1972, the Liberal-Country Party government had formalized this Commonwealth grant at 20 per cent of the per-pupil recurrent costs in government schools (the so-called 'nexus'). As one of its first acts on coming to power in 1972 the Whitlam government implemented ALP policy by establishing an Interim Committee of the Schools Commission (Karmel Committee) to propose a more equitable system of funding schools based on the actual financial 'needs' of individual schools (Smart, 1978). The Karmel Committee classified private schools into eight categories of need (A-H, A being the wealthiest or least 'needy') and proposed different levels of per capita funding for each category. It proposed a massive increase of almost a half billion dollars for government and private schools in 1974–75. Sympathetic to ALP redistributionist ideology, it also proposed that federal aid to the two wealthiest categories of private school (A and B) be phased out altogether over the two years 1974–75. This latter proposal was rejected by the Whitlam Cabinet in favour of immediate cessation of aid to such schools.

Naturally, this course of action was strenuously opposed by the parents and supporters of all private schools (Weller, 1977). Surprisingly, perhaps, some of the strongest opposition came from the Catholic Bishops and Catholic education hierarchy which argued forcefully that no student should be denied a basic per capita grant by virtue of parental wealth. Ultimately, when the legislation became bogged down over this issue in the Opposition-controlled Senate, the Country Party achieved a compromise with the government, part of which conceded that all students were entitled to a basic per capita grant. In retrospect, it is clear that the conflict generated during 1973 by this ALP attempt to enforce the principle of removing aid from the few very wealthy schools was counterproductive. The amount of money to be saved was relatively small and the bad feeling, media publicity and conflict generated was disproportionate to the potential gains to be achieved. Apparently lacking a sense of history in relation to this issue, the Hawke government was to duplicate this bitter episode a decade later with essentially the same outcome!

Under Fraser between 1975 and 1983, a less sympathetic attitude to the 'needs' approach saw a collapsing of the Schools Commission's eight categories of need into just three, a re-establishing of a generous 'nexus' with government school costs for even the wealthiest category of private schools, and a consequent acceleration of the total proportion of Schools Commission funds going to private schools. (The dramatic extent of the increase in private school funding is illustrated in figure 1.) By the end of the Fraser era the 24 per cent of students in private schools were receiving 56 per cent of the Schools Commission's recurrent grant budget. The explanations for this drift of Schools Commission resources to the private schools sector are complex. They are in large measure attributable to: the failure of the Schools Commission to impose maintenance-of-effort conditions on recipient private schools; to more and more lenient categorization of private schools; to the dramatic growth of new private schools and of enrolments in existing private schools as a result of sympathetic Schools Commission policies. The Catholic system, in particular, which was near collapse in 1973, underwent significant renewal and growth as a result of Schools Commission policies and support (Ryan, 1984 *Commonwealth Record*, p. 207; Praetz, 1983, p. 39; Marginson, 1985).

Initially the creation of the 'needs' oriented Schools Commission in 1973 'defused' the state aid conflict by creating a bigger cake and by promoting a consensual settlement which effectively coopted or disarmed those in public schooling who were later to oppose its implications. Initially there was more money for all. However, by the early 1980s as a result of policies which transferred a growing proportion of Schools Commission funds to the private sector, dissatisfaction amongst state school supporters re-emerged. This dissatisfaction was further fuelled by

Figure 1: Changes in Selected Commonwealth Budget Aggregates Between 1975–76 and 1982–83 (Real Terms)

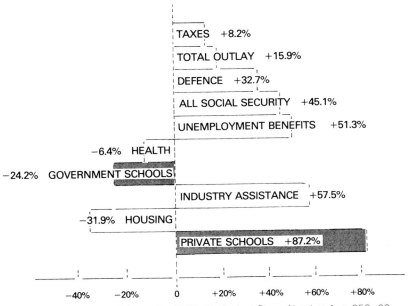

Source: Commonwealth of Australia, 1983–84 Budget Paper Number 1, p.358–63.

the change of Chairmanship of the Schools Commission in 1981. When the term of the original Labor-appointed Chairman, Dr Ken McKinnon, expired, Fraser did not renew his contract and instead replaced him with Dr Peter Tannock who was closely identified with the Catholic schools sector. Public school parent and teacher groups were outraged and openly referred to Tannock as the 'Commissioner for Private Schools'. In 1981 the state school parent and teacher representatives on the Schools Commission prepared a minority report condemning the Fraser government's interference with Schools Commission policy and the continued funding drift to the private schools. Opposition hardened, and in January 1982 the Australian Teachers Federation moved to a 'no state aid' position and when its member's term expired on the Schools Commission at the end of 1982 it refused to nominate a replacement.

The ALP Opposition Hardens Its Attitude to State Aid

This growing dissatisfaction amongst state school supporters was reflected in a hardening of ALP education policy. The revised 1982 Platform required 'that Commonwealth funds be available only to those non-government schools whose total private and public resources do not exceed the resources of comparable government schools'.

As the March 1983 election approached, the ALP articulated its concerns and fleshed out the specifics of its schools funding policy. In an official statement, Shadow Minister for Education, Chris Hurford, declared:

> Labor will end the unfairness of the Fraser government's policies. They have rekindled the wasteful state aid debate by cruelly unjust appropriations of the education dollar. This has caused the resentments which are so divisive ... Labor believes that the national government should be ensuring that the scarce education dollar must go in preference to those schools with less rather than to those schools which are already above a *community standard*.

Hurford indicated, and Hawke in his policy speech confirmed, that the fifty wealthiest private schools would have their grants (then 20 per cent of government school running costs) reduced to 15 per cent in 1984 and 10 per cent in 1985. Thus, at the end of Labor's first term, whilst all private schools would still be receiving a Commonwealth grant, the wealthiest schools would be receiving considerably less and there was an implicit assumption that the grants to these schools would be phased out.

As Dawkins and Costello noted, Labor had determined 'to make a decisive move to break the log-jam' on the 'divisive state aid issue' and this was to be done by abandoning the 'nexus' and having the Schools

Commission develop a community standard, 'a level of resources which the community at large will accept as necessary for children in various settings to get a high standard of schooling' (*Schools Commission*, 1983, p. 2). Once the 'community standard' was defined, wealthy schools which chose to remain outside it would be denied any aid at all (Dawkins and Costello, 1983, pp. 73–9).

The Hawke Government's 'Hit List' of Forty-one Private Schools

In July 1983, just a few months after taking office, Senator Ryan, Minister for Education, took the first decisive (though historically and strategically naive) step towards implementing this ALP policy. She announced in her guidelines to the Schools Commission that the nexus was to be abandoned and the recurrent grants of the forty-one wealthiest private schools were to be reduced by 25 per cent. (The remainder of the schools in the wealthiest category 1 were to receive no increase in their grant for 1984, whereas category 2 and 3 schools were to receive increases of 1 per cent and 3 per cent respectively.) In a predictable response — almost a rerun of the 1973 conflict — the private schools sector sprang to the defence of its wealthiest members. As in 1973, the Catholic sector staunchly defended the right of wealthy non-Catholic private schools to retain their grants at existing levels and argued for the retention of the percentage-link or nexus (Hogan, 1984). As Kenway (1984) has pointed out, the media fixated on this most sensational aspect of the guidelines and the wealthy schools were quickly dubbed 'victims' of Susan Ryan's 'hit list'. The fact that 90 per cent of private schools were to share an increase of $9.5m in grants for 1984 and that government schools were to receive an extra $31.4m was largely lost as attention focused on the plight of the forty-one wealthy schools.

The predictable and inevitable result, however, was that Ryan found herself in deep trouble during the latter months of 1983 as she was obliged almost daily to address large and frequently hostile gatherings of anxious private school parents across the country. For the second time in a decade, the ALP in government discovered that the wealthy private school lobby and the Catholic Bishops in combination are a formidable opposition (Kitney, 1982, p. 3). In retrospect, the $4m to be 'saved' from these forty-one 'elite' schools and redistributed was so miniscule in a Schools Commission recurrent budget of $1221.8m that it was almost laughable. Ultimately, Hawke was obliged to intervene himself. Amidst rumours that Ryan would be moved to another portfolio, Hawke joined her in the task of addressing meetings and lobby groups to reassure them that this decision was not the 'thin end of the wedge' and there was no intention to phase out aid to private schools.

Don Smart

Hawke Becomes More Conciliatory to Private Schools

In a further measure to quell the panic in the private schools, Ryan and her Department prepared a widely distributed booklet, reassuringly titled *Commonwealth Support for Non-Government Schools*, providing information about the government's 'policies for non-government schools in 1984 and beyond'. It explained the decision to 'break the percentage link' (nexus) and move to a 'community standard' as the only way to overcome the continuing inequalities in school resources by a more redistributive approach. However, it reassured schools that because there would be more money available, redistribution would harm few and 90 per cent of private schools would receive increased grants in 1984. That year was to be an interim year whilst the Schools Commission carefully researched and devised the 'community standard'. Hawke's intervention and the booklet were, of course, counter measures designed to restore the badly shaken confidence of the significant private school electorate and, as Ryan put it, to 'lay(ing) to rest some of the mistaken and sometimes outrageous claims which have been made about the policies of the government I represent' (*Schools Commission* 1983, pp. 2–3).

Clearly the government had been rocked by the extent of the reaction to its policy and by early 1984 the signs were obvious that the cautious and pragmatic government would not pursue its declared intention to 'phase out' aid to the wealthiest schools. In a speech at Geelong College in March 1984 Ryan hinted as much when she declared:

Insofar as change may be thought desirable in the national education system, under the Hawke Government *it will be gradual and reformist, rather than abrupt and radical.* Indeed, it could hardly be otherwise, given the complexity of the questions which must be asked and answered and given our commitment to *consultation and consensus* (emphasis mine). (*Commonwealth Record*, 1984, pp. 379–81).

The Schools Commission's Report on Funding Policies

In March 1984 the Schools Commission's eagerly awaited report, *Funding Policies for Australian Schools* was released. It was later dubbed an 'historic settlement' by the *Sydney Morning Herald* (14 August 1984). This controversial document of 140 pages contained minority reports from two commissioners representing government school interests. The report detailed the 'community standard' and spelled out recurrent funding options for the Commonwealth to be examined in the context of the forthcoming 1984–85 budget deliberations.

The Report acknowledged various ministerial guidelines and objectives including: the need 'to restore the community's confidence in the government's determination to give all children access to properly staffed and equipped schools'; the desire to give 'greater weighting' to the principle of 'need'; and the need to 'have particular regard to the deep concern of the government about the extent of inequality in Australian schooling'.

At the outset too, the Report acknowledged the Commission's obligations under its Act, both to have regard to 'government's primary obligation to provide and maintain public schooling of the highest standard', and to 'have regard to the prior right of parents to choose government or non-government schools for their children'. As to the former obligation, it acknowledged that 'significant modification to present funding arrangements' would be necessary to ensure that the Commonwealth more directly supported the role of public education. As to the latter, it acknowledged the continuing public debate about the *extent* to which private schools should receive public support but asserted rather forcefully:

> What cannot be denied is the entitlement of all children to resources for schooling consistent with their educational needs. This is an entitlement children enjoy in their own right, and has nothing to do with their parents' financial capacities or tax contributions.

Amongst its key recommendations, the report proposed a 'community standard' of $2195 per primary student and $3240 per secondary student with an additional loading for government schools because of their 'different circumstances' and obligations. The report also stressed the vital need for 'a period of stability and agreement about the future direction of Commonwealth and State general resource funding'. The Hawke government was well aware of this need after the turbulent debate of the preceding eight or nine months!

Urging the government to boost confidence by providing guaranteed levels of funding for the four years 1985–1988, the Commission proposed three options for the recurrent funding of government schools. Each option was premised on an annual increase in the federal contribution and the options ranged in cost over four years from an additional $140m to $240m.[2]

For private schools, the Commission recommended a new eight- or twelve-category system of need based on the percentage of the community standard or government school standard derived from private sources by 1988. The Commission expressed its preference for a twelve-category scheme linked to the community standard. This scheme would cost the Federal government an additional $106m over the four years. (The ATF has disputed the Schools Commission's estimates of costs, arguing that they are much too conservative and the real costs could be much higher.) Perhaps partly sensing the weakened resolve of the government on the issue of 'phasing out' aid to the wealthiest schools and certainly, partly reflecting the views of the commissioners representing the private sector, the report gently recommended that *all schools* be eligible for a category 1 grant.

Key Public Schools Commissioners Dissent from Report

Two of the key public school representatives on the Commission, Joan Brown (national parent body) and Van Davy (ATF), refused to endorse the report and submitted their own separate and highly critical minority reports. Both raised the by-now familiar accusation (in relation to the Schools Commission) that the document focused excessively on the funding needs of private schools in derogation of the Commission's 'primary obligation' to government schools (*Schools Commission*, 1984, pp. 115 and 121). They asserted that the annual increases recommended for private schools alone would put such a financial burden on the Commonwealth that it would seriously compete with the much-needed increases for government schools. Both were also highly critical of the enormous financial drain which the Commission's recommended continuing provision for new places in private schools would incur (from $80 –$100m extra over four years). They argued that this inevitably reduced the scope for government school funding and that the provision itself reflected the Commission's priority for the principle of access and choice over other key priorities including 'primary obligation to government schools' and the 'promotion of greater equality of outcomes'. Both were also critical of the concept and methodology behind the community standard and Brown urged retention instead of government school standard costs as the only appropriate yardstick.

In a departure from ATF official policy of 'no state aid', Davy proposed a compromise — a moratorium on *additional* Federal expenditure for private schools, with no new places to be funded and maintenance of private effort to be conditions for continued funding. In the final section of his minority report, Davy condemned the flimsiness of the methodology underlying the 'community (target) standard' and severely criticized the nature of the Commission's inquiry process:

> The procedures and the time-line have been most unsatisfactory resulting in a report that will do nothing to generate confidence in and support for the Schools Commission from those serving the government schools.

In spite of this, however, the majority view in the report gave the Hawke government the justification for reversing or halting the 'phase-out' to wealthy schools should it decide that pragmatism and consensus argued·for such an approach.

The 1984 ALP Conference Confirms 'Phase-Out' Policy

With only a month to go before the government was to announce its decisions on school funding, the July 1984 ALP Biennial Conference — the supreme policy-making body of the ALP whose decisions are technically binding on ALP politicians — in Canberra threw an obstacle (albeit not insurmountable) in the path of what might otherwise have been a smooth policy reversal. At that conference, a series of reformist resolutions were moved and passed which reflected the prevailing 'pro-government school' mood of the party. The most salient of these resolutions called upon the Federal government 'to continue to phase out all funding support for the most wealthy private schools ... and redirect these funds to government and non-government schools on the basis of need'. The conference also recommended that an additional $260m of recurrent funds be provided by the Federal government for government schools by 1986. Ironically, the Federal Minister for Education, Susan Ryan, was one of the prime movers in the adoption of these policies at the conference (ALP Biennial Conference, Canberra, July 1984, Education Resolution No 3 — see Ramsay, 1984).

Table 1: Commonwealth General Recurrent Grants for Non-Government Schools 1985–1992

Category	1985 $	1986 $	1987 $	1988 $	1989 $	1990 $	1991 $	1992 $
Primary								
1	277	277	277	277	277	277	277	277
2	370	370	370	370	370	370	370	370
3	378	387	398	414	431	449	455	460
4	559	559	559	559	559	559	559	559
5	565	574	584	603	619	631	640	644
6	571	586	606	631	661	692	704	712
7	576	598	627	666	708	752	772	781
8	768	779	792	811	828	843	848	850
9	771	786	808	834	859	880	890	896
10	774	796	824	857	892	919	935	942
11	777	804	840	881	923	960	980	988
12	781	812	855	906	956	999	1024	1034
Secondary								
1	440	440	440	440	440	440	440	440
2	586	586	586	586	586	586	586	586
3	594	602	613	631	649	667	674	678
4	889	889	889	889	889	889	889	889
5	893	898	906	918	930	940	946	950
6	901	917	938	968	1001	1032	1046	1051
7	909	936	973	1021	1070	1120	1143	1154
8	1211	1218	1226	1234	1243	1249	1253	1255
9	1216	1231	1251	1272	1294	1312	1319	1323
10	1222	1246	1277	1311	1345	1372	1385	1390
11	1227	1258	1297	1344	1392	1429	1450	1458
12	1232	1269	1319	1379	1436	1482	1514	1526

Source: Commonwealth Schools Commission Report for 1986, pp. 9–10.

Don Smart

Hawke and Ryan Reject 'Phase-Out' and Opt for Consensus

On 14 August 1984 the government announced its new funding policy for schools. Both Hawke and Ryan took great pains to describe it as an historic settlement designed to 'take off the political agenda of the 1980s the tired old state aid rhetoric of the 1960s' (Ryan, 1984a). On close analysis, it is revealed to be an extremely generous funding policy, pragmatically designed to defuse the state aid debate and ensure consensus by making more money available for virtually all schools and simultaneously giving long-term stability by promising legislation guaranteeing levels of funding for four years (see tables 1 and 2).

The Schools Commission's 'twelve-category option' and 'community standard' was endorsed as was the recommendation that all schools receive aid. The wealthiest schools categories (1 and 2) were guaranteed their existing money grants would be maintained *in real terms* though without the real increases applying to schools in all other categories. Government schools were to be given a real increase in Commonwealth funds of 50 per cent over eight years – as contrasted with a real decrease of 1.9 per cent during the seven years of the Fraser government.

Table 2:   Commonwealth Allocation for Schools, 1986

1986 National Allocations
Commonwealth General Resource Programs for Schools
(expressed in estimated December 1984 prices)

	1985 ($'000)	1986 ($'000)
GOVERNMENT PROGRAMS		
General Recurrent (a)	354 414	373 740
Capital	165 501	150 890
NON-GOVERNMENT PROGRAMS		
General Recurrent (b)	660 947	671 074
Short Term Emergency Assistance	64B	643
Capital (c)	59 727	54 406
TOTAL	1 241 232	1 250 753

(a) As this program operates on a per capita basis, final costs will be subject to actual enrolments each year.

(b) Based on latest available year's actual enrolments (1984); final payments are dependent on actual enrolments for 1985 and 1986, the distribution of increased enrolments among the funding categories the outcome of appeals by schools against their funding categories and the number of new schools to qualify for Commonwealth per capita and establishment grants; based on projected enrolments, total costs are estimated at an additional $13m–16m in 1985 and $25m–$27m in 1986.

(c) Includes amount to be transferred from Department of Community Services in 1986. An amount has also been included in 1985 for reasons of comparison.

National Allocations 1986
Commonwealth General Resource Programs for Schools
(expressed in estimated December 1984 prices)

	1985 ($'000)	1986 ($'000)
GOVERNMENT PROGRAMS		
Primary Basic Learning	5 549	5 549
Participation and Equity	40 698	20 349
Computer Education	5 251	5 251
English as a Second Language		
—General Support	42 458	40 855
—New Arrivals (a)	10 004	10 004
Disadvantaged Schools	30 034	30 034
Special Education		
—Recurrent	18 845	18 072
—Integration	1 419	1 361
Early Special Education	1 668	1 668
NON-GOVERNMENT PROGRAMS		
Primary Basic Learning	1 466	1 466
Participation and Equity	4 768	2 384
Computer Education	1 313	1 313
English as a Second Language		
—General Support	17 958	17 084
—New Arrivals (a)	1 070	1 070
Disadvantaged Schools	5 833	5 833
Special Education		
—Recurrent	4 819	4 621
—Integration	407	390
—Support Services (b)	13 000	12 467
Early Special Education	426	426
JOINT PROGRAMS		
Participation and Equity	1 701	850
Early Special Education	1 780	1 780
Multicultural Education	4 975	4 771
Ethnic Schools (a)	5 037	5 037
Country Areas	10 228	9 809
Children in Residential Institutions	2 289	2 289
Severely Handicapped Children	3 738	3 738
Professional Development	11 301	11 301
Education Centres	2 393	2 393
Projects of National Significance	1 818	1 818
TOTAL	252 246	223 983

(a) As these programs operate on a per capita basis, final costs will be subject to actual enrolments each year.
(b) Amount to be transferred from Department of Community Services in 1986. An amount has also been included in 1985 for reasons of comparison.

Source: Commonwealth Schools Commission Report for 1986, p. 57.

Many ALP Supporters Feel 'Betrayed'

Naturally this consensus solution was seen as the sacrificing of long-term ALP principles for short-term electoral pragmatism by many ALP members and public school supporters. Thus an ATF Research Paper described it in the following terms:

> It is hard to capture in words the sense of outrage and betrayal amongst government school teachers and parents following the release of the federal government's guidelines for schools funding on 14 August this year.
>
> In one stroke the Hawke government silenced the militant minority opposition of the private school supporters by giving them everything they wanted, stroked the captains of industry with a promise that education would be brought into line with their needs, guaranteed the fiscal 'rationalists' that there would be no Whitlamite expansion of education funding (except to private schools), soothed the 'back to basics' lobby by adopting their rhetoric and reassured all those who fear the teacher unions with a very public declaration of the government's intention to shut the unions out of any influence over education policy.
>
> It was a spectacular conservative coup. Hawke had become Fraser, only this time there was no alternative waiting in the wings.
>
> Given the finely-tuned electoral pragmatism and neo-conservative economics of the Hawke Government, these outcomes in retrospect look less surprising. (Marginson, 1984).

Ryan's speech to the National Press Club of 15 August 1984 confirms the impression of a Minister and a government extremely anxious to find a compromise and willing to spend their way out of trouble.

> ... This package of decisions means that there is no legitimate way in which the State aid debate can be pursued, and that a real basis for consensus in schools funding has been achieved... Too much of the government's time has been taken up with arguments about dollars.

It was not only the ALP ideologues who felt this solution smacked of expediency. For example, the widely respected political commentator, Alan Ramsay (1984) was cutting in his criticism of Ryan's speech and the turnabout:

> Thus the government that seventeen months ago pledged its primary obligation to the state school system, and built its education policy on the priority of money for the neediest, will now enshrine financial support for even the wealthiest private schools in the statutes.

Participation and Equity in Schools

The sense of betrayal felt by some public school supporters over the Hawke 'historic settlement' in the school funding arena should not be permitted to obscure the efforts made by the mildly reformist Hawke government to implement ALP platform in relation to enhancing access to and participation in education at all levels.

Perhaps the single education program which best captures the long-term educational goals and ideals of the ALP is the so-called PEP program. During 1983, Ryan said of PEP:

> The new program ... will be the centrepiece of the overall framework of youth policies ... The program will have the twin objectives of increasing participation in education and introducing greater equity in the government's overall provision for young people ...
>
> Government wishes to achieve a situation where, by the end of this decade, most young people complete the equivalent of a full secondary education, either in school or in a TAFE institution, or in some combination of work and education. (CPD, Senate, 25 August 1983, pp. 240–1).

However, it would be wrong to see this program as a unique ALP innovation, evolving neatly from pre-existing ALP education policy which, rooted in the Walker (1944) and Karmel Reports (1973), has had a long-standing concern with the issue of equality of educational opportunity. Rather, it is an amalgam of ALP educational idealism with elements of existing Fraser government policies[3] and the pragmatism of Hawke, responding swiftly to the unprecedentedly high levels of youth unemployment confronting the incoming government. This was linked to a desire to 'correct' simultaneously Australia's remarkably low secondary school retention and completion rates (only 36 per cent of students were completing grade 12 in 1982) and increase participation in post-compulsory education.

However, the largely instrumental nature of the catalyst for PEP should not detract from the government's clear commitment to placing a high priority on the educational and employment needs of young people and its 'recognition of their significance in national recovery and reconstruction'. Right from day one, the Hawke government set in train a number of initiatives to promote a more coordinated approach to the area of youth policy. The recent Priority One and Youth Traineeships programs and the Kirby Report on Labour Market Programs are all testament to a strong concern for youth.

The government allocated $74m for PEP in 1984, all but $4m of which was for government educational institutions including TAFE and the universities and colleges. Most of it was to be targeted at the approximately 40 per cent of schools with the lowest retention rates and to be used to reduce the number of students who leave school prematurely by seeking to stimulate broadly based changes in secondary education (Commonwealth Schools Commission, 1984, p. 1).

The Apparent Success of PEP

Probably through a combination of fortuitous circumstances and sound policy the outcome for the Hawke government has been remarkably satisfying. Partly through a firming trend in school retention rates which preceded PEP and partly through the PEP strategy, national retention rates through grade 12 have climbed dramatically from around 35 per cent in 1982 to 45 per cent in 1984 and probably around 50 per cent in 1985 (Schools Commission, 1985). The apparent combined effects of Hawke economic strategy as well as secondary and tertiary PEP were also gratifying. In the first two years of the Hawke government, unemployment in the 15–24 age group fell by 76,000 whilst the number in the same age cohort participating in full-time post-compulsory (age 16 +) education rose by 56,000. According to the Chairman of the Commonwealth Tertiary Education Commission: 'it is clear that the expansion in education has been a more important factor in reducing unemployment of young people than has improvement in economic activity' (Hudson, 1985, p. 49). A recent federal government committee optimistically predicted that the bulk of Australia's youth unemployment might be eliminated by 1992 through a combination of continued expansion of full-time education opportunities and the introduction of a new federal youth traineeship scheme (QERC, 1985).

Criticisms of PEP

Despite these statistics, PEP is not without its critics. This is partly, no doubt, because PEP highlights a central dilemma for Australian secondary schools in the 1980s — how to balance the demand for a uniform academic curriculum against the need to provide for new types of non-tertiary-bound students. The NSW Teachers Federation has criticized PEP for lacking direction and failing to analyze the needs of students. As a consequence, it argues, schools are taking the 'soft options' approach and providing non-academic students with 'bread and circuses' whilst they spend their final school years avoiding the dole queues (Dawson, 1985). Max Charlesworth, the Liberal Catholic philosopher summed up the growing anxieties about PEP in other quarters:

Paradoxically, in the name of helping under-privileged youth, a dual system of education is being set up, which in effect perpetuates the structure of privilege in our society, a structure in which knowledge and power remain in the hands of the few (quoted in Smart *et al.*, 1986).

In a surprise move too, in the May 1985 mini-budget, the Hawke government provided a further source of disenchantment to its reformists when it slashed the schools PEP budget by \$23m — or 50 per cent (*Schools Commission Report for 1986*, Canberra, September 1985).

Quality of Education Review Committee

The emergence of the Quality of Education Review Committee (QERC) was consistent with the trend in other western countries including the US and UK. As Scott (1986) has noted, economic difficulties have increasingly led western governments of both the left and the right to 'perceive their education systems as predominantly aimed towards producing an internationally competitive workforce'. Two overriding concerns were responsible for the emergence of QERC and dominated its terms of reference — establishing 'value for money' from federal expenditure (whilst simultaneously 'putting the lid' on federal spending on schools) and gearing the education system more closely to labour market needs (Smart *et al.*, 1986).

Undoubtedly, widespread community concern about educational standards and the enormity of the Federal deficit were mutually reinforcing pressures which pushed the Hawke Cabinet in what might have been considered an unusual direction for a Labor government. QERC appears to have been 'forced' on the Minister for Education as a result of 'intervention' by senior econocrats in the Departments of Finance and Prime Minister and Cabinet. In their review of the Education Department's 1984 pre-Budget submission, the bureaucrats demanded evidence that the massive increase in Federal per pupil expenditure (50 per cent between 1973 and 1983) had improved the quality of education. Thus, unlike the Karmel Report of 1973 which was primarily concerned with financial and educational *inputs*, QERC was required to establish that there were identifiable educational *outcomes* from federal aid. It appears likely that the Minister for Education was virtually obliged by Cabinet to agree to this inquiry as a precondition to Cabinet approving the expensive 'historic settlement' schools funding package (Smart *et al.*, 1986).

Given that it was to enquire only into the schools sector, the membership of the Committee raised some eyebrows. The members were Professor Peter Karmel (Vice-Chancellor of the Australian National University) as Chairman, Hugh Hudson (Chairman of Commonwealth Tertiary Education Commission), Dr Barry McGaw (Director of Australian Council for Educational Research, recently resigned as Professor of

Education at Murdoch University), Mr Peter Kirby (Assistant Director General of Employment and Training in Victoria) and (later) Ms Helen Williams (then Deputy Secretary of the Commonwealth Department of Education, later Secretary). The ATF and State Directors-General of Education unsuccessfully sought membership of the Committee, arguing that it was dominated by unsympathetic tertiary educators and Commonwealth bureaucrats. It is also noteworthy that no member of the Schools Commission was appointed, for implicit in QERC's establishment was the government's concern to evaluate the role of the Schools Commission itself. As we shall see, QERC's creation may well have been from the outset part of a wider strategy to downgrade the role of the Schools Commission. Even if no such strategy existed, certainly QERC was to have that effect.

Predictably, perhaps, QERC was unable to come up with conclusive measures or evidence of the beneficial effects of massive Federal aid between 1973–1984. However, its 'impressions' were that schools had 'produced results superior to those which would otherwise have been the case'. Whilst essentially supportive of continued federal aid to schools, QERC's major recommendations emphasized the need in future to devise better means for agreeing on the goals to be achieved and monitoring and gauging the educational outcomes. Thus it recommended:

- future recurrent grants should be based on 'negotiated agreements' between the Commonwealth and the other parties (state governments and non-government education authorities) which declared priority areas (for example, basic skills, disadvantaged students, etc);
- triennial accountability statements describing changes in prescribed educational indicators relating to the priority areas (for example, levels of attainment in general skills, post-compulsory education participation rates by socioeconomic class/gender/rural-urban location, etc);
- reducing the number of existing specific purpose (categorical) programs and tightening up the reporting requirements associated with these.

Whilst the Federal government was quick to endorse QERC, there has been limited progress towards implementation — for neither the State Education Departments, nor the private schools, nor the Commonwealth's own Schools Commission have been very enthusiastic about the proposed 'negotiated agreements' and 'accountability statements' with their heavy emphasis on evaluation indicators. The state departments, in particular, have expressed unwillingness to jump through inconvenient 'Commonwealth hoops' for the sake of relatively minor funds which constitute only 7 per cent of their total recurrent schools expenditure.

The views of the NSW Education Minister are probably fairly

representative:

> QERC is less concerned with quality and standards of attainment than with justifying a transfer of funds from schools which cater for all comers (public) to schools which cater for particular sections of the population (private) and to tertiary institutions. It is also an attempt to dictate to the states what their priorities and policies for education should be ... I regard this as a direct attack on the constitutional responsibilities of the states (Scott, forthcoming).

In the final analysis, I find myself very much in agreement with Scott's (1986) assessment of QERC:

> The origins of QERC, arising as it did out of Cabinet discord over education spending, the 'value for money' thrust of the Committee's terms of reference, and the extraordinary speed with which it operated, all tend to lend credence to the view that the intention behind establishing the Committee was the result more of financial than educational considerations.

Just one month after the release of the QERC Report, the Treasurer's May mini-budget carved $48.2m off the Schools Commission's total $1,474b budget for 1986 — a net reduction in real terms of 1.3 per cent on 1985. Ironically, public schools suffered the brunt of the cuts (2.7 per cent reduction) whilst private schools achieved a 1 per cent increase (Schools Commission Report for 1986).

QERC was clearly a highly political exercise which was as much about keeping the lid on future schools spending and justifying a shift in emphasis to the funding needs of the tertiary education sector as it was about educational standards. Furthermore, it became a vehicle for assisting in the downgrading of the Schools Commission's previously central role in school funding and policy determination.

Shifting Priorities and Power in Canberra: The Emasculation of the Schools Commission

During the Hawke government's first three years of office a significant shift of bureaucratic power and influence has been occurring. Gradually, a somewhat vulnerable and relatively uninfluential Department of Education has been strengthening its power and influence with the Minister — partly through changes in its leadership and partly through expansion of personnel and budget at the expense of the Schools Commission and Department of Aboriginal Affairs. Simultaneously, the Commonwealth Tertiary Education Commission — partly through the political skills of its new Chairman, Hugh Hudson, and partly through the increasingly obvious signs of neglect in the tertiary sector — has climbed to prominence as a key advisor to the Federal Education Minister and Cabinet.

The ascendancy of the Department was undoubtedly assisted by the rising prominence of its new Permanent Head, Helen Williams, during a period of hiatus and vulnerability in the Schools Commission's leadership. Dr Peter Tannock resigned at the end of 1984, leaving the Commission's leadership in limbo. Despite being a Fraser appointee and being labelled by many public school supporters as primarily a private school sympathizer, Tannock was an able bureaucrat who competently defended the Schools Commission's turf. Once he left the knives were out. During the first half of 1985, whilst a new Chairman was being sought, QERC and a Public Service Board Review were instrumental in ensuring that Cabinet would agree to the transferring of the Schools Commission's two key programs — together with their billion dollar budget — and almost half of its staff to the Department of Education. By the time the new Chairman, Garth Boomer — a curriculum, rather than policy, specialist — was in place, the Schools Commission was clearly destined for a significantly downgraded role. Ostensibly freed from major program administration so that it could play an 'enhanced policy advice' role, the Commission is looking increasingly as though its main function will, in fact, be to, run a Curriculum Development Centre.

The Shadow Minister for Education, Senator Peter Baume, alleged that Senator Ryan had been single-minded in her determination to 'gut' the Commission and predicted that deprived of its database, it will become a powerless advisory body whose advice will be ignored as irrelevant to the implementation process (*Canberra Times*, 10 July 1985).

In July 1985, a union survey revealed massive alienation among Schools Commission staff as a result of chronic understaffing and organizational uncertainty:

> The constant movement of people out of the Commission, the internal changes necessary to meet workloads ... has resulted in staffing instability for the programs administered by the Commission. There is a serious morale problem as staff at all levels attempt to carry out complex administrative tasks ... while under pressure to provide policy advice as well (*Sydney Morning Herald*, 17 July 1985).

It is difficult to avoid the conclusion that the Labor government has deliberately emasculated the Schools Commission. Perhaps concluding that the Commission had become too oriented towards the private schools and too difficult to control, Cabinet decided to pull more financial and policy responsibility back into the hands of the ministerially-controlled Department — a decision which coincided nicely with the territorial imperatives of a Department striving to justify its own continued existence.

Conclusion

Under the radical reformist Whitlam ALP government from 1972–1975, education was viewed as a central instrument for making society more equal and for promoting social reform. However, between the early 1970s and the early 1980s the western world underwent a severe economic recession and an accompanying pendulum swing from fairly liberal to much more conservative social, political and economic values and attitudes. The education policies of Reagan, Thatcher and Fraser reflected that pendulum swing. When the Hawke Labor government came to power in 1983, whilst some of the educational rhetoric of the Whitlam era remained in Labor's platform, the reformist zeal and the determination to use education as an engine of social reform had largely evaporated. Under Hawke, Labor has become a much more cautious party of the middle ground. The politics of electoral pragmatism and consensus have largely replaced the politics of idealism and reform. Anxiety about the budget deficit has ensured that 'sound economic management' has remained the predominant priority and largely pushed social and educational redistributionist policies into the background. As a result, the major determinants of education policy have been economic rather than ideological.

During the latter half of 1985 a number of respected and influential ALP elder statesmen dating from the Whitlam era (including Hayden, McLelland and Whitlam) began warning the Hawke government about the dangers of losing sight of its traditional Labor goals and philosophy in its desperation to win acceptance by big business and the advocates of privatization. McLelland warned the Party:

> If the only reason you're in politics is to stay in office you're not going to be making much difference to the obvious inequities in society (*Weekend Australia*, 13–14 July 1985).

The Hawke 'scoreboard' in educational reform to date suggests that the Party is pre-occupied with staying in office. Nevertheless, its reading of the conservatism of the electorate is an essentially accurate one and its pragmatic and consensual policies are totally understandable, if not acceptable to the ideologically pure within the ALP.

Notes

1   For the benefit of American readers the following Australian terminology needs explanation: the Federal government and the Commonwealth (government) are synonymous; private schools are also commonly referred to as independent or non-government schools.
2   Option 1 would result in the Commonwealth reaching a target of contributing 10 per cent of the community standard by 1988. Option 2 would result in the

Commonwealth meeting a constant 8 per cent of the community standard. Option 3 would involve an annual 10 per cent increase in Commonwealth contribution over the four years.

3 See for example Commonwealth Tertiary Education Commission (1982) *Learning and Earning: A Study of Education and Employment Opportunities for Young People*, Canberra, AGPS. This report was prepared for the Fraser government and recommended PEP-type solutions.

References

COMMONWEALTH SCHOOLS COMMISSION (1984) *Participation and Equity in Australian Schools — The Goal of Full Secondary Education*, Canberra, Commonwealth Schools Commission.

COMMONWEALTH TERTIARY EDUCATION COMMISSION (1982) *Learning and Earning: A Study of Education and Employment Opportunities for Young People*, Canberra, Commonwealth Tertiary Education Commission, AGPS.

DAWKINS, J. and COSTELLO, R. (1983) 'Education progress and equality' in REEVES, J. and THOMPSON, K. (Eds), *Labor Essays 1983: Policies and Programs for the Labor Government*, Melbourne, Drummond.

DAWSON, C. (1985) 'Government under fire as PEP starts to flag', *The Australian*, 6 February.

HOGAN, M. (1984) *Public Versus Private Schools*, Ringwood, Penguin.

HUDSON, H. (1985) 'Economic and political change — Its implications for tertiary education', *The Australian TAFE Teacher*, November.

KENWAY, J. (1984) 'Ideology, the media and private schooling — The year of the "Hit List"', paper delivered at the Australian Association for Research in Education conference, Perth, November.

KITNEY, G. (1982) 'Dawkins stakes future on rolling private schools', *National Times*, 7–13 November.

MARGINSON, S. (1984) 'The schools guidelines: Hawke in Fraser's clothing', *ATF Research Notes*, 2, 6 September.

MARGINSON, S. (1985) 'The collapse of the 1973 Karmel consensus', *AFT Research Papers*, 9, 15, December.

PRAETZ, H. (1983) 'The non-government schools' in BROWN, R. K. and FOSTER, L. E. (Eds), *Sociology of Education*, Melbourne.

QUALITY OF EDUCATION REVIEW COMMITTEE (QERC) (1985) *Report of the Quality of Education Review Committee*, (Chairman Prof P. H. Karmel), Canberra, AGPS.

RAMSAY, A. (1984) 'The turnabout of a state-aid advocate', *National Times*, 24 August.

RYAN, S. (1984a) Statement by the Minister of Education to Parliament, 14 August.

RYAN, S. (1984b) Address to the National Press Club, 15 August 1984.

SCHOOLS COMMISSION (1983) *Commonwealth Support for Non-Government Schools* Canberra, Schools Commission.

SCHOOLS COMMISSION (1984) *Funding Policies for Australian Schools* Canberra, Schools Commission.

SCHOOLS COMMISSION (1985) *Quality and Equality* Canberra, Schools Commission.

SCOTT, A. (forthcoming) 'The QERC Report' in SMART, D. (Ed) *Major National Reports in Australian Education*.

SMART, D. (1978) *Federal Aid to Australian Schools*, St Lucia, University of Queensland Press.

SMART, D. *et al.*, (1986) 'The Hawke government and education 1983–1985', *Politics*, 21, 1, May, pp. 63–81.

WELLER, P. (1977) 'The establishment of the Schools Commission: A case study of the politics of education' in BIRCH, I. K. F. and SMART, D. (Eds), *The Commonwealth Government and Education 1964–1976*, Drummond, Melbourne.

Chapter 8
Balancing Public and Private Schools: The Australian Experience and American Implications*

William Lowe Boyd

The growing demands for excellence, diversity, and choice in American education have raised with renewed vigor a perennial issue of educational policy: Should private schools receive public funds and, if so, on what basis? The American tradition, bolstered by our Supreme Court's interpretation of the Constitution's provision on the separation of church and state, has been to bar the use of public funds by non-government schools. But, as many critics point out, most democratic nations have not found it necessary to take such a strict stand on this issue.

Among the nations that demonstrate this point, Australia in particular stands out. Indeed, it has been proposed as a success story, a model for how the United States might undertake public funding of private schools (Doyle, 1984; Finn, 1985; Sherman, 1982 and 1983). Unfortunately, the reporting on this subject has glossed over some significant problems. Along with the successful features of the Australian approach go some disturbing features that constitute the subject of this chapter. A consideration of both sets of features suggests, at the least, that Americans should be cautious about emulating the Australian model. More broadly, cross-national research shows that a delicate balance in public policy must be struck if there is to be parity of esteem between public and private schools and equality of opportunity as well as excellence and choice in education.

The Australian Experience

As an example for Americans, Australia stands out because, beyond being an English-speaking democracy with numerous cultural similarities to the

* Reprinted with permission from Boyd, W. L. and Smart, D. (1987) *Educational Policy in Australia and America*, Lewes, Falmer Press.

United States (like Canada), it even has a Constitution consciously patterned in many respects after the American model. Yet, in a dramatic departure from the American experience, Australia's nearly identical constitutional language on the separation of church and state has been interpeted to permit state aid to sectarian schools. In the celebrated DOGS (Defenders of Government Schools) case the nation's High Court ruled, in 1981, that so long as public monies are distributed even-handedly, rather than for the purpose of creating one state-sponsored religion, there is no breach of the Australian Constitution (Sherman, 1983). This ruling, along with the breadth, minimal regulations, and apparent social acceptance of federal aid to private schools in Australia, has made it a favorite example for American proponents of educational choice, tuition tax credits, and educational voucher plans (for example, Doyle, 1984; Finn, 1985).

Although there are many similarities between Australia and the United States there also are striking differences (West, 1983). For instance, the educational traditions of the two nations are quite different. American visitors are struck by the legacy in Australia of the British dual-system of education: elite private schools for a few and government schools for the masses. Although the British legacy has been tempered by Australia's commitment to equality of opportunity, restrictive arrangements for entry into higher (tertiary) education — combined with free tuition upon admission — reinforce the perceived advantages of the grooming provided by elite private schools. However, the fundamental political basis for public funding of private schools comes not from the elite school sector but from a third important sector: the Catholic schools, most of which are not elite in admissions, fees, or resources.

In 1971, Catholics constituted 27 per cent of Australia's population, a segment of the electorate that politicians must respect.[1] The distribution of students among the three sectors of schools in 1970 was 17.8 per cent in Catholic schools, 4.1 per cent in non-Catholic private schools, and 78.2 per cent in government schools. Since the level of state aid increased in the mid-1970s, the trend has been for the non-government school enrollment to increase. Thus, by 1982 the figures were 18.3 per cent in Catholic schools, 5.5 per cent in non-Catholic private schools, and 76.2 per cent in government schools.[2]

Like many countries, Australia initially relied on schools provided by church groups.[3] In 1872, however, the Colonial parliaments passed legislation making education 'free, compulsory, and secular' and, at the same time, abolishing the financing of religious schools. This arrangement continued until 1952, when a law was passed allowing small tax deductions for schools fees. Then, in 1964, at a time when the Catholic schools were in severe financial straits, Prime Minister Menzies introduced a program of more substantial state aid. Initially, it consisted of a modest federal program of grants to public and private schools for science buildings and equipment.

Sherman (1982), who sees in the Australian experience a recipe for how to introduce state aid for private schools in the US, glosses over the controversy which ensued in Australia.[4] He reports that, 'With the initiation of aid ... public hostility to government aid gradually dissipated. Once in place, aid programs tended to be accepted by the community at large, if not by the established educational interest groups' (p. 397). West (1983, p. 414) sharply disagrees with Sherman's assessment, noting that the Defense of Government Schools lobbying group was formed as a result of the initiation of aid. Similarly, Hogan (1984, p. 3) reports that, 'For the rest of the 1960s the conflict over education funding at the Commonwealth and state levels was the most important domestic issue in Australian politics. Only Vietnam rivalled the issue of "state aid" for media attention and in its divisive social effects.'

Sherman is correct, though, about the general acceptance of state aid in the long run. As time went on, the government began to contribute substantially to the recurrent (operating) costs as well as capital costs of private schools. The expansion of state aid continued in the 1970s under both the Whitlam Labor government and the succeeding Fraser Liberal government. This trend was less controversial while the economy was strong, budgets were expanding, and support appeared to be concentrated on impoverished (mainly Catholic) private schools. To the dismay of public educators in Australia, however, by the end of the 1970s the private school share of Federal aid exceeded the government school share and was increasingly available to elite 'establishment' schools (Sherman, 1982). Moreover, there was some perception that Federal aid was helping non-government schools expand and increase their enrollments at a time when government schools were confronted with a shrinking total pool of students.[5] It was no coincidence, therefore, that the legal challenge to the constitutionality of this arrangement was brought at this time, and that in 1981 'for the first time in the history of the [Commonwealth] Schools Commission, the parent and teacher representatives on the commission filed a minority report, dissenting from the commission's recommendations on aid to the two school sectors, (Sherman, 1982, pp. 400–1).

The Commonwealth Schools Commission had been established in 1973 by the Whitlam government to provide a mechanism for forging national education policy. That same year the Karmel Report defined the terms for the Commission's initial effort at financing non-government schools on the basis of their *wealth* and *needs*. As Hogan (1984) observes:

> The terms of the modern debate were set by the Karmel Report in 1973. It is not whether there is to be aid for private schools, but how much, in what kinds of ways, according to what principles, and for what purposes? Consequently the main protagonists can be redefined according to their attitude to the Karmel values. Defenders of public schools tend to accept the needs principle whereby some schools get more government money while others get less or

even none. Supporters of private schools tend to see the needs principle as a threat and consequently they argue for a stricter equality of treatment by governments in their funding decisions. (p. 24).

The great success of the Australian approach to funding private schools thus is the establishment of principles for the financial maintenance of educational choice combined with a concern for equalizing educational opportunity via a needs-based funding approach. This approach ensures alternatives to the government schools for those who desire a particular religious education or who object to the educational philosophy, methods, or secularism of government schools. In the latter regard, for instance, many non-Catholic immigrant groups tend to prefer the Catholic schools to the government schools.

The great defect of the Australian approach is that, despite the needs-based principle, in practice significant portions of state aid nevertheless continue to subsidize and encourage an elitist sorting dynamic. This dynamic creams off upper-middle class students and weakens the government schools which still must serve three-quarters of the student population. Thus, at the heart of the continuing tensions over state aid to private schools in Australia are divisive issues of social class, privilege, and elitism versus social justice and the maintenance of quality schools for the masses (Hogan, 1984; West, 1983).

Visitors from North America are surprised by the robust and remarkably extensive array of elite private schools in Australia and even more by the fact that these schools, despite their frequent wealth and 'posh' facilities, receive generous amounts of Federal funding. Indeed, not a few Australians also are surprised and perplexed by this established, but still controversial, fact. Even though there is wide acceptance of the principle of state aid for private schools, many Australians wonder why wealthy private schools should receive substantial aid so long as numerous government schools have less than ideal educational arrangements and facilities (Hogan, 1984; West, 1983). What compelling public purposes justify this policy? The answer seems to be that there are no compelling public purposes, only compelling political reasons for this policy.

In 1983, when a new Labor government in Canberra proposed to end recurrent funding for forty-one wealthy private schools around the nation, this triggered a major and successful protest from the upper-middle class patrons of elite schools (Hogan, 1984). For example, over 5000 attended a protest meeting held at Sydney Town Hall. Though no Catholic schools were on the government's 'hit list', Catholic leaders, fearing that their schools might be next to be hit, joined forces with those demanding a continuation of recurrent funding for the elite schools. Commenting on the influence of the upper-middle class, Hogan (1984) observes that:

In the matter of school funding the case for the schools of the poor is argued (not very well) by the public school teachers' unions and, more disinterestedly, by the [Commonwealth] Schools Commission. Neither, however, has been as effective in the politics of school funding of the last twenty years as have been the organizations supporting middle class independent schools. (p. 2)

That government schools indeed have unmet needs and suffer from the creaming-off process is made clear by one of the most knowledgeable Australian educational experts, Professor Grant Harman. Speaking of Victorian high schools, he says they are:

undoubtedly inferior compared to the better non-government secondary schools. They are also seen to be inferior by parents who send their children to non-government schools, and often too by many parents and students who support public education. I know of no other high school system in the world where so many of those who run the system, from senior officials to school principals and to classroom teachers, send their own children to non-government schools. It is no wonder then that morale and aspirations in high schools are low, especially when so many high school buildings confirm the message of inferiority or mediocrity. (Harman, 1983, p. 31)

In a similar vein, Davidson (1984), commenting on the growing exodus from government schools, remarks that. 'If present trends continue, the middle classes will cease to be represented in Australia's [state] secondary schools except in front of the blackboard.' [6]

Although the dominance of non-government schools over state secondary schools is said to be especially pronounced in Victoria, I heard much the same message that Davidson and Harman articulate from people all around Australia.[7] At the least, it is clear from conversations I had in all six states that academics and leaders in state education systems rarely send their own children to government secondary schools. This is something less than a resounding vote of confidence for government schools. Indeed, the upper-middle class abandonment of government secondary schools (with the exception of a few that are selective and, hence, elite) is such that among intellectuals even committed socialists usually send their children to private schools, being unwilling to disadvantage them by subjecting them to the impoverished academic atmosphere of the depleted student bodies of state schools.

I experienced this problem first-hand when two of my children attended what was described as one of the best government high schools in Geelong, the second largest city in Victoria. By contrast with their experience in the United States, they found that very few of their peers at the school, which was in a middle-class neighborhood, had any academic orientation or any plans to go on to higher education. Some people told us that we had made a mistake, that we should have sent our children to one of the elite private schools in the city.

Our experience gave us a clear perception of how Australian youth are divided and labeled according to whether they belong to the prestige and elite networks of the 'old school tie'. The stark differences are apparent at a glance, as Harman (1983) notes, in the contrast between the frequently inferior quality of state school buildings and grounds and the elegant facilities and grounds typical of the elite schools. But the differences go far beyond such cosmetic considerations; they affect the life chances of Australian youth. For just one poignant example, parents of students at our school lamented that local employers would hire the graduates of local private schools who had *failed* the Higher Schooling Certificate exam in preference to graduates of even middle-class state schools who had *passed* the same important, culminating exam.

In sum, Australian education, like American education, has obvious weaknesses as well as strengths. Both societies desire not only quality and liberty in education, but also equality. This requires a balancing of competing values, which in turn requires a delicate balance between public and private schooling. Clearly, neither society has achieved an ideal balance (*cf.* Boyd, 1984; Murphy, 1980). In the United States, our approach has given the public schools a near monopoly on schooling in many locales. Frequently, this has produced monopoly pathologies, including insensitivity to consumers' desires and a coercive restriction of choice and diversity. Our judicially enforced neutrality toward religion often borders on outright hostility. Local control of schooling via local school districts permits some choice, diversity, and responsiveness to local consumers, but also produces great inequalities due to disparities in local wealth and *de facto* segregation by race and social class.

In Australia, by contrast, the highly centralized state-wide school systems provide a high level of equality in educational services within states, but generally little opportunity for local control or discretion.[8] The tendency toward highly bureaucratized and standardized state schooling is offset by the options provided by non-government schools subsidized by government funds. But the vast majority of Australian youth do not benefit by these options and must rely on the state schools, which are hurt both by the creaming-off process fostered by government support of the elite private schools and by invidious comparisons with them.

If private schools are disadvantaged by the American approach, the opposite is the case in Australia. Indeed, many Australians feel the balance has tipped too much in the direction of non-government schools (Aitkin, 1986; Davidson, 1984 and 1985; Randell, 1984). They fear that this trend could lead to such a decline in support for state schools that there could be a reduction in 'the standard of public education available to the more disadvantaged sections of the community' who cannot afford private school fees (Randell, 1984, p. 7). As Don Aitkin (1986), professor of political science at the Australian National University, observes:

> I am still looking for the hard evidence that supports a view that private schools should be preferred now, where public schools would have served a generation ago. What I can see without difficulty is the continual erosion of support for our public school system, which is the single most important institution in the building of Australian society.

Similarly, Davidson (1985) notes that:

> Under Mr Whitlam, the objective of state aid was equality of educational opportunity by bringing Catholic schools up to the standards of the state schools. We have since moved a long way from that ideal as the rich vie for relative advantage for their children in an increasingly competitive market for jobs and tertiary places, while demanding public funding for their private ambition as of right.

Rather than reducing elitism and social class distinctions, the present scheme of funding Australian schools tends to reinforce these problems. It seems to reflect Aitkin's (1986) comment that:

> In my more cynical moments I come to the view that Australia is a reluctant democracy with hundreds of thousands of would be aristocrats screaming to be let out. That perception always seems most accurate when schools and education are in the field of vision.

These issues of elitism and class conflict are what make state aid remain controversial despite acceptance of the principle of funding sectarian schools. Indeed, the tension between public and private schools in Australia seems to be increasing, as witnessed by the fact that the Australian edition of *Time* magazine featured a ten-page cover story on the problem in May 1987 (Ashenden, 1987).

Because of the high level of state-aid now received by non-government schools in Australia, there really are *two* publicly-funded systems, one *inclusive* (the state schools) and one *exclusive* (the private schools) in student admission policies.[9] The exclusive system is also remarkably free of regulation by the government. Indeed, state-aid comes with so few strings attached that Davidson (1985) contends that private schools escape accountability for the funds they receive. On the other hand, defenders of private schools contend that government regulation has increased greatly and has become not only a burden but a serious threat to their autonomy.

Finally, a point that seems to go unnoticed is that present policies in Australia actually provide the wealthy with a *double subsidy* in education.

They not only have their elite private schools subsidized, but also benefit disproportionately from the absence of significant fees at the universities, where, because of their educational advantages, they qualify for more than their proportional share of the inadequate supply of places available.[10] Thus, higher education for the privileged is substantially subsidized by the less well-off.[11] While the policy of free tuition at universities is attractive because it facilitates attendance by the poor, it also encourages the affluent to spend on expensive and exclusive private schools and rewards them disproportionately for doing so.

Implications for America: Dilemmas of Choice and Elitism

The question for Americans is, would public funding of private schools lead to the same kind of problems here that are experienced in Australia, not to mention many other countries? There is a real danger that it could. What most likely would occur, however, would depend a great deal on the details of the policy adopted and whether sufficient safeguards could be built in and maintained despite political lobbying to relax them. In the Australian case, an influential segment of the population favors elite private schools and even Labor governments committed to needs-based funding have been unwilling (or unable) to cut off, or substantially reduce, aid to wealthy private schools. Thus, they have continued subsidizing a dynamic that tends to undermine the public schools. However, there is some evidence from other nations that aid to private schools can be provided without necessarily undercutting the public schools or promoting excessive elitism. But while the idea of enhancing liberty and choice in education is most appealing, it is critical to recognize that the dynamics fostering negative outcomes are all too easily set in motion.

Since the Australian experience includes many distinctive features that have promoted a preference for private schools, it is hazardous to project from it to what might occur with state-aid in the United States. These features include such considerations as: (i) a British colonial/aristocratic legacy (undisturbed, as in the American case, by a revolution); (ii) a British tradition of dual school systems accentuated by convict colony origins; (iii) highly centralized, bureaucratized statewide school systems and, concomitantly, generally strong statewide teachers unions (iv) a large Catholic population; (v) a much smaller total population and economy than the United States, perhaps increasing the perception of career advantages to be gained via private schooling; (vi) a very large immigrant population in government schools since World War II, which may reduce their attractiveness to the advantaged and upwardly mobile; and (vii) free tuition for tertiary education, making the cost of private schools somewhat equivalent to American families' investment in higher education.

Despite these distinctive features, it is possible to put the Australian experience into perspective by referring to the comparative international research on public and private schools conducted by Estelle James (1984a, 1984b, 1985 and 1986). Her findings demonstrate the delicate balance that must be struck in funding and regulating public and private schools if parity of esteem between them is to be maintained. To begin with, she finds that the greater the cultural heterogeneity in a society, the more people seem to desire homogeneity in their schools and the larger is the private sector of schooling. The frequently superior school climate and student achievement in private schools are associated with their tendency toward homogeneity of values, purpose, and student bodies compared with the more heterogeneous situation usually found in public schools, since they have the responsibility to serve society generally (James, 1986).

Noting that one of the most significant types of heterogeneity involves academic ability, James (1986) comments on the consequences of the sorting of students that is likely to occur between public and private schools: [12]

> Suppose the amount learned by each student depends positively on the ability and prior achievement of other students in the classroom. Then, each student will prefer to be in an environment where the average level of ability is high and, in a mixed group, education can be said to be 'redistributed' from the more to the less bright. In a public school monopoly [involving heterogeneous schools], bright students have no recourse against this redistribution . . . [However,] once private schools are permitted and particularly if they are facilitated by public subsidy, high ability students may opt out of the public system, thereby preventing educational redistribution. Some private institutions will announce that they admit only superior students and superior students will be attracted, even if these schools spend less per student than the public schools, because the superior student input enhances the educational climate and produces greater learning at lower cost. Of course, learning will be similarly hurt in public schools as average student quality falls there (pp. 5–6).

There is an alternative to this outcome, however. Public schools can adopt policies making them more like private schools. As James (1986) puts it:

> If we allowed competition among public schools, many of them would become differentiated according to academic criteria, with students seeking the best school and schools seeking the best students within a large catchment area. Each school would then be more academically homogeneous than the typical public school is today. This is the system used in Holland, where public and private secondary schools are equally subsidized, equally selective and

equally preferred. It is also used in most Japanese high schools and universities. There, the private sector is very large and not heavily subsidized, but the public institutions compete for students, are highly selective and (consequently) are considered the elite first-choice institutions. Similarly, the few competitive public high schools we have in the US ... are relatively homogeneous academically and are on top of the educational hierarchy (pp. 6–7).

One of the problems in both Australia and America is that too many public high schools seem to have erred in the direction of excessive egalitarianism, thereby undercutting their academic standards and reputations (cf. Boyd, 1984; Cusick, 1983; Powell, Farrar and Cohen, 1985). On the other hand, educational systems organized according to highly competitive, meritocratic principles can easily err in the direction of excessive elitism. James (1986) observes that American high schools usually have tried to strike a balance by offering a variety of courses and academic tracks within a single school, which necessitates a large facility, staff, and student body. But what frequently results is the 'shopping mall high school' (Powell, Farrar and Cohen, 1985) in which many students are lost in a confusing melange of offerings, purposes, permissiveness, and people.

Unfortunately, there are no simple solutions to the tension between elitism and egalitarianism. Unless restrained in some way, the 'sorting and creaming' dynamic set in motion by selective, competitive schools quickly creates a number of vexing problems. For one thing, what is to become of the less able and less motivated students who are difficult to teach? As Murnane (1983, p. 406) notes, 'since the population of students is fixed, it is impossible for all students to attend schools with the most desirable student bodies'. Because of compulsory education laws and students' rights to a free public education, 'students who are not sorted into private schools must be educated in public schools' (*ibid*). This ensures that some public schools must bear the burden (and reputation) of educating the less attractive, lower achieving students. Even where public school systems successfully create selective 'magnet' schools that are attractive to middle and upper-middle class families, as in New York City, there is the problem of those left behind in the regular, 'unspecial' public schools.[13] The experience in places such as New York City and Buffalo, New York makes clear what is obvious on the face of it: the morale and character of the regular schools are likely to suffer by comparison with the 'special' schools. If the average or 'unspecial' student is neglected in the comprehensive high school, as Powell, Farrar, and Cohen (1985) show is the case, can we hope they will be better served in an 'unspecial' school?

On the other hand, if the public schools do not create some attractive (and, hence, usually selective) schools, there is the likelihood that their more affluent and ambitious clients will abandon them whenever acceptable private school alternatives are available. By lowering the cost of private school alternatives, state aid to private schools will greatly increase the rate of middle class abandonment of public schools. And, as the economist, A. O. Hirschman (1970) clearly demonstrates, contrary to the popular expectation that competition will spur public sector monopolies to improve their performance, there is a good chance the *opposite* will happen. While competition ordinarily may spark higher levels of performance, when the organization in question is a tax-funded, public quasi-monopoly, such as public school systems, the reverse may be the case. Under these circumstances, the gradual exit from the organization of dissatisfied clients 'is ineffective as a recuperative mechanism, but does succeed in draining from the firm or organization [many of] its more quality-conscious, alert, and potentially activist customers or members' (*ibid*, p. 55). Moreover, as Albert Shanker (1983), President of the American Federation of Teachers, has noted, even a small percentage loss of such clients can be quite serious: 'These are the parents who are active in the PTA, who campaign for adoption of the school budget and who lobby for state and federal aid. [These are the] parents [who] provide a disproportionately large share of the parental participation and political support for public schools.' (p. 475).

Indeed, it would be naive to think that a small percentage loss of the more advantaged and articulate clients would be of little political signif-cance to the public schools. Yet Secretary of Education William Bennett went well beyond this position in advocating tuition tax credits (*Education Week*, 1985). He said that they would not undercut public schools because no more than 20 to 30 per cent of our students would end up in private schools, a mere 10 to 20 per cent increase over the 10 per cent now in private schools. By contrast, Shanker worries about the political clout that would go with an increasing pool of private school patrons. Wouldn't they desire to increase the amount of state-aid they received? Shanker (1983) observes:

> At the present time, the private schools have only 10 per cent of the students, yet the political influence of this single-issue constituency was strong enough to win passage of tax credits in the House and fail only narrowly in the Senate in 1978. In 1980 it succeeded in getting the Republican Party to adopt a platform plank in favor of tax credits — and it won the support of Ronald Reagan. If the 10 per cent now in private schools have so much political power, what can we expect if the public school/private school balance shifts modestly from 90/10 to 80/20 — doubling the private school constituency? (p. 475)

Shanker also underscores the unfair nature of the competition that will occur between public and private schools if the latter receive state-aid but, as the proponents of aid (including Secretary Bennett) desire (*Education Week*, 1985), few state regulations along with the aid. Public schools still would have to meet their diverse obligations to racially integrate students and staff, to educate the handicapped, to retain disruptive students, to employ only certified personnel, and to bargain collectively with their employees. 'What meaning', asks Shanker (1983), 'can competition have when the government compels [public] schools to live with policies which are largely unpopular, exempts private schools from the same policies — and then offers tax credits to help parents take their children from schools which comply to those which do not?' (p. 476).

What easily can develop under these circumstances, and what Shanker (1983) fears, is that the public schools can get caught in a downward spiral of decay, disillusionment, and abandonment, ending up as schools of last resort, populated by those who cannot escape: the disadvantaged of society. What many observers fear has been well stated by Bailey (1981):

> Looking ahead, it is easy to become increasingly pessimistic about public support for the common schools. Major signs, especially continuing inflation, ... an aging population, and an increased interest in voucher schemes and federal tuition tax credits all point to a privatization of educational services and to fewer public resources for education generally. The logical result of these trends is unsettling, to say the least. At the end of this road may well be ghettoized schools for the urban poor, non-English-language schools for Hispanics, racially pure schools for the bigoted, religious schools for the devout, and for the well off, a wholesale reversion to the private academies of the nineteenth century. It is difficult to see how any coherent value consensus in the society at large could possibly survive such fragmentation of educational programs, institutions, and support services. (p. 38)

In regard to these fears, the Australian experience, at least with respect to the well-off, is not very reassuring. We must not forget that at the heart of the success that American public schools have enjoyed historically has been their ability to attract and retain the support of the middle and upper middle classes. As Peterson (1985b), concludes, from his study of the evolution of schooling in Atlanta, Chicago, and San Francisco, the 'common' public school in America:

> did not develop automatically; it had to compete with alternative models of providing education. Its chief competitor was [the European] two-class, dual system of schooling ... If public schools were defined as charity schools for the poor [as under the dual system], they would acquire the ignominious image reserved for almshouses and homes for the incurable. If they were to depend solely on the eleemonsynary instincts of the public, they would have limited scope and be starved for resources. The drive for common schooling ... was thus not simply or even primarily a campaign to bring schooling to the masses. On the contrary, the

campaign focused on making public schooling sufficiently attractive so that middle-class parents would choose these schools over
private forms of education. (p. 11)

As many now recognize, demographic trends in the United States
suggest that, even without aid for private schools, it may be increasingly
difficult for the public schools to retain the support of non-minority middle
and upper-middle class parents. Particularly in urban areas, the public
school population is increasingly composed of racial, ethnic, and language
minority groups (Garms and Kirst, 1980). These groups tend to be less
active and influential politically, and have a higher incidence of learning and
physical disabilities and of single-parent families. As minority groups
increasingly characterize the population of public schools, majority groups
may become less willing to finance these schools and to send their children
to them. Already there is some evidence that the affluent segment of the
baby-boom generation is less committed to support of the public schools
than their counterparts in earlier generations (Odden, 1985). They desire
quality and choice in schooling and can generally pay to get it since they
tend to be double-wage earner families.

If government aid subsidizes educational choice and encourages
abandonment of public schools, within a policy framework that places few
restrictions or obligations upon private schools, what real assurances do we
have, particularly in the present demographic situation, that the societal
outcome will be as desirable as the advocates of unrestricted state-aid
claim? Will Adam Smith's 'invisible hand' really cause innumerable private
choices to cumulate into a desirable 'public good'? Will we be able to
celebrate both pluralism and social cohesion, relying on the tender
ministrations of the mass media to supply the glue that holds together our
diverse society? Or will the absence of more constructive shared socialization erode the fabric that binds us together? One thing is clear: There is a
whole body of theory and research on collective choice that abundantly
demonstrates that rational private choices frequently produce irrational
societal outcomes, the proverbial 'tragedy of the [overgrazed] commons'
(see for example, Barry and Hardin, 1982).

Unfortunately, there is an inescapable trade-off between, on the one
hand, promoting social democracy and social cohesion and, on the other
hand, maximizing educational choice and achievement via selective and
socially segregated schooling. Estelle James is sensitive to this problem and
it is worth quoting at some length her conclusions regarding the experience
in Holland, since they make clear the delicate balance that must be struck in
regulating the balance between public and private schools:

> The extensive reliance on private schools in Holland has reinforced
> the religious segmentation within society. If all groups prefer such
> segmentation, it is pareto-efficient; but a social dilemma exists if
> one group prefers segmentation while another group prefers

integration. Then, a choice between the two policies also implies a choice about the distribution of utility between the two groups. In Holland, the separatists won a clear victory in this struggle.

The separatist-integrationist division did not, however, correspond to a class division; nor has the private school system contributed to class segmentation. This is partially because specific mechanisms, such as restrictions on tuition charges and teacher salaries, have been adopted to maintain equality, and partially because class stratification is, instead, provided by other structures within the educational system. The Dutch system has probably strengthened ... public education, since private school budgets are directly tied to public school budgets, and non-governmental financial sources are limited. This suggests that privatization does not necessarily contribute to elitism, perpetuation of class differences, and weak public schools — but elaborate structural differences between the Dutch and American educational systems and their role in society preclude easy transferability of this result. (James, 1984a, pp. 623–4)

The American tradition has been to resist promoting separatism in schooling, but to preserve the independence of non-government schools. Private schools understandably prize their autonomy, for it is central to their ability to create their distinctive character (*cf.* Rodman, 1985). Thus, present day proponents of aid for private schools want to have things both ways; they want aid but with few or no strings attached. Yet research on many countries, from Australia to Zimbabwe, consistently shows — despite what Milton Friedman says (Friedman and Friedman, 1980) — that if a society desires to subsidize educational choice but retain equality of opportunity, private as well as public schools must be regulated by the government. This is why Richard Bates (see Andrews, 1984) contends that much of the debate over state aid in Australia has been misguided; instead of arguing about the levels of aid that public and private schools should receive, the focus should be on the *principles* underlying the aid and the regulations necessary to support these principles.

Of course, regulating private schools as the price they pay for the aid they receive always is unpopular. Moreover, it produces an irony that often is noted: as state aid increases, state regulation of private schools tends to increase and in time the differences between public and private schools begin to disappear.[14] James (1984a) notes that:

[P]rivate schools in the Netherlands are heavily regulated by government with respect to inputs. Also, but to a lesser extent we find regulations over output characteristics ... These are partially designed to achieve equality, but they come at the expense of choice which the system was designed to ensure... [A]s the private sector grows, through governmental subsidies, it becomes more like the public sector. (p. 624)

An alternative to increasing the regulation of private schools, of course, is to deregulate the public schools and make them more responsive to market forces. But this is controversial and problematic for all the reasons already discussed. The fact that introducing either *more or less* regulation of public and private schools is controversial shows just how difficult it is to close the gap between public and private schools. Ideally, we should seek a desirable middle ground in regulation that avoids the problems associated with the extremes of regulative and laissez-faire approaches. Clearly, it is the excessive bureaucratization and impersonality of many public schools that makes private schools attractive to many parents. The responsiveness of public schools to their clients is greatly diminished by their bureaucratic (non-market) governance system and employee unionization, both of which feed on each other (Boyd, 1982; Michaelsen, 1977). Indeed, a major recent survey of the attitudes of public and private school teachers and administrators shows that the political/ bureaucratic ethos of public schools, unlike the market ethos of private schools, tends to foster attitudes that are inconsistent with the attributes of effective schools (Chubb and Moe, 1986). Consequently, there is a substantial case for efforts to introduce some aspects of the market dynamic into public schools through some measure of deregulation.

Thus, both public and private schools can benefit by emulating each others' strengths (Powell, 1986; Powell, Farrar and Cohen, 1985). And, the end of the road for public and private schools, when both are government funded and regulated — at least to some degree — need not necessarily be bland bureaucracy, mediocrity, and a loss of freedom. Depending upon what a society desires, and what is politically feasible, there is evidence that it is possible to achieve a balance between the extremes of regulative and laissez-faire approaches (James, 1984a, 1984b and 1986). In turn, this will involve striking a balance between elitism and egalitarianism in schooling arrangements, one that provides for excellence and choice, but also equal opportunity, dignity, and respect for the worth, contributions, and rights of all (*cf.* Gardner, 1961).[15] The competition between excellence and equity in American education today, as Strike (1985) observes, is too often cast in terms that pit the need for human capital and economic competitiveness against the Jeffersonian ideal of human dignity and participation (see also Bastian *et el.*, 1985; Katznelson and Weir, 1985). In debating and shaping educational policy for public and private schools in Australia, America, and elsewhere, we need more attention to thoughtful discussions of the full range of issues involved, such as those found in *Schools for the A.C.T.* (1983) and in the works of Hogan (1984) and James (1984a, 1984b, and 1986). Otherwise, we may find ourselves embarked on a dangerous course. In a pluralistic and unequal society, private choice in a subsidized, but unregulated education market easily can lead to divisive societal outcomes that few would desire.

To reiterate, this does not mean that we cannot strike a desirable balance between equity and choice, only that to do so requires a *regulated* education market including private as well as public schools. Besides the options for achieving this suggested by the lessons from Holland and Japan, another alternative lies in some sort of *regulated* educational voucher plan, one with adequate safeguards against racial, ethnic, religious, and social class discrimination.[16] But as attractive as such plans seem to many people, they nevertheless elicit opposition. This was vividly demonstrated in California in 1979–80, when one of the most eloquent advocates of vouchers, John Coons, led an ill-fated campaign to place a voucher proposal on the state ballot (Catterall, 1982). Coons' voucher proposal represented a very sophisticated attempt to balance the values of choice and equity. However, the degree of regulation of private schools embodied in Coons' proposal was unacceptable to the parochial school lobby in California:

> Despite a wealth of state and national publicity, and despite a year-long campaign by Coons to secure the support of organized private school interests, including the Catholic schools' associations, the petition drive did not come close to attracting the needed number of signatures to have it placed on the ballot. In fact, it garnered only a handful of active volunteers and failed to win the endorsement of a *single* organized interest group in the state, including those of private schools, during the campaign. (Catterall, 1984, p. 438, emphasis added)

Significantly, as van Geel (1978) has shown, the uncertainty and complexity introduced by voucher proposals, and especially those that attempt to build in safeguards against what might happen under unregulated plans, become an obstacle to public understanding and political success.

In the final analysis, then, Americans are left with this question: Is it politically feasible and socially desirable to undertake public funding of private schools if it can work constructively only through changes in the system of regulations that are sure to provoke strong political opposition from *both* public and private school supporters? If policy were made solely on rational grounds, and if the advocates of public and private schools were willing to accept regulatory changes that would modify the character of *both* sectors, we might easily achieve and maintain the delicate balance necessary for parity in this arena. But in the rough and tumble world of American politics, with committed lobbies on both sides of the issue, it is far more likely that the balance will shift substantially one way or another. This is what happened historically with the ascendance of the 'common' public schools. We may agree that a more equal balance between public and private schools is needed now, but do we have the political wisdom and ability to achieve and maintain it?

One possible scenario is that public discontent with the status quo in American education will continue to grow, eventually providing enough political support for the forging of a new balance between public and private schools. For instance, mounting national concern about the need for policies that will promote US economic 'competitiveness' — coupled with revelations about such matters as the continuing poor math perform-ance of American students when compared to students from other nations — is likely to bolster the view that improved educational achievement is necessary for better economic performance in this technological age. Suppose, then, that the 'excellence' movement falters, public school performance lags, and there is growing acceptance of research claiming to document the inefficiency of public schools as compared to private schools (for example, Coleman and Hoffer (1987); Chubb and Moe, 1986, forthcoming). If this happens, we then could witness the political sea change necessary for the creation of a new balance between public and private schools (Boyd, 1987).

What is more likely, though, is that we will eschew not only variants on the Australian approach of directly funding private schools, but also tax credits and vouchers as well. Two other scenarios seem more likely. First, the public schools may well be able to maintain the status quo, essentially, through a combination of habituated loyalty, public apathy, gradually improving performance as a result of the excellence movement, and massive institutional strength (see Peterson, 1985a). On the other hand, a middle-ground scenario is quite possible, one that would increase parental choice but still leave private schools without public funds. An important component of the 'second wave' of reform now underway (see, for example, Pipho, 1986) is the increasing recognition of the need for measures to enhance parental choice among public schools and thereby to ameliorate the monopoly performance problems of our public schools.[17] Similarly, as part of the 'second wave' effort to revitalize the performance and career and incentive structures for teachers and school administrators, it is necessary to break up the complacent, consumer-insensitive monopoly relationship that public schools enjoy in relation to most of their clients. All of these goals can be advanced by fostering curriculum variety and differentiation among public schools and then competition among them for clients (Clark, 1985a, 1985b). To be sure, this still leaves private schools out of the picture and liberty still would be inhibited, particularly in terms of family preference for religious education. Consequently, we may look forward to a possible improvement in the balance of choice and equity in education, but the precarious balance necessary for *full choice with equity* between public and private schools is likely to remain elusive.

Notes

1   See table 15 in *Schools for the A.C.T.*, Vol. 2, 1983, p. 67.

2   Figures from table 1.6 in *Australian School Statistics*, 1984, pp. 8–9.

3   For an overview of the history of funding of public and private schools in Australia, see *Schools for the A.C.T.*, Vol. 1, pp. 10–19.

4   Sherman's (1982) analysis is sophisticated, informative, and insightful, but even within the limitations of what he reports about the Australian experience his data could almost as easily be used to make a case *against* the Australian approach to public funding of private schools.

5   This tension particularly comes to fore when there are proposals to expand existing private schools or build new ones in areas where existing government schools are underutilized or are facing the prospects of declining enrollments. In Canberra, this situation led the Minister for Education and Youth Affairs, Senator Susan Ryan, to appoint a 'Committee of Review' to study and report on the potential impact of Radford College, a proposed new Anglican private school (*Schools for the A.C.T.*, 1983). Similarly, *The Australian* reports that, 'The NSW [New South Wales] Teachers Federation has applied under FOI [Freedom of Information] legislation for documents on the [government's] decision to fund years 11 and 12 extensions to [a Catholic systemic senior high school in Dubbo], despite claims by three nearby public high schools that the subsequent drop in their student numbers would affect curriculums in all schools' (Houghton, 1986).

6   Davidson (1984) cites figures drawn from a Commonwealth Schools Commission report showing that the state schools' share of all Australian secondary students declined from 76 per cent in 1975 to 72 per cent in 1982, and that a further decline to 68 per cent is projected by 1987.

7   The author was a Visiting Fulbright Scholar at Monash and Deakin universities during the first half of 1984.

8   The state of Victoria is in the midst of a major effort at decentralization and devolution in its state school system. See Boyd (1984) and Chapman and Boyd (1986).

9   According to Lawton (1985), Australian private schools currently 'receive grants that average about 60 per cent of the expenditure levels of government schools' (p. 82). Less affluent private schools receive substantially more.

10   Underfunding of university-based education in Australia in recent years has produced an annual outcry and debate about the number of additional student places that are needed.

11   For an economic analysis of this problem in the case of free tuition for higher education in California, see Hanson and Weisbrod (1969). For a discussion of the scholarly controversy this research prompted, see Garms, Guthrie and Pierce (1978, pp. 436–40).

12   On this sorting dynamic, see also the similar analysis by Murnane (1983).

13   See the discussion by Metz (1984) of the organizational and political dynamics set in motion by magnet schools.

14   Erickson's (1982) research in Canada suggests that the special qualities of private schools are indeed fragile and easily upset by the addition of government financial aid and regulations.

15   Resnick (1986) reports that recent cognitive research shows that features of the higher order thinking skills associated with elite education are implicit in the basic skills

emphasized in mass education. If, as Resnick thinks, there is some promise that mass schooling might be restructured to make explicit and enhance these thinking skills, then some of the achievement gap might be closed that now makes elite education attractive. See also Berman's (1985) discussion of the Minnesota Plan for school reform, which delays student tracking and specialized programs until the last two years of secondary education.

16   For discussions of the merits of various kinds of educational voucher plans, see Coons and Sugarman (1978); Jencks *et al.*, (1970); Levin (1980);'West (1982).
17   On this increasing recognition, see *Time for Results* (1986); Clark (1985a and 1985b); Chubb and Moe (1986).

References

AITKIN, D. (1986) 'Public education needs disinterested champion,' *The Age*, Melbourne, 16 January.
ANDREWS, N. (1984) 'Private schools promote elitism,' *The Mercury*, Hobart, 18 May.
ASHENDEN, D. (1987) 'Private or state? A collapse of confidence drives parents from government school systems,' *Time* (Australian edition), 4 May, pp. 56–65.
BAILEY, S. K. (1981) 'Political coalition for public education,' *Daedalus* 110, 3, summer, pp. 27–43.
BARRY, B. and HARDIN, R. (Eds) (1982) *Rational Man and Irrational Society? An Introduction and Sourcebook* , Beverly Hills, CA, Sage.
BASTIAN, A., FRUCHTER, N., GITTELL, M., GREER, C. and HASKINS, K. (1985) *Choosing Equality: The Case for Democratic Schooling*, a report of the New World Foundation, New York, The New World Foundation.
BERMAN, P. (1985) 'The next step: The Minnesota plan,' *Phi Delta Kappan*, November, pp. 188–93.
BOYD, W. L. (1982) 'The political economy of public schools,' *Educational Administration Quarterly*, 18, 3 summer, pp. 111–30.
BOYD, W. L. (1984) 'Competing values in educational policy and governance: Australian and American developments,' *Educational Administration Review*, 2, 2 spring, pp. 4–24.
BOYD, W. L. (1987) 'Public education's last hurrah? Schizophrenia, amnesia and ignorance in school politics, *Educational Evaluation and Policy Analysis*, 9, 2, Summer, pp. 85–100.
CATTERALL, J. S. (1982) 'The politics of education vouchers,' unpublished doctoral dissertation, Stanford University.
CATTERALL, J. S. (1984) 'Politics and aid to private schools,' *Educational Evaluation and Policy Analysis*, 6, 4, winter, pp. 435–40.
CHAPMAN, J. and BOYD, W. L. (1986) 'Decentralization, devolution and the school principal: Australian lessons on statewide educational reform,' *Educational Administration Quarterly*, 22, 4, fall, pp. 28–58.
CHUBB, J. E. and MOE, T. M. (1986) 'No school is an island: Politics, markets, and education,' *The Brookings Review*, 4, 4 (fall), pp. 21–8.
CHUBB, JOHN E. and MOE, TERRY, M. (forthcoming) *Politics, Markets, and School Performance* Washington, DC: The Brookings Institution.
CLARK, B. R. (1985a) 'The high school and the university: What went wrong in America, part 1,' *Phi Delta Kappan*, February, pp. 391–7.

William Lowe Boyd

CLARK, B. R. (1985b) 'The high school and the university: What went wrong in America, part 2,' *Phi Delta Kappan*, March, pp. 472–5.

COLEMAN, J. S. and HOFFER, T. (1987) *Public and Private High Schools: The Impact of Communities*, New York, Basic Books.

COMMONWEALTH SCHOOLS COMMISSION (1984) *Australian School Statistics*, 1st ed. Canberra, Commonwealth Schools Commission.

COONS, J. E. and SUGARMAN S. D. (1978) *Education By Choice: The Case for Family Control*, Berkeley, CA, University of California Press.

CUSICK, P. A. (1983) *The Egalitarian Ideal and the American High School: Studies of Three Schools*, New York, Longman.

DAVIDSON, K. (1984) 'Hidden asset of private schools,' *The Age*, Melbourne, 26 April.

DAVIDSON, K. (1985) 'State aid: Time for an accounting,' *The Age*, Melbourne, 28 November.

DOYLE, D. P. (1984) *Family Choice in Education: The Case of Denmark, Holland, and Australia*, Washington, DC, American Enterprise Institute.

Educatin Week (1985) 'Bennett opposed to increased private-school regulation,' 27 March, p. 9.

ERICKSON, D. A. (1982) 'Disturbing evidence about the "one best system"' in EVERHART, R. B. (Ed.), *The Public School Monopoly*, Cambridge, MA, Ballinger.

FINN, C. E. JR. (1985) 'Education choice, theory, practice, and research,' testimony before the Senate Subcommittee on Intergovernmental Relations, Committee on Governmental Affairs, Washington, DC: US Department of Education, 22 October.

FRIEDMAN, M. and FRIEDMAN, R. (1980) *Free to Choose: A Personal Statement*, New York, Harcourt, Brace and Jovanovich.

GARDNER, W. (1961) *Excellence: Can we be Equal and Excellent too?* New York, Harper and Row.

GARMS, W. I., GUTHRIE, J. W. and PIERCE, L. C. (1978) *School Finance: The Economics and Politics of Public Education*, Englewood Cliffs, NJ, Prentice-Hall.

GARMS, W. I. and KIRST, M. W. (1980) 'The political environment of school finance politics in the 1980s,' in GUTHRIE, J. W. (Ed.), *School Finance Politics and Practices, The 1980s: A Decade of Conflict*, Cambridge, MA, Ballinger.

HANSON, W. and WEISBROD, B. A. (1969) 'Distribution of costs and direct benefits of public higher education: The case of California,' *The Journal of Human Resources*, 4, 2, spring, pp. 176–91.

HARMAN, G. (1983) 'The White Paper and planned change for education in Victorian government schools,' *Research working paper no. 83.10*, Parkville, Centre for the Study of Higher Education, University of Melbourne.

HIRSCHMAN, A. O. (1970) *Exit, Voice, and Loyalty; Responses to Decline in Firms, Organizations, and States*, Cambridge, MA, Harvard University Press.

HOGAN, M. (1984) *Public Versus Private Schools: Funding and Directions in Australia*, Ringwood, Penguin Books.

HOUGHTON, K. (1986) 'Teachers plan FOI "guerilla war" on school funding,' *The Australian*, 10 January.

JAMES, E. (1984a) 'Benefits and costs of privatized public services: Lessons from the Dutch educational system,' *Comparative Education Review*, 28, 4 November, pp. 605–24.

JAMES, E. (1984b) 'The public/private division of responsibility for education: An international comparison,' paper presented at Conference on Comparing Public and Private Schools, Stanford University, 25–26 October.

JAMES, E. (1985) 'Public versus private education: The Japanese experiment,' unpublished paper, State University of New York at Stony Brook.

JAMES, E. (1986) 'Comment on public-private school research and policy,' paper presented at conference on Research on Private Education: Private Schools and Public Concerns, What We Know and What We Need to Know, Washington DC, Catholic University of America, 24 February.

JENCKS, C. *et al.* (1970) *Education Vouchers: A Report on Financing Elementary Education By Grants to Parents*, Cambridge, MA, Center for the Study of Public Policy.

KATZNELSON, I. and WEIR, M. (1985) *Schooling for All: Class, Race, and the Decline of the Democratic Ideal*, New York, Basic Books.

LAWTON, S. B. (1985) *A Survey of the Governance of Roman Catholic and Denominational Education in Canada, the United Kingdom, Ireland, Australia and New Zealand*, study prepared for the Ontario Planning and Implementation Commission, 30 September.

LEVIN, H. M. (1980) 'Education vouchers and social policy' in GUTHRIE, J. W. (Ed.) *School Finance Policies and Practices: The 1980s: A Decade of Conflict*, Cambridge, MA, Ballinger Publishing Co.

METZ, M. H. (1984) 'The life course of magnet schools: Organizational and political influences,' *Teachers College Record*, 85, 3, spring, pp. 411–30.

MICHAELSEN, J. B. (1977) 'Revision, bureaucracy, and school reform,' *School Review*, 85, February, pp. 229–46.

MURNANE, R. J. (1983) 'How clients' characteristics affect organization performance: Lessons from education,' *Journal of Policy Analysis and Management*, 2, 3, pp. 403–17.

MURPHY, J. (1980) 'School administrators besieged: A look at Australian and American education,' *American Journal of Education*, 89, 1, pp. 1–26.

ODDEN, A. (1985) 'Education finance 1985: A rising tide of steady fiscal state?,' *Educational Evaluation and Policy Analysis*, 7, 4, winter, pp. 395–407.

PETERSON, P. E. (1985a) Economic and political trends affecting education. Unpublished paper, Washington DC: The Brookings Institution.

PETERSON, P. E. (1985b) *The Politics of School Reform, 1870–1940*, Chicago: University of Chicago Press.

PIPHO, C. (1986) 'Restructuring the schools: States take on the challenge,' *Education Week*, 26 November, p. 19.

POWELL, A. G. (1986) 'School complacency and the future of research on private education,' paper presented at conference on 'Research on Private Education,' Washington, DC: Catholic University of America, February 24.

POWELL, A. G., FARRAR, E. and COHEN, D. K. (1985) *The Shopping Mall High School: Winners and Losers in the Educational Marketplace*, Boston, MA, Houghton Mifflin Co.

RANDELL, S. K. (1984) 'Challenges facing educators in the 80s in Australia,' *Unicorn*, 10, 1, pp. 6–15.

RESNICK, L. B. (1986) 'Instruction and the cultivation of thinking,' paper available through the Educational Research Forum, an AERA sponsored computer network and database operating on CompuServe, 4 March,

RODMAN, B. (1985) 'Independent schools fear reforms threaten their autonomy,' *Education Week*, 13 March, pp. 1 and 14.

Schools for the A.C.T.: How Public, How Private? (1983) Report of the Committee of Review into the Impact of Radford College, Volume 1: Report Volume 2: Appendixes. Canberra, Australian Government Publishing House.

SHANKER, A. (1983) 'The first real crisis,' In SHULMAN, L. S. and SYKES, G. (Eds), *Handbook of Teaching and Policy*, New York, Longman.

SHERMAN, J. D. (1982) 'Government finance of private education in Australia: Implications for American policy,' *Comparative Education Review*, 26, 3 October, pp. 391–405.

SHERMAN J. D. (1983) 'A new perspective on aid to private education: The Australian experience,' *Phi Delta Kappan*, May, pp. 654–5.

STRIKE, K. A. (1985) 'Is there a conflict between equity and excellence?,' *Educational Evaluation and Policy Analysis*, 7, 4, winter, pp. 409–16.

Time for Results: The Governors' 1991 Report on Education (1986) Washington, DC: National Governors Association.

VAN GEEL, T. (1978) 'Parental preferences and the politics of spending public educational funds,' *Teachers College Record*, 79, 3, February, pp. 339–63.

WEST, E. G. (1982) 'The prospects for education vouchers: An economic analysis' in EVERHART, R. B. (Ed.) *The Public School Monopoly*, Cambridge, MA, Ballinger Publishing Co.

WEST, P. (1983) 'Australia and the United States: Some Differences,' *Comparative Educational Review*, 27, 3, October, pp. 414–6.

Chapter 9
Public, Private and Separate Schools in Ontario: Developing a New Social Contract for Education?

Stephen B. Lawton

Abstract

When Premier William Davis announced, on June 12, 1984, that government funding of Roman Catholic separate schools in Ontario would be extended from grade 10 to grades 11 through 13, many questions that seemed resolved when Ontario entered Confederation in 1867 were reopened. What, for example, is the role of the public school in society? Why should the state fund the schools of one religion (Roman Catholic) and not others? Perhaps recognizing the inevitability of these questions, the Premier also announced that a Commission would be set up to look at the funding and governance of private schools in the province.

To understand how it is that Ontario, and four other Canadian provinces that are home to almost eighty per cent of the country's population, have more than one government funded and operated system of education, one must recapture the religious fervour and divisions of the mid-nineteenth century. At that time, the Protestant religious revival and economic dominance in the English-speaking community which led to a single system of schools in countries such as the United States, New Zealand, and Australia, failed to achieve this goal in Canada due to the preponderance of francophone Roman Catholics in Quebec. Instead, both Catholics and Protestants sought protection in their own 'separate' schools, whenever either was in a minority. This legacy, protected in the Canadian Constitution, has imposed a structure on education that has sometimes thwarted reformers, but has resulted in strong public support for education. Yet in Ontario today, given the steady transition of the majority education sector into a secular system of schooling, extension of the Roman Catholic school system is seen as an opportunity for other religious groups to demand public funds for their schools. The tenor of recent court decisions and the general disregard of the report of the Commission on private schools, however, suggest that this opportunity may be lost. An epilogue reports the resolution of the issues by the 1987 decision of the Supreme Court of Canada.

On June 12, 1984, Ontario Premier William Davis announced in the legislature that the government of Ontario would begin to fund Catholic high schools starting in September 1985. This announcement was without precedent, in that it reversed a government policy that had stood since at least 1908, and perhaps since Confederation in 1867, a policy which had been successfully defended in the courts in the 1920s (Sissons, 1959, pp. 96–112).

With the new policy, the Premier announced the formation of three commissions: one to deal with the planning and implementation of the extension of funding to Roman Catholic separate schools (which were already funded at the elementary level by government); one to consider the methods by which government financed education; and one to investigate matters related to the governance and possible direct funding of private schools (Davis, 1984). These actions took place at a time when government was preparing to enact legislation that would guarantee francophones in Ontario the right to control the education of their children, a right contained within the new *Canadian Charter of Rights and Freedoms*.

Taken together, the breadth of the government initiatives suggested an opportunity was at hand to develop a new social contract for education, one which would reflect a broader view of what types of education were in the public interest and deserving of public support, and one which would take into account the religious and ethnic pluralism of Ontario in the 1980s. Yet, even from the start, there were barriers to such a full discussion. First, the government never provided a forum for discussing whether or not it should fund Catholic high schools; the decision had been taken without public debate. Second, since public funding of these schools was the policy not only of the governing Progressive Conservative party, but of both the opposing Liberal and New Democratic parties, as well, there was no debate on the fundamental question in the legislature.

The purposes of this chapter, then, are to describe the historical background of the question of separate school funding in Ontario; to summarize the findings of the private school commission; to note recent court decisions related to the Ontario school system; and to suggest likely outcomes of the current debate on the structure of education in Ontario.

Historical Precedents.

Education in Canada is matter reserved for its ten provinces by the *Constitution Act, 1867* and the *Constitution Act, 1892* with two major exceptions: the federal guarantees for the preservation of denominational and dissentient schools that existed by law in the respective provinces at the time of their entering Confederation (guaranteed by both *Acts*), and the right of French or English minorities to be educated in their own language (guaranteed by the second *Act*).[1] Since the situations differ in each of the provinces, the overall situation is complex.

In the case of religious schooling, Newfoundland has four denominational systems (Integrated Protestant, Roman Catholic, Pentacostal, and Seventh-Day Adventist); Quebec has denominational systems (Roman Catholic and Protestant) in its two major centres but public and separate (or dissentient) systems elsewhere; Ontario, Alberta and Saskatchewan have public and separate systems; and the other provinces have but one public system, though several have made accommodations for Catholic schools within the public system, accommodations not receiving constitutional protection.

In the case of minority languages, one province (New Brunswick) has set up a school system for francophones; in the others, schools for francophones exist within the existing public, denominational, or separate systems. Attempts to recast Quebec's school systems along language rather than religious lines have been stymied by the courts, which have found that government proposals to date violate protections for denominational and separate schools. Ontario is about to try its own foray into this field, with a proposal to set up a homogeneous French-language school system in the Ottawa area.[2] In addition, private schools exist in all provinces, and are given public aid in five (British Columbia, Alberta, Saskatchewan, Manitoba and Quebec).

The history of schooling in Ontario, the subject of this chapter, is closely tied with that of Quebec since, before the formation of the current Canadian Confederation in 1867, the two were governed by a single legislature for a period of twenty-seven years. This legislature often passed distinct laws for Upper Canada or Canada West (Ontario) where both the Protestant majority and Catholic minority were English-speaking and for Lower Canada or Canada East (Quebec) where French-speaking Catholics formed the majority and English-speaking Protestants a politically and economically powerful minority.[3]

The Ontario System to 1985

By the laws in effect in Ontario at Confederation, the residents of a given community could elect a school board of three trustees to build and operate a common school. This school board could requisition property taxes in support of the school and was eligible for provincial grants. However, if the trustees of this common school appointed a Protestant teacher, then Roman Catholic residents had the right to elect their own school board, referred to as a separate school board, and erect their own school, hire their own Catholic teacher, direct their property taxes to that school, and collect provincial grants. Conversely, if the first school board formed in a community appointed a Roman Catholic teacher, then Protestants in the area had the right to withdraw and form their own Protestant separate school board.

Politically, it is clear that provision for separate schools in Ontario, with its large Protestant majority, would not have been made but for the mutual desire of Protestants in Quebec for their own schools in that primarily Catholic society, and the willingness of Catholic legislators there to unite with Catholic legislators from Ontario to assure symmetrical rights for Ontario's Catholics.

At the same time, various Protestant denominations in Ontario repressed their own differences with one another and chose not to demand separate schools for each denomination. It was a great disappointment to Protestant school leaders in Ontario that they were not able to win over all Catholics, and especially the Catholic hierarchy to the ideal of a 'common school' for all.

Through the years, amalgamation of school boards into larger units has brought about some changes in the relationship of the two types of school boards. All but one of Ontario's Protestant separate school boards have ceased to operate schools or merged with the non-denominational boards of education. The one active Protestant separate school board enrols only about 160 elementary pupils in its one school. Catholic school boards, including both Roman Catholic separate school boards and those common school boards where Catholics were in the majority, have been merged into Roman Catholic separate school boards. The level of education these boards are allowed to offer, though, has been a matter of controversy for some time.

In 1871, the Province of Ontario moved to set up a system of secondary schools, and in doing so defined all common schools, including that special form of the common school, the separate school, as elementary schools. Secondary school boards were created to operate non-denominational secondary schools for teaching subjects in grades 9 to 13 (Sissons, 1959, pp. 96–112). Hence, Roman Catholic separate school boards were limited to offering instruction in grades 1 through 8, though subsequent decisions allowed them to operate 'continuation schools' teaching subjects in grades 9 and 10.

Since in 1871 few children were completing grade 8, let alone grade 13, the Province's decision was not immediately challenged by Catholic educators, citizens, or the church hierarchy. But as secondary education became more widespread towards the turn of the century, Catholics pressed for high schools of their own, noting that, in fact, common schools had sometimes offered instruction in higher grades even before Confederation.

In the early 1920s, the Province agreed with Catholic leaders to submit a test case to the courts in order to resolve the question of whether the Province had acted constitutionally in providing for only non-denominational high schools. The final decision was not made until June 12, 1928, when the Privy Council in England (which under the *British North America Act, 1867* served as the last court of appeal) ruled in *Tiny Township v. The King* (1928) that the Province had, in fact, acted constitutionally; that is, the right to separate schools existed only at the elementary level (Sissons, 1959, p. 100).

Between June 12, 1928 and June 12, 1984, the issue of extending the separate school system (or completing it, to use the language of Catholic advocates) was rarely raised publicly. Perhaps the most notable exception was in the 1971 election campaign when both opposition parties, the Liberals and New Democratic Party, took positions favouring such an extension. They were soundly defeated by Premier William Davis' Progressive Conservatives, who argued such a move would require unnecessary duplication of services and would be socially divisive.

Nevertheless, significant changes were taking place. Post-war immigration had led to an increase in Ontario's Catholic population; Irish and French Catholics were joined by co-religionists from countries such as Italy and Portugal.[4] With the increased wealth of the post-war period, Roman Catholics had been able to expand their own private high school system to about eighty schools enrolling 30,000 students in grades 11 to 13. Usually, these private schools operated in the same buildings that housed publicly funded separate school grades 9 and 10. Thus, they were hybrid institutions, part private and part separate, with a given teacher often being employed by both the private school (usually owned by a diocese or religious order) and the elected Roman Catholic separate school board. As well, in the late 1960s French-language high schools, which had operated as private Catholic schools, became part of the non-denominational public boards of education.

Extension Announced

Between the 1971 election and his announcement in the legislature in 1984, Premier Davis had made no indication that the policy of no government support for Catholic high schools was being reconsidered. Though the government has since changed (no doubt in part due to the unpopularity in some quarters of the reverse in policy on this issue by the Progressive Conservatives), the party that has formed the current government, the Liberal Party, continued with the original schedule to extend the separate school system one grade at a time, beginning with grade 11 in September 1985, and to facilitate the *en bloc* transfer of French-language high schools to Roman Catholic separate school boards. It introduced and, in mid-1986 passed, a bill, designated as Bill 30, *An Act to amend the Education Act*, which applied retroactively to legalize the steps the government had already taken.

The entire process has not been without its critics. Yet, with all three provincial parties supporting the policy in principle, there was no political forum in which the decision to extend separate school funding could be challenged. For that reason, a number of opponents sought to have the constitutionality of the proposed bill tested. In particular, they questioned whether the bill is constitutional under the *Canadian Charter of Rights and Freedoms*, which was adopted at the time the Canadian constitution was patriated in 1982 and which came into full effect in April 1985.

Constitutional Issues

The constitutional issues can be separated into two groups: those concerned with the original rights and privileges under the *Constitution Act, 1867* and those related to the *Charter of Rights and Freedoms*. The first category also has two subsidiary questions, whether the Province must extend financing, or whether it may do so under the existing provisions for separate schools or by enacting new provisions for Roman Catholic secondary schools (Finkelstein, 1985).[5]

While it appeared that the question of whether the Province was forced by the Constitution to fund secondary grades in separate schools was answered in the *Tiny Township* case, some argued that either the Privy Council was in error or that new evidence is available that requires a rehearing of the case. Regardless of the argument, if the courts were to find that the Constitution requires funding of high school grades in separate schools, then the same arrangements and restrictions that now apply for grades 1 to 10 in Roman Catholic separate schools would apply.

On the other hand, a more conservative position is that the Province *may* extend financing to grades 11 to 13 in separate schools. This argument is based on the regulatory powers granted by the *Education Act* to the Province over both separate school boards and non-denominational boards of education. That is, just as the Province can set standards for teachers, approve textbooks and the like, so can it determine what programs are offered, as long as it does not 'prejudicially' affect the rights of Roman Catholics to their own separate schools. Certainly, adding grades 11 to 13 or transferring French-language high schools could hardly be seen as prejudicially affecting the rights of Catholics.[6]

An alternative to this latter position is the view that the Province is free to create, as new entities, Roman Catholic secondary school boards (even if it required existing separate school boards to administer these schools) but cannot 'extend' the separate system *per se* since it has been legally defined as an elementary system (a factor 'solved' in the regulations promulgated to fund grade 11 in September 1985 by simply defining grade

11 as an elementary grade). As distinct new creations, the schools of these new secondary boards would be free from any constitutional restrictions that might apply to separate schools — but their creation might be more likely to be seen as a violation of the *Charter of Rights and Freedoms*.

One of the key sections, section 15(1), of the *Charter* states,

> Every individual is equal before and under the law and has the right to equal protection and equal benefit of the law without discrimination and, in particular, without discrimination based on race, national or ethnic origin, colour, religion, sex, age or mental or physical disability.

Further, section 27 states,

> This Charter shall be interpreted in a manner consistent with the preservation and enhancement of the multicultural heritage of Canadians.

In view of these sections of the *Charter*, if the Province now grants a new right or privilege to Roman Catholics, must it not also do so to other religious and even ethnic groups? Indeed, this is the argument of those supporting greater choice and diversity in education in Ontario. They argue that if the Province is to fund high schools for Roman Catholics, they must do so for Jews, Anglicans, Hindus, Moslems, evangelical Christians, and, perhaps, Chinese, Italians, and so forth. Indeed, some argue that Roman Catholic rights to separate schools at the elementary level ought to be extended to other groups as a result of the new *Charter*, even though the rights of Catholics have existed since before Confederation and have therefore been seen as special. Yet others use this same clause in the opposite way, suggesting that it forbids the extension of funding to Catholics and others. (Clause 29 of the *Charter* ensures existing rights to separate schools are not infringed by the *Charter*.)[7] These issues, among others, were considered by the Commission on Private Schools in Ontario.

Commission on Private Schools

In his statement to the legislature regarding the government's new policy of funding Roman Catholic high schools, the Premier acknowledged that the new policy,

> legitimately raises questions about the place of independent schools in our province... (and that) it is timely and useful to review the role of these schools in educating our children (Davis, 1984).

Pursuant to this announcement, Bernard J. Shapiro, then Director of the Ontario Institute for Studies in Education and now deputy minister of education, was appointed as the sole Commissioner for the Commission on

Private Schools in Ontario, advised by a committee of fifteen members appointed by the government. His commission required inquiry on four points:

a) to document and comment on the contribution of private schools in elementary and secondary education in Ontario;
b) to identify and comment upon possible alternative forms of governance of private schools ...;
c) to comment upon whether, with reasonable attendant obligations, public funding of private schools ... would be desirable and compatible with the independent nature of such schools; and
d) to identify and comment upon existing and possible relationships between private schools and publicly supported school boards (*The Report of The Commission on Private Schools in Ontario*, 1985, pp. 1–2).

The Commissioner's report was submitted to the government on October 31, 1985 and released soon thereafter. To date, there has been relatively little public or official interest in the report, in large part due to the salience of the separate school funding issue and, more recently, implementation of the minority (French) language governance legislation. The report is of particular interest, though, because it enunciates principles clearly and possesses a vision of a more heterogeneous educational scene with greater public involvement with private schools through funding and regulation. In considering this report, two matters will be focussed upon: the scope of private education in Ontario and the place of public funding and regulation of private schools.

The Scope of Private Schooling in Ontario

In September 1984. there were 535 private elementary and secondary schools operating in Ontario, enrolling 87,126 students. Overall, about 48 per cent of the schools offered elementary education, 24 per cent secondary education, and the balance both levels (The Commission, pp. 5–6).

Enrolment in private schools grew throughout the 1970s from 2.3 per cent of all students in the province in 1973 to 4.7 per cent in 1983. Growth was higher at the secondary level (a 90 per cent increase) than at the elementary level (a 60 per cent increase), a difference largely reflecting the accelerated growth of Catholic high schools during this period.

Of the 535 private schools, eighty-eight were Roman Catholic secondary schools, all but one of which has indicated they will become part of the separate school system as financing is extended. Excluding these, Ontario has 447 private schools enrolling 53,417 students, 69 per cent in elementary and 31 per cent in secondary programs. Of these 447 schools, 285 (about two-thirds) were religiously defined while the balance (i.e., 182) were non-sectarian. The largest religious sub-groupings, other than Roman Catholic, included the Alliance of Christian Schools (9826 pupils), the Jewish schools (7837 pupils) and the Anglican schools (5089 pupils). Many of the non-sectarian schools reflected a particular philosophy (for example, a Waldorf school, a Montessori school, a military academy, etc.), provided special education for children with learning disabilities, or served as preparatory schools for foreign students wishing to attend an Ontario university.

In comparison to many jurisdictions, the percentage of Ontario's 1,850,000 students enrolled in private schools seems quite small. It should be remembered, though, that most Catholic students in Ontario attend publicly owned and operated Roman Catholic separate schools; in countries such as the United States, Australia and the United Kingdom, Roman Catholics who desire confessional schooling are found in the private sector.

Regulation and Funding

The Commissioner states eight principles that guide his report; three are relevant to discussions here:

III   That ... schooling should be made available in such a way as to: ... c) ensure that, in a pluralistic and multicultural society, schools can contribute to the strengthening of the social fabric by providing a common acculturation experience for children.

VI.   That there should be no legal public monopoly in education, and private schools that meet the minimum standards specified by the government in terms of its obligations to both society and individual children should have a clear status in recognition both of the rights of citizens to make alternative choices and of the general value of diversity; and...

VIII.   That, as a matter of public policy, and so long as the public policy objectives outlined above are not substantially eroded, new initiatives both in the public support of private schools and in the relationship of these schools should be actively developed and tested (The Commission, 1985, pp. 39–40).

To act on these and other principles stated, sixty-one recommendations are made.

To carry out what the Commissioner saw as government's obligation to children and the maintenance of the social fabric, he recommended that all private schools be required to offer a satisfactory standard of instruction covering a basic curriculum including English or French as a first language, the arts, Canadian and world studies, language, mathematics, physical education and science. As well, no school should be allowed to promote or foster racial or ethnic superiority, religious intolerance or other values inconsistent with a democratic society. That some private schools currently fall short of these standards is clear from the Commissioner's report on his visits to over forty private schools.

After some sixteen recommendations calling for the closer monitoring of all private schools, the Commissioner turned to the issue of funding private schools, in whole or in part. He believes, 'constitutional issues aside, Ontario has no obligation to fund schools and school systems other than those currently being supported, but that, nevertheless, new initiatives in this area might be wise public policy' (The Commission, p. 48).

However, in view of constitutional issues, 'the Commission believes that the argument against the status quo on the grounds that it is discriminatory against non-Roman Catholics is a very strong one. On moral grounds, limiting public support to Roman Catholic schools seems indefensible. ...' (The Commission, p. 48). It is even less defensible in view of the proposed extension of funding for Catholic secondary schools since 'this appears to be more clearly an act of political will than a fulfillment of constitutional obligation' (The Commission, p. 49).

Given this position, the Commission felt obliged to make recommendations that would provide equity for other groups, without undue risks, as he saw them, to the ability of public schools to offer equal educational opportunity, something that might be threatened if generous unrestricted funding of private schools were to provide an opportunity for high achieving and more affluent students to become concentrated in private schools.

Recommendations for funding were made in two groups. First, four recommendations suggest modest amounts of direct aid to all private schools (which would be required to meet the conditions previously outlined), either in the form of funding for learning materials or in kind in the form of transportation and classroom space:

> The Commission does not ... believe that such schools have a right to public funding in any way commensurate with that provided to the Province's public schools. The breadth of public purposes served, the access to and the accountability of the schools responsible to publicly elected boards of trustees are such as to (a) place them in quite a distinctive position and (b) entirely fulfill the Province's basic obligation to provide elementary and secondary schooling for its young. Nevertheless, the Commission has also acknowledged that the Province's independent schools both contribute to the richness and diversity of Ontario education and serve some important public purpose by providing schooling for a small but not insubstantial proportion of the Province's elementary and secondary school children. The programmes of limited support

outlined in the recommendations ... are designed to acknowledge this contribution (The Commission, p. 18).

However, to provide an opportunity for equitable treatment, the creation of a new type of school, one which though private would be associated with a school board, is recommended:

That an associated school be defined in law as an independent school that has come to an agreement with a local school board to operate in association with the board and in addition to offering satisfactory instruction ...:
(i) employs only Ontario certified teachers ...;
(ii) charges no tuition;
(iii) is, within enrolment and academic constraints, open without distinction as to race, ethnic background or religion to all persons of compulsory school age who, subject to the appropriate constitutional protections, agree to participate fully in the programme of the associated school;
(iv) is a non-profit organization;
(v) is not designed primarily to offer special education programmes and services;
(vi) reports annually to the school board with which it is associated on its financial and instructional operation;
(vii) is operated by a board of governors, at least half the membership of which shall be composed of parents of students attending the school (The Commission, p. 55).

For funding, it is recommended an annual operating grant (linked to the annual per pupil operating costs of the local board) be shared between that associated school and the school board. Further, it is recommended the two share programs in order to broaden student choice in both.

The Commission rejected the idea of recommending the 'establishment and full funding of elaborate and publicly-elected trustee systems for groups of whatever size that wish to establish an independent, but publicly funded, school' (The Commission, p. 55), an option that would parallel the operation of Roman Catholic separate schools.

The creation of associated schools, the Commissioner believes, would facilitate the maintenance of schools of distinctive character without undermining the public system. To those who might see associated schools as a threat to the common school, he commented that, 'in all but official rhetoric, Ontario has already parted from the common school idea in many ways (for example, the establishment of the separate school, the legitimization of independent schools based on the ability to pay, the frequently homogeneous grouping of children by neighbourhoods, the profound programmatic differentiation both at the secondary level and for young people with special needs, and the self-selection of students into French immersion programmes), each of which can be regarded as socially divisive' (The Commission, pp. 56–57). In all, twelve recommendations are related to associated schools.

Most remaining recommendations concern items beyond the Commission's formal mandate. Eight (Recommendations 33 to 42) are concerned with adding diversity and responsiveness to public and separate schools by requiring school advisory committees, heritage language classes in day school programs, and the like. Two (43 and 44) are concerned with home schooling; three (45 to 47) with religious education; seven (48 to 54) with special education; two (55 and 56) with the Ministry of Education's structure for monitoring private schools; and the remaining six with procedural matters.

The key recommendations in the *Report*, it seems, are those concerned with associated schools. Such an option would be similar to associate schools in Alberta, integrated schools in New Zealand, and grant-aided schools in England and Wales. Though the Commission suggests creating associated schools is a 'low risk' option as far as their impact on public schools is concerned, it is not altogether clear that commentators in those jurisdictions would agree (Snook, 1981). The Commissioner's recommendations clearly represent an attempt to provide greater diversity and choice within Ontario education, and to eliminate the apparent discrimination that exists with public funding of Roman Catholic separate schools.

The Courts Speak

In the first test of the constitutionality of Bill 30 and the extension of funding to Roman Catholic separate schools, the Court of Appeals of the Supreme Court of Ontario, in *Reference Re. Roman Catholic Separate Schools' Funding* (1986) was asked by the Province to answer the following question:

> Is Bill 30, An Act to amend the Education Act (to provide full funding for Roman Catholic Separate high schools) inconsistent with the provisions of the Constitution of Canada including the Canadian Charter of Rights and Freedoms and, if so, in what particular or particulars and in what respect?

In a three to two decision, the Court found the proposed *Act* to be constitutional. Further, they found that once the school system was extended, government support for separate secondary schools would hereafter be guaranteed by the *Charter*.

In their judgment, the majority argued that the collective rights guaranteed by section 93 of the *Constitution Act, 1867* to Roman Catholics and to Protestants could not be infringed upon by the individual rights guaranteed by section 15 of the *Charter*. Further, they rule that section 29 of the *Charter* exempts from the *Charter* any new legislation affecting the educational rights of these groups. Their judgment is based on the use of the word 'under' in the phrase, 'Nothing in this Charter abrogates or derogates from *any rights or privileges guaranteed by or under the Constitution of Canada* in respect of denominational, separate or dissentient schools.' Since legislation by provinces is made pursuant to the Constitution, it qualifies for exemption if it is concerned with Roman Catholic (or Protestant) separate schools.

Thus, if the Province had the power to extend separate schools and separate schools alone *before* the *Charter* came into force, then this power could not be removed by the *Charter*. That is, the *Charter* could not force the province to extend a right or privilege to all religious groups as far as education is concerned in order to extend it to Roman Catholics.

The majority found that, in fact, the province did have the power to fund secondary education in Roman Catholic separate schools before the *Charter* by virtue of its power to regulate education, though they accepted by virtue of the *Tiny* decision that there was no right to this funding. Therefore, the province may provide funding for Catholic high schools now, without providing comparable benefits to members of other religious groups.

'This conclusion' they write', 'does not mean, and must not be taken to mean that separate schools are exempt from the law or the Constitution. Laws and the Constitution, particularly the *Charter*, are excluded from application to separate schools only to the extent they derogate from such schools as Catholic (or in Quebec, Protestant) institutions. It is this essential Catholic nature which is preserved and protected. ...' The judges chose not to rule on whether or not certain sections of the Bill, such as those requiring separate school boards to hire non-Catholic teachers displaced as a result of the policy for a ten-year period or requiring the admission of non-Catholic students in certain circumstances, violate constitutional rights, preferring instead to deal with these matters on a case by case basis. 'In any event, the individual sections to which objection was taken care are severable and do not pertain to the critical aspects of the Bill providing for full funding of separate schools.'[8]

In the dissenting opinion, virtually all of the points made above are rejected. The dissenting judges 'do not accept the proposition that any benefit given to separate schools in Ontario by post-Confederation legislation enacted after the *Charter* by the province under its s.93 power to make laws in relation to education is shielded from scrutiny under the *Charter*. ...':

the *Charter* is part of Canada's Constitution, our supreme law; it establishes a new relationship between the individual and the state. Its text marks the metes and bounds of government authority and individual autonomy. If Bill 30 is inconsistent with the *Charter*, it is the duty of the courts as guardians of our Constitution, to declare the Bill of no force or effect.

In our opinion, Bill 30 is inconsistent with the s.15(1) of the *Charter* which gives to every individual the right to equal benefit of the law without discrimination based on religion. If this right is to mean anything, it must mean at least that the followers of one religion are not to be the beneficiaries of greater benefits provided by law than the followers of other religions. Bill 30 provides benefits on the basis of religion to one religious group only and is therefore in direct conflict with this right.

The dissenters agree that Bill 30 would have been a constitutional use of provincial powers before the *Charter*, but hold this is no longer the case. Further, they hold that section 93 rights are not expandable, so that even if the Bill had been legislated at that time the rights and privileges it provides would not be guaranteed in the same way the right to separate elementary schools are guaranteed. In particular, they 'cannot accept that the word "under" imports the broad and all-encompassing consequences attributed to it.'

> We reject the notion that every future piece of legislation enacted by the province under s.93 which confers rights or privileges on Roman Catholic separate schools is placed by s.29 beyond the purview of the *Charter*. In our opinion, this *Charter* provision cannot properly be construed so as to sweep within its ambit all those statutory enactments with respect to separate schools which may at some future time be passed by the legislature pursuant to its plenary power over education simply because the legislature is acting within its legislative competence.

Instead, section 29 of the *Charter* is seen to apply only to the rights and privileges that existed in 1867 and were guaranteed by the section 93 of the *Constitution Act, 1867*.

In stating that Bill 30 violates section 15 of the *Charter*, the dissenters note it must be given a 'large and liberal interpretation ... particularly so in dealing with religion, so as to give full effect to s.27 of the *Charter* which recognizes the multicultural mosaic of contemporary Canadian society and requires that:

> 27. This Charter shall be interpreted in a manner consistent with the preservation and enhancement of the multicultural heritage of Canadians.

Thus, they see section 15 as pertaining to both individuals and groups. They note Bill 30 is opposed by 'the Ontario Alliance of Christian Schools, by the Coalition for Public Education Ontario Inc. which includes the Anglican Church, the Baptist Convention of Ontario and Quebec, the

Presbyterian Church, and the United Church of Canada, and by the Seventh-Day Adventist Church, the Canadian Unitarian Council and representatives of the Jewish and Hindu communities.' Further, no consideration appeared to have been given by the government,

> to the desirability of extending state support, or further state support, to the denominational education of any religion. While the government appointed a Commission on Private Schools in Ontario ..., the report, issued subsequent to hearing, is not part of these proceedings. As matters presently stand, no government policy has yet been formulated which takes into account the reality that denominational schools other than Roman Catholic exist in Ontario or which seeks to accommodate the *Charter* rights of supporters of those schools or promote the proclaimed objective of s.27 to preserve and enhance the multicultural heritage of Canadians.

Conclusion

What conclusions can be drawn about the evolution of the Ontario educational system? Is a new social contract evolving, one in which the cultural wealth of Canada's many different groups, religious and ethnic, would be preserved and enhanced? In view of the public and governmental response, or lack of response, to the *Report of The Commission on Private Schools in Ontario* and the decision of the Court of Appeal, it appears that this is not the case.

Government policy, supported by the court, is to provide full funding to a complete system of elementary and secondary Catholic schools, and full funding and control over French-language education to franco-Ontarians, but to offer nothing new to all other groups. Why is this the case, given the apparent commitment to equal benefits from the law and to multiculturalism in the *Canadian Charter of Rights and Freedoms*?

This situation may reflect a particular political strategy. That is, the government may believe it is smarter to move one step at a time: first, complete the Catholic system; next, implement French governance of minority language education; then extend support to other groups. To move on all fronts at once would be too much for the public, especially those of British Protestant origin, to accept.

The majority on the Court of Appeals, it has been suggested by some rather cynical commentators, made its decision first and then sought a legal rationale for the decision. This may well be the case; as the review of the constitutional aspects of the issue in the first section of this chapter suggested, there were reasonably sound arguments that could be used to defend any of at least three positions. The Court simply chose to ignore the argument that secondary schools are an institutional form that arose, historically, after the common school, both in Canada and many other countries. Since the functions of the two overlapped due, especially, to low population densities and low participation rates in higher grades in rural areas, one can choose to emphasize either their commonalities or differences. The Court's majority chose the commonalities and concluded government regulatory powers included the power to add secondary grades to separate schools.

Quite clearly, the Court wanted to guarantee government funded and operated Catholic high schools in Ontario, a policy that parallels the rights of Protestants in Quebec and of Catholics in Saskatchewan, Alberta and Newfoundland. Ontario would no longer stand out as the only province with separate or denominational school boards that allowed them to offer only elementary education.

Had the court not taken the view it did, what might have occurred? To consider this, it is useful to focus on who the intervenants were in support of and opposed to Bill 30 and the government's position.

The intervenants supporting the view the court took were, not surprisingly, primarily Roman Catholic separate school boards. It was in their interest to do so.

The composition of opposing intervenants is more complex. Some, such as public boards of education and the federations with teachers in these boards, were opposed not only to extension of Catholic system but also to the possibility of government support for schools for other groups without constitutional protection. Others, however, such as the Alliance for Christian Schools and the Canadian Jewish Congress, may have had an alternative motive. For them to gain the equal benefits promised by the *Charter of Rights and Freedom* , it was first necessary for Bill 30 to be declared unconstitutional. Only then could a bill meeting their desires, one which would recognize the plurality of preferences for different types of education, be developed and introduced. That is, for them, broadening of the education system must be done at once, not in stages. Further, if Bill 30 were unconstitutional, they could then gain the Catholics as their allies in support of a new, broader bill. No such alliance probably would be possible if Catholics achieved their objectives first, independent of the others. This alternative strategy would not have appealed to Catholics in the first instance since it was less likely to succeed than going it alone, particularly once the government had committed itself publicly to funding Catholic high schools.

Bill 30 still has one more hurdle, the Supreme Court of Canada, to which the Ontario decision has been appealed. If this Court, which is expected to decide the case by June 1987, sustains the decision made by the Ontario Court of Appeals, then the issue of the provision of high schools for Roman Catholic schools will be settled, though skirmishes over issues such as student access and equitable funding will no doubt occur (Lawton, 1986; 1987).

For other groups, however, the fight will continue. After a proper interval, Ontario may, in the name of fairness, extend some more generous form of assistance to them as well. In this, it would again be following the lead of the other provinces with complete separate school systems.

If, however, the Supreme Court overturns the decision on appeal, something that is certainly possible, a new phase will be entered, in which Roman Catholics ally with other groups in order to achieve the objectives held in common. In all likelihood, the government would then be obliged to find a solution that reflects the idea that the province would be stronger for supporting its diversity.

Epilogue

On June 25, 1987, the Supreme Court of Canada unanimously upheld the constitutionality of Bill 30. In reaching its decision, the Court addressed three distinct questions:

> First, is Bill 30 a valid exercise of the provincial power in relation to education under the opening words of s.93 and s.93(3) of the *Constitution Act, 1867* ? Second, is Bill 30 a valid exercise of provincial power because it returns to Roman Catholic separate school supporters rights which were constitutionally guaranteed them by s.93 (1) of the *Constitution Act, 1867*? The Court was urged to decide this question regardless of its answer to the first question in order to obviate any further controversy concerning the rights and privileges of Roman Catholic separate school supporters in Ontario. The final question was, if an affirmative answer were given to either or both the above questions, whether the *Constitution Act, 1982*, and in particular the *Charter* [*of Rights and Freedoms*], is applicable to Bill 30 and, if so, to what extent and with what effect.[10]

In the Court's decision, these questions were answered in the most sweeping manner, astonishing even those who had fought long and hard for the extension of Catholic rights. The majority of the Court held (1) 'Bill 30 was a valid exercise of the provincial power to add to the rights and privileges of Roman Catholic separate school supporters under the combined effect of the opening words of s.93 and s.93(3) of the *Constitution Act, 1867*'; (2) 'Bill 30 was also a valid exercise of the provincial power to return rights constitutionally guaranteed separate schools by s.93(1) of the *Constitution Act, 1867*'; and (3) 'Bill 30 ... is protected from *Charter* review... The protection from *Charter* review ... lies not in the guaranteed nature of the rights and privileges conferred on denominational schools by the legislation passed under it but in the guaranteed nature of the province's plenary power to enact such legislation [in relation to education].'

Thus, the Court not only affirmed the constitutional validity of extending the Roman Catholic separate school system in Ontario to include secondary education, it also overturned the 1929 *Tiny* decision of the Privy Council and, by emphasizing the province's complete powers over legislation in the realm of education, indicated that the new *Charter of Rights and Freedoms* has no force as far as educational matters are concerned.

In reaching this decision, the Court commented on the muddled reasoning in the decision of the Ontario Court of Appeal, even though it upheld that decision:

> It is unclear, however, from the reasoning of the majority, if I may say so with the greatest of respect, whether it upheld Bill 30 under the plenary power conferred on the provinces in relation to education ... or because the legislation returned separate school supporters rights and privileges... There are passages which would support either interpretation.

The minority of the Supreme Court, although supporting the decision of the majority, indicated an unwillingness to overturn the *Tiny* decision, finding it sufficient to argue that Bill 30 was a valid exercise of provincial power to regulate education which was beyond the reach of the *Charter*.

The Supreme Court's decision clearly answered the constitutional issues identified in the body of this chapter. Its arguments were internally consistent and logical, having the strength of the arguments used by the minority in the Ontario Court of Appeal's decision.

The Supreme Court's decision was a major disappointment to both supporters of the non-denominational public education system and many private school groups. Little or no public debate on the issue of extending government support to private schools has taken place since the decision, although leaders of private Jewish schools have called for action in the name of equity and one private Christian school has entered into an agreement with a public school board that is reminiscent of the associate school model proposed in *The Report of the Commission on Private Schools in Ontario*.

In the past year, the focus of public debate and, in some cases, a cause of bitter conflict, has been the transfer of facilities from public school boards to Roman Catholic school boards. To date, the provincial government has contributed almost $100m additional funding for school construction in order to salve the wounds (Young, 1988).

There is a new social contract for education in the province of Ontario, but it is one that not all members of the society have signed. The new contract is between mainstream Protestant supporters of the non-denominational public system, English-speaking Roman Catholics, and French-speaking Ontarians. Other groups have been left outside the reworking of the original bargain struck in 1867; their hopes that the new *Charter of Rights and Freedoms* would extend educational rights to them has been committed by the Supreme Court of Canada to an early and final grave.

Notes

1 From 1867 to 1982, the *British North America Act, 1867* (BNA Act), an act of the British Parliament, served as the Canadian constitution. During this period, the final court of appeal concerning constitutional disputes was the Privy Council in England and all amendments to the Act had to be approved by the British Parliament. In 1982, by action of British Parliament on recommendations from the Canadian Parliament, the Act was patriated to Canada and renamed the *Constitution Act 1867*. It can now be amended only in Canada and the Supreme Court of Canada is now the final court of appeal on constitutional matters. The accompanying *Constitution Act, 1982* included the *Canadian Charter of Rights and Freedoms*, which came into full effect in April 1985.

   The key section of the BNA Act regarding education is section 93, which granted exclusive jurisdiction in the field of education to the provinces, with the exception that 'nothing in any law shall prejudicially affect any Right or Privilege with respect to Denominational Schools which any Class of Persons have by law in the Province at Union.' Further, religious minorities with separate schools were granted the right of appeal to the Federal government against 'any Act or decision of any Provincial Authority affecting any Right or Privilege' that they possessed in law at the Union, and the Parliament of Canada was granted the authority to make remedial laws as circumstances required. In Ontario and Quebec, Roman Catholics and Protestants (but not individual Protestant denominations or sects) are treated as a 'class of persons' under Section 93.

   Section 23 of the *Charter of Rights and Freedoms* extended to the two dominant language communities in Canada rights similar to those provided earlier on a religious basis. It states, in part, 'Citizens of Canada (1) whose first language learned and still understood is that of the English or French linguistic minority population of the province in which they reside, or (2) who have received their primary school instruction in Canada in English or French... have the right to have their children receive primary and secondary school instruction in that language....'

   The plans of the Ontario government to realize this right in legislation for its French minority was the subject of a decision of the Ontario Court of Appeal in *Reference re. Education Act of Ontario and Minority Language Education Rights* (47 O.R.(2d)1). The Court's decision recounts the history of French-language instruction for franco-Ontarians. Final action on the minority language governance question took the form of Bill 75, *An Act to amend the Education Act, 1986*, (S.O. Ch. 29 S.257-277.). In general, French-language trustees, with exclusive jurisdiction over French-language instruction for francophone children, are to be elected to public and separate school boards which operate French language schools. (See Humphreys, *et al.*, 1986).

2 Plans for a distinct, French-language school board in the Ottawa area were the

focus of The Ottawa-Carleton French-Language Advisory Committee's 1986 report, *Establishing a French-language School Board* (The Roy Committee).

3   Constitutional protection for Catholic and Protestant schools gave the English minority in Quebec *de facto* control over its own schools since the vast majority of anglophones were Protestant. However, language and religion did not align in Ontario. According to the Census of 1860–61, Ontario had 258,141 Roman Catholics but only 33,287 people of French origin (Forsey, 1987). Most French immigration to Ontario from Quebec occurred between 1880 and 1920.

4   According to the 1981 census, of Ontario's 8,625,107 residents, 3,036,245 or 35 per cent were Catholic, 4,418,960 or 51 per cent were Protestant, 167,320 or 2 per cent were Eastern Orthodox, 148,255 or 1.7 per cent were Jewish, 618,600 or 7 per cent expressed no religious preference, 137,110 or 1.6 per cent were Eastern non-Christian and 7770 had other beliefs. Classified according to origin, 4,487,800 or 52 per cent reported British origins, 652,900 or 8 per cent French origins, 2,610,915 or 30 per cent other single origins, and 782,645 or 9 per cent multiple origins (Statistics Canada, 1983).

5   The appendix to Finkelstein (1985) provides a description of Section 93 clauses on a province by province basis.

6   The creation of a French language school board, such as that proposed in the Ottawa-Carleton area, on the other hand, may well be considered prejudicial, even though proposals would maintain both Roman Catholic and non-denominational French-language schools. (See note 2.).

7   *Canadian Charter of Rights and Freedoms*, s.29, states, 'Nothing in this Charter abrogates or derogates from any rights or privileges guaranteed by or under the Constitution of Canada in respect of denominational, separate or dissentient schools.'

8   *Reference re Bill 30, An Act to amend the Education Act* , Supreme Court of Ontario, Court of Appeal, February 19, 1986. Majority opinion.
    It might be noted the Court's majority ignored the rights of Protestants to separate schools in Ontario and of Catholics to separate schools in Quebec. The original pre-Confederation legislation was very tailored to local situations rather than whole provinces. Had they taken account of this, they might have found Bill 30 faulty in view of section 15 of the *Charter* because the Bill does not offer full funding for separate Protestant high schools in Ontario. That is, though the *Charter* may not guarantee benefits to groups without Section 93 protection, ought it not at least apply to both groups that have such protection? Of course, the question is academic given the small size of the one active Protestant separate school board in Ontario.

9   *Reference re Bill 30, An Act to amend the Education Act*, Supreme Court of Ontario, Court of Appeal, February 19, 1986. Dissenting opinion.
    One could argue that in accepting Bill 30 for themselves and not insisting that the government extend assistance to other religious groups, Roman Catholics in Ontario are falling short of the ideals set in Vatican II's *Declaration on Christian Education*, which states, '...the (Roman Catholic) Church esteems highly those civil authorities and societies which, bearing in mind the pluralism of contemporary society and respecting religious freedom, assist families so that the education of their children can be imparted in all schools according to the individual moral and religious principles of the families.'

10 *Reference re Bill 30, An Act to Amend the Education Act (Ont.)* [1987] 1 S.C.R. 1148.

These questions parallel those identified in the body of the chapter: the first two concerns rights guaranteed by the original constitution, concerning whether the province *may* extend funding and whether the province *must* extend funding; the third concerns application of s.15(1) and s.27 of the *Charter*.

11   The Supreme Court of Canada's arguments parallel, in many ways, those used in a 1904 decision by the Supreme Court of Kansas in disallowing the levying of student fees in Kansas high schools on the grounds that they were part of a system of free 'common schools' (*Board of Education of the City of Lawrence v. Dick et al.*).

References

Board of Education of the City of Lawrence v. Dick, et al. Supreme Court of Kansas, December 1, 1904, 78 Pacific 812.

Canada Act 1982 (UK) (1982) c.11.

COMMISSION ON PRIVATE SCHOOLS IN ONTARIO (1985) *The Report of The Commission on Private Schools in Ontario*. (The Shapiro Commission) Toronto, The Commission.

A Consolidation of the Constitution Acts 1867 to 1982 (1986) January 1, Ottawa, Department of Justice, Canada.

DAVIS, W. G. (1984) Statement to the Legislature, June 12, 1984. Appendix A in (1985) *The Report of the Commission on Private Schools in Ontario*, Toronto, The Commission on Private Schools in Ontario, October, pp. 73–76.

FINKELSTEIN, N. (1985) Legal and Constitutional Aspects of Public Funding for Private Schools in Ontario, Appendix D in (1985) *The Report of the Commission on Private Schools in Ontario*, Toronto, The Commission on Private Schools in Ontario, October, pp. 81–108.

FORSEY, E. (1987) 'Separate Schools' *The Globe and Mail*, 4 March.

HUMPHREYS, E. H., LAWTON, S. B., TOWNSEND, R. G., GRABB, V. E. and WATSON, D. M. (1986) *Alternative Approaches to Determining Distribution of School Board Trustee Representation, Vol. I: Trustee Representation: Theory and Practice in Canada*, Toronto, Ontario Ministry of Education.

LAWTON, S. B. (1986) A Case Study of Choice in Education: Separate Schools in Ontario. *Journal of Education Finance*, 12: 1 Summer 36–48.

LAWTON, S. B. (1987) *The Price of Quality: The Public Finance of Elementary and Secondary Education in Canada*, Toronto, The Canadian Education Association.

THE OTTAWA-CARLETON FRENCH-LANGUAGE ADVISORY COMMITTEE (The Roy Committee) (1986) *Establishing a French-language School Board*, December Ottawa, The Committee.

Re. Education Act of Ontario and Minority Language Education Rights, (1984) 47 O.R. (2d)1.

Reference Re Bill 30, An Act to Amend the Education Act (Ont.) [1987] 1 S.C.R. 1148.

Reference Re. Roman Catholic Separate High Schools' Funding, (1986) 13 O.A.C. 241.

Roman Catholic Separate School Trustees for Tiny v. The King, (1928) A.C. 363.

SISSONS, C. B. (1959) *Church and State in Canadian Education* , Toronto, The Ryerson Press.

SNOOK, I. (1981) The Integration Act and Its Aftermath, in MCGEORGE, C. and SNOOK, I. (eds) *Church, State and New Zealand Education*, Wellington, Price Milburn, pp. 45–58.

STATISTICS CANADA (1983) *1981 Census of Canada*, (Volume 3-Profile series B) Catalogue 95-942. Ottawa: Statistics Canada.

YOUNG, M. (1988) 'The history of the conflict in Hamilton over the transfer of schools to the separate board'. The Ontario Institute for Studies in Education. Unpublished class paper.

Chapter 10
Financing Private Schools:
The West German Case

Manfred Weiss

Introduction

Although the right to establish private schools is constitutionally guaranteed in the Federal Republic of Germany and considerable public subsidies are granted to many privately run institutions, non-state education traditionally plays a less important role than in most other Western countries. In 1986, only 5.8 per cent of pupils at general schools and 6.7 per cent of pupils attending vocational schools were enrolled in private institutions. However, a comparison of the development of enrollments at private and state general schools since the mid-1970s does indicate a growing interest in private education (see table 1).[1] This coincided with shrinking public budgets and a severe decline in enrollments that started in 1972 at the primary level and has now reached the secondary schools.[2] This development intensified the competition between private and state schools (which particularly the latter found threatening) and has made the relation between public and private schools a topic of growing public concern and scholarly debate. In this context, an important issue is the financing of non-state education. The problems related to this area are the focus of this contribution. After a brief survey of the development of enrollments at state and private schools, some of the fundamental legal regulations which are of importance for the financing of private schools will be outlined. This will be followed by a short description of the financing structure (sources of finance) of private educational establishments. The final section will evaluate the system of private school financing as currently practiced in the Federal Republic of Germany, whereby different criteria will be applied.

Structure and Quantitative Development of the Private School Sector in the Federal Republic of Germany

From the statistics compiled in tables 1–3, the following conclusions can

Manfred Weiss

be drawn:

- In 1986 nearly half of the pupils attending private general schools were enrolled in *gymnasien*, representing about 11 per cent of the total of pupils at this type of school (see table 1). The majority of the pupils (48.5 per cent) of private vocational schools attended specialized technical colleges (39.8 per cent of the total of pupils) (see table 2).
- From 1960 to 1986 the proportion of the total student population attending private general schools increased from 2.8 per cent to 5.8 per cent, the proportion attending private vocational schools from 4.5 per cent to 6.7 per cent.
- A comparison of the changes in enrollments in the state and private *general* educational sector since the mid-1970s, when the decline in pupil numbers set in, reveals a distinct trend in favor of the private schools (with one exception — evening schools/*Kollegs*). The private pupil population was in part still expanding when the state schools were already experiencing a significant drop in pupil numbers.[3] This disparate development is especially conspicuous in the case of the comprehensive schools and is a result of the major expansion of the Waldorf schools (see table 3a).[4]
- An inconsistent picture emerges when trends in the vocational sector are compared according to type of school. Seen as a whole, there was a development in favor of the public sector, due to increased state involvement in vocational education. While enrollments in the public sector increased by 24 per cent between 1975 and 1986, in private schools they remained nearly at the 1975 level (see table 3b).
- When compared according to providing body, the quantitatively most important group of private schools turn out to be the church schools, which were attended in 1983 by more than 80 per cent of the pupils at private general schools (62.8 per cent Roman Catholic, 18.6 per cent Lutheran Protestant schools); about 10 per cent attended schools which belong to the 'Association of Freely Supported Schools'; 7.5 per cent were enrolled in Waldorf schools and about 1 per cent in private boarding schools (*Landerziehungsheime*).

Legal Regulations

The right to establish private schools is guaranteed in the Federal Constitution (Article 7). Private schools cannot, however, operate independently

Table 1: Pupils at private general schools according to types of schools (1960–1986)

Year	Total	Percentage of the private school pupils in:						Private school pupils as percent of the total of pupils in:					
		primary schools and Hauptschulen	special schools	intermediate schools (Realschulen)	grammar schools (Gymnasien)	comprehensive schools/ Waldorf schools	evening schools and Kollegs	primary schools and Hauptschulen	special schools	intermediate schools (Realschulen)	grammar schools (Gymnasien)	comprehensive schools/ Waldorf schools	evening schools and Kollegs
1960	200079	12.6	6.8	17.6	57.2	5.8		0.5	9.5	8.2	13.4		
1965	229706	11.5	6.6	19.9	55.2	5.3	1.6	0.5	7.9	8.0	13.2		23.0
1970	289782	11.9	8.5	19.0	53.0	5.1	2.6	0.5	7.6	6.4	11.1		28.2
1975	352211	12.9	9.7	17.8	50.6	6.3	2.8	0.7	8.7	5.5	9.6	13.3	26.1
1980	417776	12.0	10.0	19.9	48.4	7.7	1.9	1.0	11.8	6.1	9.5	14.6	20.4
1981	422293	11.9	9.9	19.9	48.2	8.1	2.0	1.1	12.4	6.3	9.7	15.2	19.7
1982	421504	11.7	9.8	19.7	48.1	8.7	1.9	1.1	13.0	6.5	9.9	16.3	18.7
1983	418808	11.8	9.8	19.6	47.9	9.1	1.8	1.2	13.7	6.8	10.2	17.0	17.7
1984	412233	11.8	9.8	19.3	47.6	9.7	1.8	1.2	14.3	7.0	10.6	18.2	17.3
1985	405556	11.8	10.0	18.9	47.3	10.3	1.7	1.2	15.0	7.3	10.9	19.3	16.9
1986	400703	11.7	10.1	18.6	46.5	11.3	1.8	1.3	15.4	7.5	11.1	19.0	17.5

Source:
DER BUNDESMINISTER FÜR BILDUNG UND WISSENSCHAFT (BMBW), 'Grund- und Strukturdaten' 1986/87, 1987/88; Statistisches Bundesamt, 'Bildung im Zahlenspiegel' 1987; own calculations.

Table 2: Pupils at private vocational schools according to types of schools (1960–1986)

Year	Total	Percentage of the private school pupils in:						Private school pupils as percent of the total of pupils in:				
		part-time vocational schools	institutions for supplement vocational training	full-time vocational schools	senior technical schools	specialized technicals schools	vocational schools in total	part-time vocational schools	institutions for supplement vocational training	full-time vocational schools	senior technical schools	specialized technicals schools
1960	88282	14.9		46.5		38.7	4.5	0.8		29.5		24.1
1965	101629	15.7	3.7	41.2		39.5	4.7	0.9	7.2	25.0		27.5
1970	121636	18.9	3.1	35.2	1.6	41.3	5.9	1.4	9.3	20.9	3.2	30.0
1975	186471	14.3	1.4	33.1	2.4	48.8	8.1	1.6	9.4	20.9	3.7	43.1
1980	171422	22.5	1.3	27.7	2.0	46.5	6.4	2.0	10.0	13.5	2.5	41.6
1981	181999	22.4	1.1	26.6	1.9	47.9	6.8	2.1	9.1	13.1	2.2	42.8
1982	185594	22.2	0.8	27.3	1.8	47.8	6.9	2.2	7.5	12.8	2.1	42.7
1983	185446	23.4	0.7	27.1	1.7	47.1	6.8	1.6	7.9	12.4	2.1	42.5
1984	186622	23.9	0.6	26.6	1.7	47.3	6.8	2.4	9.0	12.4	2.2	42.5
1985	188525	23.9	0.4	25.8	1.7	48.2	6.8	2.4	8.4	12.4	2.3	42.5
1986	180516	24.7	0.3	25.0	1.9	48.5	6.7	2.3	6.7	11.9	2.5	39.8

Source:
DER BUNDESMINISTER FÜR BILDUNG UND WISSENSCHAFT (BMBW), 'Grund- und Strukturdaten' 1986/87, 1987/88; Statistisches Bundesamt, 'Bildung im Zahlenspiegel' 1987; own calculations.

Table 3: Pupils at state and private general and vocational schools according to types of schools in indices (1975 = 100)

a)

Year	Total		primary schools and Hauptschulen		special schools		intermediate schools (Realschulen)		grammar schools (Gymnasien)		comprehensive schools/Waldorf schools		evening schools/Kollegs	
	prive.	state	prive.	state	prive.	state	prive.	state	prive.	state	prive.	state	prive.	state
1975	100	100	100	100	100	100	100	100	100	100	100	100	100	100
1980	119	90	111	78	123	87	133	113	114	114	146	131	81	112
1981	120	86	111	74	123	82	134	111	114	114	156	133	84	121
1982	120	82	109	70	121	77	133	107	114	110	167	132	80	123
1983	119	78	109	66	121	72	131	101	113	104	173	136	74	122
1984	117	73	107	62	119	68	127	94	110	98	182	126	73	122
1985	117	70	105	59	119	64	122	87	108	92	190	122	71	124
1986	114	67	103	58	119	62	119	81	105	88	206	135	72	119

b)

Year	Total		part-time vocational schools		institutions for supplementary vocational training		full-time vocational schools		senior technical schools		specialized technical schools	
	prive.	state	prive.	state	prive.	state	prive.	state	prive.	state	prive.	state
1975	100	100	100	100	100	100	100	100	100	100	100	100
1980	92	121	144	120	84	78	77	147	157	112	88	93
1981	98	121	153	118	79	82	79	155	155	126	96	97
1982	100	121	155	116	61	77	82	167	153	134	97	99
1983	100	122	163	117	47	57	81	170	144	126	96	98
1984	100	124	167	121	42	44	80	168	143	118	97	99
1985	101	125	169	122	32	36	79	165	146	114	100	102
1986	101	124	167	120	23	34	73	160	153	115	95	109

Source:
DER BUNDESMINISTER FÜR BILDUNG UND WISSENSCHAFT (BMBW), 'Grund- und Strukturdaten' 1986/87, 1987/88; Statistisches Bundesamt, 'Bildung im Zahlenspiegel' 1987; own calculations.

197

of the state. They are subject to state supervision and 'substitute schools', i.e. a school of a type which also exists in the state educational sector, must have a license from the state (the Ministry of Education of a Land). The state is legally obliged officially to recognize the substitute school if it meets the criterion of 'equivalence', i.e., if it is not inferior to public schools in terms of its educational aims, facilities, teachers' qualifications, and as long as it does not promote discrimination of pupils according to parental means. The constitution requires the fulfillment of additional conditions for the establishment of private primary schools.[5] The main motive for this restriction is the interest of the state in pupils from all sectors of the population receiving a common basic education.

Those private schools which have no counterpart in the public school system ('supplementary schools') are not obliged to have a license, but must give formal notice of their establishment. These schools are to be found almost exclusively in the vocational education sector.

The division of private schools into 'substitute' and 'supplementary' schools has manifold and far-reaching consequences, especially for the financing of the schools. According to a ruling by the Federal Administrative Court in 1966, only the substitute schools have a legal claim to state financial support.[6] Supplementary schools do not belong to the official circle of beneficiaries (although some *Länder* nevertheless grant support). As to the extent of the claim, the Federal Administrative Court only concedes financial support for the *maintenance* of the schools (not for their establishment). It is important to point out, that the state is not legally bound either to provide complete alimentation or to safeguard the existence of a particular substitute school, but only that of the private school *system*.[7] The Federal Administrative Court has ruled that the minimum level of the claim to financial support should be adequate effectively to prevent financial decline and eventual collapse. The costs of the corresponding regular public schools represent the upper limit for the claim to financial support.

Detailed legal regulations for the private school system including its financing are to be found in the relevant laws of the individual *Länder*, which are according to the constitution (Article 20,1) responsible for the educational system (for details, see Vogel, 1984). Although there is a clear regulation in the Federal Constitution, the legislation of the *Länder* is by no means uniform and usually contains stipulations for the granting of public funds which go beyond the legal preconditions anchored in the Constitution (the schools, for example, must be non-profit institutions; in some *Länder* they must relieve state education). Considerable differences exist especially with regard to the regulation of state financial assistance: schools entitled to official support, stipulations of the purpose for which the money is to be used, and amount of financial assistance.

Sources of Financing

The most important financial sources for private institutions, the quantitative significance of which may vary according to the type of school ('substitute' or 'supplementary', primary or secondary, providing body etc.) are: (1) school fees, (2) public subsidies, (3) grants from the providing bodies, and (4) donations. In a wider sense, services that are performed free of charge have to be added, for example, free teaching by members of religious orders at denominational schools.

The vast majority of private schools depend on *school fees*. According to an investigation by the author in 1985, Lutheran Protestant schools with residences for pupils charge on average 850DM per month for accommodation. Schools without residences charge either no fees or only a small amount (30–100DM per month). A similar system is reported for Roman Catholic schools. Catholic boarding schools charge an average monthly amount of 500 to 600DM. The Association of German Private Schools (non-denominational schools) quotes a monthly rate of 170 to 280DM for 'substitute' schools. The fees for private (non-denominational) boarding schools are considerably higher (1500 to 2000DM per month). At the Waldorf schools, the amount of school fees is fixed by the parents themselves on the basis of their financial capacity and willingness. Tables of standards provide a means of orientation. In 1986, the standing contributions of parents amounted to an average of 176DM, with donations included, per pupil and month.

Public financial aid is given in different ways (Vogel, 1984, pp. 126ff.):

(1) *as a regular financial aid* in the form of contributions to the recurrent costs[8] differentiated according to types of school;
(2) as *subsidies* (in some *Länder*), for example, as old-age pensions for teachers, building costs, expenses for teaching materials;
(3) as *reimbursement of school fees* (in Bavaria only) and costs for student conveyance (in some *Länder*);
(4) as *leave* granted to teachers of public schools to perform educational services at private schools, partly with continued payment of wages, set off against the financial aid, partly without continued payment, but with a contribution to the old-age pensions.

On average 4578DM were spent per private pupil (general schools and vocational schools) by the *Länder* in 1983 (Holtappels and Rösner, 1986, p. 232).[9] Between 75 per cent and 90 per cent of the recurrent costs of private schools are covered by these subsidies. *Grants from the providing bodies* of private schools are particularly important for the denominational schools. Since they usually receive state aid at the same time, these schools either charge small amounts or sometimes no fees at all. Representative figures on the support of church providing bodies are not yet available. The same applies to private donations.

Manfred Weiss

Evaluation of the System of Private School Financing

This section is concerned with the evaluation of the system of private school financing in the Federal Republic of Germany and proposed modifications with regard to the following four criteria:

(1) responsiveness to consumers,
(2) internal efficiency: cost and effectiveness of production,
(3) compatibility with goals of distributional policy,
(4) equity and social equality.

Responsiveness to Consumers

The provision of educational services in accordance with parents' preferences, which has become a question of growing concern in recent years, requires consideration of two aspects: (a) the *structure* and (b) the *quantity* of educational supply and demand.

Structure

As regards the structure of educational supply, there should be no doubt that state financial aid, which is made subject to a large number of conditions, has a restrictive effect on the provision of a manifold educational supply. The main beneficiaries are the 'substitute' schools, which tend to be closely aligned to state schools (exception: Waldorf schools). The present practice of private school financing leaves little room for special types of education. Yet recent developments suggest that a growing number of parents prefer those schools that clearly deviate in their profile from state schools. This can be observed not merely in the case of the established, traditional alternative schools, such as the Waldorf schools; new concepts such as, for instance, those offered at the 'free schools', are also enjoying increased popularity, particularly among followers of the ecologist and counter-cultural movements (Preuss-Lausitz and Zimmermann, 1984). A change in the restrictive state financial assistance as currently practiced would be desirable in order to achieve greater responsiveness to consumers, and has in fact repeatedly been called for by representatives of private educational institutions.

However the limits to the realization of greater plurality should not be disregarded. An expansion of freedom of choice in the educational system may conflict with societal interests. This aspect plays a role, for example, in conjunction with the recognition of 'free schools' in Germany. Should state approval and public financial aid be granted to schools that radically reject the functions of socialization and allocation, traditionally regarded as being

constitutive of educational institutions, and consider it their main purpose
to qualify their pupils for a counter-cultural, post-materialist lifestyle?

From a societal point of view, due consideration must also be given to
the possible repercussions which an expansion of choice may have for
social cohesion. Since parents tend to choose schools that match their
religious, ideological and political attitudes most closely, greater variety
will inevitably reinforce segregation. Some scholars are evidently prepared
to accept this, arguing that a system of unfettered educational choice would
not only best serve private interests but also help to keep out of the schools
the sort of conflicts resulting from divergent values, norms and convictions
which emerged, for example, in the Federal Republic, particularly in
connection with the controversy over the introduction of comprehensive
schools (Hanf, 1983). Other scholars, however, take the opposite view and
point out that for a democratic society to function the socialization of the
young requires heterogeneous school environments[10] that enable students
to experience the diversity of backgrounds and viewpoints necessary for
forming democratic values (understanding and tolerance of different
opinions, constructive coping with conflict, etc.) (Levin. 1983; Blue
Muller, 1983).[11]

Even if there were no societal arguments against an expansion of
educational choice, the demographic decline in the Federal Republic alone,
which will continue in the 1990s and will cause a zero sum situation at
regional level in many areas, limits the degree to which society can respond
to diverse educational demands: if the educational demands of one group
are met, those of other groups cannot be satisfied. In a conflict like this, it is
hardly possible to legitimate the fulfillment of particularistic educational
demands at the expense of the majority. In view of the demographic
development, the Federal Constitutional Court decided in a recent ruling
that the legislator is not obliged to support the private school system
without taking into consideration the decreasing enrollments in the state
school sector.

Quantity of supply and demand

The existence of 'waiting lists' for some private schools can be regarded as
an indicator for discrepancies between supply and demand, which are in
part attributable to restrictions in the financing, for example, the fact that
state financial aid generally is not available for the establishment of private
'substitute schools', but only for their maintenance. Most affected by this
are the non-denominational schools which are not supported by financially
well-situated providing bodies. What makes the establishment of new
schools all the more difficult is the practice of some *Länder* of supporting
the 'substitute schools' only after a 'probationary period' sometimes lasting
several years.

There is also the question of what influence parental participation in school financing has on the demand for private educational services. Due to the lack of empirical evidence on the 'price elasticity of demand' we can only go on assumptions. First, it can be assumed that the influence on demand depends at what level of private financial participation changes are made. If the state takes over the full costs of the 'substitute' schools, which are already supported by public resources to a large extent (particularly those provided by church bodies), there is not likely to be any change in demand worth mentioning. A stronger effect could be assumed in the case of the 'supplementary' schools.

How flexible demand reacts to changes in prices of private educational services depends on what other factors determine the decision of parents to choose private education and what weight is attached to them in comparison with the costs. An important determinant is the educational preferences of parents. As we know, these preferences reflect relatively stable value patterns that differ among social classes. Diverging preferences resulting from these value patterns are not likely to be compensated by free provision of educational services, or only to a limited extent. An empirical proof of this may be seen in the fact that in Germany the utilisation of free education at public *gymnasien* by working class children continues to remain relatively low: in spite of educational expansion and reform, in 1985 only eleven out of 100 working class children attended these schools in comparison with more than forty out of 100 children of white collar workers and fifty out of 100 children of state officials (Klemm, 1987, p. 83).

It may also be assumed that the cost factor — at least within certain limits — will not greatly restrict the realization of the educational aspirations of the education-conscious middle and upper classes. Since it is precisely parents from these backgrounds who take greatest advantage of private education, demand would probably be only slightly affected if the state were to take over the full costs (as is demanded by spokesmen for private schools with the argument that all parents should be able to choose without financial burden); the 'consumer surplus' would, however, increase.

Even if these assumptions should turn out to be wrong and full financing of the costs by the state did make private educational services attractive to groups who had not hitherto utilized them, this need not necessarily entail an increase in the total level of demand. It is quite possible that, once the selective instrument of 'school fees' were removed, the private schools would implement other mechanisms of selection to ensure that the composition of the student body, which is usually a feature of decisive impact on the attractiveness of a private school to its clientele, does not change.[12] Taken as a whole, giving new groups access to private schools may even call forth a decline in demand, depending on how severe the loss of appeal to the traditional clientele is. Thus the thesis that private educational institutions could be made accessible to large parts of the population by full state financing (Hardorp, 1983) must be met with scepticism.[13]

Internal Efficiency: Cost and Effectiveness of Production

In this section we shall focus on (a) the efficiency of regional educational supply and (b) the efficiency of the production process.

Regional Supply

Improving choice in the educational system will lead to inefficiency in the regional educational supply, if this development is accompanied by 'diseconomies of scale', i.e. higher unit costs due to the distribution of educational production to many small (public and private) schools.[14] In that case, higher average costs would be the price for greater diversity.

Particularly in times of declining enrollments, it will be difficult to reconcile diversity and efficient use of scarce resources. The currently dramatic enrollment decline in the Federal Republic has resulted in a considerable increase in the unit costs in the public school system (Weiss and Weishaupt, 1989) — in part as a consequence of underutilized school resources. The possibilities for changing this situation by adapting resources are limited.[15] It will also become increasingly difficult for the local authorities to offer secondary education with a sufficient degree of internal differentiation, especially if the traditional school structure (the coexistence of three separate types of secondary school) is retained. This can also be expected to have implications for the effectiveness of the schools. An expansion of private schooling would bring further disadvantages for the public educational system. It may therefore be assumed that in the future the policy of the Länder as regards licencing and financing private schools will become more restrictive.

Efficiency of Production

A central thesis concerning educational financing states that private participation in the costs positively affects motivation, effort and involvement of parents, pupils, and teachers.[16] The crucial question from the point of view of efficiency is whether this has — according to the concept of X-(in) efficiency[17] (Leibenstein, 1966) — implications for the costs or/and effectiveness of school operation.

As far as the aspect of *costs* is concerned, it has not yet been possible to prove convincingly the clear superiority of private schools, as was expected and as has often been claimed by representatives of these schools. Comparisons of the costs of state schools and Waldorf schools produced divergent results. According to calculations of the Free Pedagogic Centre of the Waldorf School Pedagogics (*Freies Pädagogisches Zentrum für Waldorf-schulpädogogik*), state schools are considerably more expensive (Hardorp, 1983). A comparative study conducted by Haug, 1983 applying another methodological approach, did not confirm these results. Cost comparisons like these are of little evidence anyhow, because no cost analysis is provided and it therefore remains unclear whether the differences discovered result from X-inefficiency or from other factors, such as, for example, differences in the service programme.

Private schools are also generally assumed to be more effective. The study of Coleman, Hoffer, and Kilgore (1982) in the USA is most frequently quoted as empirical proof of this. There are no comparable studies relating to the Federal Republic of Germany. The only empirical indication is to be found in a retrospective analysis of a sample of 1460 Waldorf school pupils of the age cohort 1946/47 that revealed a high school performance (Hofmann *et al.*, 1981): one third of the student population qualified for university entry, which is three to four times more than at state schools at this time; furthermore, almost half of the male graduates obtained a university degree. This result is however not surprising when the student body composition is taken into account: the proportion of the students' parents that belonged to upper social classes and had high and the highest educational credentials was significantly above average. [18]

Compatibility with Goals of Distributional Policy

A further important aspect of private school financing is related to the question as to what extent its effects on the personal distribution of income (periodical income of households) are compatible with the goals of distributional policy, i.e. the reduction of disparities in income. Redistributive effects result from the fact that each income group bears a different amount of the expenses for education and utilizes educational offers to different extents. In the case of public education, which is financed from general taxes, the distributive effect can be measured by comparing the tax burden borne by households of each income group with the educational services utilized (measured by the educational expenses for the different school types provided by the state). In the case of private education, the additional educational expenses for the households, if necessary, must be added to the tax burden. An even distribution of the use of publicly financed educational services among the income groups would result in a slight redistributive effect from the higher to the lower income groups, due to the relative impact of progressive income tax.

In the Federal Republic this applies to the primary level, not however to the institutions of secondary and higher education. Because of the relatively high social selectivity of the German educational system, the children of high income groups, already evident from the class-specific participation quotas, are represented far more than the children of low income groups. As a consequence of this, in terms of cumulative public educational expenditures for secondary schooling, the state spends about 50 per cent more on children of state officials and 38 per cent more on children of white-collar workers than it does on working class children. Similar differences become evident if we compare the monthly 'real transfer', obtained through the use of state educational services by different employee households (with two children each). According to calculations by Obersteller (1983), in 1978 households headed by a state official obtained nearly 590DM worth of real transfers, households of white collar workers 532DM, while working class households only received 385DM.

The proportion of higher income groups at general private schools is likely to be larger owing to the effect of two selective mechanisms: private participation in the school costs and the high proportion of gymnasien (*cf.* table 1). Whether full or partial financing of private schools by the state results in a net-benefit or a net-cost for their clientele depends on the tax and expenses incidence. In the case of full financing, we may assume that the obtained real transfers would not be compensated by the progressive tax system, i.e. a regressive distributional effect — undesirable from the aspect of distributional policy — would result.

Equity and Equality

Private school financing as it is presently practiced in Germany is often criticized for the fact that parents of children who attend private schools are treated unequally to parents of children at state schools as they must finance these schools through the taxes they pay, as well as participate in the financing of the private school of their choice by paying school fees. This argument disregards the fact that tax contributions and state services do not represent an exchange of payments and services. Otherwise, childless married couples, who do not use any state educational services, could demand refund of part of their taxes on the same grounds.

A further point which deserves serious discussion is the extent to which low income groups are put at a disadvantage by the present system of financing. As stipulated by the constitution, selection of pupils according to their parents' financial means is not permitted. Formally, equality is thus guaranteed, yet the actual facts reveal a different reality. It would be interesting to know the extent to which necessary private support actually causes inequalities, i.e. parents cannot choose private schools of their preference because of financial penalty. Unfortunately, there is no information on this.

However, there is empirical evidence that it is not sufficient merely to eliminate financial barriers in order to achieve an educational participation that is evenly distributed with regard to social backgrounds. As mentioned above, the educational aspiration of parents largely depends on their (class-specific) socialization and their social status. The underrepresentation of working class children at public *gymnasien* is most likely due to the mismatch between the cognitive, motivational and linguistic competencies acquired in the family socialization process by working class children and the cognitive, motivational and linguistic demands in this type of school, which are geared towards the middle class (Hurrelmann, 1985). The findings of an empirical investigation on the educational participation of children of different ability belonging to different social groups by Fend (1982) illustrate the influence that this obstacle has on the educational choice of low status parents. According to this study, the chance of a highly intelligent working class child, attending a *gymnasium* is nearly one third lower than the chance of the least intelligent children from the middle and upper class (Fend, 1982, p. 152).

If these social class impediments exist even at public schools, then they can be expected to be more severe at the corresponding private schools, which are usually more strongly adapted to the (differentiated) preferences of the middle and upper class, and some of which, such as the *Waldorf* schools, expect a degree of parental involvement that can only be met by a minority.

Also, the state of information about alternatives in education varies with social class. This becomes evident from the evaluation of the voucher experiment of Alum Rock (*cf.*, for example, Olivas 1981) as well as from the experiments with comprehensive schools in the Federal Republic of Germany.[19] In the case of private schools, which generally do not make a policy of addressing information to a wider audience, the social bias is likely to be much stronger.

Even if one agrees with the thesis that state educational policy is not fundamentally able to eliminate social inequalities, one must not conclude from this that a privately organized system performs better. 'However weak an instrument for overcoming the system of social inequality the (public, M.W.) school system may be ..., there is no historical example that an educational system developed autonomously by society has had other than the contrary effect.' (Roeder, 1979, p. 13–14). Whatever reasons may be relevant in each case for parents when deciding in favour of private education, they are all motivated by the desire to safeguard individual advantages. Critics might argue that central goals of the modern social welfare state would be violated if the state gave in to these intentions by fostering a substantial expansion of private educational supply or by leaving education completely in private hands (the market). Parents from higher social classes would benefit more from such a development and class stratification would increase. By draining off middle and upper-middle class children, an expanding private sector would have lasting negative implications for the quality of teaching and learning conditions in public schools and on the socialization of its pupils. The problems which the *hauptschulen* in the Federal Republic are confronted with, becoming more and more 'schools for the leftovers', i.e. for pupils of low ability, socially disadvantaged pupils and children of foreign workers, could then become a general feature of the public institutions in a 'dual educational system'.

This pessimistic scenario marks the possible ultimate stage of an 'unhindered' expansion of private schooling. Of course, this will not be relevant in the near future. In the coming years, policy in the Federal Republic of Germany, as in many other Western democracies, will be more concerned with the question of how to reconcile the goals of guaranteeing freedom of choice, safeguarding the social purposes of schooling, making efficient use of scarce resources, and promoting equality (see also Boyd, 1984)

This is a difficult task as may be concluded from the preceding discussion, which showed that there is a tense relationship among these goals. In the Federal Republic today policy emphasis is placed on freedom of choice. This reflects the ideological position of the governing conservative-liberal majority which thus finds itself in line with the aspirations of a growing proportion of parents to acquire greater 'consumer sovereignty'. The tendency towards greater individualism and diversity in lifestyles will further increase the demand for an expansion of choice in education. From this perspective a balance among the competing goals cannot be expected. There are indications that in a society that is becoming increasingly pluralistic (if not to say atomistic) greater responsiveness of the educational system to parents' preferences conflicts with the social purpose of schooling. The view of the school as an agent of society dominated in the 1970s during the period of reform in the Federal Republic, when a fundamental reorganization of the educational system was considered, particularly the substitution of the tripartite school structure for a comprehensive one. It seems that with the failure of this attempt the view of the school's function underwent a fundamental change: the school is no longer seen as an agent of society, but as an agent of the family. This reorientation makes the chances of the common-school idea being realized in the foreseeable future extremely slim.

Notes

1   This may be attributed to various changes in society and developments in the educational system. Among the societal changes the increasing pluralism of value orientations that is reflected in a greater differentiation of life styles and the pervasive erosion of confidence in public institutions (Weiler, 1982) may be of particular importance. As regards developments in the educational sector, the discontent with the results of the policy of educational expansion and reform and its negative side-effects (for example, mammoth schools, declining performance, increasing proliferation of legal regulations, devaluation of educational credentials) as well as the fact that the *gymnasium* lost its elite status, i.e., its function for the reproduction of socially privileged groups, made non-state education more attractive.

2   Between 1972 and 1984 the number of pupils in primary schools decreased by 45 per cent, going from 4.2 to 2.3 million, as a result of the drastic decline in births which started in the mid-1960s.

3   The delayed decline in pupil numbers at private schools could be due in part to the fact that the demographic development here first affected the 'waiting lists'.

4   The statistics do not show that the demand for the educational services of the Waldorf schools have for some years now far exceeded the capacity of the existing schools.

5   This explains the minimal quantitative significance of this type of school.

6   The Federal Administrative Court based its statement of reasons mainly on the fact that the guarantee of establishment stipulated in the Constitution implies a claim for financial support, since the conditions for authorization in accordance with Article 7 (4) of the Constitution (equivalence, no selection of pupils according to parental means, safeguarding of economic and legal position of the teachers) can only be fulfilled with the financial support of the state. Until 1966, the *Länder* agreed that no claim to the support of private schools from public funds could be derived from Article 7 of the Federal Constitution (§10 of the Agreement of the *Länder* of 1951). Nevertheless all the *Länder* eventually granted certain private educational institutions the right to financial assistance.

7   According to a ruling made by the Federal Administrative Court in 1984.

8   Two methods are applied by the *Länder* to assess the amount of regular financial aid:
   (a)   the method of financing deficits: a certain percentage of a budgetary deficit is granted to a substitute school. The school must have each single expense scrutinized and qualified for support. The corresponding state school provides the standards for comparison;
   (b)   the method of lump sum payment: the substitute school is granted a flat-rate fixed contribution (regardless of the actual expenses) that can be freely utilized. It is guided by the yearly costs of a pupil or the average wage of a teacher at a comparable state school.

9   The amount per pupil ranged from 2915DM in Niedersachsen to 5610DM in Baden-Württemberg.

10   However, the increasing social segregation of residential areas in the Federal Republic, especially in the cities, represents an obstacle to the creation of heterogeneous school environments (Auernheimer, 1984).

11   The transmission of a common school experience to pupils from different backgrounds, their social coeducation, was one of the factors which set off the comprehensive school movement in the Federal Republic of Germany.

12   For a discussion of this aspect see Murnane (1983).

13   This is particularly the case if children of foreigners ('guest workers'), who represent an extremely small minority at German private schools, are to be included. In inner city areas, an increasing number of parents choose private educational offers just because of the high proportion of foreign pupils at public schools. For these parents, the attraction of private schools will decline to the extent to which their student body composition comes to resemble that of the public schools. The experience of the USA with programs for racial desegregation provides a revealing example for this development (see, for example, Coleman, Kelly and Moore, 1975; Hannon, 1984).

14   This is the case, for example, in the Netherlands (James, 1984).

15   The negative cost implications of the enrollment decline could principally be reduced by closing down schools and/or by changing the school structure, i.e. by replacing the tripartite school system with flexible comprehensive systems, but both strategies meet with opposition: closing schools is in conflict with the policy of providing educational services close to pupils' homes and is therefore avoided, if possible, i.e. higher costs are deliberately taken into account. Changes in school structure can probably be enforced only slowly, if at all, owing to resistance from the local authorities and teachers, and also to some extent because of existing ideological objections to comprehensive systems.

16   Results of empirical studies seem to support this thesis (for example, Erickson, 1982).

17   The concept of X-inefficiency states that firms usually do not produce on their production frontier, as assumed in micro-economic theory, i.e. the actual output is less than maximum output for given inputs. According to Leibenstein X-inefficiency results from failure to exploit opportunities to improve the output-input relation, due mainly to insufficient motivation and work effort. The degree of work effort expended by an individual varies (ceteris paribus) with the contextual conditions, especially with the extent of external pressure.

18   The importance of the student body composition for student achievement is also confirmed by Murnane (1983) and Willms (1983) who reanalyzed data of the comparative study of Coleman, Hoffer and Kilgore (1982). Private schools generally have more effective mechanisms for controlling their 'intakes' — and thus the student body composition — than public schools. In the Federal Republic private schools are legally entitled to select their pupils freely.

19   Klaus-Roeder and Hässler (1977), for example, found out from an inquiry among parents that the lower down the social scale the parents were, the less informed they were as to the goals and program of comprehensive schools as an alternative to conventional education offers.

References

AUERNHEIMER G. (1984) 'Die Zukunft der Bildung'. *Forum Wissenschaft*, 84, pp. 22–25.

BLUE MULLER, C. (1983) 'The Social and Political Consequences of Increased Public

Manfred Weiss

Support for Private Schools', in JAMES, T. and LEVIN, H. M. (Eds.) *Public Dollars For Private Schools*, Philadelphia, Temple University Press.

BOYD, W. L. (1984) 'Competing Values in Educational Policy and Governance: Australian and American Developments', *Educational Administration Review*, 2, 84, 2, pp. 4 –24.

COLEMAN, J. S., KELLY, S. D. and MOORE, J. A. (1975) *Trends in School Segregation, 1968 –1973* Chicago, National Opinion Research Center.

COLEMAN, J. S., HOFFER, T. and KILGORE, S. (1982) *High School Achievement: Public, Catholic, and Private Schools Compared* New York, Basic Books.

ERICKSON, D. A. (1982) 'Disturbing Evidence About the "One Best System"' in EVERHART, R. B. (ed.), *The Public School Monopoly* San Francisco, Pacific Institute for Public Policy Research.

FEND, H. (1982) *Gesamtschulen im Vergleich* [Comprehensive Schools in Comparison], Weinheim, Basel, Beltz.

HANF, T. (1983) 'Vom pädagogischen Kulturkampf und seiner Vergeblichkeit', in AVENARIUS, H. *et al.*, (eds) *Festschrift für Erwin Stein zum 80. Gerburtstag* Bad Homburg, Gehlen.

HANNON, J. T. (1984) 'The Influence of Catholic Schools on the Desegregation of Public School Systems: A Case Study of White Flight in Boston', *Population Research and Policy Review*, 3, 84, pp. 219–237.

HARDORP, B. (1983) Die Kostenrechnung freier Schulen und ihre gesellschaftliche Bedeutung', *Recht der Jugend und des Bildungswesens*, 31, 83, 3: pp. 208–220.

HAUG, R. (1983) 'Die Ausgaben von staatlichen Schulen und freien Waldorfschulen im Vergleich' [Expenditure of Public and Private Waldorf Schools in Comparison]. Frankfurt a.M., Deutsches Institut für Internationale Pädagogische Forschung.

HOFMANN, U., VON PRÜMMER, C. and WEIDNER, D. (1981) *Forschungsbericht über Bildungslebensläufe ehemaliger Waldorfschüler* [Research Report about the Educational Life Career of Former Waldorf School Students]. Stuttgart, Pädogogische Forschungsstelle beim Bund Freier Waldorfschulen.

HOLTAPPELS, H-G. and RÖSNER, E. (1986) 'Privatschulen: Expansion auf Staatskosten', in ROLFF, H-G., *et al.*, (eds.) *Jahrbuch der Schulentwicklung* [Yearbook of School Development], Vol. 4. Weinheim, Basel, Beltz.

HURRELMANN, K. (1985) 'Soziale Ungleichheit und Selektion im Erziehungssystem. Ergebnisse und Implikationen der sozialstrukturellen Sozialisationsforschung,' in STRASSER, H. and GOLDTHORPE, J. H. (eds), *Die Analyse sozialer Ungleichheit* [The Analysis of Social Inequality], Opladen, Westdeutscher Verlag.

JAMES, E. (1984) Benefits and Costs of Privatized Public Services: Lessons from the Dutch Education System *Comparative Education Review*, 28, 84, 4, pp. 605–624.

KLAUS-ROEDER, R. and HÄSSLER, U. (1977) *Eltern und Gesamtschule* [Parents and Comprehensive School]. Frankfurt a.M., Deutsches Institut für Internationale Pädagogische Forschung.

KLEMM, K. (1987) 'Bildungs expansion und ökonomische Krise', *Zeitschrift für Pëdagogik*, 33, 87, 6, pp. 823–39.

LEIBENSTEIN, H. (1966) Allocative Efficiency vs. 'X-Efficiency'. *American Economic Review*, 56, 66: pp. 392–415.

LEVIN, H. M. (1983) 'Educational Choice and the Pains of Democracy', in JAMES, T. and LEVIN, H. M. (eds) *Public Dollars For Private Schools*. Philadelphia, Temple University Press.

MURNANE, R. J. (1983) 'How Clients' Characteristics Affect Organization Performance: Lessons From Education', *Journal of Policy Analysis and Management*, 2, 83, 3: pp. 403–417.

OBERSTELLER, A. (1983) 'Umverteilungswirkungen gruppenspezifischer Realtransfers bei Arbeitnehmern', *Mitteilungen des Rheinisch-Westfälischen Instituts für Wirtschaftsforschung*, 34, 83: pp. 25–50.

OLIVAS, M. A. (1981) 'Information Access Inequities: A Fatal Flaw in Educational Voucher Plans', *Journal of Law and Education*, 10, 81, 4, pp. 441–465.

PREUSS-LAUSITZ, U. and ZIMMERMANN, P. (1984) 'Alternativschulen und grüne Bildungspolitik', in ROLFF, H-G. *et al.*, (eds) *Jahrbuch der Schulentwicklung* [Yearbook of School Development], Vol. 3. Weinheim, Basel, Beltz.

ROEDER, P. M. (1979) 'Einleitung'. in GOLDSCHMIDT, D. and ROEDER, P. M. (eds), *Alternative Schulen?* [Alternative Schools?]. Stuttgart, Klett-Cotta.

VOGEL, J. P. (1984) *Das Recht der Schulen und Heime in freier Trägerschaft*. Darmstadt, Luchterhand.

WEILER, H. N. (1982) 'Education, Public Confidence, and the Legitimacy of the Modern State: Do We Have a Crisis?' *Phi Delta Kappan* 82, 9, pp. 9–14.

WEISS, M. and WEISHAUPT, H. (1989) 'Economic Austerity in West German Education?' *Journal of Education Policy*, 4, 89, 1.

WILLMS, J. D. (1983) 'The Myth of Private School Superiority', paper presented at the annual meeting of the American Educational Research Association, Montreal, Canada.

Chapter 11
Public and Private Education in International Perspective

Estelle James

During the past six years I have been studying the public/private division of responsibility for education in international perspective. I deal with two major issues: first, why do different countries choose widely varying systems for providing education? Second, what difference does the choice of public versus private management make, with respect to variables such as method of funding, quality, cost, efficiency and distribution of service? The present chapter summarizes some of the interim results of this project.

Part I presents demand and supply-side explanations for the differential growth of the private sector in education, arguing that this is determined by excess demand, differentiated demand, and the supply of religious entrepreneurship in the society under examination. Besides explaining differences in private sector size across countries and states within a country, I also try to explain differences across levels of education, and briefly discuss the relevance of non-profit theory to the education industry.

Part II examines three major public policy issues from the international perspective: the likelihood that a large private sector will lead to segregation along religious or racial lines; that it will create educational opportunities and elite institutions available only to the upper class; and that it implies the growth of many low quality educational institutions. Other papers coming out of this project deal in greater detail with differences in costs, quality and funding between the public and private sectors and with the related issue of whether government should subsidize and regulate private education (James, 1984, 1986a, 1986b, 1986c, 1987a, 1987b; James and Benjamin, 1987, 1988).

Examples are drawn heavily from a group of industrialized and developing countries whose educational systems I have been studying during the past few years. Non-availability and non-comparability of data have been constant problems in this study, precluding heavy reliance on econometric analysis. Therefore, while some statistical analysis is used, my

Estelle James

main approach has been to examine each country intensively, to understand how and why its private educational sector developed, and to look for common forces at work. In fact, the degree of commonality with respect to private sector origin, funding and costs, across very diverse educational systems and societies, is impressive. More tentative evidence suggests that these same generalizations apply to other countries, as well.

It should be noted at the outset that the definition of 'private' is by no means clear-cut in a situation where many 'private' schools are heavily funded by the state and regulations often accompany these subsidies. 'Source of funding' and 'type of management' may then yield different public-private categories, and many mixed rather than polar cases. This is particularly true in advanced industrial societies. In this chapter I define the private sector to include all schools with substantial non-governmental decision-making authority, which usually goes together with some degree of reliance on private funding, however small.

Part I: Determinants of the Private Sector in Education

To what degree do different countries rely on the private sector in their provision of education? How can we explain the diverse choices made by different societies and for different levels of education? The relative size of the private sector varies from 1 per cent to 100 per cent at the primary level, from 0 per cent to 87 per cent at the secondary level. The range at higher educational levels is also substantial, although not quite as wide.

How do we explain this great diversity? Is the choice of systems by a country a random event, or are there underlying forces which enable us to predict its choice? In this and the following section I suggest two sets of demand-side variables — excess demand and differentiated demand — that throw partial light on this question. These demand-side explanations view the private sector as a market response to a situation where large groups of people are dissatisfied with the amount or type of government production. Private provision of education will develop in countries where these conditions exist. (Also see Levy, 1986 and Geiger, 1986 on this point.) Finally, I add a supply-side variable which also explains why much private production in education is nonprofit.

Demand Side Explanations: Excess Demand

Private production has been a response to an excess demand for education in the face of a limited government supply. (See Weisbrod, 1975 and 1977.) The basic idea is that people will vote to expand the public school system so long as they perceive that their incremental (social plus private) benefits

214

from expansion exceed their tax shares and cannot be purchased more cheaply in the private market; but if the capacity chosen by the majority (or by some other ruling coalition) is less than full enrollment some people with high benefits may be left out and will demand education in the private sector. The ruling coalition may choose to limit the size of the public sector because they mainly care about their own education, not the education of others; because they provide a disproportionate share of total tax revenues and wish to avoid the tax burden implied by additional public expenditures; and/or because they believe that private production is cheaper and more efficient then public. In other papers I develop this excess-demand model more rigorously (James 1986c, 1987a). Here I give some examples from my case studies and summarize the results of my statistical studies.

The 'excess demand' model most clearly applies to education in developing countries, where resources are very limited and where small scale production and subsistence agriculture, industries with a low return to education, still predominate. The difficulties in raising tax revenues from rural areas, and the reluctance of the urban upper class to subsidize a large public sector from which others will benefit, lead to a coalition of low demanders and high taxpayers that effectively restricts the supply of government schools.

One might expect this coalition of low demanders and high taxpayers to be strongest at the secondary level. At the primary level, where private benefits are substantial in rural as well as urban areas and where external benefits (i.e. benefits from the education of others, or 'neighborhood effects') are most often perceived, the group of low demanders may be relatively small. At the university level, high taxpayers may be willing to pay a disproportionate amount of the public bill, if they also get disproportionate access. At the secondary level, however, rural benefits may be lower than for primary and access not as income-biased as for university; hence the low demanders and high taxpayers form a coalition to restrict government production. At the same time, as primary school graduates increase, and as the incentive to acquire higher education (often heavily subsidized) rises, many urban middle and working class families become anxious to send their children to secondary school, even if they must pay themselves. By the above reasoning we would predict that the private sector will be relatively small at the primary level, much larger at the secondary level, and the two would not be highly correlated, in developing countries where excess demand is the moving force. We would expect to find a somewhat smaller (though still substantial) private sector in higher education as well. Indeed, this prediction is roughly consistent with the findings I shall summarize below.

Among industrialized countries, Japan best fits the 'excess demand' model at both the secondary and higher levels: over one-quarter of all high school (upper secondary) students and three quarters of those in universities attend private institutions. While Japan today can hardly be characterized as a developing country, it has made the transition to a modern industrial state more rapidly and recently than most Western countries and its large private education sector may be a legacy of earlier periods. In addition, Japan has, since the end of World War II, been controlled by the conservative Liberal Democratic Party (LDP), which has maintained the lowest rate of government expenditure and taxation among modern developed countries. This policy of limited government production, as applied to education, meant that only the minimum quantity deemed necessary for national purposes was provided publicly, while everything else was considered a consumer good, left to private enterprise. It is hardly surprising that the supporters of the LDP (top managers, small shopkeepers, farmers — i.e., groups with a low taste for education or high tax shares) constituted a majority coalition benefiting from this policy of limited public spending on education. However, demand far exceeded the limited government supply, as evidenced by high application rates, low acceptance rates, and the large number of *ronin* — students who, having failed the entrance exam to universities the first time round, spend a year or two 'cramming' and try again. (This phenomenon is also found in other countries, such as India.) Thus, private funding and management of secondary and higher education flourished, particularly in the years after World War II (see James and Benjamin, 1988).

It is instructive to contrast the Japanese with the Swedish case, since the party in Sweden during this period, the Social Democratic Party, is the mirror image of Japan's LDP. The SDP's working class constituency wanted — and got — a redistributive tax structure combined with a high quantity of government service, a vast expansion of education and other social services provided by the government at the expense of upper and middle class taxpayers. In Sweden, 90 per cent of each cohort now stays in school until age 18 and one-third go on to higher education, proportions which are very similar to those in Japan, but almost all accommodated in government institutions (James 1989). Clearly, there was no leftover demand for the private sector.

Does the ability to tax as well as the willingness to spend on public education increase with economic development, leaving less leftover demand for the private sector? We would expect the group of low demanders to decline with development, given the positive income elasticity of demand for education and the higher rate of return to education in urban, industrial areas. Thus, the number of government-funded school places should increase. In the case of Japan, as agriculture declined and the urban working class increased, the LDP did indeed find it necessary to form new coalitions in order to maintain itself in power. Policies were modified in the late 1960s and 1970s to include more government spending on education and social service programs. However, this increase took the form of subsidies to the well-established private sector rather then increased government production; sectoral shares were deliberately stabilized (James and Benjamin, 1988). In other words, a third alternative exists to the two set forth above, the possibility of government subsidized private schools, and indeed, this plays an important role in modern societies (see James, 1986a). Thus, a shift from private to public financing does not necessarily imply a shift from private to public production. The latter occurred earlier in England and Sweden but has not occurred in Japan and does not appear to be an inevitable consequence of development.

Differentiated Tastes: Another Demand Side Explanation

A second demand-side model views private production of education as a response to differentiated tastes about the *kind* of service to be consumed (rather than differentiated tastes about *quantity*), in situations where that differentiation is not accommodated by government production. The private sector would then grow larger if (1) people's preferences with respect to product variety are more heterogeneous and more intense, due to deep-seated cultural (religious, linguistic, ethnic) differences; (2) this diversity is geographically dispersed so it cannot be accommodated by local government production; (3) government is constrained to offer a relatively uniform product; and (4) the dominant cultural group is not determined to impose its preferences on others; hence private production is a permissible way out.

Differential preferences about quality, one group demanding a 'better' product than the median voter choice, may also lead to the development of a private alternative. Since educational quality probably has a high income elasticity of demand, this situation is likely to occur where the income distribution is more dispersed. This phenomenon has been observed in some American cities, in selected Japanese cities such as Tokyo, and in developing countries with a disparate income distribution, such as India, Kenya and Latin America. The 'elite' private schools play an important role in the economic and social structures of their countries. They are, however, small in number, so quality consideration does not explain the existence of large private sectors. Indeed, their very eliteness comes, in part, from their scarcity value. Moreover, the public system can and has been structured in many countries to accommodate differentiated preferences about quality (for example, selective schools, internal tracking, residential segregation). In fact, while some private schools may accommodate tastes for higher quality, average quality in the private sector cannot generally be considered higher than in the public sector, as I shall discuss later. For all these reasons, when I discuss different preferences about product type in this chapter, I will be referring primarily to cultural, not quality, variables.

In countries where different cultural groups are concentrated in their own geographic areas (as in Switzerland) local government production achieves the desired diversity. In countries where a dominant group seeks to impose its language or values on others, private schools may be prohibited or restricted; this was the position of Holland and France during earlier anticlerical periods. The 'melting pot theory' and the general belief in assimilation of minorities to majority values led to the 'common school' movement in the nineteenth and twentieth century US; the growth of Catholic private schools was a response by a group that did not want to be fully assimilated. However, the 'cultural heterogeneity' model best explains the development of the private sector in countries such as Holland and Belgium today.

Dutch society has long been characterized by deeply felt cultural (religious) cleavages. In particular, control over their own education was particularly important to the Catholics and Calvinists (orthodox Protestants) who constitute approximately 50 per cent of the population. These two groups formed a political coalition at the turn of the century which, after much battling, succeeded in bringing about state subsidy of private schools, a principle embodied in the 1917 Dutch constitution (James, 1984). In the years to come not only education but most other quasi-public goods, such as health care and social service, were to be produced by private organizations, though financed mainly by the state (Kramer, 1981). Similar cleavages along linguistic and religious lines may be found in Belgium.

In India, too, private schools and colleges are often differentiated by language (associated with region of origin), religion (Moslem, Parsee, Sikh) or caste group. The same is true of Malaysia (Chinese and Indian minorities). In Israel, most private schools are run by and for very orthodox Jewish groups, who are dissatisfied with the secular public schools.

Since densely populated urban areas will be characterized by greater diversity, with a market large enough to support several schools, the cultural heterogeneity argument leads us to expect private provision of education to be positively associated with urbanization and density indices. This is one of the hypotheses that I have tested in my statistical analyses.

I would also expect differentiated demand rather then excess demand to be the moving force behind large private sectors more generally, in modern industrial societies, at both the primary and secondary levels. Desire for cultural homogeneity is likely to be greatest at the primary level, for this is the age at which linguistic ability and religious identification develop, and values are formed. It is also true, however, that residential segregation in public systems may accomplish this purpose better at the primary than the secondary level, since the catchment area is often larger for the latter. Quality considerations as a motivation for choosing private schools are likely to be larger at the secondary level. The fact that these three forces (desire for homogeneity, size of catchment area, quality considerations) have their main impact at different levels could easily lead to a relatively large private primary sector but a relatively small disparity in private sector size at primary and secondary levels, in societies where differentiated demand is the *raison d'être* for private education. These predictions are roughly consistent with the empirical findings given below.

Who Starts Private Schools and Why: Supply Side Explanations and the Theory of Non-Profit Organizations

Who starts private schools and why? This is an important question because quite commonly, private schools are established as non-profit organizations (NPOs), i.e., as organizations which cannot distribute a monetary residual. These schools have not been started to generate dividends or capital gains, as is the case with most private enterprise. It is useful then to ask why private schools are often non-profit, what are the motives of the founders (in the absence of a profit motive and reward), and what factors determine their availability? I conjecture that differences in the supply of nonprofit entrepreneurship exert a potentially powerful influence on the size of the private educational sector and provide empirical evidence to support this hypothesis.

One major motive for founding schools is the possibility of disguised profit distribution, and there is a popular belief in many countries that this takes place, particularly in areas characterized by excess demand for education (for example, Japan, Colombia). Although called 'non-profit' these organizations are, allegedly, really profit-making entities. The illegal ways of distributing profits are only rarely brought to light, as when student places or professional appointments are 'sold' to families giving large gifts to the school's administrator or 'kickbacks' are given to influential people after successful equipment sales. The legal ways are more interesting but very difficult to detect or prove. For example, the founder may become the headmaster and be paid a salary beyond the market wage, i.e., beyond what he could earn elsewhere; he is, in effect, receiving monetary profits, albeit in disguised form. Even more valuable disguised profit distribution is said to take place in non-monetary, hence nontaxable form — expense accounts, free houses and cars (James and Benjamin, 1988).

Benefits to founders may also take intangible form: perpetuation of a family name on a school, status and prestige from being connected with an important institution. In effect, by creating these status distinctions (and therefore exacerbating prestige inequalities) a society is increasing the coinage at its disposal and using some of it to pay for nonprofit entrepreneurship. These motivations are common, too, in the US. (In Sweden, on the other hand, private philanthropy is actually frowned upon as a source of undesired status differentials.)

However, another motivation seems much more potent when we observe that most founders of private schools (and other NPOs) are 'ideological' organizations — political groups in colonial countries such as India and Kenya before independence, Socialist labor unions (as in Sweden) and, first and foremost, organized religion. Universally across countries, religious groups are the major founders of non-profit service institutions. We see this in the origin of many private schools and voluntary hospitals in the US and England, Catholic schools in France and Latin America, Calvinist schools in Holland, missionary activities in developing countries, services provided by Moslem waqfs (religious trusts), etc. Usually these are proselytizing religions, but other religious/ideological groups often start their own schools as a defensive reaction (for example, the 'independence schools' in Kenya and the caste-dominated schools in India were started partly to provide an alternative to the Western mission schools). This supply-side variable suggests that the private school sector will be more important in countries with strong, independent, proselytizing religious organizations competing for clients.

These conditions were obviously satisfied in Holland in the early twentieth century, when 95 per cent of all private schools were started by religious groups; and in Latin America in the same period, when Catholic universities were started in reaction to the secular ideology of the public universities. They are present in countries with a history of missionary activity, as in Japan, India and Kenya. On the other hand, they are absent in Sweden, the country which, as observed earlier, has a very small private educational sector. The Church of Sweden, to which 95 per cent of the people nominally belong, is an established church with little opposition, closely tied to and financially dependent on the government. Historically, the church has relied on government funding and, in return, the government has the right to make decisions about Church procedures and personnel. In effect, the Church of Sweden could be viewed as part of the Swedish government, with neither the need for nor the ability to supply a competing service. Thus, both demand and supply-side variables would predict a small private sector in Sweden, and that is exactly what we find.

This simple observation — that religious groups are the major founders of private schools and NPOs — goes far toward explaining why non-profit organizations are concentrated in areas such as education and health and it also suggests a particular reason why the non-profit form was chosen by the founders: their object was not to maximize profits but to maximize religious faith or religious adherents and schools are one of the most important institutions of taste formation and socialization. (Similarly, hospitals are a service for which people will have an urgent periodic need, hence constitute an effective way for religious groups to gain entré and good will.)

Once these religious schools and hospitals are founded they have a comparative advantage over their profit-making alternatives and, in some respects, over the public competition. First, they have a semi-captive audience; as discussed in the previous section, parents may prefer to send their children to a school with a particular religious orientation. The service suppliers, the religious group itself, may 'advertize' that this is a good thing to do. Second, some people may 'trust' such schools and hospitals precisely because they are run by religious groups. Third, religious groups have, in the past, had access to low cost volunteer labor (for example, priests and nuns) and donated capital, which allow them to undercut their secular rivals and compete with government schools. Fourth, once a school or hospital has been founded by a religious group, it develops a 'reputation' which may allow it to continue attracting a clientele even if it later loses its cost advantage. Finally, the religious group may be politically powerful enough to secure government subsidies and to require that only non-profits be eligible for these subsidies. Thus, the religious motive for funding provides a powerful supply-side explanation for where private schools are found, why the non-profit form is used, and how these institutions may compete effectively with a public or secular profit-maximizing alternative.

Statistical Testing of Demand and Supply Effects

In developing the theoretical framework set forth above, I included examples from several countries which I have studied in this project. However, the number of case studies and illustrative examples is neces-sarily limited and presents the possibilities of bias. Therefore, I have also employed statistical analyses to test these ideas against a larger set of countries and in a more rigorous way.

Statistical testing of these demand and supply-side hypotheses is not an easy task. Ideally, to explain the differential size of the private educa-tional sector across countries, we need information, for each country, on the amount of government and private production; the quality, religious and linguistic orientation and differentiation of public schools; various indicators of quantity and quality demanded; the degree of cultural heterogeneity within the population, including the strength of religious and linguistic identification; and the availability of (ideological) entre-preneurs. In practice, this data is exceedingly difficult to obtain. Data gaps and definitional differences from one country to another make cross-national statistical analysis problematic, in general. In particular, uniform data is often not available on degree of religious and linguistic differentia-tion within the public system or on subjective variables such as 'intensity of preference' for religiously differentiated schools. For example, the Cath-olics and Calvinists strongly wanted their own privately controlled schools, and made this their major political objective in Holland, a country which is almost 100 per cent Christian; similarly, the very orthodox Jews wanted their own schools in Israel, a Jewish state. These two countries would not show up as very heterogeneous by international standards, yet

the subjectively felt heterogeneity and desire to achieve more homogeneous grouping was obviously great.

Moreover, as noted above, the definition of 'public' versus 'private' is
not unambiguous. We really have a continuum of public and private
funding and control, with different countries representing different points
on this continuum. For example, the Kenyan 'harambee school', which I
treat as private, is built with volunteer contributions of money and labor
from local communities, often has a teacher whose salary is paid by the
central government, therefore faces regulations over criteria for admitting
students, and is sometimes managed (at the request of the community) by
a mission group, one of the few groups with educational managerial
experience (James, 1986b). Ideally, we should therefore have data on
degree of government funding and regulation of private schools, a practice
which is quite common. Unfortunately, these data are simply not available
for large sets of countries.

Intra-country regressions

To reduce these problems in statistical testing, I focused first on differences
in private sector size across states or provinces *within* four countries in
which I had access to data disaggregated by state or province: Holland,
India, Japan, and the US. The advantage of this approach is that definitions
are more uniform within countries, and some of the variables that are most
difficult to measure, such as degree of differentiation in and religious
control of the public schools and subsidies to the private schools may be
relatively constant across states or provinces in a given country. Therefore,
we are left with a smaller set of more easily quantifiable variables.

The public/private division of responsibility for education (percentage
PVT) was taken as my dependent variable; this differs greatly both within
and across countries. In the case of the US, Holland and India this was
measured as 'percentage of schools that are privately managed'; in the case
of Japan, 'percentage of total enrollment in privately managed schools' was
the counterpart available statistic. Somewhat different models were used
for each country, because of data availability or because the relevant models
(underlying *raison d'être* for the private sector) seemed to vary. However,
whenever possible a common set of independent variables — per capita
income, density, urbanization, per student spending in public schools and
religious variables — were tested.

Per capita income was taken as an indicator of parental ability to pay
for differentiated private education in modern industrial countries such as
the US. In excess demand countries, such as Japan, higher per capita
income implies a greater demand for education; if this is not satisfied
through the public sector, it spills over to the private sector. Thus, in both
cases, states or provinces with higher per capita income would be expected
to have a larger role for private schools — so long as the localities operate

under some centralized constraints which prevent them from responding to the differentiated tastes or greater demand of their higher income residents. The same reasoning applies to density and urbanization variables.

Per student spending was used as a proxy for public school quality and the quality motive for attending private school. I would expect this to be negatively related to 'percentage private' in modern industrial societies with open access school systems, but not necessarily in developing countries where higher public quality may imply lower public quantity.

Religious variables, as discussed above, capture both demand and supply side effects. The specific variable used varied from country to country, depending on relevance and availability of data; these included variables such as 'percentage Catholic' (US), percentage Catholic plus Calvinist (Holland) and evidence of early missionary activity (India and Japan). Differential rates of government subsidy across states and provinces were not used because these data were not available; in addition, it was hoped that the variation within a country was not great. My detailed results are presented in another paper (James, 1987a). Here I simply summarize the results.

In all cases the religious variable turned out to be positive and highly significant. While this combines both a demand and supply effect in Holland and the US, in India and Japan, where many people who attend Christian schools are not Christians, we are probably observing primarily a supply-side phenomenon. Per capita income is also generally positive and significant as an indicator of excess demand and/or the financial ability of parents to purchase a preferred type of education for their children. Density and urbanization appear to be positively correlated with 'per cent private', but this effect often disappears when per capita income is included, suggesting that these three variables are exerting a common influence. Per student spending in public schools plays a very limited role except in US secondary schools, consistent with my expectation that demand for academic quality is not the cause of large private sectors. In US secondary schools, however, this variable had a significant negative impact.

Also of interest is the importance of historical factors; i.e., the early founding of private schools. This shows up, for example, in the positive importance of the 'literacy' variable in India and 'presence of pre-World War II Christian schools' in Japan. It suggests that once private schools are founded they disappear only with a long lag, even if the initial conditions disappear. These results are all roughly consistent with the hypotheses given above concerning the impact of demand and supply variables, and, perhaps most important, the role of religious entrepreneurship in determining relative size of the private sector in education. Although the four countries considered here differ greatly in terms of stage of development, political system, cultural values and size of the private educational sector, they are remarkably similar in terms of the variables determining the geographic distribution of private schools within each country.

Inter-country regressions

To test my hypotheses further I also ran a regression analysis across a sample of fifty countries — twelve modern and thirty-eight developing — the largest number for which I could get data on most essential variables. My object was to explain the percentage of enrollments that are private (percentage PVT) in different countries and to explore whether different forces are at work in modern and developing states. This study is described in detail in a separate paper (James, 1986a) but here the results are briefly summarized.

The main independent variables included were: per capita income and degree of urbanization as demand-related variables; indicators of religious and linguistic heterogeneity as proxies for differentiated demand and private supply; and dummies for different regions, intended to capture historical or other country-specific effects. Other variables that were available for smaller subsets of countries will be noted below.

I had my strongest prior assumptions about the positive impact of the religious variable, based on the theory described earlier, my case studies and my previous statistical analyses of cross-sectional differences in percentage PVT within countries. Five alternative religious variables were used: (1) REL, an index of religious heterogeneity, defined as $\Sigma\ P_i \ln 1/P_i$, where P_i = proportion of the population constituted by religion i. As the number of religions grows, so too does REL, as an index of religious heterogeneity. The index is highest when the population is equally divided among a large number of religions. My expectation was that the greater the index of religious heterogeneity the greater the competition among them for market shares, with schools as their major instrument, and hence the higher the percentage PVT. (2) My second and third religious variables were percentage Christian (CHR) and percentage Catholic (CATH). I expected these, too, to have a positive impact, since Christianity is one of the main proselytizing religions in the world (Islam being the other) and the Catholic Church has its own educational system in many countries. (3) My fourth and fifth religious variables were NCHR and NCATH, where NCHR = CHR or (1 − CHR), whichever is smaller, and similarly for NCATH. These two variables are an attempt to measure the competitive position of Christianity and Catholicism, the idea being that Christians (or Catholics) will have larger private sectors if they are a large minority or a small majority. I expected these religious variables, which capture both a demand-side and supply-side effect, to be strongly positive in both modern and developing states.

Linguistic heterogeneity was measured parallel to REL, as $\Sigma\ L_i \ln 1/L_i$, where L_i = proportion of the population speaking language i. This was expected to be positive, particularly in modern countries, where cultural heterogeneity was postulated to be the demand-side basis for private schools.

In contrast, I could not *a priori* predict the signs on per capita income or urbanization. *Ceteris paribus*, one might expect that these variables would serve as indicators of gross demand for education in developing countries and ability to pay for differentiated or higher quality education in modern countries, both implying a positive relationship with percentage PVT. This would hold under the assumption that the public sector does not respond to the differentiated tastes or greater demand of its wealthier inhabitants. Recall that this was the case in our four intra-country comparisons. In cross-country comparisons, however, this key assumption may not hold. Instead, the political forces within wealthier and more urbanized countries may lead them to provide more and higher quality education collectively, through their public schools, thereby leaving a smaller role for their private schools. Thus it remains an empirical question as to whether per capita income and urbanization are positively or negatively related to percentage PVT in international comparisons.

However, the private rate of return to education, which was available for sixteen developing countries, was unambiguously expected to have a positive sign. Indeed. this is probably our best indicator of 'excess demand', since it implies a high demand for educated labor, hence a high derived demand for education.

Unfortunately, data on per student spending or quality in public schools are not available for most countries. Similarly, data on educational subsidies are not available for large sets of countries, continuous data are even less available, and the existence of implicit tax subsidies further complicates the situation. However, for the modern countries I was able to differentiate in a rather gross way between those which offer almost full subsidies versus those which offer little or no subsidies and I included a dummy variable NS, for the latter in some equations. It is, of course, predicted to have a negative effect.

Regional dummies were included to account for historical or other country-specific effects. The dummy for modern countries (MD) proved to be significant, as will be discussed below.

I found that the role of private education is much greater at the secondary level than the primary level in developing countries, where excess demand is the major *raison d'être*, while for advanced industrial states where differentiated demand dominates, privatization rates at the two levels were much closer to each other and highly correlated, as expected. Specifically, for the twelve modern societies, the medium percentage PVT at the primary and secondary level were 12.5 per cent and 13.5 per cent respectively and the R^2 between them was .88 while for the thirty-eight developing countries these numbers were 11 per cent, 27.5 per cent and .25.

The significance of religious competition was strongly confirmed for all levels of education and groups of countries. My five religious variables, used as alternatives because of multi-collinearity between them, were usually significantly positive (or very close to significance). This is consistent with my hypotheses that differentiated demand stems heavily from religious identification and that religious entrepreneurship is serving as an important supply-side variable in both modern and developing countries.

Linguistic heterogeneity played an important role in the modern group, but not in the developing group, consistent with our differentiated demand model. The private rate of return has a positive effect in developing countries, consistent with our excess demand model.

Interestingly, per capita income and urbanization had a negative effect, especially in developing countries, in contrast to the results in our within-country regressions. This suggests that public sector capacity increases, hence excess demand decreases in the country as a whole, as economic growth proceeds. However, the 'modern dummy' was positive in my fifty country sample, offsetting this negative effect, especially at the primary level. The existence of subsidies was also positively related to private sector size in modern countries. Indeed, the 'modern dummy' may be a rough proxy for 'government subsidy.' Wealthier countries with considerable cultural heterogeneity may choose to subsidize their private sectors and hence allow differentiated demand to grow as excess demand dies out.

These statistical regularities which are, moreover, consistent with theoretical predictions, suggest that systematic forces are indeed at work in explaining regional differences in governmental versus private production of education.

Part II: Some Policy Issues

This section deals with three important policy issues on which, I believe, the above discussion of international experience can throw some light: the likelihood that a large private sector will lead to segregation along religious or racial lines; that it will diminish support for the public schools and create elite private institutions available only to the upper classes, hence reduce equality of opportunity; and that it implies the growth of many low quality educational institutions.

Religious and Racial Segregation

An important issue that arises when the privatization of education is considered concerns the degree to which this would lead to segregation along religious or racial lines, an outcome some (but not all) would like to avoid. It is true that any system which permits choice (including choice among various government schools) will cause people with like tastes to be grouped together. The probability of cultural segregation is underlined when we realize that much of the demand for and entrepreneurship in the private educational sector comes from religious groups or from groups with particular linguistic, caste or nationality affiliations, as discussed in part I. This segmentation did not occur in Japan, largely because Japan is such a homogeneous country, culturally and ethnically. However, the extensive reliance on private schools in Holland certainly reinforced the religious segmentation within that society. In India private schools tend to be divided along caste or linguistic lines. Similarly in Sweden, students and teachers self-select themselves among the various adult educational associations, according to religious or political ideology. In the US a large majority of private schools serve the Catholic population and are therefore segregated along the religious dimension — although by some measures, these are less segregated racially than the public schools (Coleman *et al.* 1982). The recent growth of fundamentalist Christian private schools in the US further segregates along religious (as well as racial) lines.

If all groups in society prefer such segmentation, and there are no additional cost involved, it is clearly pareto-efficient, but a social dilemma exists if one group prefers segmentation while another group prefers integration. Then, a system which ostensibly gives consumers a choice cannot in fact satisfy both groups simultaneously; their preferences are mutually incompatible and society must make a collective decision about which system it prefers. In Holland, for example, society decided to facilitate segmentation for those who wanted it by permitting and subsidizing choice. A pro-integrationist decision, on the other hand, can either take the form of eliminating choice (for example, by giving the state a monopoly and bussing to achieve integration) or of permitting choice with strings attached (for example, permitting a regulated private sector, with limited rights to exclude and/or with a mandated mix of students). In many subsidized private educational sectors (for example, Holland, Kenya, France) the state does indeed exert control over criteria for selecting students. Current policy in American higher education embodies elements of such controls for institutions receiving federal aid. Thus, privatization does not necessarily imply cultural segmentation but it easily can, unless specific steps are taken to avoid this.

Class Segregation and Elite Private Schools

Another fear is that a more privatized system will lead to greater segregation by socio-economic class than a public system would, with the rich having access to higher quality education than the poor. Relatedly, the upper and middle classes might vote for low cost, low quality public schools, thereby saving on taxes, and would send their own children to high quality private schools. This too, would perpetuate class differences. Has this occurred in most countries with large private sectors?

It is clear from international experience that the private sector need not contain the elite prestigious institutions, as we in the US tend to assume. Indeed, in Japan, Kenya and most other countries characterized by excess demand, the opposite seems to be true: a few public schools are on top of the hierarchy, with numerous private institutions at the bottom. Similarly, the private sector need not be an enclave for the rich. In at least two cases I have studied for which good data are available — Dutch elementary and secondary schools and Japanese universities — the various socio-economic classes are equally represented in the public and private sectors.

In the case of Holland this is partly due to heavy public subsidies and specific restrictions imposed by the government on schools which accept the subsidy. For example, such schools are greatly limited in their ability to charge tuition, to attract better teachers by paying higher wages, or to exclude students who do not pay. Moreover, private school subsidies are tied directly to public school budgets, thereby undermining the possible tendency to cut the latter. Such government policies clearly constrain some of the potential class divisive effects of privatization (James, 1984).

However, a more fundamental explanation for the absence of elite private schools exists in many countries. Most importantly, the public sector is likely to remain on top of the hierarchy if it is differentiated and competitive, if students can choose among public schools and schools can choose among students. Given their price advantage, if public schools and universities can select and exclude, they usually can compete effectively with private institutions for the best students and acquire at least equivalent reputations. This is true in Sweden, where choice of study lines and residential segregation permit differentiation within the public sector; to a much greater extent in Holland, which features a 'streaming' system that determines at an early age the small group of students who will pursue the pre-university route; and even more so in Kenya, where the small group of selective public secondary schools are the preferred alternative. It is very true in Japan, where the public secondary schools and universities are considered the elite ones — except for Tokyo high schools where students are assigned on a more random basis. More generally, since stringent selectivity is characteristic of educational systems with excess demand, the public schools are especially likely to be the elite schools in these cases; large mass private sectors develop to accommodate the leftovers. Where the existence of the private sector is based on culturally differentiated demand the two sectors are more likely to have equivalent status if both have the same rights to select and exclude. (See James, 1984, 1986b, 1989; James and Benjamin, 1987, 1988).

The concepts of differentiation and selectivity, of course, run counter to the American ideal of open access public schools, at the primary and secondary levels. Hence, the elite schools here are the private schools, which also attract higher income students. Selectivity is, however, consistent with magnet schools that are developing in some cities, specialized high schools (such as Bronx Science or Stuyvesant) which have long had excellent reputations, wealthy suburban high schools that segregate by residence, and hierarchical public university systems such as that in California, which certainly have maintained a high position in the national pecking order.

In other words, if we desire, 'choice' can exist in the public as well as the private sectors, but we may face a trade-off between quality and equality in the public sector; also between equality in the public sector and equality overall. When differentiation and selectivity are permitted in the public schools, those with greater income and taste for education probably have better access to the 'top' public schools, and therefore satisfy their preferences within the public system. This helps to maintain its status and political support. The rich can now benefit from the 'elite' schools without paying privately, but the poor also benefit because they have access to the top schools. When the public schools are homogenized, those with greater incomes and taste for education are likely to flee to the private sector, which now becomes elite. The public system is more equal, but it is also perceived as being lower quality. Since the poor are now excluded from the elite schools by economic as well as social barriers, it is not clear that equality for society as a whole has increased. These are important trade-offs and social choice issues for the US to consider, as we evaluate policies that would lead to greater privatization of education.

Low Quality Private Schools

While critics of privatization in modern countries often fear that this will lead to low quality underfunded public schools, in many developing countries the greater fear is of low cost and quality in the private sector. This stems from the fact that private schools usually operate at much lower cost than public schools, unless they are heavily subsidized by the government. Lower costs are particularly found in developing countries, where subsidies are limited. Indeed, these lower costs are a major factor enabling them to survive and constitute a possible rationale for the government to delegate production responsibilities to private educational organizations.

Should the lower cost incurred by private institutions be interpreted as evidence of lower quality or higher efficiency as compared with public institutions? This is one of the questions we would most like answered and it is most difficult to ascertain. The former interpretation assumes that efficiency is the same in the two sectors, so lower valued inputs must mean less value added. If public schools have a higher cost per student they are assumed to have a higher net output. The latter interpretation assumes that value added by the two sectors is the same (for example, the same course credits and degrees are issued), so lower costs imply greater efficiency in processing inputs, usually ascribed to more skillful management and better incentives in the private system. Families are said to choose private schools partially because of their efficiency, which keeps fees low and competitive with (free) government schools.

A definitive examination of this question requires an accurate measure of value added, a task which is greatly complicated by differences among schools in their student inputs as well as ambiguities concerning the appropriate measure of output. The output of education has been variously interpreted as amount earned (i.e. incremental lifetime earnings), amount learned (for example, incremental scores on achievement tests) or willingness to pay (i.e. the consumer's subjective evaluation of all the investment and consumption benefits of education); these three measures may give different gross outputs. To ascribe differential output effects to a school-type requires us, furthermore, to control for student input, so that we are measuring 'net value added' by the school itself, independent of the value of the incoming student or peer group effect. Unfortunately, this data is generally not available. The most careful study of this issue, based on a longitudinal survey of high school sophomores and seniors, concluded that private schools were more effective in the US (see Coleman *et al.*, 1982), but this finding has been vigorously attacked by numerous critics (for example, see Goldberger and Cain, 1982; Murnane, 1984; Willms, 1985; Haertel *et al.*, 1988) and the net outcome is probably a draw. Thus, even when excellent data are available and supposedly objective econometric techniques are used, it turns out that the results are highly sensitive to choice of statistical methodologies with different underlying assumptions, hence the definitive answer continues to elude.

In other countries we simply do not have the data for sophisticated econometric analyses. I have, however, approached this issue in another way, conducting a careful examination of how private schools coexist with public schools and trying to evaluate whether, when costs are lower, the sources of cost-saving and the consumer response thereto imply lower quality or greater efficiency.

Consider, first, the converse case of Holland. Dutch public and private schools receive the same subsidy per student, and the private schools charge a small fee as well, so their cost per student is actually (slightly) higher than in public schools. Does this mean that their value added is also greater? The problem in analyzing this is that the student inputs are, by definition, differentiated along religious lines. For example, relatively few Catholics have historically gone on to the university; is this due to a Catholic school effect or an effect stemming from the student's cultural background?

We can, however, use a more direct market-based test to examine public-private differences in school quality and efficiency in the Netherlands. Since people have a choice, which is not biased by unequal subsidies, we can simply observe their actions to make inferences about perceived benefits and costs — the approach we generally use in economic analysis. The fact that 70 per cent of all parents choose to send their children to private schools, which charge a small fee (despite the presence of free public schools nearby), suggests they believe they are getting more for their money there. Part of this preference, of course, comes from religious identification and from the desire for religious segmentation. However, since the proportion attending private schools has not declined with the increasing secularization of Dutch society, other forces must also be at work. Many people with whom I discussed this issue believe that the private schools are more personal and responsive to consumer wishes, more careful about how they spend their funds than the publics. Private schools are considered more flexible, less bureaucratic, and effectively overseen by a board of directors specifically concerned about the welfare of the school, rather than by a generalized municipal administration. We do know that, on the average, private and public schools spend their 'discretionary funds' somewhat differently, the latter paying more for 'maintenance and cleaning', the former having more left over for various 'educational facilities.' While objective proof is not available, the majority of parents have revealed their preference for (belief in the greater efficiency of) the private schools (James, 1984).

As a second case we consider Japan which, in many ways, is a polar opposite to Holland. In Japan, public high schools and universities are generally preferred by parents, both because their tuition is much lower due to generous subsidies, and their prestige is higher. Students at public institutions, on average, achieve higher test scores and lifetime earnings, suggesting that their 'gross output' is indeed greater. However, the student input is also superior at these schools, which are highly selective, and employers may use them for their screening rather than their human capital-building function, making it unclear whether 'social value added' is also greater there.

On average, the private sector in Japan operates at much lower cost per student than the public sector; in 1973, before substantial government subsidies were instituted, the private/public cost ratio was .72 for high schools, .38 for higher education (James and Benjamin, 1988). I found that part of this cost differential stemmed from product mix differentials (for example, more teaching and liberal arts, less science and research in the private sector); these are independent both of quality and efficiency implications. Part of the cost differential stemmed from lower input-output ratios (for example, more students per faculty member, larger class size), in private schools. American consumers tend to assess large classes and low student-faculty rates as 'low quality' but the Japanese do not make the same subjective evaluation and they may be right — the objective research evidence is inconclusive despite numerous studies on this topic.

However, much of the cost differential before subsidization was due to lower wages paid to workers, especially teachers. The use of low paid teachers in Japan was facilitated by the presence of enclaves of under-employed workers who do not have full access to the labor market, namely, young women and retired men. The disproportionate presence of these groups in the private sector kept average wages low there, despite the fact that formal credentials of teachers are comparable to those in the public sector. Part-timers are also heavily employed in private universities; they are not paid fringe benefits, which they receive from their regular jobs, and the moonlighting wage rate tends to be lower as well. Lower wages are, in fact, a characteristic of unsubsidized private schools (except for a few elite ones) in most countries I have studied.

Is this evidence of greater efficiency or lower quality? Do the lower wages available to these groups stem from their lower productivity, or simply from an artificial segmentation of the labor market, which arbitrarily makes different opportunities available to different kinds of people? By the former interpretation, the private sector is offering lower quality teaching. By the latter interpretation, the private sector is able to take advantage of these labor market imperfections and hire equivalent services at lower cost, while the public sector is proscribed by custom or law from doing it. In the absence of objective measures of value added and productivity, I leave it to the reader to draw his/her own conclusions about relative quality and efficiency. Perhaps a combination of lower quality and greater efficiency (i.e., poorer student inputs, possibly lower value added per pupil but higher value added per unit of expenditure) are provided by many private educational organizations.

Conclusion

In summary, I have offered a theory which explains the size of the private sector in education as depending on three variables: 1) excess demand, stemming from a political coalition which limits government production below full enrollment levels; 2) differentiated demand, arising from deep-seated religious or linguistic diversity, in the face of a relatively uniform government product; and 3) the supply of non-profit entrepreneurship, often religious, to start the private schools. I have hypothesized that excess demand is particularly evident in developing countries, at the secondary and higher levels, while private education at the primary level, and in modern industrial societies, is often due to differentiated demand. The fragmentary evidence available seems consistent with this hypothesis. Many illustrative examples have been cited. Moreover, indicators of excess demand and differentiated demand were shown to be significant in statistical analyses of differences in private sector size within and across several developed and developing countries; but proxies for religious demand and supply (for example, size of Catholic population or missionary activity) were most consistently important.

A major potential advantage of private service provision is that this permits some reliance on voluntary payments, thereby revealing and directly implementing people's preferences and reducing the necessary amount of taxation and tax-induced disincentive effects. Excess demand which stems from a political decision to limit government spending may then be satisfied in the private market place. If the social rate of return is high, this additional production and consumption of education is desirable. The corresponding disadvantage is that low income groups may have less access to privately funded education than they would to an equivalent amount of publicly funded education. However, total enrollments may be lower under a pure public system, particularly in developing countries, and non-price devices commonly used to ration space in the public sector may be just as income-biased as price rationing in the private sector. Then, private sector growth may actually improve access.

A second source of comparative advantage for the private sector arises when product variety is possible, tastes are differentiated and economies of scale are relatively small, characteristics which are often found in the education industry. Diverse organizations may be better able than government to offer a heterogeneous product mix and enable people to make separate choices about different services, rather than tying together a bundle of public goods, as is done through local governmental provision. The corresponding disadvantage is the possible segmentation of society into many small religious, linguistic and racial groups. While this can be prevented by specific 'integration' policies, it certainly has happened in some countries with large private educational sectors and this consequence must therefore be carefully evaluated.

A third advantage of privatization is the lower cost often implied. Private organizations may be able to avoid constraints on factor utilization, wage floors and bureaucratic red tape which keep government costs high. This may facilitate large increases in quantity consumed. The corresponding disadvantage is the possibility that lower costs may mean lower quality. Contrary to common belief, the public sector is often considered the high quality sector, from an international perspective. The crucial relationship between costs, quality and degree of privateness, however, is far from clear, and this is one of the issues most needing further empirical study.

Finally, I have shown elsewhere that private sector growth and government subsidies usually go hand-in-hand. Large private sectors are rarely sustained in modern countries without government support. The subsidies facilitate private sector growth but they also enable the government to extract concessions in return, in the form of regulations over inputs, outputs and other characteristics which satisfy diverse constituencies. The subsidy and regulations, taken together, have the effect of raising production costs, increasing paperwork, bureaucratization and depersonalization. While this development is not inevitable, it certainly is common. Thus, the very factors that originally create the demand for a private sector also set in motion forces making the private sector more like the public. Ironically, as the private sector grows, with public funding and regulations, it becomes quasi-governmental.

Acknowledgment

I wish to thank the numerous people in the US and abroad, who helped me with the study that has been summarized in this chapter. I especially appreciate the capable data analysis carried out by my research assistants, R. S. Huang, H. K. Lee, and Amy Salzbury. I gratefully acknowledge the financial support received for the various parts of this study, from the Spencer Foundation, the Exxon Education Foundation, the National Endowment for the Humanities, the Social Science Research Council, the Agency for International Development, and the Program on Non-profit Organization at Yale University. This chapter uses material which is presented in greater detail in several other papers I have written during the course of this study. In addition to this acknowledgment, I have cited the other papers as they have been used, and also list them among the References. The final version of this chapter was written during my year as Fellow at the Netherlands Institute for Advanced Study.

References

COLEMAN, J., HOFFER, T. and KILGORE, S. (1982) *High School Achievement: Public, Catholic and Private Schools Compared* New York: Basic Books.

COLEMANS, V. and NOFFER, T. (1987) *Public and Private High Schools: The Impact of Communities*, New York: Basic Books.

GEIGER, R. (1986) *Private Sectors in Higher Education: Structure, Function and Change in Eight Countries* Anne Arbor: University of Michigan Press.

GOLDBERGER, A. and CAIN, G. (1982) 'The Causal Analysis of Cognitive Outcomes', *The Sociology of Education*, 55, pp. 103–22.

HAERTEL, E., JAMES, T. and LEVIN, H. (1988) *Comparing Public and Private Schools*, Volume II, Lewes, Falmer Press.

JAMES, E. (1989) 'The Private Provision of Public Services: A Comparison of Holland and Sweden', in JAMES, E. (Ed) *The Nonprofit Sector in International Perspective: Studies in Comparative Culture and Policy*, Oxford, Oxford University Press.

JAMES, E. (1984) 'Benefits and Costs of Privatized Public Services: Lessons from the Dutch Educational System'. *Comparative Education Review*, 28, 605–624. Reprinted in LEVY, D. (1986) *Private Education: Studies in Choice and Public Policy*, New York, Oxford University Press.

JAMES, E. (1986a) 'The Political Economy of Private Education in Developed and Developing Countries', Washington, DC: World Bank discussion paper EDT 81.

JAMES, E. (1986b) 'Excess Demand and Private Education in Kenya', New Haven, PONPO Working Paper #117, ISPS, Yale University.

JAMES, E. (1986c) 'The Private Non-profit Provision of Education: A Theoretical Model and Application to Japan', *Journal of Comparative Economics.*

JAMES, E. (1987a) 'The Public/Private Division of Responsibility for Education: An International Comparison', *Economics of Education Review*, 6, 1–14.

JAMES, E. (1987b) 'The Non-profit Sector in Comparative Perspective' in POWELL, W. (ed.) *The Nonprofit Sector: A Research Handbook*, New Haven: Yale University Press.

JAMES, E. and BENJAMIN, G. (1987) 'Educational Distribution and Redistribution Through Education in Japan', *Journal of Human Resources*, 22, 469–89.

JAMES, E. and BENJAMIN, G. (1988) *Public Policy and Private Education in Japan*, London, Macmillan.

KRAMER, R. (1982) *Voluntary Agencies in the Welfare State* Berkeley, University of California Press.

LEVY, D. (1986) *Higher Education and the State in Latin America*, Chicago: University of Chicago Press.

MURNANE, R. (1984) 'Comparisons of Public and Private Schools: Lessons from the Uproar,' *Journal of Human Resources*, 19, 263–77.

WEISBROD, B. (1975) 'Toward a Theory of the Voluntary Nonprofit Sector in a Three-Sector Economy, in PHELPS, E. (ed.) *Altruism, Morality and Economic Theory* New York: Russell Sage Foundation.

WEISBROD, B. (1977) *The Voluntary Nonprofit Sector* Lexington, Mass., Lexington Books.

WILLMS, J. D. (1985) 'Catholic School Effects on Academic Achievement: New Evidence from the High School and Beyond Follow-up Study', *Sociology of Education*, 58, 98–114.

Chapter 12
Issues in Public Funding and Governance

Berry H. Durston

In taking an international perspective on private schools and public policy it is important to avoid the temptation to oversimplify what is in fact a very complex phenomenon. To start with, terminology differs considerably from country to country. For example, contributors to this book refer to public, private, government, non-government, state, independent, separate, supplementary and substitute schools to name but a few of the categories employed. For convenience, the broad descriptors 'public' and 'private' are used in relation to schools to distinguish between those which are generally recognized as public institutions (owned by the community, controlled and operated by public officials and funded from public sources) and those which are private institutions (typically owned, controlled and operated by religious bodies, community groups or voluntary associations but which are funded in whole or in part from private sources). While some of the income for private schools may come from supporting organizations, the major source of private income is usually school fees the level of which depends, in large measure, on the extent of the public funding available to the school. As a consequence of receiving public funding, private schools have had to accept certain limitations to their autonomy that they might not otherwise have been willing to concede.

Scope of the Private Sector

What constitutes the private sector differs considerably from one country to another. One of the most striking features is the discrepancy between countries in the relative size of the private sector. This is true even for modern industrialized democracies with somewhat similar traditions where typically between 5 per cent and 30 per cent of school children are educated outside the public sector. For example, nearly 11 per cent of children in the United States of America attend private schools but in Australia the figure exceeds 26 per cent. Even more surprising, having regard to the legacy of common heritage between the two countries concerned, is the pronounced difference between England (roughly 6 per cent) and Australia. However, the size of the private sector depends partly on the extent to which private schools have been incorporated into the public sector. In England it can be explained by the assimilation of many sectarian schools into the public sector, through a series of compromises between church and state, to become fully funded recurrent-wise from public sources although in the case of some schools at least, without necessarily surrendering control over important matters such as staffing, admissions and religious education. The situation in New Zealand, where the proportion of students attending private schools is similar to England, also reflects the effects of integration of many private schools into the public sector in return for public funding. There is, too, the question of where the Catholic enrolments are counted. For instance, in Ontario, Canada, most Catholic students attend Catholic separate schools which form part of the public sector whereas in Australia, Catholic schools are part of the private sector.

Participation rates in the private sector differ considerably with the level of education (primary, secondary). Furthermore, even within the same country the situation can differ markedly from one state to another. This applies to both the size of the private sector and the kinds of financial provisions which are made to support it. For example, in the United States the state with the highest proportion of students attending private schools in 1980 was Delaware with 19 per cent and the lowest Utah with less than 2 per cent. In 1986 enrolments in private schools in Australia ranged from a high of over 33 per cent in the Australian Capital Territory to a low of 16 per cent in the Northern Territory. Lawton's chapter on Canada and Weiss's on the Federal Republic of Germany refer to differences in funding arrangements from one province or state to another. However, it needs to be borne in mind that enrolments in private schools may not be a true indication of demand for private schooling because the number of places available in private schools may fall far short of demand.

In her chapter, James employs concepts from the discipline of economics in order to explain differences between countries in the proportion of students educated in the private sector. While some private schools are operated on commercial lines to make a profit, more typically they are established as non-profit organizations (usually a condition for the receipt of public funding and other benefits). She points to the essential ingredient of entrepreneurship in the founding of private schools. There is no doubt that the establishment of schools by religious groups has served to stimulate other groups to follow suit. This is particularly the case where public funds are available to assist with capital development and with operating expenses.

James concludes that even among countries which differ considerably in their level of economic development, political system and cultural values, the concepts of 'excess' and 'differentiated' demand help to explain the size of the private sector of schooling. She contends that if there are insufficient places available in public schools the private sector will expand to cater for the unsatisfied (excess) demand for schooling, a situation not uncommon in developing countries. However, the situation more typical of modern industrialized democracies is one in which the private sector expands to meet the (differentiated) demand for certain types of education rather than in response to an undersupply of public education. This reflects the cultural and ethnic diversity of relatively densely populated urban areas with sufficient school age children to warrant more than one school, where those seeking a different kind of education from that provided in public schools and who have the financial capacity to pay school fees can afford to send them to private schools. It seems that heterogeneous societies seek homogeneous schools. Weiss, in turn, talks of a greater differentiation of life styles that has brought about a change in educational preferences. In his view, negative perceptions concerning the educational expansion and reform of the last two decades in the Federal Republic of Germany have contributed to a loss of confidence in public education and this has had the effect of making the private alternative look more attractive.

Thrust for Privatization

In the prevailing economic and political climate facing many western nations it is not surprising that notions of privatization which affect attitudes towards the operations of public utilities such as publicly owned communication and transport systems are beginning to influence thinking about the place of government in the provision of education. There is concern about the role and efficiency of state controlled enterprises generally. Traditionally, education has been a big spending portfolio and, in times of economic stringency such as the present, governments are looking to their education budgets to find ways of reducing public expenditure. Changing circumstances involving declining school age cohorts and dwindling real resources call for radical solutions including an appraisal of the extent to which education should be a predominantly public enterprise.

Public Funding

Public funding for private schools may take a number of different forms. It may be directed to students or to schools. Direct assistance usually is provided in the form of grants or subsidies; indirect assistance (which is much more common) includes concessions on government charges; tax exemptions, rebates or deductions; access to government services or supplies; and the payment of allowances.

Central to the prosperity of the private school sector is the attitude of government to the right of parents to choose the kind of schooling that they wish their children to receive. Depending on the policies they adopt, governments can merely condone the exercise of choice or they can actively expand and facilitate it. For example, in the United States parents have the right to choose schooling alternative to that provided publicly and while there is some indirect support, no public funding is available to private schools to assist them to operate or to subsidize access to private schooling. Governments in certain other countries, on the other hand, have acted to make private education cheaper and more accessible and, in the process, have fostered an enrollment drift from the public to the private schools.

In their chapter, Edwards, Fitz and Whitty present a case study in public policy in which public funding is directed to assisting students rather than the private schools themselves. The Assisted Places Scheme in England is a program of public support for private education on a modest scale having regard to the number of students and amount of money involved each year. It provides for fee remissions adjusted according to parental income to enable a limited number of the more intellectually able students who might otherwise have attended public schools of lesser academic repute, to enrol in academically oriented private schools.

Other countries, however, have preferred to implement programs of direct support to schools. The Australian approach, for example, has been the establishment of an extensive program of public support for private schools from both federal and state governments. Federal support is based on per capita grants that take account of the private income available to each school. In addition, there is a system of state per capita grants which, depending on the state concerned, may be paid at a flat rate or calculated on an assessment of the needs of the school. There is no doubt that public funding has been a successful means of increasing the resources available to private schools in Australia and of improving access to them, by giving many parents an opportunity to exercise a choice that they could otherwise not afford, particularly if the schools had to charge fees sufficient to meet the full costs of their operation. On a national basis, the proportion of students enrolled in private schools rose from 21.3 per cent in 1975 to 26.4 per cent in 1986. This has led to the claim that Australia has a dual system of publicly supported education: the public schools which are fully funded from public sources and the private schools which are partly funded from public sources. However, the Australian experience has highlighted a problem in the relationship between public support and private effort, namely, the difficulty of implementing a needs based system for the public funding of private schools which does not penalize private effort.

Implications of Public Funding

What are the implications for public schools of providing public funding for private schools? And what are the consequences for the private schools themselves? Boyd, in his analysis of the Australian situation, makes a number of pertinent observations. Some commentators view the very existence of private schools as a threat to the welfare of public schools. They express concern about the effect on the morale of the public schools of the drift of students to the private schools and about public perceptions of the parity of esteem between the two sectors. The apparent abandonment of public schools by certain social groups in the community is seen as an erosion of support for public schools, particularly on the part of the more affluent, articulate and politically aware members of society, precisely the people who would be expected to be vocal in seeking improvements in public education and the resources to implement them. The withdrawal of their children leaves public schools as the providers of education for those who cannot or choose not to attend private schools and weakens the representative nature of public education. This has a debilitating effect on public schools which, being open to all comers, cannot hope to compete on equal terms. The situation is compounded by dwindling enrollments and resources and the attendant problems of contraction in the public sector. There is no doubt that growth in the private sector at the expense of the public sector raises questions about the role of the public school in society. The bigger the private sector the more socially representative it will be of the broad spectrum of society and the less open it will be to challenges of elitism.

It is simplistic in the extreme to blame the private schools for the shortcomings of the public schools without first attempting to address the legitimate reasons why people prefer private schools. It is all too easy to brand the supporters of private schools as anti-social and self-interested, or to assert that somehow it is undemocratic or divisive to sustain a range of schools, both public and private, with different aims and philosophies. The question to be answered is why, when there are ample unfilled places in free public schools, would anyone choose to send their child to a private school which entailed an obligation to pay fees. It is a natural inclination on the part of parents to want to ensure that their children receive the best education available in a school with an ethos with which they can readily identify. Some hold the view that education is too important an enterprise to be left to governments alone. Private schools are seen as establishing a bench mark against which standards in the public schools can be assessed and monitored. They challenge the public schools to be better. Whether justified or not, there is a public perception of declining standards of education and behaviour in public schools, of drab uniformity in public education, of disenchantment and loss of confidence. But the withdrawal of public funding for private schools is not the way to restore confidence in the public schools. All that that would achieve would be to price private schools out of the reach of many families and cause a drift back to the public sector. The effect on government budgets would be enormous and the number of dissatisfied students in public schools would swell.

It would indeed be a pity to squash the richness and diversity which private schools contribute to the totality of schooling by applying controls that serve to restrain their growth and development in ways that remove incentives and dampen the enthusiasm of students, parents and teachers. A more apposite approach would be to address the problems of alienation and dissatisfaction in the public sector by encouraging the public schools to develop some of the acknowledged strengths and desirable characteristics of private schools including a greater degree of self-determination. Private schools, for their part, have to weigh up the costs in terms of controls and limitations on their autonomy which are a natural outcome of accepting public funding. Private schools in receipt of public funding have an obligation to demonstrate that the funds provided by government are properly accounted for and applied for the purpose for which they were granted. Fiscal accountability is an accepted condition of public funding. However, there is a tendency for government to stipulate conditions for the payment of grants that schools may regard as intrusive into their affairs and that may have the potential to limit their capacity to respond to the perceived needs of their constituency and to affect the character of the school. The fundamental issue is to define the proper relationship between government and private schools.

Politics and Public Funding

Almost all of the contributors to this section point up the intensely political nature of the funding issue in their accounts of contemporary political considerations in the public funding of private schools. In a number of instances funding is depicted as an act of political will, the constitutional validity of which ends up by being tested in the courts. Nor do governments always seem to act in accordance with their espoused philosophies or in a consistent fashion. Smart, for example, outlines events in Australia surrounding the Hawke Labor government's decision, in direct contravention of the party platform, to continue public funding for private schools which operate at a level of resources in excess of those available to comparable public schools. Lawton, in turn, describes the decision of the provincial government of Ontario, Canada, to extend public funding to Catholic high schools without providing similar benefits to other religious groups. There is no doubt that the size and political clout of the private sector as a whole, or of elements within it, has had an important bearing on these decisions.

Public Policy Issues

A number of public policy issues are raised in relation to the provision of public funding for private schools. These include:

- Is choice of schooling between public and private schools a good thing or does it run counter to the interests of the wider community by creating social divisiveness?
- If choice is a worthwhile objective in a democratic society, how should it be facilitated to improve access by a broader spectrum of society?
- What constraints, if any, should be placed upon community demands for diversity and choice in private schools which receive funding from public sources?
- Is public funding the appropriate mechanism for regulating the size of the private sector?
- What is the desirable balance between the public and private sectors of schooling?
- Who should decide what that proportion should be: government (local, state, federal) or market forces?
- What forms should public funding for private schools take?
- Should public funding be an entitlement, discretionary or differentiated according to some formula?
- What kind of organizational structure is necessary for the administration of public funding to private schools?
- What conditions should attach to the payment of public funds to private schools?
- What forms of accountability should be required of private schools for the expenditure of public funds?

A particularly useful contribution of the chapter by Edwards *et al.* is to draw attention to the political and methodological difficulties inherent in undertaking public policy analysis in an intensely sensitive area such as the public funding of private schools. Apart from the obvious concern about the possibility that researchers, or others using their findings, may try to draw conclusions regarding the effects of public policy on the basis of premature evidence, there is a natural inclination to question the impartiality of the researchers themselves. It is hard to deny that public policy needs to be informed by competently conducted research rather than the rhetoric of unsubstantiated assertions and yet the reality is that the context in which this occurs is one that is often characterized by irreconcilable philosophical differences (depending on one's view of the world) which do not lend themselves to dispassionate empirical investigation and for which objective evidence, in the eyes of some, may not be in the least bit relevant. The enduring challenge for public policy makers concerned with making the best use of scarce resources is to strike a balance between competing interests that encourages pursuit of excellence and provides choice but not at the expense of equity considerations such as equality of opportunity and respect for the dignity and worth of every child. This calls for wisdom and commitment of a high order in the face of pressure from vested interests.

Chapter 13
The Politics of Privatization: Policy-making and Private Schools in the USA and Great Britain

Bruce S. Cooper

Introduction

Private schools are no longer 'private', if they ever have been. For in virtually every Western, industrialized nation, private schooling stands at the epicenter of a major political controversy concerning the sponsorship, funding, management, and quality of education (see Dennison, 1984; Cooper, 1985; Cooper, 1987b; Boyd, 1987). A full-blown political struggle is emerging in these nations between forces which press for very different ends: At one extreme are those advocating standardized, centralized (sometimes fully nationalized), state-dominated monopolies of education which work to equalize education for all — often coupled with the limitation or complete eradication of private schools as centers of privilege and inequality.

Pressing for opposite ends are the 'privatizers', those seeking to introduce the qualities of private education — competition, parental choice, efficiency, and free enterprise — into the provision of elementary and secondary education (see LeGrand and Robinson, 1976 and 1984; Friedman, 1962: Blaug, 1984; Maynard, 1975; Wicks, 1987) As Veljanovski (1987) explains in *Selling the State: Privatization in Britain*, 'Privatization is at the vanguard of a world-wide movement in thinking and politics about the legitimate role of the state in industrial society in the 1980s' (p. 205). In a recent book review in *The Times Educational Supplement*, Parker (1987) describes these two conflicting views graphically as 'the Scylla of neo-liberalism, including the eventual "privatization" of the welfare state, and the Charybdis of full-blooded egalitarianism'.

At no time have battle lines been so clearly drawn: where national regimes have placed the control of education at the top, or near the top, of their political agenda; where governments rise and fall on what they do to

Bruce S. Cooper

improve education; And where the level of dialogue is so clearly ideological, pitting the egalitarians, nationalizers, state-controllers, and socialists up against the privatizers, decentralizers, denationalizers, divestors, and
deregulators.

In Britain, for example, 'Schools take centre stage in campaign',
screamed *The Times* of London front page headlines (May 25, 1987). The
article continues:

> Education became the central issue of the election campaign
> yesterday after teachers unveiled plans to strike in fifty-two areas
> ten days before polling. Meanwhile Mrs Margaret Thatcher gave a
> clear indication that she hoped the Conservatives' opt-out scheme
> would lead to more grammar schools (p. 1).

So, while teachers' unions plan to call selective strikes just before the
national election to protest the Tory government's policies, the Prime
Minister has made 'privatization' in education her central and most
controversial policy This 'opt-out' scheme, one among many efforts to
privatize, would mean that local (public) government schools could 'go
private' by a simple majority vote of their governors and parents. These
schools would then continue to receive direct public funding but could
operate independently: setting their own policies, admitting students
selectively (with some form of testing), and even, it appears, paying their
teachers higher salaries than the local public schools (whether these new
'government maintained' schools could also charge an additional sum as
tuition is unclear, though how else could the school raise additional funds
for higher teacher salaries?).

The relative importance of public versus private provision of education is not a new issue in these countries; not at all. This controversy has
been around since democratic government began to create systems of
public or state schools, usually '... "to fill the gaps" that the private system
has left' as West explained (1970, p. xviii). But in so doing, governments
often moved to *monopolize* education by destroying or at least limiting the
non-public schools that had carried the education burden alone for
centuries (Doyle and Levine, 1984).

Rather, we now witness two fully developed school systems, two
clearly opposing ideologies, and two conscious arguments about who
should provide education and how. What had once been a rather limited
controversy over school reform, 'aid to church schools,' 'parochi-aid', as it
was called in the USA (Erickson, 1968), for example, or over the rights of
these schools to exist at all in many countries, has now become a major
ideological struggle. In effect, those who favor a purely public education
system, governmentally controlled and funded, usually seek to guarantee
equality of opportunity, democracy and a semblance of cohesion that a 'free
market' ostensibly cannot provide (Walker, 1984). And those trying to
privatize schooling strive to enhance competition and efficiency, and allow

246

the consumer — not the state — to determine the ownership and kinds of education which children receive.

Whatever the attempt to make schooling more competitive, private, and choice-enhancing, the response of the established government schools is always defensive and strong. In both Britain and the US, as this chapter shows, efforts to introduce radical reform are met with strong resistance from teachers' unions, moderates and liberals, and from those concerned about preserving the equalitarian approach to education. We shall see that moves toward privatization in the US have been unsuccessful at the national level, though a large number of local and state education authorities have attempted to enhance choice within the system. In Britain, by way of contrast, a number of schemes are in place — such as the Assisted Places Scheme to allow children to attend elite independent schools at government expense and the newly announced independent, direct-grant City Technology Colleges (CTCs) — which allow parents and teachers to select a school outside the confines of the government school system.

Privatization Defined

No international comparison of governmental policies concerning private schools would be possible today without an analysis of efforts to 'privatize' education. Privatization in Britain, 'an ugly word that describes a wonderful process' (Clarke, 1987, p. 66; Drucker, 1970), refers to attempts by governments to divest themselves of the major provision of educational (or other) services, turning instead to the private sector to educate children; or short of total divestiture, governments might strive to introduce 'qualities' of the private sector into education. Privatizing is seen as an attempt to reverse the pressures to nationalize services and industry. That is, while socialist governments have had a penchant for buying up the means of production (the steel, coal, communications, and auto industry, for example), more conservative regimes, upon ascending to power, would promptly sell off — or 'privatize' — those same national corporations.

In education, similarly, privatization aims to foster competition between the state and non-public school sectors and amongst schools within sectors, in order to stimulate improvements and innovations; to bring private funds and local initiative into education; and to offer a wide range of schools (types, philosophies, values) to parents and to allow them to select the schools they prefer.

Stuart Sexton, in *Our Schools — A Radical Policy* (1987), makes the point well on privatization of education in Great Britain:

The only choice left is to devolve the system to the schools themselves, and to create a direct relationship between the suppliers of education, the schools and the teachers, and the consumers, the parents and their children. It is to create, as near as is practicable, a 'free market' in education. To use a popular word, it is in some sense to 'privatize' the state education system (p. 10).

In the USA, similar arguments have been made for such privatization measures as aid to private schools (direct grants and ancillary services) or direct assistance to families through tuition tax credits and education vouchers, a means by which government delivers school funds to parents, not to school districts, permitting families to select the schools of their choice. As Levin (1983) explains, 'In the context of educational choice, these approaches begin with the view that the most important educational commitment in a democratic society is that of permitting families to choose the kind of education that they want for their children' (p. 35; see also Coons, Clune, and Sugarman, 1970, ch. 2). Or, as James and Levin (1983) state in the introduction to *Public Dollars for Private Schools: A Case of Tuition Tax Credits*

> Tuition tax credits would furnish substantially higher levels of public support for non-public schools. If the proposal were enacted, it would encourage family *choice* and, many advocates argue, foster greater *competition* and *excellence* in education. Tuition tax credits would also shift some of the emphasis of public policy away from public schools, an institution presently beseiged by declining enrollments, economic retrenchment, and eroding public confidence (1983, p. 4, my emphasis).

Privatization, in the extreme, would mean total private ownership, provision, and control of education, a development not given much consideration in modern countries. Few would advocate withdrawing all public tax support for education — letting each family go it alone on its own resources — or at best having private philanthropy fill in. The well-to-do would fund their own children's schooling — and through a church or other elemosynary association fund the schools for some of the indigent. The bulk of the poor, presumably, would get no formal education at all. Even an unconcerned, middle-class family might simply 'overlook' the education of their children, or so the argument goes.

Most policy-makers, and even the most conservative of economists, have argued that using a 'pure' market — like the one for automobiles and mink coats — would mean a large, un- or under-educated group of people, posing an encumbrance to economic growth (see Schultz, 1963) and a threat to civil peace, the quality of life, and the ability of the masses to participate effectively in democratic life (Friedman, 1955 and 1962). Or as West explains,

> ...the social benefits of education are not confined to the 'educatee'

but spread to society as a whole, most noticeably in the form of reduced crime and more 'social cohesion'. This can be expressed negatively; the private actions of an uneducated person may have unfortunate consequences for others in society (1970, p. 31).

Whatever the reasoning, in the context of this chapter, education will be considered more or less privatized — to the extent that choice, openness, and competition are encouraged, or discouraged; but the idea that real, total privatization is a possibility (like the selling off of a coal mine) in modern nations is dismissed for practical political reasons. In our opinion, the government will long have a major political and financial interest in education; it is just the *nature* of the state's role that concerns us in analyzing privatization of education in the US and Britain.

Thus, political analysis of the government's relations with schools in general — and private schools, in particular — shall be considered in this essay, using a redefined notion of privatization. In so doing, we shall think of the concept as relative, that is, a kind of continuum from total state ownership and control at one extreme, as occurs in the Eastern Bloc nations (see Cooper and Doyle, 1985) where 'private' education is inconsistent with the radical-equalitarian, socialist ideals, to total privatization at the other (though as we have just shown, this condition is highly unlikely in nations where government schools are widely accepted and entrenched). As shown in Figure 1, the extremes are presented as (1) Total state ownership, funding, and control of schooling at one end, to (2) Total privatization of provision, support, and management, at the other.

It is possible to have a 'mixed' set of characteristics lying well between the extremes of strictly public or strictly private ownership/funding/control. For example, one sees private ownership of schools, with government funding, and government control, as is the case in Great Britain, with 20 per cent of the schools sponsored by religious groups but which receive full funding and major control ('voluntary-aided' schools) from the government. Or, one could construct a system whereby schools are publicly owned, yet which have substantial private funding and private/market forces at work, as one sees in the state university system in the US where parents pay tuition and where intense competition for students exists among public and private institutions of higher learning. Or, a system

Figure 1. Privatization of Education: A Continuum

Total State Control	Total Private Control
State ownership _	Private ownership
Government funding _	Private support
Government regulation _	Private market Regulation

could exist where ownership and funding are public, but a competitive, 'private market' is established among government schools, thus creating privatization of sorts through a system of (differentiated, 'open enrollment', and competitive) 'magnet schools'.

Thus, it seems clear that the politics of private education, or better yet, of 'privatization' of education, is much more complex than one might assume, particularly when one attempts to study the topic across nations and policy arenas. When politicians in the US Congress, the British Parliament, or in local school authorities begin to 'privatize', to offer choice between sectors, or within them, the political responses are much the same: strong resistance to attempts to grant parents more choice and to allow schools — both public and private — to compete. The introduction of parental choice and inter-school and inter-sector competition is perhaps more important in explaining political behavior than is whether one is discussing any particular aid scheme, whether for public or private schools.

Privatization and Politics in Britain and the USA

Policy-makers appear to have at least two major options in aiding private schools, and in turn privatizing the education service. The first, and most direct, is simply funding the individual: to give parents the equivalent amount of money (to what is currently spent on education in the locality or program) and to allow parents to 'buy' the schooling their children need and want (see Doyle and Cooper, 1987). Whether in the form of a 'voucher', a 'grant,' a 'certificate' (they are known by all these names in various laws and proposals), whether an 'unlimited' voucher whereby any choice is acceptable to the funders, or a 'restricted' one (see Seldon, 1986; Mason, 1975; Jencks, 1970) which places certain conditions on the user, this approach has recently been proposed by the Reagan Administration in its Title I/Chapter 1 re-authorization bill and by the Thatcher administration under Secretary of State for Education, Sir Keith Joseph, though not as yet enacted.

A second approach to privatization — one now being tried in both the US and Britain — is funding institutions, at the school level, schools of a variety of types, offering a set of choices. In Britain, such programs include (1) City Technology Colleges (CTC's) — secondary schools with a high-powered science/technology theme that are 'independent' schools supported by direct grants from the national government, and (2) the recent proposal in the Conservative Manifesto (1987) in which government (or public) schools can withdraw from their local education agency by a majority vote of the parents and school governors, creating the new 'grant-maintained' (GM) schools.

And America's 'magnet schools' — schools with special themes or programs, available to all students in a region — also create a 'market' by

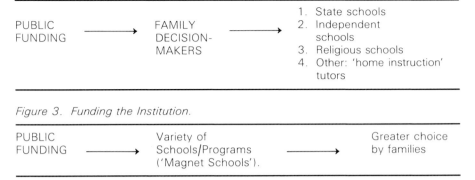

Figure 2. Funding the Individual.

Figure 3. Funding the Institution.

funding competing schools at the level of their ability to attract and hold students; by allowing parents to select these schools without restrictions of place of residence, even across city boundaries into suburban school districts; and by encouraging schools to feature special, attractive programs and to recruit widely for the 'best' students and staff. As shown in figures 2 and 3, these two approaches to organizing, funding, and controlling schools have major implications for the policy-makers.

In the next two sections, comparative US-British examples of policies for funding the individual (usually, the family) and funding the school are presented and analyzed, with the countervening political arguments by those supporting government control of schools.

1 Funding the Individual: 'Vouchers', by Any Other Name

The USA

The concept of funding pupils, not systems of schools, has been around for almost forty years, and has gone through numerous alterations. In the USA, recent legal developments have made it almost impossible to provide equitable aid to children attending parochial schools without accepting some form of *direct family subsidy* for education. For the First Amendment of the US Constitution forbids the 'Establishment' of religion through direct aid to religiously-sponsored schools. In Britain, a number of reformers have reached much the same conclusion, though not necessarily for legal or religious reasons. And in both nations, experiments using vouchers have been attempted: the county of Kent planned to issue vouchers in a limited way, though the plan was withdrawn; in Alum Rock, San Jose, California, a small voucher experiment was attempted, but strictly within the public or government school sector (in order to avoid the legal and political problems of public funding for religious schools), And the state of New

Hampshire almost adopted a total funding scheme which would have allocated school funds to the family, not the local education agencies.

In all, then, vouchers have been discussed, debated, altered, and attempted (Uzzell, 1984). As predicted, they are supported by those who seek a simple, direct, and effective way to, 'privatize' education — and to allow funds to reach public and private schools on equal footing. And as also predicted, this form of funding the individual has caused the most virulent of political reactions from those supporting the hegemony of the government school sector. Critics of vouchers see them as divisive, as a not-so-veiled way of funding elite schools and leaving the poor, the underachieving, the least desirable children behind. Vouchers are perceived as a direct attack on the qualitarian principles of universal, equitable, and high-quality education for all. Currently, voucher schemes are pending in the US Congress and are advocated by New Right reformers in Britain.

During this spring of 1987, two bills are pending in the federal funding of education. Both are concerned about 'reauthorizing' the nation's largest ($3.3 billion) federal aid to education program, Chapter 1 of the Education Consolidation and Improvement Act (ECIA). Both bills must tackle a major obstacle to easy passage of this law: how to guarantee that children attending the nation's 9000 participating private sectarian schools receive their just share of the services — those established to help the poorest and lowest achieving students in all schools — public *and* private.

These two bills represent the two sides of the aid-to-private-schools conflict: the Democratic-sponsored law seeks to maintain the primacy of public schools as the major institution in education; the Republican administration's bill attempts to 'privatize' education, in that it proposes a local option voucher — one in which local education agencies could award 'compensatory education certificates' (CECs) to poor, underachieving children (their families) who attend parochial schools for remedial services, if the LEA itself could not serve these children directly.

Background

In 1965, President Lyndon Johnson and Congress passed the largest and most important federal aid to education law, called Title I, later changed to Chapter 1, of the Elementary and Secondary Education Act, or ESEA (Eidenberg and Morey, 1969). The goal of Title I of ESEA was to offer remedial help in basic subjects, reading, writing, mathematics, to the poorest and lowest achieving students in the nation's schools.

A major compromise in the bill, to secure the support of Northern, urban, and Catholic and Jewish constituencies, was some federal aid to children in parochial schools. Since the First Amendment prevented *direct* government support of religious institutions, Congress wrote into Title I an indirect approach, or, in the language of the law-makers: an 'equitable constitutional formula': giving additional money to the local *public* schools, and allowing them to hire public school teachers to visit the parochial school and offer, in a 'neutral' classroom (all religious symbols and articles removed), the same kinds of remedial help that children in public schools were getting.

Between 1965 and 1985, the church-state compromise seemed to work. The federal government awarded funds to local school districts, based on the number of poor children. The public school hired extra staff and provided Chapter 1 remedial help on the premises of the parochial school. Church school leaders, so long concerned about depending on government school officials to delivery services, learned to trust the public schools; and public school districts found working in parochial schools rewarding. Furthermore, Title I/Chapter 1, and its various amendments over the twenty years, added provisions such that failure of local district to provide 'equitable services to private school children' could lead to the ability of the US Government to withhold funds from districts not providing equitable services to private school students, and to bypass local authorities and to fund third party providers, which has been done 106 times since 1965.

By the 1980s, some 300,000 eligible children in attendance at parochial schools were receiving direct services, in their schools, from the Chapter 1 program; about 8000 of these were being served through a bypass provision.

But, then, on July 1, 1985, the US Supreme Court, in *Aguilar* v. *Felton* ruled that bringing public employees into the parochial schools, and supervizing them there, was a violation of the separation of church and state: that mingling public and religious school staff, on the premises, was 'excessive entanglement' of religion and government, and that direct services inadvertently assisted in the 'religious mission' of the schools — all in direct violation of the First Amendment prohibition against the 'establishment' of religion.

Now, for the first time in twenty years, public schools were required to provide these equitable services to children in religiously-sponsored schools, but somehow they were expected to do it outside the parochial schools themselves. In the nearly two years since *Aguilar* districts have tried almost everything: transporting private schoolchildren to public school sites, or neutral sites at great cost and with serious losses of valuable instructional time; hooking the parochial schools into a computer or television network for remediation, even though no one could be sure that the private school staff at the other end knew how to use the equipment; or bringing mobile vans to the curbside.

These rather awkward and very expensive options (for example, to lease a van costs $105,000 each per year in NYC; and at most, it can serve only thirty students per day, six to eight at a time) have not worked overall, driving up costs and lowering the participation and quality of Chapter 1 for private school children. Enrollment in these federally-guaranteed programs has dropped by over one-third, as costs have nearly doubled (see Vitullo-Martin and Cooper, 1987). As the Rev. Thomas G. Gallagher, Secretary, of the US Catholic Conference, explained in a letter to the Chair of the House Subcommittee on Education, August F. Hawkins, Democrat from California:

> Some local education authorities are currently providing Chapter 1 services to private school children in mobile education units or in leased neutral sites. Others are bussing private school children to public schools and are providing chaperones to escort the children walking to the nearest public school. The alternatives have proven to be particularly disruptive to the regular academic programs of these students (January 15, 1987).

Chapter 1 expires in 1987. Congress and the President must decide how to reauthorize it and what means to use to reach the 300,000 or so children in parochial schools who qualify for these federal compensatory educational services. Lawmakers have two proposed bills up for consideration.

H.R.-950: The Democratic bill

One proposal, called the 'Special Educational Needs Act of 1987', HR-950, is presented by the Democratic Party majority in the House of Representatives, through Representative Hawkins and by moderate Republican William Goodling of Pennsylvania. It seeks to continue funding the local public school districts — and requiring them to provide 'equal services' to children in religiously-affiliated schools. This approach, funding public school districts and having them hire staff to help parochial school youngsters, worked reasonably well since the law was passed in 1965 and the ruling of the Supreme Court in 1985. Since then, however, it has not. And the private-public school coalition which has supported Chapter 1 since its first passage has begun to crumble over how to restructure the program to include private school students, weakening the 'education lobby' overall (Cooper and Poster, 1986).

The only concession made by the Democrat's bill is a 'sweetener' of some $30 million (to public school districts) for capital costs incurred when trying to carry out the High Court's requirement that services for parochial schools be 'off-site'. Thus, the public schools, here again, receive the extra funds for their capital costs, even though the money is targeted to serve the students in parochial schools.

The term 'capital expenses', according to the proposed legislation,

> ...is limited to expenditures for non-instructional goods and services such as the purchase, lease and renovation for real and

personal property (including but not limited to mobile instructional units and computer equipment and materials), insurance and maintenance costs, transportation, and other comparable goods and services [SEC. 117 (D)(b)(4)].

Otherwise, the law proposes to continue Chapter 1 as is: local districts, using federal funds, to attempt direct — but off-site — services to children in parochial schools. This bill represents the efforts of the Democratic Party, backed by the teachers' unions, administrators' associations, and other liberal groups to continue government-school domination of the largest and most important of federal school programs.

'Investment in Human and Intellectual Capital' Bill: The Republican law

The Republican administration has offered a competing bill for consideration before Congress in re-authorizing Chapter 1. It contains certain key elements of privatization, allowing local school systems to issue vouchers, or, as they are here called, 'Compensatory Education Certificates', to families of eligible Chapter 1 children attending the nation's non-public schools. Further, the bill is framed in the conservative language of privatizers, as its preamble explains:

> To increase investment in human and intellectual capital, to promote the development of science and technology, to enhance the protection of intellectual property, to bring about legal and regulatory reform essential to the elimination of obstacles to competitiveness, to improve the international economic environment (Subtitle A, *American Excellence Act* of 1987).

Note the emphasis on competition with foreign economic powers, the Japanese come to mind; and the concern for the developing of capacity in science, technology, and 'intellectual capital'.

The major departure from other federal aid bills, and a move toward privatization in education, is the introduction of family choice through federally-funded, local allocated 'certificates', which can be 'cashed in' for a number of remedial programs (operated by the local public school, the parochial school, other government schools, universities, and even, one presumes, to hire tutors), In particular, the law would '... allow for the provision of compensatory education certificates to parents for educationally deprived children'. The bill continues:

> The Act would authorize the LEA to provide these certificates if it determines that doing so (1) would be more effective in meeting the needs of eligible children than direct services provided by the LEA, or (2) is needed to provide services required under Chapter 1,

including services to private school children as required by section 557 of the Act [(SEC. 1011(a)].

This law shares much in common with other voucher attempts: it would allow choice amongst programs; it would create new markets for these children and their services; and it would remove the government — the LEAs — from having to deliver remedial services directly to parochial schools, thus overcoming the basic constitutional concerns about 'excessive entanglement'. In fact, Mr. Justice Powell, of the US Supreme Court, the swing vote in the *Aguilar* ruling, commented in his consenting opinion that just such a law (vouchers) would likely be found legal and constitutional, since it would be simple, open to all children, and would place the parent, not the public school, as the main agent of remedial decision-making:

> Our cases have upheld even-handed secular assistance to both parochial and public school children in some areas... [see the *Mueller* v. *Allen* decision in which a Minnesota tax deduction scheme was upheld as being 'even-handed' for children attending both public and non-public schools]. ... I do not read the Court's opinion as precluding these types of indirect aid to parochial schools. In the cases cited, the assistance programs made funds available equally to public and private schools without entanglement... The constitutional defect in the Title I programs ... is that it provides direct financial subsidy to be administered in significant part by public school teachers [and administrators] within parochial schools — resulting in both the advancement of religion and forbidden entanglement. If, for example, Congress would fashion a program of even-handed financial assistance to both public and private schools that could be administered without governmental supervision at the private schools, so as to prevent the diversion of aid from secular purposes, we could be presented with a different question (*Aguilar* v. *Felton*, 84-237, 84-238, 84-239, July, 1985, Justice Powell, occurring, p. 5).

Politically, one might think that the 'local option voucher' would be more acceptable than mandatory voucherization; yet close analysis of the reaction of the Democrats and the public school groups shows the contrary. Any form of privatization is anathema. The teachers' unions, for example, have opposed the local option voucher. Mary H. Futrell, President of the largest association, the National Education Association, condemned the Chapter 1 voucher as 'a guise for funneling public monies to private schools, ... a hoax, hypocritical, odious ... cruel' (Futrell, 1986, p. 14). During the first week of hearings, Chairperson, Representative Gus Hawkins, upon learning the preferences of the Catholic and Jewish groups for the 'certificates' over the Democratic approach, leaned back in his chair high up on the dais in the Carl Perkins Hearing Room, and said, 'There will be no vouchers from this committee!' The hearing room packed with representatives from local groups of public school principals, teachers, and superintendents' associations, nodded approval. The Democrats on the committee smiled knowingly.

2 Aid to Institutions: Funding 'Magnet Schools'

Great Britain

Britain has also explored various schemes for privatizing education, including vouchers. But for various reasons to be discussed shortly, direct aid to families in the form of vouchers was rejected in 1981, though free places in independent schools were funded for thirty-five thousand students. In 1986, the government announced a plan to create twenty City Technology Colleges, secondary schools which would be 'independent' entities funded directly by the national government. And in the 1987 party Manifesto the Conservatives announced plans to permit local public or government schools to withdraw themselves from the local education agencies, if their parent body and governing boards so voted.

Thus, privatization through family funding gave way to privatizing schools — a form of 'magnetization' — as we shall discuss next. And interestingly, attempts to privatize within the government sector, by creating competing state (magnet) schools, caused the same kind of political reactions as vouchers, with many of the same arguments heard.

Background

By American standards, British education appears more 'privatized', since most children seeking religious education can enroll, free of charge, in various Roman Catholic, Anglican, Jewish, Methodist schools, and under 'voluntary aided' status, the government will pay full (100 per cent) tuition and 85 per cent of the construction and renovation (capital) costs for private school buildings. Currently, 20 per cent of all students in England and Wales attend religiously-sponsored schools which are fully 'maintained' by the government (this means, too, that teachers in the voluntary-aided sector receive the same pay as government school teachers). Public aid to religious schools is no issue; for Britain, with its Church of England, has no laws 'separating church and state'. In fact, religious instruction is the only course of study now required in all British classrooms, public and private.

Furthermore, families in Britain have the opportunity to enroll their children in any government school to which they can gain admission, regardless of its location. Thus, while American students usually attend schools in their school district, British students have the option — if a 'place' is available — to attend a school in a neighboring local education agency and the 'home' LEA will reimburse the receiving LEA. A number of 'better' LEAs actually gain more students than they lose — having a positive 'balance of payments' and make money on their incoming students to fill empty seats. Thus, besides the options to attend, free, a denominational school, students in Britain can also elect to enroll in schools outside their immediate community or LEA, though there are obvious practical and safety limits on the numbers that an outstanding LEA can accept.

Despite access to a range of government, sectarian, and private schools, reformers in Britain are pressing hard for privatization, particularly for ways to change the basic unit of British education, the 'comprehensive' school (see Woodhall, 1977). For, in 1965 — the same year that President Johnson signed the Elementary and Secondary Education Act into Law — the Labour government under Prime Minister Harold Wilson, requested the merger of the 'tripartite' system of British schools — the elite grammar schools, the less elite secondary modern schools, and the remaining vocational schools — into the-one-school-for-all approach: the comprehensive school.

These schools were seen as more democratic and equalitarian. They replaced — or began to replace — a system based on examinations which separated the 'top' 15 per cent (who went to grammar schools) from the remaining 85 per cent (who attended secondary or vocational schools). The plan, finally accepted by most of the local education agencies, called for a two-tier approach: the first being comprehensive 'junior' schools (ages 11 to 14) and comprehensive 'senior' schools (ages 15 to 18), though the configuration varied greatly. The Labour government in its circular to LEAs, announced that 'it is the government's declared objective to end selection at eleven plus and to eliminate separatism in secondary education' (Circular 10/65: The Organization of Secondary Education, 12 July, 1965).

Privatizers in Britain point to the loss of the elite grammar schools, the homogenization of education, and the drop in standards and discipline as major problems, ones that require the reintroduction of special schools, through some kind of direct grant system. Thus, while reformers in the US must contend with the prohibitions of the First Amendment against aid to voluntary denominational schools, in Britain the issue is somewhat different. How to privatize the government school sector, dominated by mediocre comprehensive schools (Peacock and Wiseman, 1964) while contending with the power of organized groups against such efforts? As Arthur Seldon explains in *The Riddle of the Voucher* (1986).

In the thirty years since 1955, most of the grammar schools have been closed. If the 1955 Minister had been advised by his officials

..., Britain's grammar schools would have been saved, parents would have learned to choose schools, and insist on rising standards, numeracy and literacy among the school population would now be higher than ever, taxation would be much lower, the officialdom smaller, the state would not have encroached on civil life to the point at which it is now difficult to roll back (p. 12).

With the Thatcher victory and the new power of the Right in government, the pressure to create a national voucher was high. Yet funding the individual through a voucher was not implemented by Sir Keith Joseph, Secretary of State for Education in 1981, though attempts were made to influence him. For example, when FEVER (Friends of the Education Voucher Experiment in Representative Regions), an interest group, sent the Minister a practical plan for privatizing education, through direct aid to families, Joseph responded that the 1980 Education Act already privatized education, through the Assisted Places Scheme (see Chapter 6 of this volume for Edwards, Whitty and Fitz's analysis of this scheme), a means of giving scholarship aid to children attending the elite independent 'public' schools, and publishing for all to see the examination results for each government school.

And the government refused the voucher concept for other reasons as well, First, concern was expressed for whether vouchers would be available for independent schools and whether these schools would wish to participate, thus giving up some control over their admissions. If independent schools were left out of the scheme, then the program would be nothing more than an 'open enrollment' plan within the maintained sector, since students already have access to government and voluntary-aided religious schools free of charge. And if independent schools were included, these vouchers would drive up the cost of education and would diminish the level of private contribution through tuitions lost.

Second, voucherization would cause great consternation among the leadership within the government sector. Would, for example, each school be able to hire and fire, and pay teachers whatever the market would bear? If so, how would this plan affect national salary scales, which are subjects of law and national negotiations? What impact would parental preferences have on school curricula, program, and the needs of employers (local agencies)? And third, 'a voucher pitched at the average unit cost in an individual local authority's area would thus provide, to a significant degree, differently for the different conditions and management of different schools' (Memorandum, Department of Education, on Vouchers, 16 December, 1981), creating illegalities and hardship for the poorer schools. In all, then, the Minister and the Department of Education and Science rejected the notion of vouchers as too radical, risky, and uncertain.

Thus, not only did the Left attack vouchers as anti-democratic and elitist (Wagner, 1974), but the Right itself, once in office, found the concept too much of a break with past practices. In summary, Sir Keith Joseph raised these issues with vouchers:

> The above considerations raise large questions about what the function of the LEA would be and how education would be organized and run under a voucher system. Among others, the following points arise:
>
> i. Would a voucher system be compatible with individual LEAs management of the education service in its area? How would it fit in relation to an LEA's responsibilities to determine general policies in response to demographic change and in respect to the pattern of schooling?
>
> ii. In view of the substantial differences in inter-authority average units costs, how would movement across LEA boundaries be facilitated?
>
> iii. How should education outside the compulsory period be organized and financed? In particular, if vouchers are available for school sixth forms, should 16–19 education provided within the Further Education sector be financed similarly or differently?
>
> iv. What changes in the present law would all the above considerations entail? More specifically, what changes would be needed so that the voucher would in effect be a means of giving cash to parents which they would only be free to spend on their children's schooling?
>
> Department of Education and Science
> December 1981

City Technology Colleges: Magnets and Privatization

With vouchers an unlikely prospect, another approach to privatization was attempted: opening a series of government schools, with a special theme (science, technology, mathematics, and entrepreneurship) and regional enrollment patterns, which would be funded directly by the Department of Education and Science, not by the local education agencies. These national magnet schools were announced in October, 1986, by Secretary of State for Education, Kenneth Baker, and were explained in a brochure entitled *City Technology Colleges: A New Choice of Schools*

These CTCs are an interesting attempt at privatization within the government school sector. They are a cross between an 'independent school', operated by a charitable trust, and a 'government-maintained' school, which selects its own 'governing body', sets curriculum, hires staff, and sets admissions policies. The government has set certain constraints, however: they must operate as non-profit trusts and will be funded on a per pupil (per-capitation) basis, with initial start-up costs raised from the private, corporate sector; they can hire their own staff, set their own program, and work closely with the inner-city areas where they will be located.

As one can see, these are not to be 'vocational' or 'technical' schools per se; but rather they are designed to teach core courses in the sciences, mathematics, technology, business, computers — all in preparation for university and polytechnic colleges, as well as the world of work and entrepreneurship. These are schools for training the elite, the next generation of engineers, nuclear scientists, and more important, leaders in commerce, entrepreneurs, venture capitalists, the shock troops of the new post-industrial, hi-tech, marketing-financing-profiting Britain.

Interestingly, from an American perspective, the CTCs were created with such ease. While Chapter 1, for example, is tied up in committee, under debate, being chewed over by Democrats and Republicans, the White House and the Congress, the British simply announce a whole new kind of national school, paid for by the national treasury. Kenneth Baker, having cleared the innovation with the Prime Minister and the Cabinet (Tories all), restructures British education. No parliamentary hearings, no votes. As Minister of State, he moved ahead, with his party's backing, to open schools which give Tories a quick fix, something to point to.

The System Fights Back

As one might predict, defenders of the local education agencies, of urban schools, and of the record of the existing system were fast to attack this form of privatization within the government school sector. Perhaps the most cogent arguments came from the LEA group from the cities, the Association of Metropolitan Authorities (AMA). The published paper is entitled calmly, *City Technology Colleges: A Speculative Investment* (February 1987). It stakes its territory around six arguments, most of which defend the local education agency as the legitimate and effective institution to be setting up and running schools, while the Conservative government has seen the LEAs as the symbol of recalcitrance, union power, and Socialism. Here we see the forces against privatization at their lucid best.

1. *Destructive Intrusion into Local Reorganization*: Inserting CTCs into urban schools, according to the AMA, will upset the careful planning of LEAs, as they deal with declining enrollments, the need to close buildings, and make changes in buildings.
2. *Exacerbating Teacher Shortages — in Math and Science*: The AMA also claims that creating these magnet schools will only make the shortage of teachers in critical technical areas worse. If the sponsors of these schools 'bait the salaries above the nationally agreed levels' (p. 6), then 'able teachers now in the maintained sector may very well be drawn into these

schools', making the shortages more critical. This complaint by the AMA overlooks the growing interest as reported in the newspapers, of retired teachers (but often not elderly) who would *flock back into the profession* if given a chance to teach in the CTCs.

3. *Ignores 'Innovative Curriculum' in LEAs*: The AMA argues that the CTCs are hardly new or innovative, that already, the metropolitan schools are offering courses similar to the technology, science, computers and mathematics. Further, 'the authority concerned has pioneered some important developments in building up relationships with industry and commerce' (p. 8). Students in these schools are encouraged, the AMA explains, to engage in 'mini-enterprise operations in schools', and programs link up closely with British Telecom, 'Industry Year', 'Industry Matters', and 'the London Education Business Partnership'.

The AMA then accuses the CTC curriculum of being too restrictive and leading 'to a degree of specialization which other recent curriculum developments have discouraged' (p. 10). This argument is strange coming from an educational system which slots children into fields for O-levels and A-levels early on. Finally, here, the AMA lowers the boom on the CTC: 'If the aims of a CTC are worthy, *they are worthy for all pupils*, and provision cannot be justified only for a few' (p. 10).

4. *Blindness to 'the Problems of Our Cities'*: Here the anti-privatizers muster several classic arguments: first, that if the government wants to create new institutions and new jobs in the cities, then let them create a new industry which will employ people, not displace them as the CTC will do. Second by stealing the best students away from urban schools, the CTCs will only make the schools worse for everyone else.

5. *Blindness to the 'Successes' in the Cities*: The AMA report also emphasizes the progress that urban schools are currently making, and claims that the government 'misunderstands' the improvement in achievement (increased number of students for example, leaving school with five or more O-level — Ordinary level — passes). These improvements in the cities are continuing, 'in spite of the effects of economic and social handicaps and the disruption caused by industrial action [British teachers have been on a limited strike action for over two years]' (p, 13). Thus, this group claims, the CTCs may endanger the progress in education being made, by diverting resources, creaming off the brightest students and further eroding public confidence in urban schools.

6. *Difficulty of Starting New Urban Secondary Schools*: Finally, the Association of Metropolitan Authorities call attention to the immense costs and energy necessary for 'individuals and organizations in the business community and elsewhere' (p. 16) to start such schools. Capital costs (buildings, outfitting them) for old facilities could run between 3 and 6 million pounds per school; new schools, 7 to 10 million pounds each to construct. Staffing at all levels (for ages 11 to 18) will require the hiring of teachers across fields and levels, plus support and custodial staff, even as the school is attempting

to attract the necessary 1000 or so students. During the 'start-up', the AMA argues, the per-unit costs will be extremely high.

Additional costs may accrue to CTCs because they lack 'access to LEA bulk-purchasing arrangements'. Also, if these schools are totally free to parents, the school must absorb the expense of transportation, meals, examination fees, uniforms, field study; staff, too, will not have access to the LEAs in-service centers and programs. All these costs must be borne in ways outside of the regular grants from the DES, and from 'private', corporate sources which may fluctuate from year to year (and with the profitability of the firms).

The AMA may have been prescient in this last concern: Costs for start-up, housing and preparing the schools are running high; and corporate 'givers' have been cautious, though recently the Hanson Trust gave a 1 million pound grant to the DES to start the first CTC, in Solihull. Stuart Sexton and this researcher have made trips to Liverpool, a prime urban site for a CTC, to look for a building for the school. The politics of privatization comes to earth when a Conservative agent (Sexton is the father of the CTC and associated with the hard Right) enters a strong Socialist city council area, asking the Council to sell or lease him and his trust (the 'sponsor') a site to open a competing, 'independent', Technology College.

The real estate office of the City of Liverpool, which has the responsibility to buy and sell property for the city's use, showed us four buildings, one of which was ideal for a CTC. It was being closed down (merged) in July 1987; it was large and reasonably new (1948), and it was in decent condition (another building which had been closed earlier and left vacant had been vandalized). A formal proposal is now pending to sell this school to Sexton's trust. But, the likelihood that the Council will approve the deal, and create a competing secondary school, is rather slim. The Council may likely refuse the offer (1 million pounds), on ideological grounds, rather than accept the money which the city so desperately needs.

So, as of right now, no single CTC is slated to open this autumn (1987). It was hoped by Sexton and others that the first CTC might be hiring staff and admitting students by May of 1987. The Solihull CTC has funds, a 'sponsor', trust, but are still working to find a headteacher and staff. By 1990, it is likely that Britain will have twenty more such direct-grant, independent schools, a major step toward privatization within the maintained/government sector.

Analysis

As we can see, *funding institutions* may be as difficult as *funding individuals*, particularly when the purpose is moderate forms of privatization. Funding families raises the spectre of nearly unlimited choice, students' moving in and out of government schools and into a range of private and parochial ones. This, the 'producers' of education cannot accept. And funding schools directly based on their ability to attract clients, to increase diversity, quality, innovation, and choice, is also seen as 'back doors' out of the established system. With the CTCs, the establishment, the local education agency, fears the competition and the loss of students, support and hegemony. As we see from the AMAs attack on the CTCs, they claim administrative chaos, a worsening of urban problems with their introduction, and a concern that a few students may benefit while most have less.

This argument has been heard in the USA as well, as groups have attacked the system of magnet schools, the 'supermagnets' in New York City (Cooper, 1987a), for many of the same reasons. With ninety of its 113 secondary schools 'magnetized' (having special themes, competitive admissions, and open access across the city — no immediate catchment areas), groups in the city have argued against them on the grounds that they discriminate against the poor and non-white students, actually injuring the education for most students to the advantage of the few. In its *Public High Schools: Private Admissions* (1985), the Advocates for Children of NY, Inc., a public interest group, argues that:

> ... students from impoverished, segregated minority neighborhoods have a much poorer chance of obtaining acceptance to a selective school than those in more affluent, integrated, or predominately white neighborhoods. Minority students' odds are particularly bad at schools that are seeking to maintain a white majority (p. 1).

Thus, while the public schools in NYC are attempting to offer families wide options and choice, a central goal of privatization, the difficulties arise from any 'market' approach. How do consumers gain information on the choice of schools? How just and equitable are the admissions procedures? How effective is the sorting process? And what is the impact of competition and choice on the system as a whole.

In Britain, too, a whole set of similar questions are being raised by critics of the City Technology Colleges. Ian Nash, for example, wondered 'whether the free enterprise model is the best for delivering the CTC experiment, what effects the colleges [i.e., secondary schools] will have on neighboring schools, and what local education authorities should do to prepare people for the inevitable change [toward technology and competition]?' (Nash, 1987, p. 8).

Another advocacy group in New York City, the Educational Priorities Panel, also claims that the system of special schools is unjust. It believes that there is a 'lack of adequate space in schools that students want to attend' and 'a lack of adequate information and guidance for students to make informed and appropriate choices' (see *Lost in the Labyrinth: New York City High School Admissions*, 1985, p. i.).

Like any market system, competitive admissions to schools raises all the problems of logistics, advertising, screening and fairness, though CTCs in Britain may avoid some of these problems by doing the process more personally and carefully. One of NYC's problems is that over 80,000 children apply for only 61,000 places in special magnet schools. Given, too, that students may apply to as many as thirty different magnet schools, the number of applications can be as many as two million, a problem for any system.

The politics of magnet schools (whether in Britain or the US) is a good illustration of the conflict between advocates of choice, competition, and enterprise versus those favoring equity and a common, standard education for all. Whether a voucher or a special school, whether funds go to families or directly to schools ('following the student' on per capita basis), whether in the US or Britain, the issues raised pit privatizers against equalizers. It is not that total privatization is possible, given the concern of government for equality of education; rather attempts to weaken the hegemony of the educational system, as constructed, are perceived as threats. Thus, even modified, locally-controlled vouchers for the poor are perceived as attacks on the system and are resisted in Congress, as the reauthorization debate over Chapter 1 illustrates.

While these struggles appear sometimes to be ideological posturing, or election-year maneuverings, there is much at stake. In the US, the very future of private, sectarian schools may rest with how Congress decides to configure remedial aid under Chapter 1. If the Democrats — the party of Franklin D. Roosevelt and John F. Kennedy, of the ethnic and the poor — listen mainly to the teachers' unions and ignore the needs of poor children in Catholic and Jewish schools, then Congress may reauthorize Chapter 1 as is. This would virtually deny the nation's most needy children access to the largest federal aid to education program — all because the Reagan administration dares to raise the possibility of a very limited voucher plan (Lines, 1985). This denial of resources might also lead to the closing of large numbers of inner-city Catholic schools which do much for the poor.

In Britain, radical privatization of education has stalled. Vouchers are no longer likely. The CTCs, admittedly a mild and limited attempt to fund these independent schools directly, have been received with fear and scepticism by the school establishment. Why, for example, have not the local government schools opened their own CTC or other types of magnets? Rather than groan and stall, why have not the LEAs fought fire with fire: creating competitive special schools (magnets) with themes such as technology, art and music, humanities and languages? It would be ironic and true justice if local authorities competed successfully with the CTCs, rather than cursing them. Competition breeds competition.

The stakes in Britain are high as well. It is a Western nation with an unproductive and poorly educated work force (only 16 per cent of Britains go to college or university, in comparison to 56 per cent attending in the

Bruce S. Cooper

US), though improving recently. Creating high quality, high-powered secondary schools, publicly funded, and parachuting them into local authorities, upsetting the complaisant local government schools, are steps in the right direction.

So, while total privatization in education is unlikely in modern democracies, given the demand for universal, equitable services for all, a little school capitalism and privatization, may challenge the basic political assumptions about education. It may force the school monopolies off their haunches, breaking up their power and control, making them more responsive to consumer needs and national concerns. There is ample evidence in the US and Britain that introducing qualities of private education into the public system is already underway: magnets, CTCs, local vouchers, open enrollment, 'opt-out' possibilities, and enhanced access to private schools are examples of such attempts.

And these approaches may change the politics of education in Western nations forever. No longer are the debates simply about better government schools and more government funding. Instead, questions of private and public education, access and choice, are now fundamental. In the US, these concerns extend to religious rights and liberties, since poor children are being forced to decide between federal remedial services (through Chapter 1) in a public school, and a religious education, without government assistance, in a parochial school — hardly a happy dilemma in a nation founded to preserve religious freedoms. In Britain, privatization in education raises essential questions of school efficiency, quality, and choice, in a nation which is working hard to rebuild its economic system.

In both countries, school politics has become a fascinating battle-ground over fundamental concerns of choice and equity, liberty and control. And private education, with its incentives, enterprise, and consumer-orientation, stands at the center of much of this debate.

References

BOYD, W. L. (1987) 'Rhetoric and Symbolic Politics: President Reagan's School Reform Agenda', 'Commentary' *Education Week* March 18, pp. 21 and 28.
BLAUG, M. (1984) 'Education Vouchers: It All Depends on What You Mean' in *Privatization and the Welfare State* LEGRAND, J. and ROBINSON, R. (Eds) London, George Allen and Unwin.
CLARKE, P. (1987) 'The Argument for Privatisation' in NEUBERGER, J. (Ed.) *Days of Decision: Privatisation: ...Fair Shares for All or Selling the Family Silver*, London, PAPERMAC, pp. 66–91.
COONS, J. E., CLUNE, W. and SUGARMAN, S. D. (1970) *Private Wealth and Public Education*, Cambridge, Mass., Harvard University Press.
COOPER, B. S. (1985) 'Refighting the Private School Wars' *Politics of Education Bulletin* 12, 2, Winter, pp. 14 –16.

COOPER, B. S. (1987a) 'SuperMagnets: The NYC Design for 90 High Schools'. Paper at the American Education Research Association, Washington, DC, April 22.

COOPER, B. S. (1987b) 'The Uncertain Future of Nation Education Policy: Private Schools and the Federal Role', American Educational Research Association, April 21, 1987, Washington, DC, and in BOYD, W. L. and KERCHNER, C. (Eds) *The Politics of Excellence and Choice in Education*, Lewes, Falmer Press.

COOPER, B. S. and DOYLE, D. P. (1985) 'Nonpublic Schools, Worldwide'. *International Encyclopedia of Education*, London, Pergamon Press.

COOPER, B. S. and POSTER, J. (1986) 'Breakdown of a Coalition', *Education Week*, 'Commentary', May 21, p. 28.

DENNISON, S. R. (1984) *Choice in Education: An Analysis of the Political Economy of State and Private Education*, Hobart Paperback #19, London, The Institute of Economic Affairs.

DEPARTMENT OF EDUCATION AND SCIENCE (1965) *Circular 10/65: The Organization of Secondary Education*, 12 July, HMSO.

DEPARTMENT OF EDUCATION AND SCIENCE (1986) *City Technology Colleges: A New Choice of Schools*, United Kingdom, Department of Education and Science, October.

DEPARTMENT OF EDUCATION AND SCIENCE (1987) *City Technology Colleges: A Speculative Investment*, London, Association of Metropolitan Authorities, February.

DOYLE, D. P. and COOPER, B. S. (1988) 'Funding the Individual? A Chapter on the Future of Chapter 1', in DOYLE, D. P. and COOPER, B. S. (Eds) (1987) *Federal Aid to the Disadvantaged*, Lewes, Falmer Press.

DOYLE, D. P. and LEVINE, M. (1984) 'Magnet Schools', *Phi Delta Kappan*, 66, 4, December.

DRUCKER, P. (1970) *A New Style of Government*, London, Conservative Party Centre.

EIDENBERG, E. and MOREY, R. D. (1969) *An Act of Congress: The Legislative Process and the Making of Education Policy*, New York, W. W. Norton and Co.

ERICKSON, D. A. (Ed.) (1968) *Public Controls of Nonpublic Schools*, Chicago, University of Chicago Press.

FRIEDMAN, M. (1955) 'The Role of Government in Education' in SOLO, R. A. (Ed.) *Economics in and the Public Interest*, New Brunswick, NJ, Rutgers University Press, pp. 123–153.

FRIEDMAN, M. (1962) *Capitalism and Freedom*, Chicago, University of Chicago Press.

FUTRELL, M. H. (1986) 'Vouchers: The Hoax is Transparent' *Education Week*, 5, 17, January 6, p. 14.

JAMES, T. and LEVIN, H. M. (Eds) (1983) *Public Dollars for Private Schools: The Case of Tuition Tax Credits*, Philadelphia, Temple University Press.

JENCKS, C. (1970) *Education Vouchers: A Report on Financing Elementary Education by Grants to Parents*, Berkeley, Ca.: Institute of Government Studies.

LEGRAND, J. and ROBINSON, R. (Eds) (1976) *The Economics of Social Problems: The Market Versus the State*, 2nd Edition, London, Macmillan.

LEGRAND, J. and ROBINSON, R. (Eds) (1984) *Privatization and the Welfare State*, London, George Allen and Unwin.

LEVIN, H. M. (1983) 'Education Choice and the Pains of Democracy; in JAMES, T. and LEVIN, M, *op. cit.*

LINES, P. M. (1985) 'Peaceful Uses for Tuition Vouchers: Looking Back and Looking Forwards', Denver, Education Commission of the States.

Lost in the Labyrinth New York City High School Admission (1985) New York: The Educational Priorities Panel.

MASON, P. (1975) Education Vouchers Under Test, *Oxford Review of Education*.

MAYNARD, A. (1975) *Experiment with Choice in Education*, London: The Insititute of Economic Affairs, Hobart Paper #64.

NASH, I. (1987) 'Revolution Begins in Solihull', *The Times Educational Supplement*, 29 May, p. 8.

PARKER, H. (1987) 'Review: A Choice of Evils', *The Times Educational Supplement*, May 29, p. 18.

PEACOCK, A. and WISEMAN, M. (1964) *Education for Democrats*, Hobart Paper #25 London, Institute of Economic Affairs.

Public Schools: Private Admissions. A Report on New York City Practices (1985) New York, Advocates for Children of New York.

SCHULTZ, T. W. (1963) *The Economic Value of Education* New York, Columbia University Press.

SELDON, A. (1986) *The Riddle of the Voucher — An Inquiry into the Obstacles to Introducing Choice and Competition in State Schools*, Hobart paperback #21, London: Institute of Economic Affairs.

SEXTON, S. (1987) *Our Schools — A Radical Policy*, London, Education Unit, Institute of Economic Affairs.

UZZELL, L. A. (1984) 'Robin Hood Goes to School: The Case for a Federal Voucher Program', in MARCHNER, C. (Ed.) *A Blueprint for Education Reform*, Chicago, Free Congress Research and Education Foundation.

VELJANOVSKI, C. (1987) *Selling the State: Privatization in Britain*, London, Weidenfeld and Nicholson, Ltd.

VITULLO-MARTIN, T. and COOPER, B. S. (1987) *The Separation of Church and Child: Federal Aid to Parochial Schools After Felton*, Indianapolis: Hudson Institute.

WAGNER, A. (1974) 'Vouchers — Are They the Answer to Parental Choice? *Education* 144, 24, December 13, 1974.

WALKER, A. (1984) 'The Political Economy of Privatisation', in LEGRAND, J. and ROBINSON, R. (Eds) *op. cit.*

WEST, E. G. (1970 *Education and the State: A Study in Political Economy*, 2nd edition, London: The Institute of Economic Affairs.

WICKS, M. (1987) *A Future for All: Do We Need a Welfare State?* London, Penguin.

WOODHALL, M. (1977) 'Alternatives in the Finance of Education: Vouchers', *The Finance of Education*, London: The Open University, Economics and Education Policy IV.

Chapter 14
A 'Back Door' Process of School Privatization: The Case of Israel

Dan E. Inbar

In a small country with a strong, egalitarian and centralized public school system like Israel, the very discussion of a privatization process in the elementary school system is inconceivable. However, there are enough signs of just such a process taking place to trigger a discussion. The long-range implications of privatization of the Israeli elementary school system and its theoretical application justifies, perhaps requires it, even at this early stage.

Nevertheless, the following discussion is somewhat daring in our context. It analyzes buds of various socio-educational changes and attempts to perceive them as a cumulative process, arguing that they may be considered part of a more general process of growing parental involvement in schools. In addition, it offers some hypotheses for future developments.

The main purpose of this chapter is threefold: First, to point to some of the basic changes taking place in the Israeli elementary school system; second, to support and strengthen the argument that these changes can be perceived as part of a comprehensive process toward what will be termed educational privatization; and third, to speculate upon some future consequences and possible responses.

The process toward educational privatization will be defined here as a process in which parents are intensifying their influence on schools by increasing their direct involvement in school affairs, by exercising more choice, expanding direct payment for school programs, all this at a time when nationwide, centralized, normative regulation and control is being reduced. This does not imply that schools are being taken over by the private sector, but rather that privatizing characteristics are being incorporated into the public school system.

This analysis will begin with a brief historical background for, in order to understand why such a privatization process in the Israeli elementary school system is so inimical an idea, it must be comprehended in its unique historical configuration. It will also include a discussion of three examples of the privatization process and an analysis of six basic socio-educational forces for change, ending with a discussion of some hypotheses of future trends.

The School System: Background

The relatively short history of the state of Israel forces us to consider its educational system in an evolving society. (Ackerman, Carmon and Zucker, 1985), implying that that society is still going through dynamic changes. The roots of the contemporary Israeli educational system are inherent in the pre-state organizational structures, and its policies should be perceived in view of their developments before the creation of the state in 1948 (Elboim-Dror, 1985).

The Ministry of Education in fact controls the whole educational system for the entire population, Arab and Jewish. All the educational laws and by-laws, like free and compulsory education, apply to both sectors. The discussion here focuses on the development of the Jewish elementary school system only, which is concentrated in the major urban areas. For the purpose of this discussion two basic features of the Jewish Israeli element-ary educational system will be emphasized: its egalitarian ideology and its centralized structure.

The egalitarian ideology is rooted in the socialistic ideology of the founders, and, indeed, socialism has played a vital role in the foundation of the Israeli state, people with Socialist ideology having won positions of great economic and political power (Kleinberger, 1969). In the funda-mental drive to integrate the Jewish immigrants into one nation, the elementary school system, through the 1949 law which provides for compulsory and free education of all children from age 5 to 13 years, inclusive, was seen as a major vehicle to equality.

Primary schools throughout the country were divided into three categories: advantaged, partially disadvantaged, and disadvantaged, which was thereafter the basis for accomplishing the policy of special investment for schools in the disadvantaged categories. This was done through investment in manpower, teaching, compensatory programs, extended school day, and remedial instruction (Minkowich *et al.*, 1982).

Until 1953 the educational system was divided among four ideological trends which differed sharply in their educational aims. The religious trend aimed at educating pious and observant Jews in a combination of Zionism and religion. The Labor trend, which represented the Socialist movement, aimed at combining Zionism and socialism as the major educational goals. The schools of the general trend steered a middle course, with a com-promising approach to political, social and national tradition (Kleinberger,

1969; Bashi, 1985). The fourth trend was the small, non–Zionist, extreme Orthodox religious sector, which even opposed the use of the Hebrew language in their schools.

In 1953 the Knesset (Israeli Parliament) passed the state Education Law which was intended to abolish the unwholesome linkage of pedagogical and organized political trends in education. The law replaced the recognized trends with state education, still divided into two, the religious state education (about 20 per cent) and state education (in practice, secular education). The extreme Orthodox religious trend removed itself from the state education and was recognized as an independent trend at this point. However, in order to ease the change and the near-termination of the Labor trend, a provision for supplementary programs, intended to comprise no more than 25 per cent of the total number of teaching hours given in any class, was incorporated into the law.

This provision of the law, which would have offered individual schools or their local communities a limited freedom of choice, was almost never implemented. However, as will be discussed later, it is now serving as the major legitimating basis of the new process.

The elementary school system is covered by a well organized supervisory system, coordinated by six district superintendents, who are the interim echelon between schools and the central authorities. All inspectors principals and teachers are state employees and all salaries are paid centrally according to one nationwide scale. Appointments, assignments to particular schools, and dismissals are controlled by the Ministry of Education through inspectors and the district superintendents, although over the years many school principals have gained personal power to influence teachers' assignments and appointments. Furthermore, the strength of the central authorities has to be viewed within the small size of the overall system: there are 1329 elementary schools in the country.

Beyond the general centralized system of Israel, the state Educational Law had in the first three decades considerably strengthened the powers of the Ministry of Education by placing it in effective control of the whole of elementary education through the authorization to prescribe a uniform and obligatory basic curriculum (Kleinberger, 1969).

Another factor which is important to this discussion is the country's pluralistic character. Although Israel is considered a country of Jewish immigrants crystallizing into a unified nation, its pluralistic nature, culturally and politically, must also be seen as one of its basic characteristics (Inbar, 1986).

In summarizing the background, two basic characteristics are of major importance to the present discussion. First, the Israeli elementary school system is structurally as well as procedurally highly centralized. Second, since the creation of the state, equality as a major social philosophy and political ideology has been considered one of the basic goals and operative guidelines of the whole system. The combination of the two characteristics

— a strong, centralized, egalitarian elementary school system in a democracy which legitimizes pluralism — sets the necessary foundation for the following discussion.

The Privatization Process

Three types of examples will be used to illustrate the various developments in the Israeli elementary school system toward what is here termed the privatization process, with each type focusing on a different, unique characteristic of the phenomenon. The common denominator of all three types, however, is the increasing involvement and influence of parents on school affairs, increasing diversification of programs, and weakening of centralized normative regulations and controls. The three types of examples are the development of:

a) 'specialty' schools;
b) 'ideological' schools; and
c) in-school programs.

a) The 'specialty' schools, which be considered as a type of alternative school, are schools which focus on special types of programs. The major examples are the art elementary school and the natural/science-oriented elementary school. Beyond the emphasis on certain contents, these schools have several notable aspects. First, they do not have bounded registration zones, students can enroll in this type of school from all over the city. Enrollment is based on two major criteria: parents' choice and entrance tests. Both criteria are a meaningful departure from regular public elementary school practise, where parents have essentially no choice between schools and elementary schools do not administer entrance tests.

In addition, if all public elementary schools offer free education, in these schools special payment, although relatively moderate is required. In those cases where parents cannot afford the special payment, they will either pay less or be exempt.

A third interesting characteristic of these schools is that students who do not stand up to school requirements, either in general scholarship achievements, behavior, or talent in special programs (music, drama, art, crafts, etc.) may be asked to return to their original elementary school. Although the number of such cases is small, the very principle is significant.

Finally, one of the prerequisites of these schools is a high degree of parental involvement. Parents are required to participate in school programs, such as trips in the natural/science programs or working with students in workshops in art and crafts programs.

In general, these schools reflect a considerable change in some basic norms underlying the public elementary school system in the last thirty-five years. They allow parental choice of schools, on the one hand, but at the same time allow administration of school selection. Hence, they pose a direct threat to the egalitarian values that are so basic to the Israeli public school system and increase direct parental participation in everyday school teaching. Similarly, these schools, by requiring special payment, are moving away from the Free Education Act. These schools, as well as others, as will be discussed in the following, have enjoyed acceptance as legitimate educational endeavors from the very beginning. Although there are only a few schools of this type, basic principles are changed and broken, which might have long-range implications.

b) The 1953 decision to abolish trends in the elementary school system and to develop religious state education and state education, leaving the extreme Orthodox religious independent schools in the shadowy background, is a circumstance which has existed for more than three decades. However, some meaningful changes are taking place. Some schools although a limited number still, are defining themselves around distinct social philosophies, ideologies, and beliefs. These have two basic organizational shapes. First, some schools are leaving the state education frame and are becoming recognized as unofficial schools, still supported financially by the Ministry of Education, similar to the status of the Independent schools. Second, other schools in the state education frame have become officially distinguished as having a certain ideological or philosophical identity.

The first group consists only of religious schools as yet. Parents not satisfied with the religiousness of the religious state schools fought, often through the courts, strikes and political pressure, to establish schools adjusted to their level of religiosity. The nearly forgotten independent schools indirectly influenced the Ministry of Education's policy. In order to avoid the drift of pupils from the religious state schools to the independent, the Ministry approved the opening of the special types of religious schools. This may seem to be an internal religious affair on the surface, but a precedent has been established and a principle has been broken: schools, under parents' pressure, may leave the state education frame.

The second group of schools, although still part of the state education frame, are identified mainly with the Labor movement philosophy, and one school identifies itself with increased Judaic studies. Again, an important precedent has been established by infringing upon a principle. Schools may now be ideologically identified, under parental pressure, within the state education frame.

Beyond the legal status and the ideological identification of both groups of schools three characteristics deserve some elaboration. First, all schools have extended their registration zones beyond the regular community zones of the state education schools. Second, in all schools there is intensive parental involvement, while in some schools, as in the Labor-oriented school, for instance, parental involvement is a prerequisite for enrollment. Third, all of these schools have additional money sources,

Dan E. Inbar

either from parents or from various organizations, which, of course, again raises the question of equality.

c) In-school programs can be seen as one of the most fascinating developments in the Israeli elementary school system. In this case schools, through direct parental participation, are developing and offering special programs to students. The domain of these programs includes topics such as art, crafts, ceramics, drawing, dancing, music, theater, drama, etc. However, beyond these relatively traditional extracurricular programs, due to parents' demands, programs such as history-through-museums, story-telling, logic, mathematical games, natural science, and computers have been introduced. These programs are very closely related to the central core of education beyond classical enrichment programs.

The programs are implemented mainly in two versions. First, after condensing all regular school activities into five days by adding one hour to each one of them, the sixth day may be devoted entirely to the special programs. (The school week in Israel is six days, as is the work week.) Or second, the special program may be provided in one or two days by extending the schooling day.

Parents are directly involved in developing these programs. In most cases a group of parent representatives, with the principal, form a steering committee which decides upon contents and runs the programs. Furthermore, there are cases where one of the parents, either paid or volunteer, is responsible for and operatively runs the program. Parents have to pay for these programs, but no child is denied participation if, in rare cases, parents cannot afford the fee.

The amount of fee is decided upon by the steering committee and covers all expenses. The teachers of the various subjects are specially hired by the steering committee and are paid by the parents in various ways, but never directly by the school and of course not at any time by the Ministry of Education. Salaries are in many cases negotiated and are relatively high, far beyond what might have been paid by the central educational authorities. The special teachers, generally not from the same school in which the program is provided, can be replaced if their work does not meet expectations. Furthermore, in many cases pupils are asked to fill in questionnaires, expressing their level of satisfaction with the various courses they attend.

These types of programs are spreading very rapidly around the country, mainly in the big cities, Tel Aviv, Haifa and Jerusalem and their surrounding small towns, where these areas account for almost 80 per cent of the country's student body. Parents learn about the programs and are requesting them from their schools. The central authorities of the Ministry of Education are aware of this phenomenon, although there is no consensus about it among them. However, because of problems created by drastic budget cuts, and because these programs derive their legitimation from the provision that parents and schools have the right to develop 25 per cent of

274

school programs, they silently condone them. The whole phenomenon is quite new and without any central organization, and therefore no systematic information has been gathered on the subject.

This process, which may seem peripheral to the foundation of schooling, will ultimately have long-range implications for the whole elementary school system. Parents, suddenly engaged in hiring teachers and paying salaries, have to form local school judicial entities and pedagogical committees, act as fiscal role holders, get involved and be directly accountable for education programs. The new teacher payment procedures are endangering the nationwide salary scale which is deeply ingrained in the egalitarian social philosophy. Furthermore, these teachers, in contrast to all elementary school teachers, are untenured, and liable to replacement. Thus, a merit system is beginning to evolve. Similarly, the idea that pupils have the privilege to choose a special program and, in many cases, have their satisfaction taken into consideration, might again be seen as the start of a dramatic change in the traditional Israeli elementary school system.

After some hesitation, school principals have started to encourage the introduction of such special programs. A change in their traditional role has begun to occur. They now engage in direct curriculum planning and policy development, whereas in the past they perceived this as something they rarely had the opportunity to do because of their overwhelming administrative responsibilities (Goldstein, 1973; Inbar, 1977).

What are the general socio-educational forces which are driving this process? What are the environmental conditions which enable it to flourish?

The Socio-Educational Forces for Change

After elucidating some of the basic signs of change, in the following analysis six broad forces and conditions for change will be discussed. These forces might offer some insight into the quite surprising changes in the centralized-egalitarian elementary educational system in Israel, and strengthen the basic argument that these signs of change may be perceived as preliminary buds of a long-range comprehensive change in the elementary school system.

The six socio-educational forces are:

a) the increasing volition of parents to choose among educational preferences;
b) the desire of parents to increase their influence on educational philosophies;
c) the readiness of parents to pay for choice, influence, and extra programs;
d) a shift of emphasis from equality to quality;

e) the centralized intention to promote school autonomy; and

f) the drastic decline in resource allocation to the public school system.

Obviously, the six forces should not and cannot be analyzed separately. They are interdependent and derive from similar broader socio-political tendencies. Hence, they should be considered as complementary and their full power springs from their configuration.

a) Volition to choose. There is a general uneasiness in the Israeli public with the achievements of the elementary educational system and an increased disbelief in the central authorities' ability to improve things. The feeling is that schools have become more uniform and bureaucratized and have fallen under too much central control. Parents are looking for better schools and better programs and are trying by various means to break out of official registration zones, where they have no influence on the school. They are searching for a way to find the best for their children. Parents are trying to exercise choice.

The roots for this tendency may be seen as a combination of inner factors and outer influence. It is possible to argue that in the local arena there is a steady process of 'public maturation' — a reduction of public confidence in the central authorities and an increased desire for choice. Indeed, this tendency to exercise more choice in education is not an exception. It is evident in the health system, in housing, and in other community activities. Although it is difficult to trace clear channels of outside influence, the openness of the Israeli system to a flow of information and the history of ideas that have been introduced into the educational system enable such a claim to be made. The influence might be derived from ideas such as alternative schools and the voucher system. Both are examples of the drive for increased choice and efficiency by promoting competition among schools and programs (Mecklenburger and Hostrop, 1972; Fantini, 1973; Coons and Sugarman, 1978).

Similarly, studies on private schools in the US (Coleman *et al.*, 1981 and 1982) and the growing debate about the private school in that country (Cooper *et al.*, 1983) are another example of this outer influence. Consequently, local conditions are setting the need for more and better choices, and international developments provide some degree of legitimation.

b) Influence on philosophy. Direct political ideology was ruled out of the elementary system in the state Educational Law of 1953. And the right of parents to influence schools — the famous 25 per cent provision — was really never exercised in the past. However, in recent years this provision has been brought into use, directly or indirectly, enabling parents to influence the philosophy of schools. Increasing numbers of parents are seeking a more defined philosophy of education, either directly related to pedagogy, such as open or liberal education, or ideological ones, such as Labor-oriented philosophy, or Jewish traditional and religious-oriented values.

Indeed, it might mean diversification of schools according to differentiation of school philosophy, drifting away from the idea of a unified educational value system. The public is less reluctant to accept the possibility that pluralism, according to social and pedagogical philosophy, can be represented to a certain degree in the educational system. These tendencies might also be seen as a reflection of the ideological and religious extremism which has developed in recent years in the Israeli public. But this is not the institutionalization of extremism; rather it is an opposing effect by creating an educational buffer against unacceptable ideological and religious extremism.

Perhaps the strongest controversy is around the question of religious education, religious aspects in education, and the relationship between the secular and religious in the Israeli educational system, some of it reflecting the ongoing public debate about the question of Jewish identity, its relation to the Jewish religion, and to Jewish tradition. This tendency can be seen as a special case of parents exercising their right to choice. However, the emphasis here is not directly on educational content or level of excellence in schools, but choice among basic social philosophies, beliefs and ideologies. The schools themselves, by availing themselves of certain selection procedures and obtaining greater resources privately, are indeed offering better education.

c) Readiness to pay. Desire for improved educational programs and for being able to choose programs to suit children's perceived needs and talents can be seen as inherent in parents' aspirations. The question is twofold: what is the intensity of such volition, and to what degree are parents ready to translate these aspirations into action and directly invest resources for them. Informal education, through private institutions fuctioning in the afternoon, community centers, and private lessons have been utilized by sections of the population for many years. However, the significant difference here is that parents are now more ready than ever before to invest resources to directly accomplish their aspirations in schools. These resources consist of time, effort and money. For the majority it means, of course, only money. It is true that the public resists any general payment to schools, as for instance the idea of the Ministry of Finance that parents should pay a global sum to improve the Ministry of Education's budget, in spite of the fact that education is free. Although such payments were to have been gradual, related to income, they were rejected by the public when first introduced in 1985 and never received Parliamentary approval. Nevertheless, parents are ready to pay directly for schools and for programs, even very costly ones like the introduction of microcomputers, as long as there is a clear address and their money does not disappear into the national budget.

Such direct payment is associated with accountability, with more control over programs and consequently with stronger influence on school affairs. This direction is clearly associated, as will be elaborated later, with the general tendency of the Ministry of Finance of trying to enforce direct payment for social services. The Ministry argues, for instance, that the public should pay for health services in spite of the various health insurances, which is a significant shift in the traditional, highly socialistic, welfare-based economic system. But if, when payments were required, the public reaction was always negative, for educational purposes when payments are officially collected by parents' committees for determined school programs, resistance is minimal.

d) From equality to quality. Dialectic discussion between equality and the best interests of the child is ongoing. The question of the degree to which freedom and personal choice contradict public interest in general, and equality in particular, is intrinsic in the debate on education. The argument, on the one hand, is that society's sole objective in education should be the best interests of the individual child (Coons and Sugarman, 1978), and that enforced equality is comparable to the myth of Procrustes, who fit travelers to his bedsteads by chopping off limbs too long or stretching bodies too short (Flew, 1981). On the other hand, freedom of choice, as reflected in the voucher plan and private schools, could provide greater reproduction of social inequalities than the present public schools (Levin, 1978).

Furthermore, the challenge to private schooling is not simply on the grounds of inequality, but rather because of some of its questionable justifications. As Tawney (1952) put it thirty-five years ago 'The idea that differences of educational opportunity among children should depend upon differences of wealth among parents is a barbarity' (p. 157). Ericson's (1984) answer to the question whether a system of private providers of education is more likely than the public educational system to meet the compelling interests of the state with a minimum of bureaucracy and a maximum of personal choice is clearly negative too.

The question of equality vs. free choice cannot be overlooked in this context, even if the argument that private schooling and the voucher system are not, in themselves, intrinsically negative is accepted (Wise and Darling-Hammond, 1984). The fundamental point here is that there is a meaningful shift in the Israeli public from equality and social integration toward quality and free choice in educational philosophy. This is as yet perhaps only a relatively latent shift, but still a dramatic change in the Israeli public's ideology of elementary schooling. Operatively, it means that if, in order to achieve a higher quality of education by creating schools with preferred ideologies or beliefs, the cost is increased inequality and social segregation, the public is ready to pay it. Furthermore, as alluded to above, as long as it is not perceived as an official policy or does not endanger integration of a whole community or district, the central authorities will passively support it and implicitly approve it.

e) Promotion of school autonomy. Provoked by the recognition that a rigidly centralized educational system does not answer the needs of a pluralistic society with a diversity of needs and professional responsibilities (Ministry of Education and Culture, 1979), by professional demands for organizational and structural reforms (Minkowich and Bashi, 1973; Peled, 1976), and international advocacy of more localized control (Levin, 1970; Fantini and Gittell, 1973), the Israeli Ministry of Education declared its intention to move toward more decentralization and local control. The Ministry clearly stated, through the Director General's announcements, its encouragement of school autonomy (Ministry of Education and Culture, 1975).

The operative translation of this intention to encourage school autonomy was brought into focus in the new regulations for allocating teaching hours to the elementary schools (Ministry of Education and Culture, 1981). In these new regulations for the 1982 academic year a basic teaching hours standard was allocated to schools, with each school being able to allocate them differentially to the various classes, programs and subject matters. Furthermore, teaching hours could be converted to finance special programs and acquisition of educational equipment. These directives encountered intensive resistance and strong negative repercussions from elementary school principals.

The reason for the repercussions was that these provisions toward school autonomy were related to budget cuts, which meant reduction in the number of teaching hours allocated to schools. Furthermore, natural growth had to be absorbed in the number of classes in operation as of 1981. Only in rare exceptions would new classes be allowed to be opened (Ministry of Education and Culture, 1981). School principals felt that the central authorities in fact had shifted the burden of the budgetary cuts onto the principals' shoulders. Consequently, they resisted implementation of the idea, although supporting its principles. Meanwhile, the Ministry of Education continued to advocate and encourage schools to undertake autonomy (Planning Committee of the Pedagogical Secretariat, 1984).

For several years nothing really occurred. The elementary school principals were caught in a dualistic situation, where theoretically they could assume some autonomy but practically it meant being responsible for one-directional changes — cuts. However, in the last few years (1985–1988) an increasing number of principals have realized the opportunities open to them at a time when parents are showing willingness to pay for programs and to support the idea of more qualitative 'special' schools. This now enables principals to initiate programs and ideas and thus assume much more autonomy than suggested by the central authorities. Schools now may develop programs with fiscal independence from the Ministry of Education, and may hire and fire certain teachers, an unheard of situation before. The central authorities are aware of this, but are unable or unwilling to get seriously involved.

f) Decline in resources. Scarcity of resources is often a powerful vehicle for accelerating social processes. It seems that this is the case in the process of school privatization in the Israeli elementary school system. Since 1983 Israel has witnessed one of its worst economic situations. Cutting public expenditures was one of the main means of overcoming the trend toward 800 per cent inflation. In 1985 the most severe budget restrictions were employed and, by 1987, the rate of inflation was brought down to less than 20 per cent per annum. This venture had a direct effect on the educational budget. During the years 1980–1986 the number of pupils in the elementary school system grew about 12.9 per cent, the number of teachers until 1985 followed suit, although at a slower pace, and grew about 7.7 per cent, but has been reduced again, since 1985, by 7.9 per cent. From 1984–1985 to 1985–1986 the national educational expenditure as a percentage of the GNP was reduced by almost 1 per cent (Ministry of Education and Culture, 1987).

This affected the system in various ways. The total number of teaching hours at the primary level was reduced during 1981–1986 by 28.5 per cent, and after closing small schools, making a great effort to increase the number of pupils per class, and improving administrative efficiency by cutting administrative employees, the average number of weekly teaching hours has been reduced in the elementary schools — except for the first and second grades — by 11.6 per cent (*ibid.*, 1987). Teachers' assistants have been abolished, classes have become more crowded, and many of the programs in art, music and natural sciences were drastically reduced.

In parallel, one of the ways the Ministry of Education balanced the national budget was by promoting more direct public payment for services, thus moving away from the highly centralized welfare system.

These severe constraints put upon schools accelerated the privatization process in two complementary ways. First, they really depreciated educational quality to a degree that parents felt it immediately, as children started to return home from school earlier. Thus parents' general uneasiness about school quality turned to clear frustration. Second, it served as a real justification and a convenient rationalization for parents to pursue the changes and for the Ministry of Education to approve them, although it was conscious of the possible inequalities and segregational implications.

Summary

Socio-educational changes are almost inherently long-range processes and rarely unidimensional. The socio-educational changes discussed here should be considered in this light. The six major forces driving the changes that have been elaborated should be seen as interacting in a unique configuration, when each force alone is not strong enough to force the change. In a situation where disappointment in the educational processes and outcomes exists, and there is frustration at the central authorities' inability to improve them, the public tendency is to resist state paternalism and to try to exercise more personal choice, even if this means cracking one of the fundamental principles of the educational system — the idea of equality.

On the school level, principals are starting to realize that parental involvement might increase their professional autonomy. With local financing, many school programs can be developed independently of the central authorities' control. Furthermore, schools can develop overall programs, and be identified with that program, i.e., get the status of 'specialty' school around a certain specialization, philosophical as well as contextual, again even if it may mean some shift in the balance of equality and quality. The central authorities are well aware of this process. In the opening statement to the 1987 Ministry of Education and Culture booklet, the Minister writes: 'A heavy shadow is spreading over the educational system in the last years... A process is starting which differentiates between the rich and the poor. Rich parents are financing programs and subjects in schools that the poor cannot afford. A gap between rich and poor institutions is starting to develop... There is a need to gather strength and to stop these processes soon' (*ibid.*, p. 1). However, the ability of the Ministry of Education to halt these developments is limited.

Although it is hard to predict the long-range socio-political reaction to privately-oriented schooling in the Israeli elementary school system, some basic options can be identified and deliberated. The first option — to stay the process — seems to be impractical. In the contemporary situation reversing the changes is untenable and freezing them impossible. The second option — differential investment to match all schools to the leading privately financed schools, i.e., centralized egalitarianism — seems to be only a partial solution. It can be done only in very extreme cases. A third option — free development toward more privatization — seems unlikely. There are limits in the educational gaps a small nation in the unique socio-political situation of Israel can absorb.

The fourth option — some kind of cooptation — seems to be the most plausible one. The process of privatization discussed here does not eliminate government control of education; it redefines it. The examples given illuminate a process of growing privatizational elements within the public system. Hence, it is reasonable to assume that in time the Ministry of Education will become more involved in it, and this in three complementary ways. First, more authority will be delegated at the municipal level, enabling urban areas to assume more responsibility and to be more involved in contextual issues. The burden might thus be divided among all levels. Second, to encourage more schools to assume more autonomy and to get more parents involved might thus raise the level of education on a much broader scope. This may be accompanied by a well developed and comprehensive advisory system. Third, considering the centralized educational stucture, the development of comprehensive regulations and guidelines seems to be a reasonable, balancing step. These would probably

concentrate on a determination of boundaries to private programs in schools, allowing them up to a certain percentage of the total program, and the development of special pay scales which would be high enough to draw good teachers, but still be limited. More attention, also, would be paid to balancing school populations. 'Specialty' schools would be required to enroll a minimal percentage of disadvantaged pupils.

The state will then continue to be interested in improving educational quality. However, because equality is so central a value'in Israeli society, the state has to insure itself by a restricted and, from the central authorities' angle, hopefully controlled, acceptable level of inequality. This would be accomplished through means of legislation, regulation and an elaborated advisory system.

Under the current system of financing elementary schools, private interests are pursued in the public system, i.e., state education through private funding. Whether inequality can be controlled and coexistence between private and public interests can be maintained in such conditions remains to be seen.

References

ACKERMAN, W., CARMON, A. and ZUCKER, D. (eds) (1985) *Education in an Evolving Society* Jerusalem, Van Leer.

BASHI, J. (1985) 'The Primary Education, in ACKERMAN, W., CARMON, A. and ZUCKER, D. (eds) *op. cit.*

COLEMAN, J., HOFFER, T. and KILGORE, S. (1981) *Public and Private Schools* New York, Basic Books, Chicago, NORC.

COLEMAN, J., HOFFER, T. and KILGORE, S. (1982) *High Schools Achievements: Public, Catholic and Private Schools Compared* New York, Basic Books; Chicago, NORC.

COONS, J. E. and SUGARMAN, S. (1978) *Education by Choice: The Case for Family Control* Berkeley, Calif., University of California Press.

COOPER, B. S., McLAUGHLIN R. H. AND MANNO, B. V. (1983) 'The latest word in private school growth', *Teacher College Record*, Vol. 85, No. 1, pp. 88–98.

ELBOIM-DROR, R. (1985) 'Educational Policy-Making in Israel', ACKERMAN, W., CARMON, A. and ZUCKER, D. (eds) *op. cit.*

ERICSON, D. P. (1984) 'Liberty and equality in education: A summary review', *Educational Theory*, Vol. 34, No. 1, pp. 97–102.

FANTINI, M. D. (1973) *Public Schools of Choice: A Plan for the Reform of American Education* New York, Simon and Schuster.

FANTANI, M. D. and GITTELL, M. (1973) *Decentralization and Achieving Reform* New York, Praeger Publications.

FLEW, A. (1981) *The Politics of Procrustes: Contradictions of Enforced Equality* London, Temple Smith.

GOLDSTEIN, J. (1973) 'School system personnel's attitudes towards the elementary school principal in Israel', *Studies in Educational Administration and Organization*, Vol. 1, No. 1, pp. 61–101.

INBAR, D. E. (1977) Perceived authority and responsibility of elementary school principals in Israel, *Journal of Educational Administration*, Vol. XV, No. 1, pp. 80–91.

INBAR, D. E. (1986) 'Educational policy-making and planning in a small centralized democracy', *Comparative Education*, Vol. 22, No. 3.

KLEINBERGER, F. A. (1969) *Society, Schools and Progress in Israel* London, Pergamon Press.

LEVIN, H. M. (ed.) (1970) *Community Control of Schools* Washington, DC, The Brookings Institute.

LEVIN, H. M. (1978) 'Private schools in a societal framework', Essay prepared for a book on private schools in honor of Helmut Becker, edited by D. Goldschmidt, Stanford, California.

MECKLENBURGER, J. A. and HOSTROP, R. W. (eds) (1972) *Education Vouchers: From Theory to Alum Rock* Homewood, Illinois, ETC Publications.

MINISTRY OF EDUCATION AND CULTURE (1975) *Director General Special Announcement No. 6* Jerusalem.

MINISTRY OF EDUCATION AND CULTURE (1979) *Special Director General Announcement: State Committee Report on the Teacher and Teaching Profession Status*, Ministry of Education and Culture, Jerusalem, December.

MINISTRY OF EDUCATION AND CULTURE (1981) *Educational Administration Announcement* No. 159, Article 178, Jerusalem, March 19.

MINISTRY OF EDUCATION AND CULTURE (1987) *The Ministry of Education and Culture* Jerusalem, February 7.

MINKOWICH, A. and BASHI, J. (1973) *A Reform Proposal of the Inspectory and Supervisory Structure*, Submitted to the Ministry of Education and Culture, Jerusalem, April.

MINKOWICH, A., DAVIS, D. and BASHI, J. (1982) *Success and Failure in Israeli Elementary Education*, New Brunswick, NJ., Transaction Books.

PELED, E. (1976) *Education in Israel for the 1980s*, The Ministry of Education and Culture, Jerusalem.

PLANNING COMMITTEE OF THE PEDAGOGICAL SECRETARIAT (1984) *Educational Autonomy — Meaning and Application*, Ministry of Education and Culture, Jerusalem.

TAWNEY, R. H. (1952) *Equality* (revised ed.), London, Allen and Unwin.

WISE, A. E. and DARLING-HAMMOND, L. (1984) 'Education by voucher: Private choice and the public interest', *Educational Theory*, Vol. 34, No. 1, pp. 29–47.

Chapter 15
Can Poor Parents Make Wise
Educational Choices?

Patricia A. Bauch

Introduction

Poor parents' ability to make wise educational choices is a much debated subject and affects public policy concerning parental choice of schooling alternatives for their children. In the United States, access to precollegiate private education is frequently limited to wealthy families who can afford to pay private school tuition since no government subsidies are available to support parental choice of an alternative to public education. The inaccurate assumption that primarily the rich can afford and thereby have the right and privilege to attend private schools has worked against the development of a favorable social and political climate in which government support for family choice can be intelligently discussed in a democratic society. What has been neglected is an understanding of the right, privilege, and ability of all parents freely to select an educational alternative for their children from among options that can be discriminated one from the other either on the bases of what is proper or improper for their children or on the bases of what parents perceive as preferable differences among available choice options.

Researchers and policymakers cite numerous objections to entitlement plans that would provide the poor with access to private schools. Among them are concerns about equity and the information needs of the poor. If public support for non-public education were forthcoming, it is argued that an even greater segregation of social groups would occur than is already the case (Levin, 1983; Catterall, 1983). Some fear that public support for private schools would benefit the rich who are more highly motivated and have greater information-seeking opportunities than the poor (Bridge, 1978). Based on data analyzed for the Alum Rock Voucher Experiment, Bridge and Blackman (1978) claim that the poor, disadvantaged by low income and less education, are less aware of school program alternatives and have less access to information regarding them making it unlikely that they can or will make potentially good decisions about school placement that will benefit their children. Bridge (1978) rallies support for his findings by citing social science research which has consistently shown a positive correlation between information levels and social class for a wide range of subjects including child-rearing practices (Anderson, 1936; Kohn, 1969), education (Mann, 1974; Bridge, 1974), nutrition (Food and Drug Administration, 1974) and general information (Hyman, Wright, and Reed, 1976). By implication, then, poor families may not have the necessary information nor be motivated or 'fit' to seek appropriate educational experiences for their children (Coleman, 1977; Wise and Darling-Hammond, 1984) thus jeopardizing the social equity objectives of voucher or entitlement systems and casting doubt on the positive outcomes for poor children that such systems might provide.

Despite these and other objections, reform proposals calling for the restructuring of public education include the idea of providing parents with various types of choices that would permit schools to respond to student diversity. Support for the idea comes from a number of sources and is receiving considerable press attention. Recently, *Time for Results*, a report of the National Governors' Association (1986), criticized the lack of choice in public education as a denial of the nation's diversity, arguing that choice is the best way to increase school effectiveness.

According to the latest Gallup Poll, 76 per cent of public school parents would like to have the right to select their children's school (Gallup and Clark, 1987); and Black parents more than white parents favor the idea of tuition vouchers to pay for schooling (Gallup, 1986). A recent study of educational choice in Minnesota (Treichel, 1986) indicates that poor and minority families are more supportive of voucher plans than the white middle class. In addition, such families were less likely than the white middle class to report that schools are responsive to their needs and effective in serving their children. They, more than the white middle class, were likely to say they would transfer their children to private schools if vouchers were available and to favor 'open enrollment' plans that would allow them to choose rather than having to accept a public high school assignment for their children.

The choice movement, begun quietly in the late 1960s as the public school alternatives movement supported mainly by middle and upper class whites, has emerged in the 1980s as a lively and growing debate surrounding the establishment of diversified public schools, schools-within-schools, and the call for public financial support for private schools supported primarily by minorities and lower-income parents.

Although the sociology of education literature is replete with studies showing the influence of family background on children's educational experiences (for example, Coleman, Campbell, Holson, McPartland, Mood, Weinfeld and York, 1966; Jencks, 1972; Sewell and Hauser, 1976) little is known about the characteristics of those poor families who do choose private schools. If the school-related attitudes and behaviors of poor families in private schools are similar to those of non-poor families, we might have some basis from which to argue in favor of a public policy that democratically supports educational choicemaking.

This chapter presents evidence that poor families in Catholic high schools act capably and responsibly in exercising school choice in the education of their children. Many poor parents, at great financial sacrifice, seek schools they believe will benefit their children and be responsive to their specific educational needs (Bauch, 1987; Cibulka, O'Brien, and Zewe, 1982). Poor parents want what is best for their children as do non-poor parents. The evidence suggests that mechanisms could be found that would facilitate the adequacy of choicemaking behavior among poor families if they were given the opportunity to choose from among educational alternatives for their children. The ability of poor parents to adequately assess and care for their children's educational needs is of utmost concern to educators and has implications for school effectiveness and public policy related to school choice.

Evidence from a voucher experiment at 'Alum Rock' offers insights into the information-seeking habits of parents, especially poor parents, who over time acquire the same information levels as upper income parents in choosing a school. Findings from a recent study of parents who choose to send their children to inner-city Catholic high schools conducted at The Catholic University of America (CUA) show that poor parents are similar to non-poor parents in their educational motivations and parent involvement behavior which indicates a comparable commitment to their children's education. Similarities between family groups, despite economic and social differences, suggest that many poor families act responsibly in their choice-making behavior. If so, the current school reform effort might be bolstered considerably by policy provisions permitting poor and minority families to make the same educational choices that middle-class parents frequently make.

Theoretical Background

Private Schooling and the 'Effectiveness' of School Choice

An array of major studies over the past twenty years show that parental cooperation and involvement are essential components of effective schools (Bloom, 1964, 1981; Bronfenbrenner, 1974; Clark, 1983; Walberg, 1984) and that parent expectations and involvement influence student attitudes and achievement (Henderson, 1981, 1987; Kagan, 1984). Although some would argue that private schools attract parents who are already highly motivated and want to be involved (Cibulka *et al.*, 1982), nevertheless, the choice of a private school appears to foster greater parental involvement compared to assignment to a public school, presumably because these schools by design extend opportunities to parents for satisfying involvement (Coleman and Hoffer, 1987). Also, school choice in itself may enhance parent involvement if it is based on mutual values and expectations between family and school.

Private schools also appear to foster greater academic achievement than public schools, especially among minority and lower-income students (Coleman and Hoffer, 1987; Greeley, 1982; Benson, Yeager, Wood, Guerra, and Manno, 1986). While some would argue that achievement differences between public and Catholic schools are trivial (for example, Alexander and Pallas, 1983; Keith and Page, 1985), some school practices, organizational characteristics, and value orientations of private schools are beginning to be described that are associated with school effectiveness such as an academically-focused curriculum, a decreased emphasis on within school tracking, and a school climate that promotes moral and value development (Bryk, Holland, Lee, and Carriedo, 1984; Chubb and Moe, 1986). Although the literature on private-public school comparisons does not adequately examine within and between sector differences among the many types of schools that offer choice (i.e., public magnet schools, schools-within-schools, open enrollment plans; independent schools, religious schools, community schools) private schools generally appear to share characteristics different from public schools that enhance school effectiveness such as order, discipline, mutual selectivity, and a value orientation (Erickson, forthcoming; Kilgore, forthcoming).

In a choice system, such as is found primarily in private schools, parents exercise some autonomy, control and efficacy concerning their children's educational development. Bandura's (1986) theory of efficacy suggests that parents who make choices act in a way that contributes toward their school children's success. Parents want to believe that the choices they make for their children are efficacious, and therefore, they will work harder to insure that their children are successful in school as a result of parental decisions. The efficacy of choice presumably is similar for all parents despite socio-economic advantages.

The Deficit-Difference Controversey

Poor families and perceived deficits in family functioning related to school perform-ance. Based in the classical sociological literature, 'deficit' thinking about poor families views students from these families as culturally 'deprived' and thus unable to perform well in school. Kohn (1969) argues that poor families do not share middle-class values concerning achievement and its concomitant values of delayed gratification, discipline, and hard work necessary for school success. Even if this is an adequate description of some poor families, the assumption ought not to be made that the culture of elites includes these characteristics or is somehow intrinsically more valuable than that of the lower classes (Valentine, 1968).

In addition, deficit thinking assumes that cultural and social class differences contribute to family disorganization, poverty, the lack of effective concept acquisition, and other intellectual and cultural deficits which need to be remediated through prescribed school intervention strategies (Banks, 1987). This view served to undergird some aspects of the Johnson administration's War on Poverty (Bereiter and Engelman, 1966) mandating educational programs aimed at fostering middle-class social and economic values. It is currently experiencing a resurgence in the neocon-servative Reagan movement of the 1980s (Banks, 1986; Wilson, 1987) and in the excellence movement in public education with its emphasis on increased accountability, higher standards, and identical criteria and requirements despite social class background and cultural differences among students (Raywid, 1987). This deficit model of family functioning feeds the contention that poor parents cannot make effective educational choices for their children.

Based on the flawed social pathology research of the 1960s with lower-class families, the typical school intervention strategy became one of devising ways to alter the cognitive, personality, and motivational disposi-tions of minority children in order to exact from them a middle-class model of competent task/test performance.[1] Schools typically overem-phasize achievement while neglecting to acknowledge the developmental and cultural needs of students. Schools eventually alienate lower-class families from the educational process when they devalue parents' needs, expectations, and experiences. Such parents become discouraged from active school participation, contributing to poor student performance in school.

Cultural Differences, Family Functioning, and the School Performance of Poor Children

A less pejorative view of family functioning has recently emerged from the literature on which school and public policy are rarely based. It views all families as culturally different, not deficient; and as passing through various stages of development. This difference-dynamic view of family life sug-gests the need for a diversity of responses from schools.

Boykin (1986) demonstrates how the social mobility attitudes and child-rearing practices of minorities and poor families include negotiating a dominant and oppressive culture. Discontinuities between the cultural backgrounds of students and the culture of the school are associated with distinct types of school problems. Coping and other adaptive mechanisms are part and parcel of everyday life, but in most schools these are severe for the poor and for some racial groups (Ogbu, 1982). Minority families have a tapestry of socialization needs including mainstream culture, minority culture, and a specific ethnic culture. This three-fold socialization press places them in a triple quandary (Boykin, 1986).

Blacks are a poignant case for the United States where the Afro-American experience is not well-understood. Neisser (1986) and McAdoo and McAdoo (1985) present an impressive array of revisionist scholars who see the need for a multiplicity of responses from schools for minority students. Boykin (1986) describes the dimensions of Black culture as emphasizing spirituality, harmony and movement, communalism, expressive individualism, and oral tradition as opposed to Western emphasis on materialism, dualism, competitiveness, authoritarianism, and logical formulations as emphasized by schools. Blacks learn in a relational mode that emphasizes caring and relationships to persons as opposed to objects. They draw upon a different epistemological framework that they intuitively use — symbolic imagery and rhythm, elements sadly lacking in the school curriculum (Nichols, 1986). Banks (1986) argues that schools fail to emphasize appropriate pedagogy, content, and other curriculum elements that would facilitate Black learning. Many teachers do not understand the culture of Black children and thus have little insight into their learning styles (Hale-Benson, 1982).

Boykin (1986) and Boykin and Toms (1985) elaborate on the quandary of Black socialization. While the African-American experience is fundamentally bicultural, not all minority and poor families share all aspects of biculturality uniformly. Many lower-class parents typically want their children to function successfully in mainstream America, even while they retain many unique Afro-American propensities in their psychological transactions. Some researchers find that the goals and values of child-rearing in many Black families are much like those of the American middle-class ideal (Baratz and Levine, 1978; Billingsley, 1968) with a strong occupational and educational orientation (Hill, 1972; Moos and Moos, 1976). Black students have educational and vocational aspirations as high or higher than their white counterparts (Simmons, 1979), and Black teenagers' parents have goals similar to whites for their children. Many parents may approve children's using Black English at home and in the community, but prefer the use of standard American English in school and at work (Hoover, 1978).

Families differ regarding the value they place on higher education. Richardson (1988) proposes three categories of minority students: a) those who come from professional families and are already attending, or plan to attend, elite, white colleges and who have a lifelong commitment to education; b) students who have college aspirations and who value education but whose college preparation is inadequate; and c) students who do not have college aspirations and who doubt that higher education will make a difference in their adult lives.

Families have different preferences and needs as they evolve through developmental stages in their attempts to negotiate the various socialization agendas. Epstein (1986a) recognizes the important role schools have of providing for these various points of development or dissimilar needs among families and their members at different stages, such as providing the necessary guidance and counseling that would help those who aspire to college or who are discouraged about college to make effective pre-collegiate educational choices.

A cultural difference, dynamic view of family functioning focuses on the diversity and heterogeneity of poor and minority groups, and the need to provide school choices that will embrace cultural pluralism in an equitable and healthy way. The cultural difference view provides an alternative family perspective from which to argue in favor of educational choice for the poor.

The poor, however, have practical problems as consumers that some would argue are less of an obstacle to middle class families concerning information acquisition and the development of school choice behaviors. The Alum Rock voucher demonstration project and the CUA study of parents who choose to send their children to inner-city Catholic secondary schools are helpful in examining these problems.

The Information Needs of Poor Parents and the Alum Rock Voucher Demonstration

During the 1970s, efforts to stimulate voucher experiments were made by the Office of Educational Opportunity and the National Institute of Education. The Alum Rock, California voucher demonstration project began during the 1972–73 school year and lasted for five years. Designed as a 'regulated compensatory' plan, it was conducted by Christopher Jencks and his colleagues from the Center for the Study of Public Policy at Harvard. Inspired by the immigrant experience in Catholic schools, he proposed that his plan be used for inner-city Black children. Jencks' initial idea was to help poor parents help themselves by providing them with unlimited choice, subject to certain 'necessary' controls (Doyle, 1977). Although private school participation was planned in the Alum Rock demonstration, it was precluded at the outset by state law and never materialized even after state enabling legislation was passed. Parental choice of educational programs was therefore limited to those offered by the mini-schools in the participating public schools.

Evaluation of the Alum Rock experiment focused on the impact of educational choice on parents, teachers, administrators, schools and students. Evaluators placed a great deal of importance on parent decision making, claiming that 'parents must have accurate *and* timely information' in order to make intelligent decisions. They stated that 'information imperfections present a particularly difficult problem for family choice in schooling plans, because a lack of information among parents ... means that some children, perhaps the children who can least afford it scholastically, are likely to end up in programs that are not good for them' (Bridge and Blackman, 1978, p. 27).

A brief overview of Bridge and Blackman's assessment reveals that while economically advantaged families were initially more aware of schooling options and consulted more information sources, namely printed information, than did economically disadvantaged families, the differences were only slight. Poor families gained information over time more rapidly than did non-poor families indicating their ability to eventually negotiate the voucher process. For example, at the end of a four-year period, parent awareness of the existence of alternatives exceeded 97 per cent of the population involved, although in the first year of the experiment fewer parents were aware. Regarding levels of awareness, a difference of only four percentage points separated families from the lowest and the highest income levels (Bridge and Blackman, 1978, Table 6, p. 34) in the fourth year. Blacks and Anglos were aware of the existence of program alternatives at about the same rate whereas the Spanish-speaking Mexican-American group lagged behind. Although percentages are not given by ethnicity or income levels from the first through the fourth year, the general findings state that 'Over time, the differences between parents' information levels are reduced as parents gain more experience with the choice system, given that the rules of the system stay relatively constant' (Bridge and Blackman, 1978, p. xiii).

Similarly, results showed that Anglos and more educated families exceeded other ethnic groups and those with less education in the use of various information sources. However, the gap is based on a mean difference of only half a point with the exception of Spanish-speaking Mexican-American groups which tended to be slightly greater. The mean differences among all groups indicate use of four different sources of information to learn about the Alum Rock choice system as compared to the use of three different sources. An analysis of variance indicates that parents' education, rather than ethnicity, 'explains' the one source difference among parents. Expectedly, Spanish-speaking Mexican-Americans had the lowest level of education (Bridge and Blackman, 1978, Table 8, p. 38).

Regardless of ethnicity and levels of education, more parents said they preferred face-to-face encounters over printed information: school publications (30 per cent), talks with parent counselors (22 per cent), and talks with teachers and principals (22 per cent). Those with higher levels of education preferred school publications as a source of information only slightly (5.3 per cent) more frequently than those with lower education levels. Again, expectedly, Spanish-speaking Mexican-Americans were about 14 per cent less likely than Anglos to prefer school publications.

Poorer parents initially tended to want their children to attend schools that were geographically closest to their homes; however, as parents became more familiar with the voucher plan, they were less likely to base their decisions on nonsubstantive educational factors such as transportation. Interestingly, families did not separate themselves racially in choosing program alternatives.

At best, results are mixed regarding parents 'information imperfections' that accompanied this voucher experiment. The authors concluded that parents varied *widely* in their awareness of schooling alternatives and in the accuracy of their information about the rules governing choice. The evidence does not seem to support this conclusion; rather, parents varied slightly, if at all, based on levels of education and income, and over time these parents were able to learn what was going on by utilizing verbal information that takes longer to disseminate than printed information. Parents' information imperfections were just that — imperfections and not serious flaws.

Much has been made in the literature of these overinterpreted conclusions based on an uncritical assessment of these data to argue against choice for the poor, far beyond what they deserve (for example, Kutner, Sherman and Williams, 1986; Wise and Darling-Hammond, 1984), and used to bolster the argument that poor parents cannot make potentially wise educational choices.

The Catholic School Setting

Catholic secondary schools provide an apt setting in which to examine the educational motivations and choicemaking behavior of poor parents. Historically, many lower-income and minority families, chose to attend private schools, especially Catholic schools, which worked to their advantage in securing for them middle class status and a place in the mainstream of American society.[2] As mainly European third and fourth generation Catholics grew more affluent following World War II, they abandoned inner-city parishes and joined the flight to the suburbs leaving behind half-empty churches and schools free of debt. The influx of 'new' poor and minority families into the inner-city and the willingness of Catholic schools to keep their tuition rates low made these schools especially attractive to these new city dwellers who exercise school choice by sending their children to these schools rather than to the public schools and for reasons that differ from an earlier era.[3]

Catholics, predominantly whites, previously chose Catholic schools primarily for reasons of religious instruction (Greeley and Rossi, 1966; Greeley, McCreedy, and McCourt, 1976; Neuwien, 1966). Black parents, who are non-traditional users of Catholic schools, are more interested today in an academic education in a religious setting than in formal religious instruction (Bauch, 1987; Convey, 1986). Along with affordable tuition costs, this shift away from religious reasons has made these schools more attractive to non-Catholics, especially Blacks. This increase in educational choicemaking among lower-income and minority families provided an opportunity for a study to probe the issue of parent motivations and involvement among these families and the seriousness with which they take responsibility for their children's education.

Parent Motivation and Involvement in Inner-City Catholic High Schools

An on-going study of families and Catholic schools at The Catholic University of America (CUA) demonstrates that poor families are as highly motivated as non-poor families in their educational aspirations for their children and in their reasons for choosing Catholic schools. Parental groups differ in their school participation only by degree. Findings from the study are presented below. Information concerning the methodology is in the appendix.

Family Characteristics

The survey results from the CUA study establish several facts about the economic, social, motivational, and behavioral characteristics of the parents as a whole and permit comparisons between economically poor and non-poor families concerning parent motivations and school involvement in inner-city Catholic secondary schools. Differences are examined for four income groups: poverty families, or those whose annual income is $10,000 or less, the federal poverty level for a family of four for the year 1985 (32.3 per cent; N = 317); moderately poor families with incomes between $10,001 and $20,000 (29.4 per cent; N = 288); moderately non-poor families with incomes between $20,001 and $30,000 (19.8 per cent; N = 194); and non-poor or upper income families with incomes of $30,001 a year or more (18.5 per cent; N = 181).[4] While the income of this latter group may indicate a certain affluence, this study did not investigate other assets such as property, stocks, bonds and other investments that would more accurately describe the financial status of affluent families.

Approximately 60 per cent of the families are Black, 27 per cent are Hispanic, and 13 per cent are white. Three of the five schools are predominantly Black, one is Hispanic, and one white. Although each school is economically diverse within, the median income levels at the five schools follow an ethnic pattern; that is, the predominantly white school has a higher median income level than the Hispanic school, but not as high as any of the three Black schools.

For purposes of this study, families earning less than $20,000 (61.7 per cent of the sample) are designated as economically poor or poverty families. Compared to the non-poor, poverty families are burdened with the greatest number of financial and social 'deficits'. Concerning a number of economic-related factors, poverty families use 18 per cent of their disposable income for school tuition compared to 3 per cent used by families earning more than $30,000 annually.[5] Only one-fourth of poverty families receive financial aid from the school in the form of partial or full tuition assistance, twice as many as non-poor families. Besides paying tuition, other financial outlays include participation in fundraising activities such as purchasing raffle tickets, and paying for books and school uniforms. The vast majority also pay public transportation costs, since, with the exception of one school, students commute from a wide geographic area, sometimes travelling several hours a day. Thus, the financial sacrifice incurred by poverty families in choosing these Catholic secondary schools is especially great and may be indicative of family motivation.

Lee (1987) argues that financial sacrifice is a useful behavioral measure of 'value of education'. She shows that the degree of financial sacrifice is related positively to student achievement. That is, the degree to which families are willing to sacrifice financially to pay for private schooling affects children's school performance. This finding is a correlate to those of Erickson (1986) in his British Columbia study. He found that government subsidies to private schools resulted in decreases in volunteerism, commitment and loyalty among parents, teachers, and students and rendered private schools less distinctive in the eyes of their clientele. How financial sacrifice directly motivates students is evidenced by those who made remarks to interviewers similar to the following: 'My mother has the attitude that she is not going to pay so much money so I can mess around in [private] school. She says she works hard for it [=money] and she does not expect me to go out and louse up'.

All income groups possess some social 'deficits', but poverty families are more likely than other groups to lack the social and cultural capital associated with high social status (Coleman and Hoffer, 1987; Lareau, 1987) that supposedly facilitates parent involvement and thus school learning. These include factors such as time, money, and other material resources, educational skills, social networks, and occupational prestige. From this perspective, poor families in this study could be expected to possess hardships beyond income, more than upper income families, and thereby could be expected to be less involved in their children's education.

Similarly, poverty families were 40.7 per cent more likely than families earning more than $30,000 to have the mother in the home than in the workforce but 44 per cent less likely to have two parents in the home. The higher the family's income, the greater the likelihood that the mother is employed, a 'deficit' less restricted to lower-income families. Having the mother in the workforce is even more the case for two-parent families earning more than $30,000 where virtually all mothers work, suggesting that there is a need for both parents to work in order to pay for private schooling. Having two parents in the home is certainly important for economic reasons, especially for minority families who may not have other financial assets.

Milne, Myers, Rosenthal, and Ginsburg (1986) show that mothers' employment has negative effects for white students from two-parent families but generally positive effects for Black students from single-parent families. In a German study, Koliadis (1975) found that lower-income working mothers had higher levels of satisfaction regarding their children than their counterparts who were not employed but who wanted to work. These latter mothers had less trusting relations with their children and less sureness in their own maternal and pedagogical qualities. The establishment of social networks among co-workers and increased income may offset the disadvantage of having the mother in the workforce, especially for poor and minority families. This was illustrated in this study by the interviews, especially among Black, non-Catholic students, who sometimes mentioned their mother's workplace as the source of information regarding her decision to send the student to a Catholic school. Thus, having the mother in the workforce could be viewed as an educational and economic advantage for poor and minority students.

Besides being more likely to have the mother at home and being single parents, poverty families were significantly more likely than families in the highest income range to be Catholic, to have attended Catholic schools themselves, and to be non-Black. Sharing religious and cultural goals with the Catholic school, although they lack certain socio-economic advantages, poverty families have a potential for greater integration into the school's religious community than those who lack these characteristics.

In sum, for this sample, as income increases, educational prestige, the likelihood of being Black, being non-Catholic, never having attended a Catholic school, having two parents in the home, and having the mother in the workforce increases, indicating the presence of an upwardly mobile, Black, non-Catholic constituency that is highly motivated in its effort to acquire and pay for a private school education. These family characteristics are similar to those of Blacks in other studies of Catholic schools (i.e., Convey, 1986). A second identifiable group, the very poorest families, have greater economic-related deficits including not having the mother in the workforce. They are likely to be Hispanic or Black. Since their financial sacrifice is greater and since they are more likely to be Catholic, their integration into the school may be accomplished in ways different from the non-poor, upwardly mobile Blacks whose additional socio-economic resources may aid their integration. Obviously, these schools serve groups with widely varying socio-economic characteristics. This diversity makes it difficult to determine what kinds of characteristics are deterrents to parent involvement and school performance in Catholic schools.

Parent Motivations

The most common feature all families share in this study is parent motivation. Regardless of income and other background factors, parents have exceedingly high expectations for their children's future level of educational attainment. They consistently cite academic goals, particularly college preparation, as their reason for choosing a Catholic high school. They place a high value on the substantive aspects of school learning. Poor families are no different from non-poor families in that they value education and want what is best for their children.

Table 1 indicates that no significant differences were found across income levels concerning parents' expectations that their children will obtain a bachelor's or higher degree. The vast majority have this expectation while over 40 per cent expect their children also to obtain a master's degree or an advanced degree such as a PhD, MD, or a law degree.

Parents overwhelmingly endorse 'academics', 'discipline', and 'religion and values' as very important reasons for choosing a Catholic school regardless of income. They assign less importance to noneducational or nonsubstantive reasons such as 'convenience/safety', 'child's choice'. 'affordable tuition', and 'athletics'. There were some differences regarding 'convenience/safety' and 'athletics' reasons. Poor parents, especially parents of girls, were more concerned about how safe the school was and whether or not it was located in a safe neighborhood. Only a small percentage of parents considered athletic programs to be a very important reason for choosing a school; however, poor parents were considerably more likely than non-poor parents to choose this response.

When asked to select their most important or priority reason for choosing the school, some differences emerged. There is a tendency for poor families to select discipline reasons as 'most important' although discipline reasons are not a priority compared to academic reasons which were cited *first* by slightly more than half of all parents. The other half chose non-academic reasons over academic ones indicating parents' concern for an educational environment that emphasizes more than just academics. As indicated in Table 1, 'religion and values' and 'discipline' were the second and third ranked reason. None of the other reasons received more than 7.6 per cent of parents' response with the exception of 'child's choice' which was chosen as a priority by 11 per cent of parents with income beyond $30,000. Presumably, children from high income families exercise more choice options than those from poor families and their parents take their school choice preferences under advisement. For the

Patricia A. Bauch

Table 1   Distribution of Parent Responses to Motivation Items by Income

Variables	$10,000 or less	$10,001– 20,000	$20,001– 30,000	$30,001– or more	Totals
			Income Range		
Expectations for Child's Education Attainment					
Bachelor's degree +	219	203	145	139	706
	70.0%	71.5%	75.5%	77.7%	72.9%
Master's Degree +	118	129	81	74	402
	37.7%	45.4%	42.2%	41.3%	41.5%
Reasons for School Choice — Very Important					
Academics	261	238	161	145	805
	87.0%	86.9%	87.5%	83.8%	86.5%
Discipline	261	254	167	149	831
	84.2%	88.5%	86.5%	82.8%	85.7%
Religion/values	252	247	168	143	810
	83.4%	87.9%	89.4%	82.7%	85.8%
Convenience/safety	106	94	53	37	290
	35.3%	34.8%	28.5%	21.4%	31.2%*
Child's choice	102	94	53	38	287
	33.4%	33.6%	27.7%	22.1%	30.3%
Affordable tuition	189	175	107	92	563
	51.4%	61.8%	55.7%	52.6%	58.8%
Athletics	61	48	23	14	146
	19.7%	17.1%	12.0%	8.0%	15.3%*
*Reasons for School Choice — Most Important***					
Substantive					
Academics	131	129	111	84	455
	47.5%	50.4%	62.0%	53.5%	52.4%
Religion/values	38	46	29	24	138
	14.1%	18.0%	16.2%	15.3%	15.9%
Discipline	46	25	14	14	99
	16.7%	9.8%	8.8%	8.9%	11.4%
Nonsubstantive	60	56	25	35	176
	21.7%	21.9%	14.0%	22.3%	20.3%

* significant at the .05 level
** significant at the .01 level

majority of parents, academic as well as personal development reasons guide their choice of school.

In examining parents' motivations related to other family characteristics such as religion, ethnicity, single parents, and mother's employment, some interesting relationships were found. Catholics, expectedly, prefer religious reasons more frequently than non-Catholics, regardless of income levels. Blacks were significantly more likely to choose academic reasons than whites or Hispanics; but again, non-poor Blacks were only slightly more likely to do so than poor Blacks. There were no differences concerning reasons given by single parents compared to those of two-parent families. However, academic reasons as well as higher income levels were positively related to the frequency of mother's employment.

Parent Involvement

The noticeable difference between poor and non-poor parents concerning school participation and communication is the frequency with which they are involved. (See table 2.) Parents' whose incomes exceeded $30,000 were twice as likely to talk with their children's teacher three or more times a year. However, this does not mean that poor parents are not in contact

Table 2   Distribution of Parent Responses to Involvement Items by Income

| | Income Range | | | | |
Areas of involvement	$10,000 or less	$10,001– 20,000	$20,001– 30,000	$30,001– or more	Totals
Parent Knowledge of School: *					
Parent knows a great deal	110 35.1%	91 31.9%	83 43.7%	52 28.9%	336 34.7%
Parent knows a moderate amount	174 55.6%	166 58.2%	97 51.1%	114 63.3%	551 56.9%
Parent knows very little	29 9.3%	28 9.8%	10 5.8%	14 7.8%	81 8.4%
Parent Communication:					
Talks with teachers (3+ times a year)	70 22.2%	70 24.6%	75 39.7%	77 42.8%	292 30.2% *
No contact with school personnel	9 2.8%	10 3.5%	7 3.6%	5 2.8%	31 3.2%
Usually initiates school contacts	92 34.1%	87 33.5%	62 36.0%	66 39.1%	307 35.2%
Parent Participation:					
Helps at school (3+ times a year)	78 24.6%	100 34.7%	70 36.1%	66 36.5%	314 32.0% *
Attends school meetings (3+ times a year)	204 64.4%	205 71.2%	154 79.4%	134 74.0%	697 71.1% *
Monitors homework	212 72.6%	220 81.5%	155 83.3%	140 80.9%	727 78.9%
Parent Decision Making:					
Advises or is consulted by school	129 40.7%	98 34.0%	60 30.9%	49 27.1%	336 34.3%
Is not consulted, but would like to be	179 56.5%	173 60.1%	117 60.3%	117 64.6%	586 59.8%

* significant at the .05 level
** significant at the .01 level

with the school. There were no differences in income levels among parents who say they do not communicate with the school at all. Poor parents are more likely than non-poor parents to use a variety of communication modes. Those who do not communicate three times a year or more with their children's teachers, indicate that they talk with other school personnel such as school counselors and the principal or talk with a teacher once or twice a year, or read letters and bulletins from the school, or respond to parent surveys. Poor parents indicated that they were more likely to talk with school personnel by phone than other income groups (not shown). Other studies show that poor parents have positive attitudes toward contacts with teachers comparable to those of higher income families and want to cooperate with them (for example, Snow, 1982).

Similarly, there were no income differences related to the frequency with which parents said they initiated contacts with the school rather than waiting for the principal or a teacher to contact them, presumably when there was a problem, a matter of obtaining information, or for other reasons. This lack of difference in income groups suggests that poorer parents were as aggressive as non-poor parents in contacting the school when they found it necessary to do so and were no more likely than non-poor parents to avoid school contacts.

Although there is a tendency for parents in the highest income group to report that they participate in school-related activities more frequently than lower-income parents, a clear trend is not evident. Moderately poor parents are as likely as moderately non-poor parents to help at school three times a year or more including serving as advisory, school board or parent board members, and assisting as teachers, classroom aides or substitute teachers. School meetings are reportedly well attended, again by approximately the same proportion of all parents with the exception of the poorest parents who are somewhat more unlikely to attend three meetings or more a year. More than 80 per cent of parents at all income levels, with the exception of the poorest parents, say they monitor homework.

Only about a third of parents reported that they advise or help make school decisions in the area of school policy, goals, and curriculum. As with knowledge of the school, more lower than higher income parents claimed they were involved in the school's decision-making process. However, there were no significant differences among income groups concerning parents' desires to be involved in school decision making. More parents who thought they were not consulted wanted to be involved than were actually involved. In the schools, parent decision-making generally took the form of making decisions about their children's initial course work during parent-child screening interviews, serving on arbitration and discipline boards, responding to school surveys, and participating in decisions at home-school meetings.

Although parent decision-making is not emphasized at these schools, it does appear that other forms of parent involvement, especially activities directly related to children's school performance such as attending school meetings and parent-teacher conferences and monitoring homework do receive greater attention than in public schools (Bauch, 1988; Cantril, 1979; Coleman and Hoffer, 1987; Epstein, 1986b).

In sum, the findings from this study indicate that: i) poor and minority parents place a high value on education as indicated by the financial sacrifice they make to send their children to private schools. Financial sacrifice seems greater for poor parents who pay a substantially higher proportion of their income for tuition and related expenses. ii) Despite economic and social hardship, poor families are just as motivated as non-poor families in wanting a good education for their children. They do not choose these schools for trivial reasons such as the attendance of their children's friends; rather, they give substantive reasons just as frequently as do non-poor parents. Parents choose these schools for developmental reasons as well as academic reasons. iii) Poor as well as non-poor parents are involved in these schools at a moderate to high rate of participation. Poor parents tend not to speak directly to their children's teachers or go to the school as frequently as do non-poor parents who are likely to have the additional resources that promote these activities including transportation, child care arrangements, and perhaps a flexible work schedule. However, that does not mean they are not involved. Despite economic differences, parents uniformly want to be involved in school decision-making. Poor parents do not perceive themselves as knowing less about the school than non-poor parents.

Conclusions

Private schools are not just schools for the wealthy. Many poor and minority parents who choose them, most at great financial sacrifice, value education highly and want what is best for their children. They take steps to insure that their children perform well in school, just as wealthy parents apparently do. The information and communication gap between these groups is not as serious as some would contend and can be remedied by providing extra assistance to poor families.

Admittedly, success in choice making is governed, in part, by the ability to develop certain behaviors such as consumer 'strategies' and the acquiring of needed information to make 'informed choices'. Parents' intentions for choosing a school and their education-related behavior constitute a type of strategizing. The fact that poor parents are just as likely as non-poor parents to have substantive reasons for choosing a school lends credence to their ability to make potentially wise educational decisions for their children; that they are actively involved in them demonstrates their motivation and support for their choice behavior.

Despite what some would fear, it is not that poor parents are not able to practice consumer choice behavior. Rather, poor parents take longer to acquire information; over time they catch up and become aware at the same level as non-poor parents. They are also just as likely as the non-poor to practice consumer strategies that insure that school expectations are fulfilled; however, they make use of different strategies and practice some behaviors less frequently than non-poor parents such as communicating with school personnel by telephone rather than coming to the school. If parents are actively involved in a school, it is questionable that a slight increase in the number or kinds of contacts contributes positively to children's school performance. What is more important is that parents do have contacts with the school. More time and more diverse opportunities to practice consumer behavior need to be alloted to poor and minority parents in order to accommodate them.

No doubt, highly motivated poor and minority parents, are eager for information about schooling and would welcome its provision to assist them in locating a school they select, if they had such an option. Their reliance on face-to-face information could lessen the possibility of misinterpretation to which even the non-poor are liable.

While the availability of consumer information is important, informed choice may not be as important as parents' positive feelings about the school, especially if parents have an opportunity to choose it. Parents who choose private schools may not perceive differences between the public and private school curriculum, its methods of instruction or educational philosophy and that of the private school chosen; however, they may strongly believe schools of choice provide a better learning environment and therefore a better education and preparation for life than their children could obtain in most public schools. It may not be as important that parents are able to distinguish among program options as it is for them to select schools related to their values and to the kind of environment in which they feel their children will do well and where they feel their cultural values are respected.

Glenn (1986) remarks that even highly-educated parents, in choosing schools for their children, tend to make judgments based upon intangibles such as school climate, ethos and reputation, often based on personal recommendations, not on sophisticated research findings. Currently, poor parents are helpless in the face of decisions by school administrators. Such decisions may contribute to the learned helplessness and passivity that is expected of poor parents and the belief that they cannot make informed choices. Neither of the two research studies discussed above leads to this conclusion. Allowing poor parents to make educational choices on a par with the middle and upper middle class parents would afford them an opportunity to find the type of school they feel is best for their children. The perception of possessing educational options would in turn translate into specific expectations and vigilance that the expectations be met.

In considering the role that Catholic schools might play in the education of poor and minority children, such families may choose Catholic schools because they perceive them as more accepting of cultural differences, and as more empathetic about individual student's needs in the form of attention, personal interest, high expectations, and intensity of involvement that is less frequently found in public schools. Catholic schools may be viewed more positively than public schools by Blacks as places of social integration in the negotiating of the triple quandary.

Equity concerns about choice do not appear to be a problem in these studies. In the Alum Rock Study parents tended not to sort themselves by ethnicity whereas at the five schools in the CUA study, parents were more likely to sort themselves by ethnicity, not by income. Each school had a predominant ethnic group, an historical characteristic of Catholic schools, but wide economic diversity within each school. Socio-economic, ethnic and religious differences were down-played. For example, teachers and students consistently and universally told interviewers that they were not aware of which students came from poor families. In racially-mixed schools, the school administration took specific steps to insure that students of different races were not separated in classes and school acitivities and to support the development of inter-racial friendships. In Black schools with large proportions of non-Catholic students, such students appeared to be integrated into the study body. They not only attended religion classes and participated in other religious functions, but teachers commented that they were often more knowledgeable about the Scriptures than their Catholic peers. Some schools went out of their way to make these students feel at home. An ideology present in all the schools that did not put a premium on a student's race, religion, nor economic level provided the background for a high level of social integration into the school community for all students suggesting consonance with Coleman and Hoffer's theory that Catholic schools provide functional communities that assist lower-income and minority students to perform better in Catholic schools than in public ones.

Coleman and Hoffer (1987) and Coleman (1987) propose an explanation for achievement and other effects for poor and minority students, especially in Catholic schools. Catholic schools not only place greater curricular demands on students, but they also maintain a relationship to the parental community that is not found generally in public schools. This community surrounding the Catholic school, a community created by the church, constitutes a social network, Coleman (1987) argues, in which certain agreed upon norms about raising children exist and where relationships between adults and children extend beyond the family to include a certain intrusiveness of one adult in the activities of someone else's child. These adult-child relationships create a kind of social capital beyond the family that aids them in their child-rearing tasks and is especially beneficial for children without extensive social capital in the home.

A neglected factor in the Coleman-Hoffer thesis is the many successful Catholic schools which are not religiously homogeneous schools. In these schools, families do not share the same setting for religious worship, nor do they necessarily agree on many topics that are fundamental to Catholic Church teaching and to the raising of children, and yet, most poor and minority students do well in these schools. Why?

Going beyond the Coleman-Hoffer thesis, there may be something that Catholic schools do that helps integrate students into the school community that is not necessarily nor directly church-related, despite Coleman's (1987) observation that there is nothing specifically that goes on *within* the schools to which such integration can be attributed. Rather, I submit, that there may be two reasons. First, Catholic school philosophy views individuals as unique and capable persons (Congregation for Catholic Education, 1988; National Conference of Catholic Bishops, 1973). There are expectations for parents as well as for children. Second, because Catholic schools are chosen by parents and the school chooses its clients, presumably there are fewer discontinuities between home and school in regard to parents' values. It would seem that mutual selectivity is vital to student success at any school. Mutual selectivity can be arrived at only through choice.

Policy Implications

The denial of education choice based on the assumption that poor parents cannot make wise decisions concerning their children's education because they are poorly motivated or lack appropriate information seems weak. The evidence shows that many are highly motivated and would be able to choose appropriate schooling for their children. Given the *supposed* deficits or disadvantages that such families have to overcome that accompany poverty, educational and social policymakers should ease their burdens, where possible, by enacting policies that will strengthen family autonomy, motivation, and self-determination. They should provide information and other social supports, especially when the poor are willing to make considerable financial and personal sacrifices to obtain the type of schooling they wish for their children. The denial of choice to these families seems elitist and undemocratic in that it treats poor families as second class citizens who require caretakers to make appropriate decisions for them. Such status does nothing to enhance the family autonomy and efficacy that illicits the incentive for effective school performance.

A voucher plan for poor and for minority families whose children must negotiate several socialization agendas, might incorporate some aspects of Jenck's original plan (Doyle, 1977; Jencks, 1968). A limited, voluntary, compensatory plan in which vouchers would be issued to qualified families, much like food stamps, would be exchanged by schools of choice for a committed, fixed amount of government funding to cover a part, if not all, of a student's school expenses. A limited, voluntary voucher plan would permit motivated poor and minority families to have a wider range of school choices which can be justified by their diverse background needs and greater educational and socialization needs. Other precautions would also have to be taken as suggested by Nathan (1987), especially the need constantly to correct features of a voucher plan so that choice does not produce unintended consequences. It would be surprising to see the extent to which, over time, most poor and minority families would become familiar with and wish to participate in a voucher system.

Parents should be free to choose to have their children educated in either an ethnically homogeneous or a heterogeneous setting. For example, there is nothing intrinsically wrong with an all-Black school as long as it is of high quality and responsive to its students; in fact, it is racist to hold such a view (Coleman, 1977; Lines, 1987). Students who are particularly difficult or who have learning problems should receive a higher voucher amount in order to make them more attractive to schools and to assure that the schools that accept high numbers of these students are well-equipped and have highly-trained teachers.

Since such a system would stimulate competition among schools, there might not be as much movement from school to school as expected. Effective schools would strive to become more responsive to their families in order to retain them and in order to attract new, voucher families. Since all schools would be competing with one another, the schools of poor children of non-voucher parents would improve also. Schools that failed to attract families would be forced to consolidate with other schools or close.

Choice schools should require extensive parent involvement and inclusion in school decision-making by way of boards, committees, homework, and so on, but should take special care to accommodate poorer and single parent families who have child care and transportation needs. The assumption should not be made that the poor are less likely to want to be involved in the school and in school decision-making.

The implementation of a limited, voluntary voucher plan could provide valuable information and experience to educators, policymakers, and government officials about how choice might improve schooling for all students, especially poor and minority students who seem not to do well under the present educational system. After a limited pilot program, depending on its outcomes, such a plan might be adjusted and expanded. Through thoughtful design and commitment, the twin goals of school improvement and equality of educational opportunity are attainable through public policies that enable poor families to perform competently in the education of their children.

Additional research would be helpful about parents' reasons for school choice, their informational needs and the strategies they use for choosing schools. There is also a need to explore patterns of mutual selectivity and the meaning and impact of a 'good fit' between family and school in schools of choice.

Patricia A. Bauch

A Cautionary Note

While the majority of families in the CUA study are considered economically poor, they appear to be highly committed to college preparation for their children and are highly motivated in choosing a Catholic high school. What may distinguish them most from other poor families not in Catholic schools is their level of demonstrated motivation and aspirations, qualities which may be latent in other poor families who do not make the decision to sacrifice financially to send their children to private schools. These are not the discouraged poor who do not see the value of higher education (Richardson, 1988). Perhaps it is this type of family who is encouraged about higher education but discouraged about public education in its present form as a means of obtaining it for whom vouchers would work best. Their encouragement, I submit, could be attributed to their exercise of choice.

It cannot be shown conclusively that poor families can make potentially good educational choices for their children, if given the opportunity to do so. However, it can and has been demonstrated that where poor families do exercise choice, they behave like non-poor families and have motivations and strategies aimed at school success. In order to unleash the motivational potential of poor families, opportunities for choice must be made available to them. They would then have the incentive to develop their own educational strategies for helping their school children succeed. The implementation of a voucher system for the poor has the potential to provide hope for many poor families, reform our ailing schools, and bring the United States a step closer toward realizing its national commitment to educational equity.

Appendix

This study was conducted by researchers, under the direction of the author, at the Center for the Study of Youth Development at CUA. The purpose of the study was to examine the impact of Catholic secondary schools on low-income and minority students. We collected data during Spring 1985 from five schools representative nationally of 'successful' inner city Catholic high schools. The study was a part of a larger one funded by the Ford Foundation and undertaken by the National Catholic Educational Association to develop a national profile of Catholic secondary schools (Yeager, Benson, Guerra, and Manno, 1985; Benson *et al.*, 1986).

Six university researchers spent the equivalent of ten days at each school. We gathered questionnaire data for the family study reported here from 1070 parents in five inner-city Catholic high schools, 64 per cent of the population surveyed. The researchers obtained other data through

306

formal and informal interviews with parents, students, teachers, and administrators, and through participant observation. We wrote extensive case studies detailing the daily life of the schools and their participants (Bauch, Blum, Taylor, and Valli, 1985). For this report, we made comparisons among parents at various income levels to determine differences in parental motivation and school involvement. Comparisons were also made based on parents' educational levels with similar results. More detailed information concerning the research design, conduct of the study, and types of data gathered is available from the author (Bauch, 1987; Bauch and Small, 1986; Bauch *et al.*, 1985).

For purposes of this study, we measured parent motivations according to parents' responses to a series of survey questions concerning their children's expected future educational attainment, and their most important reasons for choosing to send their children to a Catholic high school. Response options for predicting their children's future educational attainment level ranged from 'not graduate from high school' to 'obtain an advanced degree after college (PhD, MD, or law degree)'. For the questions that probed parents' reasons for choosing a Catholic school, we asked: 'Listed below are some reasons parents frequently give for choosing a Catholic school. First: How important was each reason in helping you decide to send your child to this school? Second: Which reason was the most important? (Mark only one).' The twenty-five reasons presented were derived from an extensive review of the literature. These reasons, or response items conceptually and statistically formed four categories representing four different types of reasons: 1) academic and curriculum, 2) discipline, 3) religion and values, and 4) non-substantive reasons (for example, safety, child's choice, transportation, location, affordable tuition).

As a measure of parent involvement, we analyzed parents' responses to questions concerning their knowledge of the school, nature and extent of home-school communication, and their participation in school-related activities and school decision-making. Concerning school knowledge, we asked parents: 'How much do you feel you know about what goes on in your child's school?' Concerning home-school communication, we measured the frequency with which parents reported that they, rather than the principal or teachers, initiated contacts with the school; and the number of times in a school year they talked with their children's teachers. We asked questions about parents' mode of communication (i.e., telephone, group meetings, home visits, parent-teacher conferences). We also asked parents to indicate their participation in a number of parent participation roles described by twelve items concerning: 1) helping at school including serving as advisory, school board or parent board members, and assisting teachers as classroom aides or substitute teachers; 2) monitoring homework, and 3) attending various types of school meetings. Lastly, we asked parents whether they advise or help make decisions for the school in the areas of school policy (i.e., discipline, admissions, goals, and curriculum);

and, if they did not advise or help make decisions, whether they would like to be consulted by the school.

Among other demographic and family factors, parents provided information about whether they are Catholic, whether they attended a Catholic school, the number of parents and children living in the home, parent's educational attainment, family income, employment, ethnic background, and sources of financial aid for schooling.

The schools are located in metropolitan city districts in four geographic regions of the country. In the selection process, we chose schools that were representative nationally of inner-city Catholic secondary schools. Thus, the schools have a diversity of organizational arrangements including size, gender and racial composition, and governance structure (for example, private or diocesan-owned, and religious order or diocesan-operated). The schools are also socio-economically diverse. They vary considerably in the proportion of lower income families served ranging from 15 per cent to 46 per cent. Four of the five are predominantly minority schools. The fifth school is a white, working class school with a one-third Black enrollment. Examining parents' educational motivations and school involvement by income in diverse inner-city settings provides a baseline of data for a critical assessment of family educational choice arrangements by poor and minority parents.

Acknowledgment

The author acknowledges with gratitude the suggestions of James G. Cibulka, Eleanor D'Armour-Thomas, Sally M. Flanzer, Patricia M. Lines, and Linda R. Valli, and the generosity of the National Academy of Education's Spencer Fellowship Program under whose sponsorship this chapter was completed.

Notes

1 A critical overview of the social pathology research of the 1960s with its emphasis on the 'disadvantaged' that spawned deficit thinking regarding poor families reveals serious inadequacies. Ginsburg (1986) argues that the research of the 1960s that contributed to social policy directed toward school improvement employed narrow methodologies that were not based on an understanding of children in general or the poor in particular (for example, Deutsch, 1967; Hess and Shipman, 1967), For example, behavioral scientists examining the parent-child interaction of lower-class families performing an artificial task noted behaviors that differed from those of middle-class families. The Piagetian perspective which formed much of this work did not take into account the role of the environment in concept acquisition. From

an ecological perspective, scientists could have viewed insufficient laboratory performance as distinctive, rather than deficient. Presumably poor and minority children develop special kinds of adaptation, skills not possessed by middle-class children. For lower-class families, the laboratory situation may have been uninteresting, threatening or condescending. From such situations, lower-class family interaction is difficult to interpret. Ginsburg considers much of the psychological research conducted on poor mothers and their children insensitive, narrow-minded, and wrong.

2 See Andrew A. Greely (1976), 'The Ethnic Miracle' for elaboration on this point.
3 Since 1969, the proportion of minority students in Catholic schools has more than doubled from 424,520 or 10.4 per cent of total enrollment to 586,500 or 22.4 per cent in 1987. During this period, the percentage of non-Catholics has also increased significantly from 2.07 per cent to 11.2 per cent. Although Catholic school enrollment continues to decline from its peak enrollment of 5.1 million in 1965, the increase in minority enrollment, especially Black and Hispanic, in Catholic schools is a fact that cannot be ignored (Bredeweg, 1988).
4 For this study, average family size is four persons—generally two adults and two children per family. This did not vary by income levels.
5 This was determined using a simple calculation comparing the average cost of school tuition (i.e., $1190) to the mean income for each ethnic group.

References

ALEXANDER, K. L. and PALLAS, A. M. (1983) 'Private Schools and Public: New Evidence on Cognitive Achievement in Public and Private Schools', *Sociology of Education* , 56:3, October, pp. 170–181.

ANDERSON , J. E. (1936) *The Young Child in the Home: A Survey of Three Thousand American Families* New York, Appleton-Century.

BANDURA, A. (1986) *Social Foundations of Thought and Action* New Jersey, Prentice-Hall.

BANKS, J. A. (1986) 'Race, Ethnicity, Class, and Education: A Critical Analysis of Concepts and Paradigms.' Presented at the annual meeting of the American Educational Research Association, San Francisco.

BANKS, J. A. (1987) 'Ethnicity, Class and Cognitive Styles: Research and Teaching Implications.' Presented at the annual meeting of the American Educational Research Association, Washington, DC.

BARATZ, K. W. and LEVINE, E. S. (1978) 'Childrearing by Black Parents: A Description and Comparison to Anglo and Chicano Parents', *Journal of Marriage and the Family*, 40:2, November, pp. 709–19.

BAUCH, P. A. (1987) 'Family Choice and Parent Involvement in Inner-City Catholic High Schools: An Exploration of Psycho-Social and Organizational Factors.' Presented at the annual meeting of the American Educational Research Association, Washington, DC.

BAUCH , P. A. (1988) 'Is Parent Involvement Different in Private Schools?', Educational Horizons, 66:2, Winter, pp. 78–82.

BAUCH, P. A., BLUM, I., TAYLOR, N. and VALLI, L. (1985). *Final Report to the National Catholic Educational Association on a Field Study of Five Low-Income-Serving Schools* Washington, DC, The Catholic University of America.

BAUCH, P. A. and SMALL, T. W. (1986) 'Parents' Reasons for School Choice in Four Inner-City Catholic High Schools: Their Relationship to Education, Income, and Ethnicity.' Presented at the annual meeting of the American Educational Research Association, San Francisco.

BENSON, P. L., YEAGER, R. J., WOOD, P. K., GUERRA, M. J. and MANNO, B. V. (1986) *Catholic High Schools: Their Impact on Low-Income Students* Washington, DC, National Catholic Educational Association.

BEREITER, C. and ENGLEMANN, S. (1966) *Teaching Disadvantaged Children in the Preschool* Englewood Cliffs, NJ, Prentice-Hall.

BILLINGSLEY, A. (1968) *Black Families in White America* Englewood Cliffs, NJ, Prentice-Hall.

BLOOM, B. (1964) *Stability and Change in Human Characteristics* New York, John Wiley.

BLOOM, B. (1981) *All Our Children Learning: A Primer for Parents, Teachers and Other Educators* New York, McGraw-Hill.

BOYKIN, W. A. (1986) 'The Triple Quandary and the Schooling of Afro-American Children', in NEISSER, U. (ed.) *The School Achievement of Minority Children* New Jersey, Lawrence Erlbaum Associates.

BOYKIN, W. A. and TOMS, F. D. (1985) 'Black Child Socialization: A Conceptual Framework', in McADOO, H. P. and McADOO, J. L. (eds) *Black Children· Social, Educational, and Parental Environments*, Beverly Hills, Sage Publications.

BREDEWEG, F. H. (1988) *United States Catholic Elementary and Secondary Schools: 1987–1988*, Washington, DC, National Catholic Educational Association.

BRIDGE, G. (1974) *Parental Decision-making in an Educational Voucher System*, Santa Monica, CA: Rand.

BRIDGE, G. (1978) 'Information Imperfections: The Achilles' Heel of Entitlement Plans', *School Review*, 86:3, May, pp. 504–29.

BRIDGE, R. G. and BLACKMAN, J. (1978) *A Study of Alternatives in American Education, Vol. IV: Family Choice in Schooling*, Santa Monica, CA, Rand.

BRONFENBRENNER, U. (1974) *Is Early Intervention Effective? A Report On Longitudinal Evaluation of Preschool Programs, Vol. 2.* Washington, DC, United States Department of Health, Education, and Welfare.

BRYK, A. S., HOLLAND, P. B., LEE, V. E. and CARRIEDO, R. A. (1984) *Effective Catholic Schools: An Exploration*, Washington, DC, National Catholic Educational Association.

CANTRIL, A. H. (1979) *The School-Home-Community Relationship: An Interpretive Summary of the Public's View*, Washington, DC, Community Education Program, US Office of Education.

CATTERALL, J. S. (1983) 'Tuition Tax Credits: Issues of Equity', in JAMES, T. and LEVIN, H. M. (eds)*Public Dollars for Private Schools: The Case of Tuition Tax Credits*, Philadelphia, Temple University Press.

CHUBB, J. E. and MOE, T. M. (1986) 'No School Is an Island: Politics, Markets, and Education', *The Brookings Review*, 4:4, Fall, pp. 21–28.

CIBULKA, J. C., O'BRIEN, T. J. and ZEWE, D. (1982) *Inner-City Private Elementary Schools; A Study*, Milwaukee, Marquette University Press.

CLARK, R. (1983) *Family Life and School Achievement: Why Poor Black Children Succeed or Fail*, Chicago, University of Chicago Press.

COLEMAN, J. S. (1977) Choice in American Education', in COLEMAN, J. S. (ed.) *Parents, Teachers, and Children: Prospects for Choice in American Education*, San Francisco, Institute for Contemporary Studies.

COLEMAN, J. S. (1987) Families and Schools, *Educational Researcher*, 16.6, August–September, pp. 32–8.

COLEMAN, J. S. and HOFFER, T. (1987) *Public and Private High Schools: The Impact of Communities*, New York, Basic Books.

COLEMAN, J. S., CAMPBELL, E. Q., HOBSON , C. J., MCPARTLAND, J., MOOD, A. M., WEINFELD, F. D. and YORK, R. L. (1966) *Equality of Educational Opportunity*, Washington, DC, United States Office of Education.

CONGREGATION FOR CATHOLIC EDUCATION (1988) *The Religious Dimension of Education in a Catholic School*, Rome, Vatican Polyglot Press.

CONVEY, J. J. (1986) 'Parental Choice of Catholic Schools as a Function of Religion, Race, and Family Income.' Presented at the annual meeting of the American Educational Research Association, San Francisco, CA.

DEUTSCH, M. (ed.) (1967) *The Disadvantaged Child*, New York, Basic Books.

DOYLE, D. P. (1977) 'The Politics of Choice: A View from the Bridge', in COLEMAN, J. S. (ed.) *Parents, Teachers, and Children: Prospects for Choice in American Education*, San Francisco, Institute for Contemporary Studies.

EPSTEIN , J. L. (1986a) 'Parents' Reactions to Teacher Practices of Parent Involvement', *Elementary School Journal*, 86:3, January, pp. 277–94.

EPSTEIN, J. L. (1986b) 'Toward an Integrated Theory of School and Family Connections, Report No. 3', Baltimore: Center for Research on Elementary and Middle Schools, The Johns Hopkins University.

ERICKSON, D. A. (Forthcoming) 'Effects of Privatism in Public and Private Schools: An Interpretation of Pertinent Research', in BAUCH, P. A. (ed.) *Private Schools and the Public Interest*, Westport, CT, Greenwood Press.

ERICKSON, D. A. (1986) 'Choice and Private Schools: Dynamics of Supply and Demand', in LEVY, D. C. (ed.) *Private Education: Studies in Choice and Public Policy*, New York, Oxford University Press.

FOOD AND DRUG ADMINISTRATION (1974) *Consumer Nutrition Survey, Part I: 1971–73*, Washington, DC, Government Printing Office.

GALLUP, A. M. (1986) 'The 18th Annual Gallup Poll of the Public's Attitudes Toward the Public Schools', *Phi Delta Kappan*, 68:1, September, pp. 43–59.

GALLUP, A. M. and CLARK, D. L. (1987) 'The 19th annual Gallup Poll of the Public's Attitudes Toward the Public Schools', *Phi Delta Kappan*, 59:1, September, pp. 17–30.

GINSBURG, H. P. (1986) 'The Myth of the Deprived Child: New Thoughts on Poor Children', in NEISSER, U. (ed.) *The School Achievement of Minority Children: New Perspectives*, New Jersey, Lawrence Erlbaum Associates.

GLENN, C. L. (1986) 'Letting Poor Parents Act Responsibly', *The Journal of Family and Culture*, 2:3, Autumn, pp. 1–18.

GREELEY, A. M. (1976) 'The Ethnic Miracle', *The Public Interest*, 45, Fall, pp. 20–36.

GREELEY, A. M. (1982) *Catholic High Schools and Minority Students*, New Brunswick, Transaction Books.

GREELEY, A. M., MCCREADY, W. C. and McCOURT, K. (1976) *Catholic Schools in a Declining Church*, Kansas City, Sheed and Ward.

GREELEY, A. M. and ROSSI, P. H. (1966) *The Education of Catholic Americans*, Chicago, Aldine Publishing Company.

HALE-BENSON, J. E. (1982) *Black Children: Their Roots, Culture, and Learning Styles*, revised ed., Baltimore, Johns Hopkins University Press.

HENDERSON, A. E. (ed.) (1981) *Parent Participation — Student Achievement: The Evidence Grows*, Columbia, MD, National Committee for Citizens in Education.

HENDERSON, A. E. (1987) *The Evidence Continues to Grow: Parent Involvement Improves Student Achievement*, Columbia, MD, National Committee for Citizens in Education.

HESS, R. D. and SHIPMAN, V. (1967) 'Cognitive Elements in Maternal Behavior', in HILL J. P. (ed.) *Minnesota Symposia on Child Psychology, Vol. 1*, Minneapolis, University of Minnesota Press.

HILL, R. B. (1972) *The Strengths of Black Families*, New York, Emerson Hall.

HOOVER, M. R. (1978) 'Community Attitudes Toward Black English', *Language in society*, 7:1, April, pp. 65–87.

HYMAN, H., WRIGHT, C. R. and REED, J. S. (1976) *The Enduring Effects of Education*, Chicago, University of Chicago Press.

JENCKS, C. (1968) 'Private Schools For Black Children', *New York Times Magazine*, 118:40:461, November 3, pp. 30 and 132–140.

JENCKS, C. (1972) *Inequality: A Reassessment of the Effect of Family and Schooling in America*, New York, Harper and Row.

KAGAN, S. L. (1984) 'Parent Involvement Research: A Field in Search of Itself, Report No. 8', Boston: Institute for Responsive Education.

KEITH, T. Z. and PAGE, E. B. (1985) 'Do Catholic High Schools Improve Minority Student Achievement?' *American Educational Research Journal*, 22:3, Fall, pp. 337–49.

KILGORE, S. B. (Forthcoming) 'Differences in Public and Private Schools: What We Do and Do Not Know', in BAUCH, P. A. (ed.) *Private Schools and the Public Interest: Research and Policy Issues*, Westport, CT, Greenwood Press.

KOHN, M. (1969) *Class and Conformity: A Study in Values*, Homewood, IL, Dorsey Press.

KOLIADIS, E. (1975) *Working Mothers and the Socialization of Children*, Weinheim and Basel, Beltz.

KUTNER, M. A., SHERMAN, J. D. and WILLIAMS, M. F. (1986) 'Federal Policies for Private Schools', in LEVY, D. C. (ed.) *Private Education: Studies in Choice and Public Policy*, New York, Oxford University Press.

LAREAU, A. (1987) 'Social Class Differences in Family-School Relationships: The Importance of Cultural Capital', *Sociology of Education*, 60:2, April, pp., 73–85.

LEE, V. E. (1987) 'The Effect of Family Financial Sacrifice on the Achievement of Disadvantaged Students in Catholic Schools.' Presented at the annual meeting of the American Educational Research Association, Washington, DC.

LEVIN, H. M. (1983) 'Educational Choice and the Pains of Democracy', in JAMES, T. and LEVIN, H. M. (eds) *Public Dollars for Private Schools: The Case of Tuition Tax Credits*, Philadelphia, Temple University Press.

LINES, P. M. (1987) The Denial of Choice and *Brown v. Board of Education. Metropolitan Education*, 1:4, Spring, pp. 108 –27.

MCADOO, H. P. and MCADOO, J. L. (eds) (1985) *Black Children: Social, Educational, and Parental Environments*, Beverly Hills, Sage Publications.

MANN, D. (1974) 'Public Understanding and Education Decision-making', *Educational Administration*, 10:2, Spring, pp. 1–18.

MILNE, A. M., MYERS, D. E., ROSENTHAL, A. S. and GINSBURG, A. (1986) Single Parents, Working Mothers, and the Educational Achievement of School Children, *Sociology of Education*, 59:3, July, pp. 125–39.

MOOS, R. and MOOS, B. S. (1976) 'A Typology of Family Social Environments', *Family Process*, 15:1, March, pp. 357–71.

NATHAN, J. (1987) 'Results and Future Prospects of State Efforts to Increase Choice Among Schools', *Phi Delta Kappan*, 68:10, June, pp. 746–52.

NATIONAL CONFERENCE OF CATHOLIC BISHOPS (1973) *To Teach as Jesus Did: A Pastoral Message on Catholic Education*, Washington, DC, United States Catholic Conference.

NATIONAL GOVERNORS' ASSOCIATION (1986) *Time for Results: The Governors' 1991 Report on Education*, Washington, National Governors; Association Center for Policy Research and Analysis.

NEISSER, U. (ed.) (1986) *The School Achievement of Minority Children: New Perspectives*, New Jersey, Lawrence Erlbaum Associates.

NEUWIEN, R. A. (ed.) (1966) *Catholic Schools in Action* , Notre Dame, University of Notre Dame Press.

NICHOLS , E. J. (1986) 'Cultural Foundations for Teaching Black Children', in RATTERAY, O. M. T. (ed.) *Teaching Mathematics, Vol. 1: Culture, Motivation, History and Classroom Management*, Washington, DC, Institute for Independent Education.

OGBU, J. U. (1982) 'Cultural Discontinuities and Schooling', *Anthropology and Education Quarterly*, 8:4, Winter, pp. 290–37.

RAYWID, M. A. (1987) 'Excellence and Choice: Friends or Foes?' *The Urban Review*, 19:1, July, pp. 35–47.

RICHARDSON, R. (1988) 'Minority Participation in the Teaching Profession.' Presented at the south eastern regional meeting of the Holmes Group, Washington, DC.

SEWELL, W. and HAUSER , R. M. (1976) 'Causes and Consequences of Higher Education: Models of the Status Attainment Process', in SEWELL, W., HAUSER , R. M. and FEATHERMAN, D. L. (eds) *Schooling and Achievement in American Society*, New York, Academic Press.

SIMMONS, W. (1979) 'The Relationship Between Academic Status and Future Expectations among Low-income Blacks', *Journal of Black Psychology*, 6:1, August, pp. 7–16.

SNOW, M. B. (1982) 'Characteristics of Families with Special Needs in Relation to Schools', Charleston, WV, Appalachia Educational Laboratory.

TREICHEL, I. (1986) *Educational Choice: A Survey of Minnesota Parents*, St. Paul, Minnesota Citizens for Educational Freedom.

VALENTINE, C. A. (1968) *Culture and Poverty: Critique and Counter Proposals*, Chicago, The University of Chicago Press.

WALBERG, H. J. (1984) 'Families as Partners in Educational Productivity', *Phi Delta Kappan*, 65:6, February, pp. 397–400.

WILSON, W. J. (1987) *The Truly Disadvantaged: The Inner-City, the Underclass and Public Policy*, Chicago, The University of Chicago Press.

WISE, A. E. and DARLING-HAMMOND, L. (1984) 'Education by Voucher: Private Choice and the Public Interest', *Educational Theory*, 34:1, Winter, pp. 29–47.

YEAGER, R. J., BENSON, P. L., GUERRA, M. J. and MANNO, B. V. (1985) *The Catholic High School: A National Portrait*, Washington, DC, National Catholic Educational Association.

Chapter 16
Elitism and Patterns of Independent Education

Peter Mason

There is general agreement in democratic countries in Europe west of the iron curtain, in North America and in Australia and New Zealand about the importance of freedom of parental choice in education and about the right of individuals and associations of various kinds, confessional and lay, to found and run private schools, subject, as is only reasonable, to minimal controls by government to ensure the health, fair treatment and basic educational needs of pupils. This agreement is based on two concepts, both fundamental to the accepted definition of justice in the free world — firstly, that this aspect of freedom of choice is a human right, an agreed principle expressed as a major clause in the various international declarations of human rights which have received the assent of almost all democratic countries and which include the European Convention adopted by all members of the European Economic Community; and secondly that freedom of choice in education is an essential element in the preservation of freedom in a democratic society.

Nevertheless, it is natural in a world largely conditioned by what Professor Mead and others have called an underlying system of inherited inequalities, that educationalists in particular and sociologists and economists in general should be especially concerned to promote, if not absolute equality, at least some real equality of opportunity; and that some political parties both in Europe and elsewhere should have attempted to legislate to this end by limiting or curtailing what they see as privilege in the private sector. How best to foster equality of opportunity and how far it is possible to achieve any real shift has been, of course, the subject of continuing controversy from the time of Adam Smith and more recently Jencks to the present day, Jean Floud (1975), in a strongly critical article on the Jencks view that education offers little if any hope of equalizing opportunity argues that the appropriate question to ask is not whether schools can change people, but whether, other things being equal, the self-perpetuating momentum of the closed system of inherited inequalities can be checked

Peter Mason

by the injection of outside resources in the form of publicly provided education and training. She went on to say that if the distribution of public funds on education is selective according to ability or 'merit' or choice the effect will be to increase inequality even though more children from humble homes are numbered among students at advanced levels. Further-more, though parents who pay fees at independent schools increase the amount of educational resources available for general distribution, they reinforce the conservative influences which stem from the closed circle of friendship and intermarriage fostered by closed communities — which, as will appear, independent schools tend to encourage.

The very limited objective of the present enquiry is not to dispute Floud's general contention or to attempt to solve the equation of social justice, but to demonstrate from the factual and comparative study of independent education in Europe, North America and the Antipodes in which I have been engaged for the past four years how what are usually called in the jargon élitist tendencies of independent education (to say nothing of similar tendencies in public systems) vary in degree and force, depending firstly on the constitutional, legal and managerial framework in which such schools operate, and secondly on the historical development of educational patterns and social mores, and in particular on the involvement of the churches in education in the society in question. I shall also try to demonstrate something of the different ways in which governments have tried to achieve a degree of balance between, to most people, the equally desirable aims of freedom of choice in a pluralistic society and the promotion of greater equality of opportunity; and, perhaps more impor-tantly, to isolate the key factors by which this balance is determined. This may do something to clarify the issues at stake which cause such marked differences in the acceptability, the scope and the cost of private education in the different countries and in the degree of variety of choice and equality of opportunity they achieve; and it will demonstrate how, by examining the factors which determine the nature of the independent sector in a given society, we can discover how it stands on the scale of reference whose equally unattainable poles are complete freedom of choice for parents and autonomy for schools at one end and complete equality of opportunity at the other. It will help, too, to site it on the élitist spectrum by the degree to which it appears to be socially divisive and privileged and so tends to create or at least perpetuate an élite or privileged group in the society to which it belongs — a charge to which, as will appear later, the British independent schools have proved to be especially vulnerable.

I shall endeavour to use the word 'élitist' in a neutral sense, despite any personal commitment to increasing equality of opportunity — firstly because, as suggested above, it seems beyond doubt that the equally desirable goals of freedom of choice for the individual and equality of opportunity are, at least partially, mutually exclusive and presuppose the need for compromise; and secondly because the creation of an élite of some

316

kind seems to be a natural and unavoidable by-product of every society, so that the only sensible goal must be to ensure, in platonic terms though not, please God, with a platonic model, that those who belong to it are as civilized and public-spirited as possible.

As was suggested above, the factors or controls which determine the nature and function of an independent sector arise from a number of different causes. The most obvious and formal controls stem from clauses in written constitutions (where these exist) which define the role of the state, the rights of the individual, the relation of church and state and the delegation of powers to regional and provincial authorities. For example, the First Amendment of the US constitution, with its separation of church and state as subsequently interpreted by the Supreme Court, does much to explain the composition of the private sector in the US and the fact that up to the present it has received only the minimal fiscal support from federal and state governments; while the 'due process' clause of the Fourteenth Amendment establishes the right to parental choice of private education as long as it meets reasonable standards as laid down by the States, and has made possible the growth of a strong and varied private sector. On the other hand, article 208 of the 1814 Constitution of the Netherlands, as revised in 1922, establishes the principle of freedom of parental choice and at the same time attempts to secure freedom of access (and therefore equality of opportunity for all) by ordering public funding of both sectors on equal terms, and, as will be explained more fully in a later section, forbidding private schools to charge fees. The result is that Dutch private schools are not markedly different from state schools. By contrast, article 33.3 of the Italian Constitution states 'Corporate bodies and individuals have the right to set up schools and educational institutions *so long as no expense to the State is involved*, and in the next sub-section lays the ground for what has turned out to be a very stringent legal control of the management and curricula of a growing private sector which, except for some Catholic schools supported by the Church, is exclusive because it lacks public subsidy.

Next in order are the controls and/or benefits laid down by the legislature at national, or, where devolution of educational control occurs (as in the US, Canada, Australia and Germany), at state or provincial level. These controls take the form of clauses in Education, Finance and other Acts and of Standing Orders and Administrative Regulations issued by ministers and civil servants. They may either impose extra financial and administrative burdens on private schools or grant them relief from rates, taxes and payment for public services; and, where schools are non-profit-making or form charitable trusts, may entitle them to receive tax-free donations or share educational services provided for state schools. This heading accounts for very varied degrees of regulation of such things as school buildings, school attendance at least during the years of compulsory education, and pupil registration, which are evident, for example, in the practice of the different American or Australian States. It also covers the varying complication and stringency of regulations in some administrations governing curriculum, the examination and assessment of pupils and the certification of teachers, to say nothing of the control of teachers' terms of service and salaries. All these bear upon the status of independent schools and their place on the élitist spectrum. Other laws may encourage or, as in Australia, require that independent schools be non-profit-making trusts or charities rather than commercial enterprises or limit the possibility of financial aid or relief to the first category of school. Independent schools may be further advantaged by the grant of tax concessions by way of tax deductions or tax credits to parents who pay fees, or whose children are educated away from home, or who make charitable gifts to independent schools.

Both constitutional and legislative controls and benefits of this kind are clearly important factors in determining the status of independent schools and the relative breadth of the social and intellectual hinterlands from which they recruit pupils. No less important is the effect of the patterns and philosophies of education which are enshrined in their own statutes or prospectuses — especially when, as in Australia, France, Spain and the Low Countries, the great majority of private schools are directly controlled by a religious denomination or at least in sympathy with a particular creed or church, while being at the same time partly or wholly subsidized by state funds, and as a result able to recruit from a wide range of home backgrounds. Confessional schools in many countries rely on their appeal to believers and the involvement of pupils, parents and teachers rather than on superior facilities to those of the state system, especially when, as in the Low Countries they are fully funded by the state and are not permitted to charge regular fees. They may and often do include a number of schools which are both more exclusive and more expensive than the rest and which in all countries alike confer advantages of status and quality of education of a more strongly élitist kind; but even in the US, where independent schools are by reason of the constitutional bar disqualified from regular subsidy, Catholic schools in particular educate many children from very disadvantaged homes and are low on the élitist scale both in terms of cost and of academic selectivity.

At the other end of the religious spectrum, the growing group of fundamentalist schools in the North American continent, in the Antipodes and, to a lesser extent, in Europe are élitist only in terms of offering and demanding membership of a *soi-disant* élite group without other than religious pretensions to special status or advantage, and are mostly wary of any form of state control or subsidy. Some indeed refuse to comply with compulsory requirements for registration by state authorities. Yet again, 'free' and community-based schools, as well as those which promote secular educational theories like those of Steiner and Montessori, are often in principle egalitarian but are in fact mainly supported by the middle and professional classes, who can afford to back their educational predilections no less than those who pay fees to more orthodox independent schools. They do, however, increasingly qualify for recognition and subsidy in countries such as the Netherlands, Denmark and Germany and in the Antipodes, so adding to the extent and variety of choice.

The controls exercised either restrictively or beneficially upon the independent sector by law and by its own philosophies of education are, however, a reflection of broader societal influences. These, of course, evolve and change with time, but they have their roots in the historical and spiritual past of the society in question. For example, the aims and ethos of the traditional nineteenth century English boarding school for the upper classes with its inherited tradition of godliness and good learning, which spread through the English-speaking world, remain potent in many schools belonging to the National Association of Independent Schools (NAIS) in the US, to CAIS in Canada and to the Association of Heads of Independent Schools in Australia and New Zealand and have influenced patterns of state education, while a very different and more meritocratic concept of the role of the secondary school and of the content of education continues to inform both public and private sectors in many continental European countries. More recently, the current of egalitarianism and the pursuit of equality of opportunity which have since the 1940s gained force and influence in all countries alike, though to different degrees, have in turn greatly influenced the attitude both of governments and of the public to private education and contributed to attempts to reduce the autonomy of the private sector. In some countries, notably France, Spain and the United Kingdom and more recently in Australia and New Zealand, the effect has been to bring the private sector under direct attack either by threatening the public subsidies which make the schools available to the less well-off or, as in Great Britain, aiming at the abolition of all fee-paying education on grounds of élitism and divisiveness.

This perhaps rather obvious summary may serve to demonstrate the complication of interacting factors which determine where the independent sectors and their individual components in our different countries should be placed on the élitist spectrum, from which I would remind you that there is no escape. It is now time to illustrate a bit more precisely by reference to more specific examples from within Europe and from North America and Australia and New Zealand how the various factors we have discussed combine to determine the profile of the private sector in particular countries. It may be helpful to summarise them once again under four brief heads as follows:

a) The constitutional and legal guarantees of the right of parental choice and freedom of belief and association.
b) The combined effects of:
    i) the nature and extent of direct subsidy to independent schools

        from public funds and of indirect subsidy through the pro-
        vision of public services and taxation relief.
   ii) legislation for the control of buildings, attendance, admissions,
        curricula, examinations, the certification and employment of
        teachers, for inspection and for the control of accountability.
  c) The amount in indirect aid to parents (and so to schools) by way of
      state scholarships, remission of fees and tax deductions for school
      fees and for charitable gifts to schools.
  d) The historical development of educational patterns and social
      mores; and in particular the involvement of the churches. [1]

In the Netherlands in 1982/3 71.7 per cent of all children attended Catholic, Protestant or lay private schools, which by law receive support from government equivalent to that given to state schools in terms of provision and running costs. They may not charge fees, apart from small means-tested charges for school visits and amenities, must follow state norms in salaries, curriculum and examinations and are open to inspection by state inspectors. These controls permit no more than two hours of each week to be devoted to a school's private initiative, though the wind is tempered increasingly to accommodate the education systems of Steiner and similar schools. These now receive financial subsidy at primary and occasionally at secondary level and have increased in number rapidly in the last ten years. Any educational superiority Dutch private schools can claim comes from the greater dedication of staff and involvement of pupils rather than from superior resources — and there is no evidence that attendance at a private school, as opposed to university or other qualifications, influences career chances through the nepotism of a powerful school-based old-boy network. Clearly these schools are low on the élitist scale, and being without cost, except for extras, are able to attract pupils from all kinds of social background. Catholic schools in particular are often situated in downtown areas in the cities and the fact that a number of better-off middle-class Catholic parents choose to register their children there rather than in a school with a more affluent catchment area is an indication that this openness appeals to their Christian sense of social justice and to the highly democratic instincts shared by the mass of Dutch people generally. Nevertheless, Dutch private schools tend to foster and reproduce the mainly middle-class ethos of the majority who use them and, for the 85 per cent in denominational church schools, some degree of commitment to a particular brand of institutional Christianity or at least to Christian ethics. They also tend, by reason of their sectarian differences, to perpetuate the separate identities of their particular congregations. Much the same is true of Belgium, where 62 per cent of the school population in Flemish speaking and 44 per cent in French speaking areas attend subsidized denominational and mostly Catholic independent schools which may not charge tuition fees, and must submit to government control of curricula and examinations. Here too the sector includes a small but growing number of secular schools on Steiner and Decroly principles operating on the same terms as the Catholic and Protestant schools. The price paid by independent schools in both countries is one of very real inroads into their autonomy and a comparatively poor standard in material provision compared with even partially fee-paying schools elsewhere. This has led James (1986) to describe them as 'an alternative mode of delivering quasi-public services, services that provide private as well as collective benefits'. She points out in the same chapter (pp. 132ff) that although government controls of expenditure, curriculum and examinations are no doubt partially at least intended to secure equality of opportunity their result is in fact to limit choice and variety overall as well as perpetuating divisions based on faith.

Germany shows a different and instructive pattern. While the strict academic standards of the nineteenth century remain strong in terms of curriculum and comprehensive education is only patchily accepted, reaction to the trauma of the Hitler era has engendered a determination to achieve a genuinely democratic society, and this is clearly visible in legislation about private education. Though responsibility for education rests with the eleven *Länder*, the Federal Constitution of 1949 is exceptional amongst its European counterparts in the extent of support and protection offered to the independent sector. Article 7 guarantees for all regions of West Germany public inspection of schools, the establishment of religion as a required subject and the right of existence of private schools. Subsections 4 and 5 state that private schools equivalent to schools in the state system (*Ersatzschulen*) must, to obtain official recognition, fulfil certain requirements about aims, premises and staffing; and go on to lay down that there must be no discrimination between pupils by reason of parental means. As a result, many private schools began to receive subsidies from 1951 and in 1966 the Federal Constitutional Court ruled that, because of the 'no discrimination' clause, *Ersatzschulen* were legally entitled to subsidy from the regional governments. Though the SDP is less friendly than the CDU and CSU to private schools, all *Länder* give support at the rate of on average 70 per cent of equivalent cost in a state school to 'recognized' independent schools which follow one of the official state patterns; and in some regions this has been extended to Steiner and similar schools whose ethos and curriculum are idiosyncratic. Furthermore, *Land* governments do not quibble about social divisiveness when school fees are limited to less than a third of total cost. In addition, many schools either receive subsidy from the churches (especially from the Catholic Church in Bavaria) or grant bursaries to parents in need. Furthermore, parents of children under 18 who are boarders or living away from home are eligible for a tax rebate worth DM1800 in 1985, while children over 18 undergoing training as a home student qualified for DM2400 or if away from home DM4200 — a valuable perk since many pupils stay at secondary school until 19 or 20.

Of a total of 604,254 private pupils in 1983 (representing 5.6 per cent of the total school population) 310,000 attended Catholic, and 42,000 Protestant schools, many of them boarding. The remainder attended either the increasingly popular *Waldorfschulen* (Rudolf Steiner based), one of the *Landerziehungsheime*, which are country boarding schools on English lines, or one of the large group of 'neutral', non-confessional schools belonging to the *Verband deutscher Privatschulen*. Comparatively few (1.2 per cent) were in private primary schools, with 9.4 per cent in secondary schools and 6.8 per cent in vocational schools.

Faced with economic recession in the last two or three years and reductions in rolls in state schools caused by the declining birthrate, regional governments, and especially those with an SDP majority, have made efforts to reduce the level of grant, despite objections in the courts by the independent schools which fear increased fees will make them less attractive to the less well-off. Nevertheless, German independent schools are in terms of social intake open to children of parents of restricted means who choose them either on grounds of belief or of educational opportunity; and they make possible a form of upward social mobility not otherwise easily available in regions which have adopted a comprehensive pattern in their state system. Some schools, many of them Catholic or Protestant boarding schools, have a special cachet in later life, but in general the five main groups of schools belonging to the umbrella organization, *Arbeitsgemeinschaft freier Schulen*, are valued for their variety, their independence and the quality of education they provide in a society which sets high value on qualifications as well as on freedom of choice. On the élitist scale they rank in academic terms *pari passu* with the better state schools and resemble them more than they differ from them, except in their independence and in benefits accruing from the involvement of parents, pupils and staff in an enterprise to which all subscribe. The price they pay in terms of autonomy is the degree of control exercised by the *Land* authorities over curriculum, examinations and budgets; but in some regions at least this has been much more flexible for Steiner and similar schools than might have seemed likely. The school organizations have shown themselves to be active and resourceful in putting the case for freedom of choice and diversity on which depends the accessibility of private schools to children whose parents could not afford the full cost of fees.

In Denmark all the factors work together to maintain a long-standing tradition of private education, reflecting deeply-felt convictions about liberty of choice and respect for individual beliefs as well as an intensely democratic instinct for social justice evident in many different aspects of Danish life. A law of 1814 sanctioned the existence of a private sector which was extended in the 1840s by Grundtvig's folk high school movement for young adults and confirmed by article 76 of the Constitution of 1949. This establishes the right of parents and guardians to provide comparable education outside the state system. Subsequent government legislation ensured financial subsidy for up to about 80 per cent of running costs to private schools of all types, philosophies and religious beliefs provided they reach a modest standard of comparability to state norms and teach the Danish language; and in addition gives help with loans and interest on loans and offers free places to children of the less well-off during compulsory education. Most schools are non-profit-making and are founded by groups of parents to meet their special needs (for example, Steiner or Montessori programmes) or to serve a confessional, political or ideological group. New and quite small schools are encouraged to apply for grant if they can muster at least seven pupils, a principal and funds for a building. Each school enjoys the same and quite extensive choice of educational methods; and the impartial neutrality of government allows aid to socialist- and marxist-oriented and even to international schools alongside confessional and ethnic ones. While most pupils come from middle-class and lower-middle-class homes the modest fees attract working-class parents to economize to pay them; and the free-place fund also helps.

As a result Danish private schools reflect the pluralism of a highly democratic society and are a virtually undisputed and welcome element in the national provision for education. On the élitist scale and in terms both of autonomy and accessibility they qualify for the lowest rating. There is no evidence that going to a private school gives any special social advantage in career or life generally, apart from the natural ones of a good home background and a good education — although it must be admitted that in academic quality the group of fourteen or so private *gymnasia* achieve high standards and by reason of their modest fees and the provision of bursaries and remission of fees are accessible to able children from quite humble homes. Denmark illustrates very clearly that a combination of favorable legislation and a tradition of liberal democracy can effectively minimize élitism in independent education. The only foreseeable threat to the private sector in Denmark would come from a major increase in its size from the present 9 per cent with the financial costs to government involved; and the grant system is at present under threat of amendment because of economic stringency. Here is a situation which makes possible cooperation between the sectors rather than rivalry, though this is not entirely absent — and it is in cooperation and not in competition that the best hope of progress lies, as will be clear from recent experience in the United States.

Great Britain provides a very striking contrast. Firstly, of course, there is no written Constitution sanctioning the rights of parents and the principle of freedom in education; but education has been for centuries defined as one of the four main categories qualifying for charitable status under English charity law, and until the beginnings of state education in the middle of the nineteenth century was mostly provided by charitable foundations, many of which dated from the sixteenth century or even earlier. While many of them were absorbed into the state sector as it developed in the first half of this century, those which remained independent have continued to be largely responsible for the education of the professional classes. This explains why the private sector, which now educates about 6.5 per cent of the school population in England and Wales and 3.4 more than 7 per cent in Scotland, provides at the end of the secondary stage almost 25 per cent of students in higher education and 45 per cent of students at Oxford and Cambridge. The boys' and girls' so-called 'public' schools, which now prefer to be called 'independent', and the preparatory schools (for children from 5 or 8 to 13), are the largest group in the total of roughly 2500. They are, as was made clear above, charitable foundations or trusts, some of great antiquity and all to varying degrees socially, academically and financially selective. The long-standing influence of 'public school' pupils and especially of old boys (*alumni*) of Eton, Winchester, Rugby, Westminster and other famous schools in Parliament, the professions and the City of London, together with their dominance of Oxford and Cambridge, though now much reduced, has aggravated public hostility to private education even in liberal democratic circles, which advocate the withdrawal of charitable status and financial aid such as it is; and it is the declared though somewhat impracticable policy of the British Labour Party ultimately to abolish private education entirely, despite British adherence to the various declarations of human rights which guarantee freedom of parental choice and the right of citizens to establish private schools. There are also those who argue that the decline of the British economy is the fault of a pattern of education which sets too much store on the liberal professions and too little on commerce, technology and engineering. All the same, as the state system crumbles visibly and the hope pinned on the social engineering expected from the comprehensive schools fades into disillusion, the demand for places in independent schools grows daily and new schools are born and flourish.

Government aid is limited to the present government's Assisted (i.e., means-tested) Places Scheme for a maximum of some 5000 children annually who show outstanding ability in admission tests set by the schools themselves; and to help with boarding costs for diplomatic and military personnel serving abroad. The schools themselves do their best to offer scholarships and bursaries and many parents contrive to pay the very high fees through insurance schemes taken out early in a child's life. As charities the schools are relieved of half the local rates and of taxes such as VAT and can receive donations under covenant which are increased by the return to the charity of income tax paid by the donor; and apart from the requirements of public examinations they have complete freedom in educational matters, religious instruction, choice and payment of staff, etc. The former Direct Grant Scheme under which some 170 established independent schools, fifty of them Roman Catholic, received financial aid from the Ministry of Education in return for educating a proportion of pupils free and others at fees dependent on income and topped up from public funds, was abolished in the 1970s by a Labour government, with some loss of upward mobility for able children of less well-off parents. A somewhat similar scheme, however, still exists in Northern Ireland. The private sector in Great Britain has therefore clearly preserved a very real degree of autonomy but is open to the charge of élitist exclusiveness both in terms of cost (ranging in schools in membership of the Independent Schools Joint Council, whose acronym is ISJC, from £1500 to £5250 per annum for day pupils and £3500 to £7050 + for boarders at the secondary stage) and of academic selection, since admission to senior schools depends on the attainment of a variable qualifying standard in examination; and the historical accident of an established church created by Henry the Eighth at the Reformation has increased this exclusiveness by making possible the incorporation of most local Anglican and Catholic grammar schools and many equivalent primary schools into the state system as 'voluntary-aided' schools, a process which many of the secondary schools at least have more recently come to regard as restrictive of their liberty in terms of organization and selection. For this reason, even though most of the best-known public schools are either affiliated to the Anglican church or are owned and controlled by Catholic orders, the British private sector lacks firstly the breadth of support from both lay church members and the Church authorities which has recently proved so strong a bulwark against attack from left-wing governments in France and Spain; and secondly the broadening of its intake in terms both of social origins and ability, which would have been assured by the retention in the independent sector of the now voluntary-aided schools whose independent equivalents in most European countries, in the US, in some provinces in Canada and in Australia give their respective independent sectors a much broader and less élitist image.

Nevertheless, the sector as a whole does offer some variety of choice. Amongst schools not in membership of ISJC some are local and modest both in cost and degree of selectivity by ability and others tend to cater for those who have fallen behind in state schools. Others again offer different and sometimes experimental patterns of organization and educational theory, such as Neill's Summerhill and the London Free School, to say nothing of Steiner, Montessori and similar schools. Its strength lies in the degree of autonomy schools enjoy to control their own destiny with only a minimum of regulation by the state to ensure reasonable standards of health, equipment and efficiency. Overall, therefore, even within the established schools it caters for quite a wide range of ability; but without increased government assistance, preferably to parents rather than to schools, it cannot hope to widen much further accessibility and variety of choice regardless of parental ability to pay the full cost of private education. It is worth noting, however, that a recent survey showed that in the 'élite' group of ISJC schools 66 per cent of parents of present pupils had not been themselves educated in an independent school, as against 50 per cent twenty years ago — a result which suggests that the circle of privilege, if this is what it should be called, is far from being self-regenerating and affords some real opportunity of upward social mobility to those who can pay the price.

If we look a little more closely at the North American scene, where there is no serious opposition either in the US or in Canada to the existence and use of private schools and freedom of parental choice is now largely taken for granted, the picture is of a broader and more diversified range of schools, educational objectives and costs, which supplement rather than compete with the public systems of education, which in both countries are under the legislative control of the States or Provinces. Neither the American nor the Canadian Constitutions make direct reference to parental choice or the right to establish private schools, but the famous Supreme Court judgment in the Pierce v. Sisters Case, 1925 is generally held to guarantee them in the States, while in Canada the 1952 Charter of Rights is held to override any restrictive provincial legislation. The devolution of power results in quite wide differences both in law and practice in the regions and in the extent of controls and benefits to independent schools.

In the US, where 12.4 per cent of the school population attend private schools, (all but 15 per cent of which are denominational and for the most part Catholic), the right of private schools to receive financial aid by subsidy or exemption from federal and state taxes is limited by the Supreme Court's not always consistent interpretations of the 1st Amendment to the Constitution and its separation of Church and State referred to in an earlier section. It has been held to bar most kinds of subsidy to schools and parents, including the supply of text books and materials; but both federal and some state authorities provide aid of different kinds and non-profit making schools are mostly exempt from federal and state taxes. On average 10 per cent of private school income comes from direct and indirect federal and 17 per cent from state and local funds. State regulation varies widely from the minimal to control as stringent as that of the public system, as does the degree of collaboration between the public and private sectors.

In Canada there is a difference between provinces such as Ontario, where Catholic schools have a special status within the state system, others which run dual Catholic and Protestant state systems and those where no formal arrangement is made. Five provinces subsidize private schools and seven do not, though a majority provide shared services, text books and other materials. These differences help to explain why the private sector educates only 4.6 per cent of the total school population of Canada. As in the States, independent schools benefit to the extent of perhaps 35 per cent of costs from direct or indirect local, provincial support and from special federal programmes.

Non-profit-making schools in both countries also benefit from the incentive of tax deductions for donors; and the relatively tiny but powerful group of traditionalist élite schools in membership of the American National Association of Independent Schools and its Canadian equivalent, CAIS, raise huge sums annually to fund their own scholarship schemes and so to extend their accessibility to the less well-off. The private sectors as a whole comprise firstly a wide range of denominational schools in which the Catholics predominate alongside Anglicans, Methodists, Presbyterians, Baptists, Dutch-Reformed, Seventh Day Adventists, Mennonites and the rapidly growing Fundamentalist Christian schools and secondly a smaller non-sectarian group of Montessori, Waldorf and other experimental or 'free' schools. The breadth of both sectors increases their general influence, decreases their vulnerability to charges of élitism, and ensures that there is virtually no controversy about the desirability of a pluralistic system of education in either country. The burning issues are the advantages and disadvantages of increased subsidy from public funds by way of vouchers or tax-credits in terms of equality of opportunity and the danger of increasing loss of autonomy as a result — something which the fundamentalist schools in particular, often already refusing to fulfil state requirements, will not contemplate. Arguments for and against private schools turn more on the issues of freedom of choice, and of belief and morality than academic excellence, despite much popular discontent with state schools, especially in downtown areas of the big cities; indeed, in terms of academic élitism state schools in socially favored areas are often more vulnerable to attack than top private schools.

In Australia and New Zealand, as in North America, there is no specific reference in a Constitution to the rights of parental choice of school and of private education. In Australia, educational legislation is a state and not a Federal responsibility and varies in detail from state to state, but in all explicitly recognizes the existence of private schools and parental choice. In both countries private schools are accepted sectors of the national provision of education.

In Australia 27 per cent of the total school population attend 'non-government' schools, 68 per cent, of which are Catholic. The range of schools is much as in North America and includes both non-sectarian schools and every kind of denominational foundation. Although the private sector was modelled from early times on the English and Scottish 'public' schools and like the government system much influenced by English patterns in general, the élite schools in membership of the Australian Association of Heads of Independent Schools form only a tiny, though influential minority. All are non-profit-making as a condition of receiving financial subsidy from both Federal and state governments upon a twelve-point categorization theoretically depending on 'need'. The present government is redefining the categories and has frozen grants to the 'better-off' schools for the future, but the principle of subsidy is strongly established and would be politically impossible to abolish in the face of popular support and in particular of the strength of the Catholic vote, despite some support for abolition from the left wing of the Labour party. Grants from Federal and state sources account on average for roughly 75 per cent of the costs of all but the more élite Catholic schools, and just under 40 per cent of those of non-Catholic schools. The price of subsidy is quite strict control of the use of resources and of building and other standards by both Federal and state authorities and by state regulations for the curriculum and teacher certification, which result in the refusal of aid by some fundamentalist Christian schools, which are growing no less rapidly than in North America, and increasing hesitation among the more established schools about receiving gifts from Greeks in the shape of government subsidies.

In New Zealand, where in the late 1970s Catholic and a few other schools accepted integration in the state system with a status somewhat akin to but more independent than that of voluntary-aided schools in the UK, the private sector has been reduced from 9.3 per cent to 3 per cent of the total school population. Otherwise it shows the same wide range of affiliation as in Australia. Schools are exempt from taxation on terms similar to those for charitable status in the UK, and benefit from charitable gifts which qualify donors for tax relief. The Education Act requires them to be registered and regularly inspected, but other controls are few. Until 1986 they have been eligible for loans at reduced interest, a complicated salary subsidy ranging from 20 per cent to 50 per cent of salary costs and allowances for text books and materials. The Labour government is in process of reducing the level of support ostensibly for reasons of economy, but might well be happy to abolish it altogether in its second term of office. The change has already resulted in withdrawals of pupils from less well-off homes, particularly from remote rural areas where farming incomes have suffered and boarding is essential.

As in some European countries and in North America, the combina-tion of subsidy with a broad spectrum of types and affiliations of schools has so far ensured in both countries a considerable variety of choice with a fair though still inevitably incomplete degree of equality of opportunity, which has been further strengthened since very few schools in either country are overtly selective in terms of ability and even the most 'élite' schools cater for a very wide spectrum. In neither country has subsidy so far involved serious loss of real autonomy, beyond the requirements of conformity with quite tolerable regulations for the general conduct of education, although once again a few highly sectarian schools opt out of the system and refuse to comply with any kind of regulation. The most significant contrast is in the schools' relative ability to resist further encroachment by socialist education ministers. With the strength of the Catholic Church, which in Australia significantly refused the kind of offer of integration it accepted in New Zealand, to support it the private sector in Australia can hope to continue to offer a fair degree of equality of opportunity to match the relative comprehensiveness of its intake in academic terms. Its main concern is with the growing tendency of federal government to demand a much higher degree of accountability for the expenditure of state funds received by way of grant.

To sum up, it seems fair to argue from these accounts of different systems of private schooling that, given a desire for collaboration and complementation by both government and the private schools, it is feasible for the private sector to achieve a balance between preserving independence and autonomy and ensuring a fair measure of equality of opportunity. This in turn will help to foster a pluralistic national system embodying freedom of parental choice and variety of allegiance and educational philosophy. Some degree of élitism is natural and inevitable in education as in all other human activities, but is demonstrably less obtrusive in the context of a broadly based, widely varied and accessible system of private schools which are partly funded or in other ways aided by the state. Élitism will be most apparent, though not necessarily anti-social, where selection by cost, by ability and by traditional allegiance reduces social mobility; but at the other end of the spectrum a private sector may lose much of its effectiveness if, as in the Low Countries, it abandons the autonomy which allows of real differentiation and is the only real basis of freedom of choice and variety.

Note

1 More information including statistics about private schools in each of these areas will be found in the author's three studies, *Private Education in the EEC (1983)*, *Private Education in the United States and Canada (1985)* and *Private Education in Australia and New Zealand (1987)* all published by the Independent Schools Information Service in London. *Private Education in South Africa* will be published later in 1989.

References

JAMES, E. (1986) in LEVY, D. C. (ed.) *Private Education — Studies in Choice and Public Policy*, New York, OUP, p. 123 and pp. 132ff.
JENCKS, C. (1975) *Qualities and Inequalities in Education*, London, Academic Press, pp. 37ff.

Chapter 17
Elitism and the British 'Public' Schools

Irene Fox

Introduction

Private education in Britain has been the subject of long standing academic and political debates which extend well beyond educational arguments to include a consideration of the very nature of the society in which the schools are to be found.

Before looking at these debates in any detail, and presenting evidence on the subject, it is necessary to identify what is meant by the private sector of education. With the exception of the workhouse schools, educational provision in Britain remained exclusively in the hands of the private and voluntary sectors until 1870. It was not until 1833 that the state first sought to assist voluntary (largely church) effort through the introduction of a parliamentary grant for education, £20,000, to be used in the towns where the rapidly expanding population had outgrown the resources available to make even the most rudimentary provision for the children of the poorer classes. Secondary provision, the focal concern of this chapter, remained outside the state until the passing of the 1902 Education Act and was initially composed of three main types of school: the public, the endowed grammar and the private. Whilst the private schools could be distinguished by their total dependence upon the market for the supply of their pupils and the endowed grammar schools by the fact that they had been endowed at various points in history to train poor scholars as choristers or to teach them Latin grammar (hence the name grammar schools), the public schools were (and remain) in their turn less easy to identify.

Deterred by the limited curriculum offered by the grammar schools, the aristocratic and landed families favoured the use of private tutors. A few grammar schools, notably Westminster, Eton and Winchester, received aristocratic patronage as early as the eighteenth century but it was not until the reforms inspired by Arnold of Rugby in the first half of the nineteenth century that the demand for institutional schooling grew such that an increased number of the grammar schools came to find favour with the aristocracy, giving rise to the term 'the great schools' — the forerunners of the public schools. These schools were mainly, but not exclusively, boarding schools, able thereby to serve the needs of a geographically widely scattered population. The term 'public' used to describe the most prestigious of the endowed and the proprietary schools is of uncertain origin. The historians Lawson and Silver identify it as a term which strictly belongs to all endowed schools in order to distinguish them from their private counterparts (Lawson and Silver, 1973) whilst John Rae, the erstwhile head of Westminster School, sees these very endowments, as well as the schools' boarding facilities, as its basis for both meant that the schools were open to the public in general and were not restricted to any social grouping (Rae, 1981). A second sense in which, according to Rae, the schools merit the name 'public' is the contrast that they provided to the private tutoring originally favoured by the aristocracy and the gentry.

It was not until 1869 that the formation of the Headmasters' Conference (HMC) by Edward Thring, the headmaster of Uppingham School, provided the public schools with their first opportunity to establish a collective identity. Although only fourteen of the seventy headmasters initially responded to Thring's invitation to meet at Uppingham, gradually an increasing number of them were attracted to the idea of a committee that was formed specifically to look after the interests of their schools. The criteria for membership had not been fully formalized but the important point is that membership of the conference was by invitation and technically this remains the position today, with the proportion of pupils engaged in sixth form work being an important criterion. It is the schools which are in membership of the HMC which form the elite of the private sector of education in Britain and which are known as the public schools.

A further division within the private sector came with the introduction of the direct-grant schools. These were made possible by the provisions of the 1902 Education Act which empowered local education authorities to grant aid to fee-charging grammar schools. The 1907 Direct Grant regulations enabled such schools which offered more than 25 per cent of their places to local education authorities and central government to attract a higher rate of grant. In return, central government had control over the fees charged. The aim of the direct-grant schools was to provide a ladder of upward mobility for the bright children of poor families and they remained hybrids of the state and the private sectors of secondary education until their demise in 1976 following the publication of the Direct Grant Grammar Schools (Cessation of Grant) Regulations in 1975. After 1976, two-thirds of the direct grant schools did elect to become private schools as opposed to being completely taken over by the local education authorities. Over the years the Headmasters of the boys' direct grant schools were invited to join the Headmaster's Conference and therefore they too could be considered to be public schools.

There are 225 public schools whose Headmasters currently belong to the HMC but it is the top boys' public schools which have been the focal point of public debate. These schools have been attacked both for creating a class-divided society and for reproducing such a society by serving as a mechanism for allocating individuals to top positions within it, binding them into a unified class able to exercise hegemonic control. Its supporters defend these selfsame schools not only for preserving freedom of choice, which is seen as central to the workings of a market economy, but also for providing this economy with well educated pupils who will ensure that the academic, cultural and moral standards of society are preserved. Thus the dispute is not about whether these schools are elitist but about the nature of the elite that they produce.

Can the public schools be said to be perpetuating an already class-divided society by recruiting exclusively from the established landed and monied upper classes, or can they more accurately be accused of drawing the brightest pupils away from the maintained sector to establish a meritocracy which then monopolizes the top positions? The British sociologist Anthony Giddens speaks for many when he writes that 'the public schools ... continue to play a dominant role in the self-perpetuation of recruitment to elite positions in Britain' (Giddens, 1979, pp. 8–10). The literature overflows with terms such as 'elite', 'ruling class' and 'upper class', a proliferation of terminology which serves to confuse rather than to clarify.

Essentially one needs to consider the methods by which people come to exert power over others and to control their own life chances. In its crudest form Marxist theory states that in capitalist societies there are two classes: those who own the means of production and those who do not. The owners of the means of production consolidate their position through their control not only of capital but also of the political machinery of the state and the hold which it establishes over the production of ideas. From this perspective, a concern with the public schools is a concern with both the ways in which they produce and disseminate the ideas of the ruling class and their facilitation of access to positions within it.

The ruling class needs to be clearly distinguished from the upper class which has a disproportionate share of wealth and income and has developed a distinctive life-style but does not enjoy undisputed political power. It is in the writings of Pareto and Mosca that the political theory of elites finds its roots. They used the theory as a critique of the Marxist theory of class which attributes political power to economic power. Crucial to elite theory is the belief that power in society is so diffuse, competitive and fragmented that it is constantly subject to countervailing checks which render improbable hegemonic control by a single group. It is Pareto's second use of the term elite, the distinction between the governing elite and the non-governing elite, which brings us close to a consideration of power based on factors other than property, for he observed that the governing elite contain certain groups of people who he called 'aristocracies.' The studies of elites in Britain have come to focus upon the education of those who have reached elite positions within elite occupations.

There is undisputable evidence to show that the top positions in Britain recruit heavily from ex-public school pupils and this has been summarized in table 1 by Boyd (1973): The most comprehensive survey of the social origins of pupils entering the Headmasters' Conference Schools is that undertaken by Graham Kalton, He shows that the proportion of the boys who came from manual families was 10 per cent in the non-direct grant day schools but only 3 per cent in the boarding schools (Kalton, 1966).

Halsey's (1980) work is based upon evidence from the Oxford Social Mobility Study relating to a sample of men born between 1913 and 1952. He found that the social class composition of the secondary private schools is in direct proportion to the standing of the school such that 16.2 per cent of those in the direct grant schools had manual fathers but only 11.2 per cent of those in the non-HMC and 6.3 per cent of those in the HMC private schools.

All this evidence is, however, of limited value in telling us about the precise role that a public school education plays in allocating people to top positions: Do they achieve these positions by virtue of their middle-class origins such that a public school education is merely a '*rite de passage*', or does such an education have an independent effect in securing class position? A further limitation of these studies is that they have been confined to men; there are virtually no details about girls in the private sector.

Debates about the private sector in general and the boys' public schools in particular have not been confined to academic textbooks but serve to divide the major political parties in Britain. Essentially, whilst the Conservatives support them, the Labour party is committed to their abolition. The Labour party's political challenge to private schooling was a long time in the making. Initially the party believed that the schools should be allowed to wither away as the ever improving provisions of the

Table 1   *Percentage of Elites with a Public School Education*

Conservative cabinet	90.9
Judiciary	78.7
Army (Major Generals and above)	78.0
Ambassadors	75.6
Directors of clearing banks	72.6
Church of England (Bishops and above)	70.9
Directors of nationalized industries	63.2
Directors of private industry	56.0
Royal Air Force (Air-Vice Marshall and above)	47.8
Civil Service (Under-Secretaries and above)	47.5

Source: Boyd, D. (1973) *Elites and Their Education*, Slough, NFER.

maintained sector would render them redundant. (A not dissimilar view has been adopted by the Social Democratic party today which believes that market rather than political forces should be allowed to destroy the schools). For the past thirty years its annual conference has been debating the issue of the private school. These debates are fully recounted by Salter and Tapper (1981) but essentially they have ranged along two main axes: the desire to abolish the elite versus the wish to promote a meritocracy, and the injustice of private schooling versus the need to preserve private liberty.

It was only after Labour's election victory in 1964 that the Secretary of State for Education, Anthony Crosland, turned his attention to the public schools by setting up the Public Schools Commission and charging it with 'examining the ways of integrating the public schools with the state system of education.' Asking the commission to focus upon the possibilities of integrating the schools with the state system was seen as a compromise between leaving them alone and the demands of the left wing of the party for abolition. The first report of the commission (Public Schools Commission, 1968) actually recommended that 50 per cent of the places in the boarding schools should be made available to non-fee paying pupils who were in need of a boarding education. The fate of this report was to fall victim to its compromising terms of reference as it found favour with neither the schools and the Conservative party which opposed its recommendation to sacrifice academic standards to boarding needs, nor with the left wing of the Labour party who wished to see the schools abolished altogether, and the report's recommendations were rejected by the 1968 party conference. It was, however, the recommendations of the second report (Public Schools Commission, 1970) which led to the abolition of the direct-grant schools as already discussed. It was thus that the ultimate legacy of nearly thirty years of debate in the Labour party was to create approximately 120 new private schools. Further action over the private schools was curtailed by Labour's election defeat of 1979 and it is only in opposition that the party's commitment to abolition has become more resolute. Labour has now produced a detailed plan to abolish the schools within ten years of its return to office (Labour Party, 1981).

The Conservative party has not devoted such a large amount of time and energy to debates about the public schools, simply because it had no wish to challenge their existence. However, some concern was expressed as long ago as 1942 when the Minister of Education, R. A. Butler asked Lord Fleming to head a committee to consider how the public schools could be brought into closer association with the general system of education. The reasons for establishing this committee were as much to do with the anxiety over the schools' future as with a search for greater equality. The prewar slump and the falling birth-rate gave rise to a fear, shared by the schools and the government alike, that they would become citadels of privilege with relatively few people able to support their fees. In its report two years later, the Fleming committee recommended that the schools should be opened to all children who would be able to benefit from the education that they provided, irrespective of the income of their parents. In that event, few places were taken up by the local education authorities. It was only with the election of the 1979 Thatcher government that private schooling has come to occupy and indeed maintain a high place on the political agenda of the Conservative party. The Tories have been steadfast in their support for the private sector and within a year of its return to office the Thatcher government passed an Education Act which sought to re-establish the freedom of parental choice which had gradually been eroded since the passing of the 1944 Education Act. Part of this freedom of choice was the introduction of the Assisted Places Scheme, designed to enable children to enter the participating private secondary schools on a means tested basis. At the time of writing the right wing of the Tory party was expressing its support for the reintroduction of the direct-grant schools as a means of bridging the chasm between the two sectors of education and of widening opportunities for the able children from poorer homes to receive a quality education. Paradoxically such a proposal presents a potential threat to the vibrancy of the private sector as it is today.

The Ethos of the Public School

Much has been said about the alleged role of the public schools in reproducing a class-based society but little attention has been paid to the qualities that they foster in their pupils. The history of the emergence and development of the public schools is fraught with the tension between their academic and traditional functions. The origins of these schools have already been discussed and were shown to lie amidst the endowed grammar schools which were established to give their pupils a classical education. It was only as these schools enlarged their curriculum to include a general liberal education, no longer enslaved to instrumental ends, that the gentry began to send their sons to them. The first report of the Public Schools Commission (also known as the Newsom Report) identifies the traditional values of the Edwardian days espoused by the schools them-selves: service to the community, leadership, initiative and finally self-reliance; it is these which can be said to constitute the 'public school ethos.' At the heart of this ethos lie the 'expressive goals' of the public schools, so labelled by Lambert (1975). These are the qualities or attributes which are seen as ends in themselves — the values of behaviour, morals, taste and expression — the goals most frequently mentioned by the headmasters of the boarding schools interviewed by Lambert. Anderson (1966) identifies the manner in which these qualities derive from the culture of the landed gentry who brought the public schools to their pre-eminence in the nineteenth century. It was to the boarding schools that the gentry sent their sons and which therefore came to epitomize this ethos, and it was therefore to the boarding schools that the newly emerged nineteenth century industrialists sent their sons to be gentrified. It can be argued that the day schools modelled themselves on their boarding counterparts.

How accurate is this ethos of a public school education? Not everyone shares the view that the core feature of the public school ethos is 'service to the community.' Ostensibly expressive goals can become laced with threads of instrumentality; the emphasis upon training for leadership can ensure that leadership and therefore power is secured. Is training in leadership skills all that the public schools have to offer their pupils? Scott (1982), in discussing the upper classes in Britain today, would appear to deny this. He identifies three possible advantages that a public school can offer to those seeking access to and acceptance by these classes today. Undoubtedly there is a need for academic skills, the necessary certificates to prove technical competence but, argues Scott using data from the Oxford Social Mobility Study, the state maintained grammar schools have shown themselves to be fully competent in furnishing their pupils with such skills. Secondly, there is the importance of promoting cultural integration, ensuring that all those who belong to the upper classes, irrespective of their social origins, share a common set of values and beliefs, which in a capitalist society is an ideological commitment to the rights of property and the value of credentials. Scott denies that the public schools have a monopoly over this function and in this he is supported by Smith (1976). Smith discusses how the grammar schools served to offer a sense of cultural inclusion with the ruling elite to those who were sponsored into them by the 1944 Education Act whilst preserving a relational segregation. Thus the third and final advantage that Scott suggests a public school can offer to its pupils, over and above those offered by the grammar schools, is the web of social assets which are believed to be of crucial importance for membership of the upper class: a distinctive style of life and the possibility of forming the useful social contacts, which comprise the 'old-boy network'.

Changes in the Maintained Sector

How useful is Scott's analysis in explaining the role of the public schools today? The maintained sector of education has undergone a marked change since the time that the men studied by the Oxford Social Mobility Group, on which Scott bases much of his analysis, were at school. There have been significant alterations to the institutional character of secondary schooling in the form of the transition from grammar and secondary modern schools to predominantly non-selective comprehensive education; to the actual experience of learning; and more recently to the level of funding.

The move towards comprehensive reorganization was fuelled by the demonstrated failure of the 1944 Education Act to significantly widen class access to academic education. The provisions of the act, notably selection on the basis of merit as opposed to parental means, were aimed at satisfying the dual demand for efficiency and equity by drawing upon the available pool of untapped talent simultaneously to stimulate Britain's economic growth and satisfy the desire to promote equality of opportunity. Attempts to monitor the results of comprehensive reorganization have failed to produce consistent results; different pieces of research into the effect of reorganization on public examination results reach somewhat contrasting conclusions and do little to confirm the fears of parents whose children were destined for the grammar schools.

Progressive education, with its emphasis on child-centred education, came to be seen as a necessary accompaniment to comprehensive reorganization. At the end of the 1960s what has come to be known as the 'new sociology of education' launched its critical attack upon the 'received' view of what is problematic in education and why working-class children are failing to succeed in middle-class terms. This received view is manifested in the concern to maintain the traditional goal of education, the reproduction of inequality, whilst seeking to broaden the social base of recruitment to unequal positions. By the early 1970s the new sociology was beginning to be introduced into teacher training courses and the combination of progressive methods and social radicalism undoubtedly influenced a number of socially committed teachers. The unique autonomy of Britain's teaching profession ensured that many of those trained in the seventies were able to put their ideas into practice. The right wing press, and indeed the Conservative party, have not been slow in highlighting incidents of disruption in the classroom. As the results of academic research into examination performance have low visibility by comparison with media publicity, the parents have been drawn into the moral panic about Britain's educational standards.

Superimposed upon this essentially right-of-centre critique of educational provision in the maintained sector is the growing uncertainty about the very future of this sector as the Thatcher government looks increasingly towards both the private sector and market principles for educational provision. At the same time as 17,617 pupils are attending private schools through the Assisted Places Scheme at a cost of approximately £23 million, local education authorities are being forced to curtail their expenditure within government approved limits. As capital overheads still have to be paid for this inevitably means that classroom budgets are being cut. At the time of writing a number of proposals are being floated to make the maintained schools more accountable to market forces; these include: competing for government funding in terms of their popularity as measured by the number of pupils in the school; resurrecting the idea of the voucher system; seeking money from the City and industry for twenty city technology colleges and, perhaps the most bizarre proposal of all, selling packages of schools to the private sector which would fund and control them, forcing the remaining maintained schools to compete for pupils.

Under these conditions it would hardly be surprising if parents who could afford to do so did not turn in increasing numbers to the private sector where their children's education would seem to be more assured.

The view that the schools have undergone a remarkable change is encapsulated in the title of Rae's (1981) book: *The Public School Revolution*. In this he documents the changes that have occurred in response not only to the political and ideological challenges of recent years but also to the economic changes that have accompanied them. Rae, as the Headmaster of a leading public school and himself a past chairman of the HMC, wrote that the schools were challenged by the changes in educational ideas that were affecting the maintained sector; in particular 'the fashionable rejection of competition ... and of academic selection' confronted the public schools with the dilemma of choosing to remain unaltered, to follow this trend or to establish an alternative by returning to their original function as grammar schools, concentrating more on academic excellence. At the same time, the schools faced the challenge of a declining market, brought about by the growing success of the post 1944 grammar schools in achieving academic results (as already discussed by Scott), particularly in the competition for places to Oxford and Cambridge and, probably of even greater importance, by the inflationary crisis of 1973–9 which trebled the fees in the schools. He concludes that the schools responded to parental demand and to the ideological attack upon their elitist ethos by undergoing an 'academic revolution' which changed many of the organizational and curricular features of the schools as well as their methods of selecting pupils. Rae writes from 'inside' the system but similar conclusions are reached by Salter and Tapper (1981) writing from the 'outside', They describe how the schools are less isolated both physically and socially than in the past. Families are more difficult to keep at arm's length for today's parents are less willing to delegate to the school the upbringing of their children. The schools have responded by allowing more chances for home visits and by encouraging the parents to have closer contacts with the school.

The empirical evidence to support these conclusions is essentially limited. The 1983 survey by the Independent Schools Information Service's (ISIS) of the sixth form subjects studied in the public schools does show that the emphasis in the curriculum on the classics has been replaced by the sciences and mathematics. This is reinforced by the Independent Schools Careers Organization (ISCO) surveys of leavers from the public schools for the past twenty years which show that courses in engineering, business studies and science are the most popular amongst the ·school leavers (ISCO, 1983). Similarly the annual ISIS Census provides evidence of some of the ways in which schools have changed with respect to the type of pupils recruited. There has been an overall increase in the number of pupils that they are able to recruit, a rise from 109,477 in 1973 to 146,118 in 1985 — an increase of 33 per cent. This has been brought about exclusively by the increase in the number of day pupils such that the proportion of boarders has fallen from 42 per cent in 1973 to 32 per cent in 1985. Most of the new pupils attracted by the increase in day places have come from the maintained primary sector and have entered the schools at the age of 11 rather than the traditional age of 13, with the schools frequently opening junior departments to accommodate them.

Research Design

Given the changes that have occurred in the maintained sector of education since the period on which the work on the private sector already discussed was based, important questions about the ethos, the recruitment base, and the consequent role in class reproduction of the public schools remain unanswered.

A notable omission from any systematic research has been the views of the parents and in particular their reasons for turning in ever growing numbers to these schools. Instead we have had to rely on second hand reports as mediated either by Headmasters such as Rae or by critics of the system. For example, Marsden (1962) has concluded that whatever the reasons that parents give to researchers for choosing a boarding school for their sons, they are merely following family tradition, giving relatively little thought to their decision. It was in response to this absence of any serious study of the parents that I carried out my own research in the academic year 1979–80. By interviewing 190 sets of parents, a random sample of those who were educating their sons in the traditionally independent (as opposed to ex-direct grant) public schools in that year, I was able to establish both the socio-economic and the ideological dimensions of the classes which served as the recruitment base of the boys' public schools. I was primarily concerned to identify the extent to which the schools recruited from the existing 'elites' and to establish the main values that the parents bring to the schools in seeking an education for their sons. Accordingly the research addressed several specific questions:

1. What is the occupational and social status of the parents of the boys attending the traditionally independent public schools?
2. Can the parents who have been educated in these schools be identified by a distinctive culture with shared perceptions of the social order?
3. What advantages of a public school education were sought by the parents?

The answers to each of these questions were elicited in a different way. In the interest of saving space, I will summarize each method under the discussion of the findings pertaining to each of the research questions.

Research Findings

1   *Who are the Parents?*

The research began with the search for an elite and this was done in two ways. Following the work of Boyd (1973) it was possible to identify from their occupations that twenty-two of the fathers interviewed (nearly 12 per cent) could be termed an 'occupational' elite. A notable omission from Boyd's definition of the elite is the ownership of land. The relationship in Britain between the ownership of land and of other forms of capital is complex, but the practice of acquiring land as part of the process of gentrification which began in the nineteenth century has continued until the present time. None of those classified as members of the occupational elite gave any indication of substantial land ownership, but 8 per cent of all the fathers owned land in excess of 240 acres (the average size of farms in Britain), two-thirds of them working as full-time farmers.

The use of a second method of identifying an elite has compensated for

Table 2   Main Occupations of Fathers

	% in the sample (1)	% in the gen pop (2)	(1)/(2)
CLASS I	69.1	13.6	5.1
Administrators and Officials	25.9	2.9	8.9
Managers in commerce and public utilities	11.6	1.1	10.5
Senior civil servants	3.2	0.28	11.4
Managers in mass communications	1.1	0.03	36.7
Senior LA admin	2.1	0.36	11.4
Sales managers	3.2	0.8	4.0
Headmasters, senior police	2.6	0.14	15.0
Officers in the armed services	2.1	0.14[*]	15.0
Self-employed professionals	18.4	0.79	23.3
Doctors, lawyers and accountants	6.8	0.35	19.4
Dentists and architects	3.7	0.17	21.8
Engineers, surveyors and pharmacists	4.2	0.16	26.3
Chiropodists, physiotherapists	1.1	0.02	105
Stock and insurance brokers	2.6	0.01	260
Industrial Managers	8.9	1.4	6.4
Large Proprietors	5.9	0.02	295
Employed Professionals	10.0	4.78	2.1
ALL CLASS II	8.9	13.16	0.68
CLASS IV	20	9.4	2.1
Small proprietors	10.5	6.4	1.6
Farmers	10.0	0.79	12.6
CLASS VII	0.5	—	—
Lorry driver			

[*] Estimated by Oxford Occupational Mobility Sample (N = 9457) 1972

341

the omission of land owners from the occupational elite. Allocation to the occupational elite was on the basis of the self-reported occupations of the fathers. The second method relied on the process of ascription; that is, a third party (the researcher) decides the criteria for elite membership. By the use of various directories (for example, *Who's Who*; *Burke's Landed Gentry*) it was possible to identify twenty members of the male sample who have received public acknowledgement of their social position and who thus are termed the 'social' elite. A cross-reference of the membership of the occupational and the social elites revealed eight fathers common to both; thus thirty-four fathers or 18 per cent of the male sample can be labelled 'elite.'

However, a close inspection of table 2 reveals that with only one single manual worker amongst them, nearly 82 per cent of the public schools today are in what is conventionally known as the 'middle class.' A closer examination of the occupational titles in table 2 which are used to compose the seven classes employed by this research does begin to show some of the diversity which did in fact characterize the fathers. Included amongst them were managers in senior positions, farmers, professionals and small shop keepers.

Sixty per cent of the mothers interviewed were engaged in some form of paid work, but none of them could be identified as members of the occupational elite nor indeed as members of the social elite independently from their husbands.

A more detailed study of the social origins of the boys unmasks still further the diversity that is contained within the term 'middle class'. The Oxford Social Mobility Group's comparison of the class position of its male respondents with that of their fathers shows how the expansion of class I has produced evidence of a very considerable degree of upward mobility. Only 24 per cent of the men in this class were found to have fathers in the same class (Goldthorpe and Llewellyn, 1980). Although both the rate and the range of the upward mobility enjoyed by the fathers in this sample falls short of that found by the Oxford Social Mobility Group, the increased opportunities for such mobility are clearly reflected in their origins. Table 3 shows that over a half of all the class I fathers interviewed were first generation members of their class and the experience of mobility of the members of the occupational elite contained within it is remarkably similar, only 57 per cent of them were born into their class. It is the social elite which can be seen to exhibit the high degree of social closure which is characteristically linked with the public schools.

An inspection of the social origins of the mothers suggests that their class origins are as diverse as those of the men. With the exclusion of the social elite who are highly endogamous, there is evidence to show a considerable amount of marriage across social class such that in many cases the woman may be bringing cultural and/or financial capital into the marriage. If the majority of parents do not constitute an elite in Pareto's

Table 3

a) *Social Origins of Men Using the Public Schools*

Male Respondents:	Male respondents' fathers' class				
	I	II	III	IV	V–VIII
All class I males (129)	46	9	11	21	13
(All class I males in Oxford Mobility Study	24	13	10	13	40
Occupational elite only (14)	57		43		
Social elite (20)	90	0	5	5	0
Class I males excluding members of both elites (95)	36		64		
All Class IV males (40)	23	3	0	68	8
(All Class IV males in Oxford Mobility Study)	6	4	6	37	47

b) *Social stability of class I males*

	1st Generation	2nd Generation	3rd Generation
Occupational elite	43	28	29
Social elite	10	35	55
Other class I males	64	16	20

Note : Percentages in each row total 100

Social stability data are based on three generations of men where available

sense of the term, unable therefore to wield significant power, can they be said to constitute a financial upper class? Bamford (1967) has discussed how, historically, the top public schools showed a reluctance to widen their intake. The picture today would appear to be very different, for many of these selfsame schools ruthlessly pursue both the academic excellence on which their reputations are alleged to rest and the pupils upon which their very futures depend. However, when the research was undertaken the average annual day fees were £1200 per annum and the boarding fees in excess of £2500, so it is obvious that the financial wherewithal of the parents is the ultimate determinant of who, in the main, will receive a public school education.

In income terms alone the parents were undeniably wealthy, as can be seen from table 4. Whilst the median income of the 150 men who were both earning and answered the relevant question was £14,024, over two and a half times that of the median income of non-manual male earners in Britain in 1979, the modal income lay in the range £15–20,000. Conversely, the mothers who were earning had an income which was below the non-manual average income of women, £3432 pa. Such an income is barely sufficient to alter the economic class position of these families but is possibly of key importance in implementing the decision to educate their children privately, for table 4 shows that, in the main, it is the low income fathers who were more likely to have wives who were earning.

In considering the formation of a financial upper class, it is the ownership of capital rather than the level of earned income which is crucial; capital is associated not only with high income and the variety of fringe

Table 4   Distribution of Parents' Annual Gross Earned Income (156)

Fathers		None	U.£3	£4 −4	£4−5	£5−6	£−8	£8 +	As a proportion of total fathers
				Mothers '000s					
None	%	0	0	0	40	40	20	0	0.32
Under £6000	%	40	40	0	10	10	0	0	0.64
6−8000	%	30	30	20	10	0	10	0	0.64
8−10,000	%	33	27	13	13	7	0	7	0.96
10−12,000	%	53	21	5	0	11	5	5	0.122
12−15,000	%	42	39	3	7	3	3	3	0.20
15−20,000	%	52	36	6	3	0	0	3	0.21
20−50,000	%	68	16	0	0	0	10	6	0.20
£50,000 +	%	100	0	0	0	0	0	0	0.013

As a proportion of total mothers 0.481 0.282 0.051 0.058 0.045 0.045 0.038
Note: Percentages in each row total 100
Source: Social Trends, HMSO)
(Median Non-Manual Income 1979 Men: £5,283.00 pa
Women: £3,161.80 pa

benefits which such an income normally brings, but also with accumulation, with investment income and with power. Accurate estimates of the ownership and distribution of wealth in Britain are exceedingly difficult to obtain; in the absence of a wealth tax personal wealth holders are not obliged to disclose the magnitude of their wealth. The most comprehensive summary of the way in which personal wealth is distributed amongst wealth holders is contained in the Reports of the Royal Commission on the Distribution of Income and Wealth (the Diamond Report). The information about the wealth holding of the parents in this sample is restricted to details about personal wealth, excluding wealth held as personal chattels or the value of the principal residence, which are unlikely to be realized in order to pay for school fees. Table 5, in showing the proportions of both the fathers and the mothers holding different amounts of wealth and, comparing them with the estimates of the Diamond Report, highlights the enormous concentration of wealth that is to be found amongst some of the men in the sample. Whilst this concentration is not as marked amongst the women, there was still a disproportionately high number of very wealthy women amongst the mothers of the public school boys. Research such as this, which was seeking to distinguish a financial upper class from an essentially bourgeois population, is primarily interested in the distribution of wealth at the higher end of the scale. It is inevitable that there should be an element of subjectivity when any attempts is made to define 'the higher end', but the decision to define as wealthy those in possession of in excess of £100,000 was primarily the result of the wish to maintain consistency with comparable work (see Harbury and Hitchens, 1979). This decision resulted in the identification of 30 per cent of the fathers and 7 per cent of the mothers as financially wealthy. Whilst the research failed to locate any of the women as members of the occupational elite, this does not preclude the possibility of their membership of the financial upper class independently from their husbands. It is difficult to disentangle the source of the wealth owned by the 7 per cent of the wealthy women, for all but two of them were married to men who were similarly wealthy and who may well have rearranged their own capital within the marriage.

The true size of the membership of the financial upper class is underestimated by virtue of the fact that at least 70 per cent of the mothers and of the fathers still had at least one parent alive at the time of the interview and several of them related how legal ownership, even if not the actual control, of the family assets remain with the living parent. Although many of the remainder of the parents interviewed are undoubtedly members of the financial upper class in the sense that they stand to inherit considerable wealth, many of them felt that such an inheritance would come too late to be of much practical use.

An additional way in which linkages to the financial upper class can be identified is through the benefits of family wealth without direct participation in the ownership of capital. Thus substantial unearned income without the possession of capital or being the beneficiary of a trust fund was also considered as evidence for inclusion in the financial upper class. Six of the men and seven of the women appeared to be linked in this way. Drawing together the information received from the 155 men and the 155 women who answered all the relevant questions it can be shown that a quarter of today's public school boys are clearly drawn from the upper class as defined in financial terms. Of these, nearly a quarter have fathers who are also members of either the occupational or the social elite. Thus a total of thirty-four per cent of the boys were united by the fact that they came from an immediate family background which although part of a unified class hierarchy, extends well beyond its upper reaches. They share in common parents who by virtue of economic position, occupational role or social

Table 5   The Distribution of Wealth of All Parents in the Sample and All Wealth Holders in 1974

Range of wealth in £000s	Fathers (155)	Mothers (155)	(a) Male Wealth Holders	Female Wealth Holders
None	9.7	43.9	(Estimated to be 50 per cent)	
Under 5	23.2	25.2	51.2	60.8
5–10	11.6	8.4	23.9	12.2
10–20	9.7	2.6	17.2	13.1
20–50	11.6	7.7	5.8	5.4
50–100	12.3	5.2	1.3	1.1
100–200	7.1	2.6	0.3	0.4
200 +	14.8	4.5	0.1	0.1
Total	100%	100%	100%	100%

Source: Estimates of All Wealth Holders from the Diamond Report

standing are members of an elite. Whether these parents who included both an earl and a first generation manufacturer of pots and pans are sufficiently ideologically integrated to form a hegemonic ruling class remains to be seen.

A ruling class is distinguished from a financial upper class by its ability to exercise control both over the uses to which its wealth is put and over the dissemination of ideas. A public school education has been identified as a key element in the formation of this hegemonic class. Writing as recently as 1959 Snow has argued that an absorption rate of 25 per cent of new blood is the maximum amount tolerable if the public schools are not to lose their essential character (Snow, 1959). Table 6 gives the details of the secondary education of both of the parents and from this it can be calculated that 44 per cent of the parents are clearly drawn from outside the private sector of education, let alone the public schools.

Do the experiences of the fathers interviewed confirm the assertion that a public school education does in fact confer extra advantages upon those who have been educated in this manner? At first sight this would appear to be the case, for membership of both class I and of the social elite is

Table 6   Parents' Education

		Fathers		Mothers
a)	*Primary*	%		%
	State	45.7		43.7
	Mixed	6.5		4.2
	Abroad	6.5		6.3
	Private day	15.6		36.3
	Private board	26.0		9.5
	Total	100%		100%
b)	*Secondary*			
	Non-selective	11.2		18.0
	Abroad	7.5		2.6
	Grammar	30.0		30.0
	Mixed	1.0	Mixed/convent	10.5
	Direct grant	7.0		5.8
	Non-HMC private	10.2	Day private	9.5
	Day-HMC	9.0	Boarding private	18.4
	Boarding-HMC	24.6	Boarding public	5.3
		(Major 17.6%)		
	Total	100%		100%
c)	*Post-secondary*			
	None	37.8		29.5
	Part-time	11.4	Finishing school	6.3
	Agriculture	2.2		2.1
	Sandhurst etc.	2.7	Nursing/physiotherapy	19.0
	Professional articles	9.2	Teaching Training	12.6
	Polytechnic/HE	6.0	Secretarial/Commerce	18.0
	University	5.7		9.0
	Oxbridge	15.1		3.7
	Total	100%		100%

disproportionately associated with an education in a public school. However, table 3 reminds us that members of the social elite have largely inherited their class I positions and though type of schooling may help to consolidate this status it plays little part in initiating what is essentially a process of ascription on the basis of birth. A more detailed analysis of the fathers' class of origin and type of secondary education received shows that there is a direct relationship between the two, such that a public school education is largely, but not exclusively, dependent upon class I origins. Table 7 clearly demonstrates that of the fathers who originated in class I, those who had been to a public school were no more likely to have remained in this class than their peers educated in the maintained grammar schools. It is the fathers who have been privately, but not public school educated, who were the least likely to have secured their class I position. Not only were the public schools demonstrably not superior to the maintained grammar schools in assisting the men in this sample to retain their class I positions, but they also failed to exhibit any qualities as promoters of upward mobility. The financial status of those originating in the manual classes V–VII had virtually denied them access to a public school education but this had not prevented these fathers from achieving class I positions, for the same proportions of the maintained grammar school educated fathers from the manual classes and public school educated fathers from class I are to be found in class I positions today.

The evidence about the relationship between type of secondary education received and membership of the financial upper class suggests that there are two dominant and equally important modes of entry into this class: either by inheritance, passing through a major public school en route, or by individual, entrepreneurial success largely following an education in the non-selective part of the state system, the secondary modern schools.

The significance of these findings is limited both by the social context within which they took place and the design of the research itself. This research has concentrated upon a self-selected group of people, those who are both able and willing to pay for a public school education for their sons; hence it underestimates the extent of downward mobility amongst public school educated fathers who can no longer afford to pay school fees and it

Table 7 Relationship between secondary education and class position of those fathers originating in class I

	School			
Class	Major Boarding	Other HMC	Other Private	Grammar
I	81.0	91.3	57.1	83.3
II	4.8	4.3	28.6	5.6
IV	14.3	4.3	14.3	11.1

Note: n = 70
Percentages in each column total 100

focuses attention upon the successful as opposed to unsuccessful grammar school educated fathers. The findings of the Oxford Social Mobility Study, based upon a large sample of the whole male population between the ages of twenty and sixty do lend support to this research's conclusions about the relationship between class position and type of secondary education, although there are no details about the financial position of these men. It is these findings which have enabled Heath, a member of the group, to describe the public schools as '... fulfilling a role of perpetuation and transmission of privilege from one generation to another' (Heath, 1981, p. 473), leaving the grammar and direct-grant schools to act as the escalators of upward mobility.

Perceptions of the Social Order: A Distinctive Culture?

I now turn to the second question addressed by the research. If there is no evidence that a public school education has, to date, improved the life chances of those who received it as opposed to a grammar school education, can it nevertheless be shown that within the apex of Britain's class structure there is a sub-group which has been so educated and can be clearly identified by its distinctive culture? The search for such a culture can take many forms, but this research was primarily concerned to identify the perceptions which the different groups of parents held of both the class structure into which their sons were poised to enter as autonomous beings and the advantages which a public school education would afford to them.

About a quarter of the parents interviewed believed that there is a total freedom of social movement in Britain. They saw the class structure either in terms of a ladder with unfettered movement between all the rungs, or as containing clear boundaries which serve to delineate one class from another but not to form insurmountable barriers which can only be breached by collective class struggle. The parents defined these boundaries in terms of differences in the earning power, the occupations, and above all the attitudes and education which distinguish the members of one class from those of the others. However, these boundaries were seen as breachable by those who have the motivation and necessary skills to do so.

The majority of the remaining three-quarters of the parents did recognize limitations to the amount of individual mobility possible because they believed that there is a clearly identifiable top class, a class which is more likely to be based upon birth and breeding than upon the acquisition of power and wealth. Many of them believed that this class is shrinking in both size and importance, being associated with the values and style of life of another era when land was a dominant force in Britain. As a consequence there was inevitably a recognition of the possibility, indeed danger of downward mobility from this class, but it was not seen as an 'open' class in the sense that people cannot move into it with equal facility;

membership is essentially a matter of birth. However, like the parents who believed that there is total freedom of movement throughout the entire class structure, the majority of these parents believed that access to the positions that lie below this apex of inherited class position is not restrained by structural forces. Whilst all the parents clearly recognize the opportunities that this openness of access presents, they also recognized the attendant dangers to their sons of downward mobility.

Although there was some variation between the parents with respect to their perceptions of the class structure in Britain, this was not related to their social or educational origins. The material condition of all the parents, as we have seen, was above average in terms of both financial and occupational success, and their consciousness appears to have been shaped by this rather than by their divergent past experiences. The parents arrived at their success from very different starting points, yet this does not appear to affect the way in which they viewed the class structure. The parents who achieved upward mobility into their current class position shared very closely the perceptions of those who were second or even third generation members of their class; both groups believed, despite the evidence to the contrary, that their current success was due to their own efforts rather than to the prevailing structural conditions. Having either experienced upward mobility or witnessed it, parents believed that such opportunities as well as the dangers of downward mobility still existed at the time that they were being interviewed.

Despite all their differences, the members of this population are fundamentally united in their perceptions of the social order which has afforded them their privileged position. The parents were reluctant to specify the types of jobs that they envisaged, let alone desired, for their sons — vehemently asserting that such ambitions are both unrealistic and futile. In a world which is perceived as open to individuals to succeed and to fail according to merit and ambition, it is pointless and possibly dangerous to cherish dreams whose translation into reality cannot be ensured. The most that the parents realistically believed that they could do was to offer their sons the best opportunity to make what they can of their lives, and a public school education is part of this offering. Given the perceptions of the nature of the class structure, fluid in the middle with an upper class which was seen either as non-existent or as closed to upward mobility, it would in turn be unrealistic to believe that many parents were using the public schools to facilitate the entry of their sons into the very top positions in society. Whilst they may have wished for such a future for their sons, it is much more likely that their immediate concern was to ensure that they offered them the chance to succeed in maintaining current class position in a world which was seen as increasingly competitive and where success was believed to be dependent upon the possession not only of technical skills but also of the appropriate values — ambition, deferred gratification and, above all, the determination to succeed.

Irene Fox

The Advantages of a Public School Education

Given such circumstances, the third question this research turns to is the issue of what the parents believe that the public schools could offer to their sons which the maintained sector was failing to provide. Although only about a half of the parents were themselves educated in the private sector, in the vast majority of cases the remainder were grammar school educated. Most of the parents who have chosen to educate their sons in the public schools share a variety of 'experiences' of state education which serve to mediate their secondhand, received knowledge of it. For the majority, the experiences are more immediate than merely being the employers of state educated labour; most had friends and relatives who had recently used the maintained sector for the education of their children and three-quarters of them had had direct contact, using it for the whole or part of the education of some or all of their children. A quarter of the parents had actually educated at least one child in the secondary schools which they were rejecting and a further 50 per cent had made use of the primary schools, an experience which may have affected some of them in their choice of secondary school.

The reasons that parents actually gave for choosing a public school education are many and varied (see table 8) and are presented at different levels of abstraction which range from 'doing one's best for one's child' to the specifics of 'better facilities.' It would be wrong to assume that choosing this education always involves a conscious rejection of the state alternative, for there were some parents who were merely following family

Table 8   Reasons for Choosing a Private Education

Advantage	
Better academic results	52
Character and discipline training	48
Children treated as individuals	46
Better teachers and/or methods	40
Fuller education	36
Size of school and/or classes	34
Get on better in life	28
Mix with a better type of child	27
Develops confidence and/or independence	26
Stretch and/or develop children	22
Polish children	18
Do one's best	17
With children who want to learn	13
Freedom to choose	12
Family tradition	9
Better facilities	8
Old-school tie	8
Need a boarding school	6

Note: Totals Exceed 100% as parents gave an average of 4.4 reasons tradition and others who displayed what can best be described as a blind faith in the public schools, believing that they were doing what was best for their sons by sending them to schools which offer every single advantage. But for the majority of parents the decision to use a public school was a carefully considered one — carefully considered in the light of how the world looked to them. Again the parents displayed a remarkable similarity in the qualities that they sought from the schools, manifesting their common class position and shared view of the world and largely obscuring the variation in their social and educational origins. It is thus that the same two advantages that the public schools are believed to have over the maintained secondary schools were mentioned most frequently by all the types of parents — the ability to produce better academic results and to develop character by instilling discipline.

Academic results are essentially about examination performance and above all gaining entrance to the universities and the professions. It is in this sense that the 'academic revolution' is fuelled by parents who can no longer turn to the grammar schools to ensure that such results are achieved.

The search for development of character through discipline bears little resemblance, in the majority of cases, to the service to the community that Lambert saw as central to the public school ethos. What parents required of the schools was that they impose discipline upon the children, teaching them what is right and wrong, to dress properly and ultimately to develop a tidy mind and self-discipline in order that they can learn to live in a world which has rules. Preparation for leadership and the development of a sense of responsibility were mentioned by very few of the parents. Many of the parents saw academic success and a disciplined person as complementary rather than as alternatives. These are the qualities that the parents believed that their sons need to possess if they are to succeed in a world hallmarked by economic recession and a corresponding contraction in employment opportunities. It is in this sense that both characteristics can be understood as important determinants of individual success, the single most important motive of parents for rejecting the maintained sector and its provisions.

One of the most remarkable features of the reasons that parents gave for choosing a public school education for their sons is not the reasons themselves but the extent to which they were shared almost universally by parents from the diverse range of backgrounds represented in today's public schools. Particularly noticeable is the way in which class I parents, where the father was second or third generation within this class, and thus more likely to have had a public school education, could barely be distinguished from those where the father had been upwardly mobile into class I and therefore was unlikely to have had this form of education.

It was in the choice of a particular school that the search for clearly identifiable sub-groups of parents was most successful. The most obvious difference between the schools is the division between day and boarding schools. In simple occupational terms there was no statistically significant difference between the boarding and the day parents, although there was a disproportionately high number of farmers using the boarding schools. However, few of the first generation parents used a boarding school for their sons and it was amongst the parents of the boarders that one was more likely to find the small number of parents who gave 'family tradition' as an important reason for choosing this form of education.

Boarding is, however, only one axis along which the schools vary; an important feature of any system which thrives on the principle of the market, with freedom of choice as an important part of its philosophy, is its individuality. Within the seemingly homogeneous category 'public schools' selected for this research, there are numerous differences which serve to differentiate between schools, including the size of the school and the status that it enjoys both within and outside the Headmasters' Conference. Whilst all of the schools are academically selective in their admissions policies in the sense of administering an entrance test, all are dependent upon the fees for the major part of their income and some schools inevitably are able to be more selective than others. This is particularly true of the day schools where, as has already been discussed, the greatest demand is now to be found. It is largely these schools and the most prestigious of the boarding schools which are able to reject pupils on academic grounds.

Despite the constraint upon the parents in their choice of a particular school, such that only two-thirds of the parents were using schools of their first choice, the schools did vary with respect to their social intake such that individual categories of schools could often be identified by an ideal-typical set of parents who came to characterize a particular category but never to completely dominate it for they never formed a majority of the parents within it. For example, the parents who had a non-grammar school education in the maintained sector were virtually excluded from the largest and most prestigious day and boarding public schools. Conversely, those who had been educated in Britain's top boarding schools were relatively successful in securing places at these schools for their sons, even if not always in their own school, and it is here that the social (but not the occupational) elite educated their sons. Thus whilst the parents displayed a striking convergence in their view of the world which awaits their sons and in what they expect from the schools, they would appear to be seeking to preserve their social identity by educating their sons alongside those with whom they can identify both culturally and demographically.

Conclusions

It has been clearly established that the incumbency of elite positions is virtually monopolized by those who have been public school educated and, in turn, it has been shown that the schools continue to be distinguished by the already privileged boys whom they educate. However, up to now there has been little evidence to support the view that it is the public school education *per se* which confers advantage in the sense of securing access to these elite positions or indeed to the more bourgeois occupations valued by the parents. To date the major significance of the public schools must be seen to lie with their capacity to act as a focus of critique of the provisions of the maintained sector.

The majority of the parents of today's public schoolboys who were interviewed for this research believed that a public school education does have the power to secure position in the fluid class structure of contemporary Britain. This was seen to be the result of the schools' capacity to promote both better academic results and greater discipline. It may well be that the changing technological and political complexion of Britain means that the parents' perceptions are correct and the true significance of these schools lies not in their past but in their immediate future. At the same time as academic credentials are becoming of increasing importance in securing high status employment, the educational policy of the Thatcher government shows clear signs of applying the principles of the market to the provision of state schooling. Thus the private schools in general and the public schools in particular can be seen as increasingly threatening the maintained sector by attracting superior financial and human resources. As a result, the already financially privileged will come to depend upon the public schools to provide the academic qualifications for their children which are necessary to perpetuate this privilege within their own families.

References

ANDERSON, P. (1966) 'Origins of the Present Crisis', *New Left Review*, 23, pp. 26–53.

BAMFORD, T. (1967) *The Rise of the Public Schools*, London, Nelson.

BOYD, D. (1973) *Elites and their Education*, Slough, National Foundation for Education Research.

GIDDENS, A. (1979) 'The Anatomy of the British Ruling Class', *New Society*, vol. 50.

HALSEY, A. H. (1980) *Origins and Destinations*, Oxford, Clarendon Press.

HARBURY, C. D. and HITCHENS, D. M. (1979) *Inheritance and Wealth Inequality in Britain*, London, Allen and Unwin.

HEATH, A. (1981) 'What Difference does the Old School Tie Make Now?', *New Society*, vol. 56.

INDEPENDENT SHOOLS CAREERS ORGANIZATION (1983), Prospectus 1983/4.

KALTON, G. (1966) *The Public Schools: A Factual Survey*, London, Longmans.

LAMBERT, R. (1975) *The Chance of a Lifetime? A Study of Boarding Education*, London, Weidenfeld and Nicolson.

LABOUR PARTY (1981) *A Plan for Private Schools*, London, TUC-Labour Party Liaison Committee.

LAWSON, J. and SILVER, H. (1973) *A Social History of Education in England*, London, Methuen.

McCONNELL, J. (1967) *Eton: How it Works*, London, Faber and Faber.

MARSDEN, D. (1962) 'Why Do Parents Pay Fees?', *Where* vol. 10, pp. 19–21.

PUBLIC SCHOOLS COMMISSION (1968) *First Report*, London, HMSO.

PUBLIC SCHOOLS COMMISSION (1970) *Second Report*, London, HMSO.

RAE , J. (1981) *The Public School Revolution*, London, Faber and Faber.

ROYAL COMMISSION ON THE DISTRIBUTION OF INCOME AND WEALTH (1976) Report Nos 4 and 7, London, HMSO.

SALTER, B. and TAPPER, T. (1981) *Education, Politics and the State: The Theory and Practice of Educational Change*, London, Grant McIntyre.

SCOTT, J. (1982) *The Upper Classes: Property and Privilege in Britain*, London, Macmillan.

SMITH, D. (1976) 'Codes, Paradigms and Folk Norms: An Approach to Educational Change with Particular Reference to the Work of Basil Bernstein', *British Journal of Sociology*, vol. 10, pp. 1–19.

SNOW, G. (1959) *The Public School in the New Age*, London, Geoffrey Bles.

Notes on Contributors

Patricia A. Bauch is Assistant Professor and holder of the Elizabeth Ann Seton Chair in the Department of Education at The Catholic University of America, Washington, DC, USA.

William Lowe Boyd is Professor of Education in the Division of Education Policy Studies, College of Education, Pennsylvania State University, University Park, Pennsylvania, USA.

James G. Cibulka is Associate Professor in the Department of Administrative Leadership, School of Education, University of Wisconsin-Milwaukee, USA.

Bruce Cooper is Associate Professor of Education, Graduate School of Education, Fordham University, New York, USA.

Denis Philip Doyle is a Senior Fellow at The Hudson Institute, Washington, DC, USA.

Berry H. Durston is Acting Head of the Centre for External Studies, Curtin University of Technology, Perth, Western Australia. Formerly, he was Executive Officer of the National Council of Independent Schools, Canberra, Australia.

Tony Edwards is Professor and Head of the School of Education at the University of Newcastle upon Tyne, United Kingdom.

Donald Erickson is Professor of Education in the Department of Education, University of California, Los Angeles, USA.

John Fitz is Senior Lecturer in the Department of Education at the Bristol Polytechnic, United Kingdom.

Irene Fox, now deceased, was a member of the Faculty of Social Sciences and Business Studies at the Polytechnic of Central London, United Kingdom.

Dan E. Inbar is Associate Professor in the School of Education at The Hebrew University of Jerusalem, Israel.

Estelle James is Professor in the Department of Economics, State University of New York, Stony Brook, New York, USA.

Stephen B. Lawton is Professor of Education in the Department of Educational Administration at the Ontario Institute for Studies in Education, Toronto, Ontario, Canada.

Peter Mason is Honorary Research Director of the British Independent Schools Information Service and Chairman of the European Council of National Associations of Independent Schools.

Jacob B. Michaelsen is Professor of Economics in the Department of Economics at the University of California, Santa Cruz, USA.

Barbara L. Schneider is a Research Associate in the Ogburn–Stouffer Center for the Study of Population and Social Organization at the University of Chicago, Chicago, Illinois, USA.

Don Smart is Associate Professor in the School of Education at Murdoch University, Murdoch, Western Australia, Australia.

Manfred Weiss is Senior Researcher in the Department of Economics of Education at the German Institute for International Education Research, Frankfort, FRG and Part-Time Lecturer in the Faculty of Educational Studies of the University of Frankfort, Federal Republic of Germany.

Geoff Whitty is Chair of the Faculty of Education and Community Studies at Bristol Polytechnic, United Kingdom.

Index

Baker, Kenneth 260, 261
Bamford, T. 343
Bandura, A. 288
Baptist Convention of Ontario and
    Quebec 184
Baptist schools 327
Bates, Richard 162
Bauch, P. 82
Baume, Peter 144
Belgium, schools in 55, 218
Bennett, William 9, 99, 159
Bill 30, *An Act to amend the Education Act*
    175, 185–8
    test of constitutionality of 182–5
Black Muslim schools 34
Blackman, J. 285, 292
Blaine, James G. 47
Bloom, B. 31, 81
Boomer, Garth 144
Booth, W. C. 22, 27
Boston Latin 44
Bowles, S. 58
Boyd, D. 334, 341
Boykin, W. A. 289, 290, 291
Boyson, Rhodes 116, 118, 119
Bradford Grammar School 116
Breit, Sally
    Aideing in Education 38
Bridge, R. G. 285, 286, 292
British public schools 331–54
    advantage of education in 350–2
    charity status of 108
    ethos of 336–7
British schools 107–21, 150, 323–6
    funding of 108, 257–63
    scope of private sector 238
    see also British public schools
Bronx Science 44, 56, 229
Brooklyn Tech 56
Brown, Joan 134
Butler, R. A. 335

Canadian Association of Independent
    Schools 319, 327
Canadian Charter of Rights and
    Freedoms 172, 176, 177, 182–5,
    186, 187, 188
Canadian Confederation 172, 173
Canadian Constitution 171
Canadian Jewish Congress 186
Canadian schools 55, 326
    in Ontario 171–91
    funding 179–82

scope of private schooling 178–9
Canadian Unitarian Church 185
'Cardinal Principles' 25
Carlisle, Mark 116
Carroll, James 52
Catholic schools 31, 47, 173, 180
    in Australia 51–3, 128, 131, 150, 152
    in Canada 14, 171, 172, 173–5,
        178–88
    and the disadvantaged 75–6
    in Holland 320
    in the USA 293–301
Catholic University of America (CUA)
    287, 294
Center for Education Statistics 75
Center for the Study of Public Policy
    291
Center for the Study of Youth
    Development 306
Central Public School (Philadelphia) 44
Centre for Policy Studies 111
Chapter I 15, 250, 252–3, 265, 266
charity schools 2, 108
Charlesworth, Max 140–1
Charter of Rights (1952) (Canada) 326
choice, educational 11
    in Australia 50–3
    in Denmark 48–50
    in Holland 54–5
    in USA 43–4, 47, 55, 56
Church of Sweden 220
Church schools in Denmark 48
Cibulka, J. 81, 82, 101
City Technology Colleges 9, 11, 247,
    250, 257, 260–6
*City Technology Colleges: A New Choice of
    Schools* 260
*City Technology Colleges: A Speculative
    Investment* 261
Civil Aeronautics Board 63
class segregation 227–9
Coalition for Public Education Ontario
    Inc 184
Cohen, D. K. 158
Coleman, James 10, 33, 75, 76, 77, 99,
    100, 204, 303
Commission on Private Schools in
    Ontario 177–8, 179–82
'common school' movement 218
Commonwealth Schools Commission
    125, 127, 151
*Commonwealth Support for Non-
    Government Schools* 132